INTERNATIONAL
ENVIRONMENTAL STUDIES

First Edition

Edited by Katlyn S. Morris, Ingrid L. Nelson,
V. Ernesto Méndez, and Saleem H. Ali

University of Vermont

cognella®
academic publishing

Bassim Hamadeh, CEO and Publisher
Michael Simpson, Vice President of Acquisitions
Jamie Giganti, Managing Editor
Jess Busch, Senior Graphic Designer
John Remington, Acquisitions Editor
Brian Fahey, Licensing Specialist
Mandy Licata, Interior Designer

First published in the United States of America in 2015 by Cognella, Inc.

Front cover:
Cover image copyright© 2013 by Depositphotos / Dmytrii Minishev
Cover image copyright© 2012 by Depositphotos / imagex
Back cover image courtesy of William B. Morris.
Interior image copyright © 2012 by iStockphoto.com / Angela Schmidt.

Printed in the United States of America

ISBN: 978-1-62661-612-7 (pbk) / 978-1-62661-613-4 (br)

www.cognella.com   800-200-3908

CONTENTS

INTRODUCTION

The range and severity of environmental changes around the world can simply seem overwhelming. Should environmentalists focus on climate change or the global proliferation of electronic waste? Could they focus on both? What type of mechanism would solve such environmental problems most effectively, efficiently, and fairly: policy and governance, grassroots activism, or market-based approaches? Who gets to decide the priority issues, and who is affected? These questions point to a larger issue of how to understand environmental processes across scales, while maintaining a focus on specific people and places, their histories, and the politics of who can access, use, and govern natural resources.

We are all inextricably connected to the biophysical and social environment, and our every interaction with the environment alters it, for "good" and "bad." The actions and policies of one country affect people across the world. For example, U.S. subsidies for corn production lead to depressed corn prices worldwide, putting many Mexican corn farmers out of business because they cannot compete with U.S. prices. Likewise, the decisions of companies, communities, and individuals have far-reaching effects. Consider that at the global scale, consumer demand for oil encourages companies like Shell to continue oil exploration and drilling in Nigeria, while at national and local scales this may result in oil spills, local water and air pollution, and threats to wildlife. What opportunities do we have to use natural resources, such as land, fresh water, wood, and fuels, in ways that replenish the environment rather than degrade it? Who is responsible for environmental degradation, and who is responsible for healing these ecosystems? Although there are no easy answers to these crucial questions, this book offers readers the opportunity to think critically about the complex relationships between humans and the environment across scales and international contexts.

As authors who teach, conduct research, and engage in social/environmental efforts from coffee forests in El Salvador to international climate negotiation meeting rooms; from wetlands in the northeastern USA to the miombo woodlands of Mozambique, our collective experience has shown us the complexity of environmental issues and the importance of seeing environmental studies as inherently: 1) transdisciplinary, 2) multi-scalar, and 3) political.

In order to share this perspective with readers, we have included case studies from around the world that demonstrate the practical applications of some of the more innovative approaches to environmental studies. Some of these are more promising than others in delivering environmental results while explicitly accounting for socio-economic and political disparities among the people and ecologies involved. Others may be more focused on a particular discipline or issue. However, all of these approaches have been used as tools to address global environmental challenges, and they all provide valuable lessons on how to view and "unpack" some of the major environmental issues of our time.

A. What Makes This Book Unique?

"Environmental studies" necessitates an appreciation for the interface between planetary ecological processes and international social, cultural, economic, and political dynamics. While there are ample readings on international environmental policy *or* on global ecological systems, a text that provides a confluence of these approaches remains elusive. Integrating the disciplines and different knowledge systems is necessary, yet academics and practitioners still grapple with how best to do this. We must continue to explore not only the biophysical characteristics of our planet, but also the complex and dynamic relationships that exist between humans and the environment. Our goal is to provide students and mid-career professionals with a solid foundation with which to understand contemporary environmental issues, as well as opportunities for critical thinking and further inquiry and engagement.

Rather than separating ecological processes from social, political, and economic dynamics, we combine ecological and human dimensions of the environment throughout the text. In fact we have intentionally sought and chosen approaches and case studies that prioritize this integration. The selected readings offer breadth across the range of issues and approaches within environmental studies, and depth through case studies from diverse regions. Sections on environmental studies approaches and frameworks provide students with a solid theoretical background, while case studies ground the theory in an applied, geographically situated context. Readers should gain a clear understanding of the transdisciplinary (i.e. across disciplines and knowledge systems) nature of environmental studies, as well as gain a solid grasp of how different tools and approaches have been used to address specific ecological issues. This volume explicitly addresses the importance of diverse knowledge and approaches as a means to better understand and resolve the global environmental challenges facing our planet, making this a true "environmental studies" text.

B. Organization of the Book

The book consists of six core sections divided among key ecological issues: biodiversity, fresh water, agriculture and food systems, energy, waste, and climate change. Each section begins with a brief introduction to the key ecological and social context necessary for understanding the issue. We then feature a prominent analytical and/or applied approach within the field of environmental studies (see Table 1).

We recognize that there are many different ways to approach environmental problems and solutions. We therefore situate each approach among other frameworks and approaches, addressing key areas of overlap and distinctions. Following each "approach" Part is a case study, demonstrating a practical application of this approach to the ecological issue. Each section concludes with a set of take-home messages and common critiques of the particular approach.

We have chosen to focus on six key ecological areas that represent some of the most important contemporary environmental challenges and opportunities. Within each section, we also review select related issues (for example: deforestation and its impacts on biodiversity; food sovereignty movements within food and agriculture). Although we do not capture every possible environmental issue, we attempt to integrate those environmental issues that affect the entire planet (though they do so in different ways at different scales). Given the links between many ecological issues and approaches covered in the text, we encourage readers to make connections throughout the book. The introductions and conclusions to each section illustrate key areas of overlap between issues and offer students the opportunity to appreciate the interconnectedness of global environmental studies. We invite you to delve in and question, think, and discuss.

Table 1. Thematic Organization of the Book by Ecological Issue, Approach, and Location

Section	Ecological Issue	Approach	Case Study Location
I	Biodiversity	Protected Areas	Bwindi Impenetrable National Park, Uganda
II	Fresh Water	Ecosystem Services	Murray-Darling Basin, Australia
III	Agriculture and Food	Agroecology	Latin America
IV	Energy	Environmental Justice	Mekong River Basin, Southeast Asia
V	Waste	Political Ecology	Multi-locational
VI	Climate Change	Environmental Governance	European Union

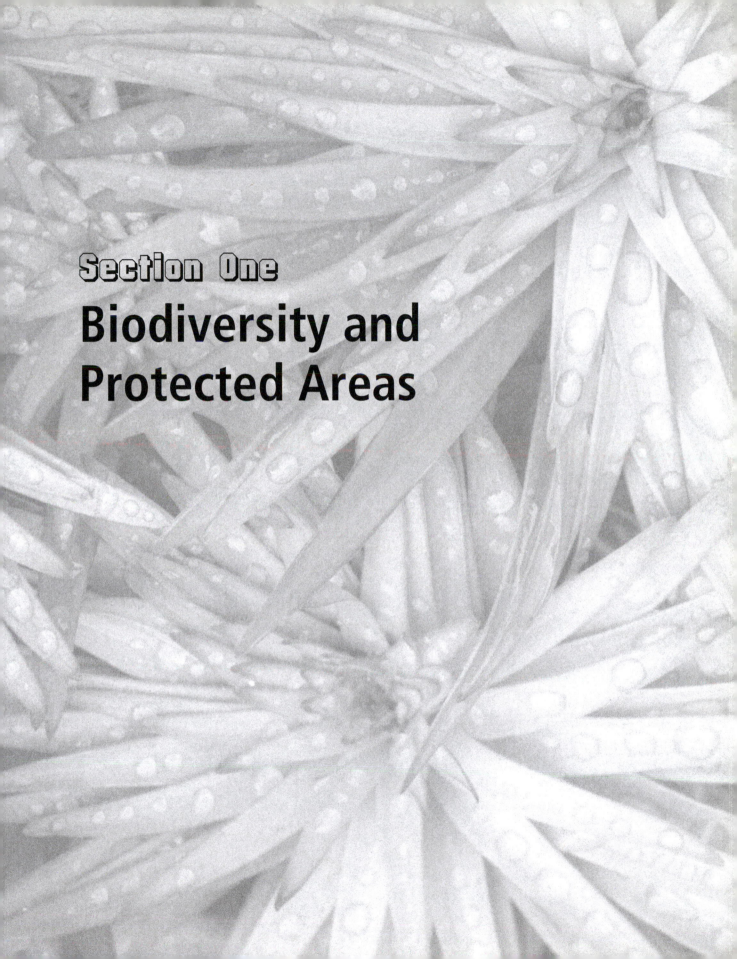

Section One

Biodiversity and Protected Areas

INTRODUCTION TO GLOBAL BIODIVERSITY

Agrobiodiversity
Fortress Conservation
Wilderness

Ecotourism
Trans-Frontier Conservation
Areas (TFCAs)

KEY TERMS

Biological diversity or biodiversity is generally "the variety of life" (Guyer and Richards 1996, 1). While many environmentalists credit ecologist Edward O. Wilson for coining the term "biodiversity," Walter Rosen utilized the term in 1986 (Guyer and Richards 1996). Wilson took up the term as part of his effort to "try and protect a specific academic interest (in whole organisms)" in a particular historical moment when many scientists were focused on understanding biological processes at the molecular level (Guyer and Richards 1996, 5). Thus, from the start, the concept of biodiversity asserted a particular way of seeing and understanding nature in terms of developing strategies for supporting and monitoring organisms, species, and habitats instead of prioritizing knowledge creation primarily through the reductive lens of a microscope.

In the late 1980s, the United Nations Environment Programme (UNEP) invited experts to develop a common definition of biodiversity and an assessment of its importance to ecology and humans, and to suggest strategies for minimizing threats to biodiversity. The product, the Convention on Biological Diversity (CBD), was presented at the United Nations Conference on Environment and Development (also known as the Earth Summit) in Rio de Janeiro in 1992 and entered into force in 1993. Article 2 of the CBD defines biodiversity as "the variability among living organisms from all sources including, inter alia, terrestrial, marine and other aquatic ecosystems and the ecological complexes of which they are part; this includes diversity within species, between species and of ecosystems." While this definition might seem fairly comprehensive, "biodiversity" is not directly equivalent to "nature," which is a much broader concept that includes processes beyond the biosphere.

Species Extinction

One of the main purposes of the idea of biodiversity was to develop a way of quantifying what had thus far eluded quantification: the number of different species, including both genetic and ecological diversity (Guyer and Richards 1996; Hellmann and Fowler 1999). Ecologists and other experts have collected samples of fossils and other material that show evidence of three to five mass extinctions of a wide range of species between 439 million years ago and the most recent mass extinction about 65 million years ago (Wake and Vredenburg 2008). Despite knowledge of mass extinctions of 10 to 95% of all species in these events (actual breakdowns and estimates vary), scientists have only estimates of how many species previously existed and they struggle to estimate how many species exist today. Scientists now warn that the globe is experiencing a sixth mass extinction event—the first mass extinction to be caused largely by human-related activities, ranging from pollution to climate change and facilitation of colonization by invasive species (Wake and Vredenburg 2008). Ecologists and policymakers recognize human impacts on living beings, but it is difficult to quantify at what *rate* we are losing biological diversity and to implement solutions to prevent further biodiversity loss.

Attempts to quantify the number of species and the rate of loss of biodiversity extend beyond mere scientific utility towards broader political-economic agendas. Scholars such as MacDonald (2010) have pointed out that the CBD codified business as usual more than it managed to radically stop threats to biodiversity because it ignored the role of consumption and capitalist expansion in driving biodiversity loss. MacDonald (2010, 526) explains that the CBD "codifies a dominant perspective of nature as capital through its emphasis on sustainable use initiatives that, when translated into practice, means the use of in situ biodiversity to realize profit through the conversion of use value to exchange value." This codification of nature into material (e.g., genetic information and material) for trade in the global market—along with the CBD's protection of a country's rights to determine who can benefit and what kinds of benefits to derive from resources within its territory—raises questions for environmentalists who embrace policies that follow the CBD model of "biodiversity" over a broader definition of nature (MacDonald 2010).

Another popular policy tool for protecting species has been the codification of species lists such as the IUCN Red List (www.iucnredlist.org), The Convention on International Trade in Endangered Species of Wild Fauna and Flora (CITES) (signed in 1973), and the United States Endangered Species Act of 1973 (ESA), which categorize the degree of threat experienced by different species (e.g., threatened, endangered, extinct) and prioritize the conservation of species deemed particularly important to the survival of broader habitats and ecosystems. Many scientists caution, however, that we tend to overly emphasize the biodiversity of charismatic mammal and reptile species, while the bulk of biodiversity exists in insect, plant, fungus, and other "animal" kingdoms (categorization of living things follows hierarchies established before the CBD, including kingdom, phylum, class, order, family, and genus categories) (Wilson 1998). Another important opportunity for the preservation of plant, animal, and microorganism biodiversity exists in agricultural systems, referred to as **agrobiodiversity**.

Agrobiodiversity includes the diversity of plants, practices, and knowledge that farmers manage and use within their farms and in the broader landscape.

Though biodiversity is often thought to exist mainly in wild ecosystems, agricultural systems have potential to incorporate significant numbers of plant species that thereby support a diversity of organisms (insects, bats, birds, soil microorganisms, etc.) (Méndez et al. 2010). Agroforestry systems producing coffee and cacao in the tropics have been shown to have levels of biodiversity comparable to forests, showing the great potential for human use of ecosystems to also support biodiversity conservation (Perfecto and Vandermeer 2008).

Biodiversity and Protected Areas

An additional tool used to protect biodiversity is the designation of ecosystems with particularly rich habitat and high levels of biodiversity as protected areas. The chapter that follows (Brockington et al. 2008) is part of a book offering a comprehensive review of the history, challenges, and future trajectories of conservation and protected areas. Co-authors Dan Brockington, Rosaleen Duffy, and Jim Igoe explore "how protected areas change nature and society" (64). The chapter highlights the major sticking points in debates about the purpose of conservation, the relationship between people, animals and park territory, and who wins and loses through the establishment of protected areas.

Brockington, Duffy, and Igoe (2008) question the notion of "**wilderness**" as "natural" spaces without people and critique a model of conservation commonly called "**fortress conservation**." Named after its reliance on enclosing common resources and lands for the enjoyment of elite tourists and its eviction of local people, fortress conservation upholds a view of nature that sees people as fundamentally incompatible with nature unless it is through the role of appreciation through tourism. Despite evidence across geographical contexts that this model is both ecologically and ethically questionable, many protected areas continue to function in a fortress-like model to this day, despite alternative experimentation with community-based conservation and other initiatives.

The next article (Laudati 2010) is a case study examining the grounded experiences of local people living within the boundary zone of Bwindi Impenetrable National Park in Uganda. In this area, endangered mountain gorillas are legally protected by **ecotourism** policies from not only being hunted by locals but from anyone approaching them or frightening them. Laudati argues that this policy aimed at protecting an endangered species translates to a livelihood threat for local farmers, who cannot protect their food crops from gorillas wandering beyond

Wilderness is a concept that differs across cultures, but in the "Western" philosophical tradition refers t nature that is untouched by humans or that is not controlled by humans and that is in need of protection. Th term has a long and controversial history in relation to conservation and conflicts along divisions of race, clas gender, ethnicity, and others.

Fortress Conservation consists of the enclosure of commonly held natural resources through the creation reserves, parks, and other bounded areas for conservation and tourism-related activities, to the exclusion local residents and users from these areas.

Ecotourism is composed of income-generating activities geared towards tourists who seek to appreciate various forms of "nature" in a wide range of locations and environments. Such activities often combine standard forms of the hospitality industry, including lodging, dining, and provision of souvenirs.

the park's boundaries and into farmers' fields (Ibid.). As gorillas have adjusted to more human activity in the park through ecotourism, and as there is territorial competition between gorilla groups, gorillas have expanded their foraging grounds beyond the park boundaries and into farmers' fields (Ibid.) This has in turn led to the effective extension of the park boundaries into the private lands of local farmers and the continued prohibition of people from taking resources from the park. This reflects a common theme with protected areas that conserve critical plant or animal habitat at the expense of local food production systems and land and resource tenure (Adams 2004; Brockington et al. 2008; Laudati 2010).

HIGHLIGHTED APPROACH: PROTECTED AREAS

The Power of Parks

By Dan Brockington, Rosaleen Duffy, and Jim Igoe

> The scientific mind does not so much provide the right answers as ask the right questions.
>
> Claude Levi-Strauss

The last two decades have seen the crystallization of fears by conservationists that there is a substantial extinction crisis looming, if not already unfolding. They have witnessed the growth of a substantial network of protected areas whose development is becoming increasingly driven by, and responsive to, the geography of rarity, endemism and land-use change. But the same period has also seen substantial critiques of conservation practice, both in terms of its impact on nature, and its consequences for society. The result has been a vigorous examination of protected areas (often euphemized as 'parks'). The discussion has often been confusing according to the questions that different protagonists were asking. We attempt to provide some clarity here.

First, we consider how well parks work. More precisely, we ask: is strong protection from human influence by states the best way to protect valuable nature, or would conservation objectives be advanced by encouraging other mechanisms that allowed more human use, development objectives or local control? We argue that there are good data demonstrating that parks protect vegetation and wildlife well from human transformation, but poor data as to their relative performance against other conservation mechanisms such as community conservation or village governed forest reserves, or other such schemes. In other words we do not understand the circumstances that might make formal protected areas the best means of achieving conservation objectives.

Second we examine the impacts on people. We consider how they have distributed different types of fortune and misfortune to their neighbours and stakeholders at different spatial scales. We examine the state of knowledge about eviction from protected areas. We argue that there are clear, sometimes widespread benefits arising from parks, many of which are hard to value in dismal economic terms, and that these have often been accompanied by varying degrees of local disempowerment, dispossession and marginalization. We argue that enquiries into eviction alone can risk displacing more important issues. We note that it is difficult to gain any comprehensive idea of the general social impacts of parks for want of any systematic data collection.

In recent years these questions have become embroiled in two other confusing conflicts. First, there is the poverty and conservation debate, which concerns conservation's role in causing and reducing poverty. Second there is the principle of local support, which states that parks without local support are bound to fail. We examine both, arguing that each is often founded on misunderstandings or confusions and that there is much more room for agreement between each side than is first apparent.

The issues we examine here have dominated discussions in conservation circles for many years and it is important that we outline our position and thinking on them. This chapter does review in detail how protected areas change nature and society. Given that our argument is that conservation and capitalism are combining to reshape the world we need to consider more carefully precisely what changes protected areas, the central conservation strategy, bring.

How Well do Protected Areas Work?

Protected areas play a vital role in conservation strategies and have been vigorously defended (Kramer et al, 1997; Brandon et al, 1998; Oates, 1999; Terborgh, 1999). These arguments are partly based on the obvious successes of the more strictly protected areas, generally termed 'parks' in protecting nature, and partly on diverse failures and uncertainties associated with alternative strategies.

With respect to protecting vegetation, there are strong debates in Canada, New Zealand and Australia about the place of grazing on public lands and the best way of protecting grasslands from unwanted change, but these are not debates about the effectiveness of parks per se. On the contrary, opponents of parks know that they will be effective in excluding grazing if established; that is why they oppose them. The disputes here are about the ecological necessity of protecting the land from livestock, with farmers disputing the findings of ecologists and the ability of the latter to know the land as they do. In New Zealand and Australia any land protected from livestock has also to be protected from introduced herbivores, carnivores and plant species (Mark, 1989; Gillies et al, 2003).

There is much more dispute about the most effective means of conserving tropical forest. With respect to tropical forests' protection, the importance of parks is strongly supported by a number of studies. Bruner and colleagues (2001a) found, on the basis of questionnaire evidence of managers and experts of a sample of 93 tropical parks in populated areas, that 40 percent had experienced improvement of vegetation cover, 43 percent had shown no further forest clearance since establishment. Naughton-Treves and colleagues (2005) compared 36 deforestation rates inside and outside protected areas. In 32 cases the deforestation rate was between 0.1 and 14 percent faster outside protected areas' boundaries. DeFries and colleagues (2005) examined the increasing isolation of 98 protected tropical forests using coarse resolution satellite data and found that two thirds experienced significant deforestation within 50km of their borders, but only a quarter had such within their boundaries.

There are problems with these studies. For example, it is not normally appropriate to use questionnaire data to assess vegetation change. It is simply not accurate, and prone to bias. In the case of Bruner and colleagues' work many of the respondents had a vested interest in showing that the parks were working because they were on the staff. Naughton-Treves et al are handicapped by the methodological problems of quantitatively comparing the rates of deforestation across different studies. They also do not say what proportion of the deforestation rates were 0.1 percent and which 14 percent lower. Nor do they, or DeFries and her colleagues, mention the possibility that in some cases gazettement may hasten land-use change beyond protected area boundaries. Nevertheless the trend in these findings is clear. There are clear suggestions that in some, if not many, circumstances, protecting a place by designating it as a park can much reduce unwanted vegetation change.

But does this mean that parks are better than other forms of protection? If we wish to protect a coastal forest in Madagascar, or a rainforest in New Zealand, is it necessary to impose state enforced regulations? Government conservation departments can be far removed from local realities, else simply absent and unable to enforce their rules. There are all sorts of situations where some form of local control may be better than distant state controls. None of the studies above, however, address that question (Bruner et al, 2001b; Vanclay, 2002). They are only concerned with how parks do compared to their surroundings, not with how they perform compared with other means of protection. Ostrom and Nagendra's review of this literature concluded that the 'debate over the effectiveness of strictly protected areas needs to be extended to a much larger landscape of tenure regimes' (2006, p19225).

This is an important issue, but has been tackled with surprisingly few rigorous studies. There are some relatively small-scale studies based on satellite data and aerial photographs. Nepstad and colleagues have compared the relative efficiency of large uninhabited parks and inhabited extractive and indigenous reserves in preventing fire and deforestation in the Brazilian Amazon using satellite data between 1997 and 2000 (for deforestation), and 1998 (for fires). They found that both forms were effective against preventing fire and deforestation, with no significant differences between either. They noted that the good performance of occupied reserves was achieved despite their being at the frontier of deforestation pressure, whereas parks benefited from their relative lack of proximate habitat change (Nepstad et al, 2006). Ostrom and Nagendra report poor performance of selected parks in South Asia that excluded local management, and better performance of community managed forests nearby (Ostrom and Nagendra, 2006).

The most ambitious attempt to test the relative efficacy of protected areas is work by Tanya Hayes and Elinor Ostrom, who have considered the relative effectiveness of parks compared to community controls in two recent papers (Hayes and Ostrom, 2005; Hayes, 2006). They looked at data collected by the International Forestry Resources and Institutions (IFRI) network on 163 forests, of which 76 were 'parks' and 87 'non-parks', where park was defined as falling in one of the six IUCN categories (Table 1). All forests in the IFRI database provide relatively standardized data about institutions governing their use, ownership, user communities and forest products used. To compare forest condition Hayes and Ostrom used assessments of vegetation density made by independent professional foresters who compared the vegetation density of IFRI forests to other forests in the same ecological zone.

Table 1. A comparison of the distribution of parks in Hayes' sample and others

Country	Hayes, 2006; Hayes and Ostrom, 2005			Naughton-Treves et al, 2005	DeFries et al, 2005	Bruner et al, 2001a
	Non-parks	Parks not in WDPA	Parks in WDPA			
Argentina	–	–	–	–	5	–
Bolivia	3	6	–	–	2	–
Brazil	2	1	–	–	32	7
Colombia	–	–	–	–	9	8
Equador	1	–	–	4	2	7
Paraguay	–	–	–	3	3	1
Peru	–	–	–	5	4	6
Venezuela	–	–	–	–	11	–
Belize	–	–	–	–	2	1
Costa Rica	–	–	–	12	2	–
Guatemala	6	1	–	2	4	–
Honduras	1	–	–	1	2	4
Mexico	2	4	–	2	–	1
Nicaragua	–	–	–	–	1	–
Panama	–	–	–	–	2	–
USA	7	–	–	–	1	–
Jamaica	–	–	–	1	–	–
Cambodia	–	–	–	–	4	1
China	–	–	–	1	3	–
India	28	11	1	–	10	–
Indonesia	–	–	–	3	29	8
Japan	–	–	–	–	1	–
Laos	–	–	–	–	–	10
Malaysia	–	–	–	–	3	–
Myanmar	–	–	–	–	1	–

(continues)

Country	Hayes, 2006; Hayes and Ostrom, 2005			Naughton-Treves et al, 2005	DeFries et al, 2005	Bruner et al, 2001a
	Non-parks	Parks not in WDPA	Parks in WDPA			
Nepal	22	23	2	–	1	–
Philippines	–	–	–	–	1	7
Sri Lanka	–	–	–	–	4	–
Taiwan	–	–	–	–	4	–
Thailand	–	–	–	–	29	3
Vietnam	–	–	–	1	2	3
Brunei D'm	–	–	–	–	1	–
CAR	–	–	—	–	1	–
Congo	–	–	–	–	2	–
Cote d'Ivoire	–	–	–	–	2	4
DRC	–	–	–	–	4	–
Ghana	–	–	–	–	–	10
Kenya	–	1	4	1	1	–
Liberia	–	–	–	–	1	1
Madagascar	4	4	–	–	5	5
Malawi	–	–	–	–	1	–
Senegal	–	–	–	–	–	2
Tanzania	1	1	1	–	–	6
Togo	–	–	–	–	–	2
Uganda	10	3	13	8	–	6
Australia	–	–	–	–	2	–
Total	87	55	21	44	198	93

Hayes and Ostrom report no difference in the vegetation density of parks and non-parks. But they found evidence that might make parks imposed and policed by government a less robust form of conservation than protection rooted in local institutions. For instance, they found that density of vegetation was higher where more forest products had rules governing use, and lower where there were no rules. They found vegetation density was more abundant where more user groups could define the rules and sparser where fewer could. Thus what makes for more effective protection (denser vegetation relative to similar forests) is not the official designation, but rather the role of residents in defining rules for forest products.

But there are several problems with this analysis. There were no data about the size of these forests, and so it is impossible to assess the relative significance of the contribution of parks and non-parks to protected area networks. There are also problems with how the term 'park' was defined. Few of the parks in the analysis were included in the World Database of Protected Areas (WDPA) (Table 1). This could reflect its incompletenesses, but it could also mean that there is simply inadequate overlap between this sample of parks and those other authors have used. The WDPA lists nearly 4700 other protected areas in the countries Hayes and Ostrom examined, including nearly 1700 forest reserves, which are not part of their analyses. The WDPA is not the ultimate authority as to what constitutes a park. But it has formed the basis for other studies (Rodrigues et al, 2004; DeFries et al, 2005; Naughton-Treves et al, 2005). Rigorous methodologies need not be based on the WDPA, but it would be useful for comparative purposes to know how samples of parks relate to the WDPA.

It is perhaps unfortunate that Hayes and Ostrom tied their work so tightly to parks. The term is a shibboleth (Redford et al, 2006, p1); it is widely used, but in ways that reinforce prejudice, obscuring more than it reveals. One could argue that parks are in fact irrelevant to their argument. They are in fact concerned with the importance for conservation of locally derived rules of resource-use control. There is a risk that the value of their findings will be lost by the confusion over the term 'park'.

But this work also shows us that Hayes' question, 'Are parks effective?', is just a little too blunt. Effective for whom, for what nature? And if Bruner and his colleagues show that 40 percent of (large tropical forest) parks 'have seen an improvement in vegetation cover', they also show that 17 percent were not 'holding their borders' against agricultural expansion and a further 43 percent merely had no further net clearing (cf. Roe et al, 2003). The question to ask in these circumstances is not whether they are failing or succeeding, but rather under what circumstances were they strong, and when were they weak? As we will argue later, it is not adequate simply to assert that they will be weak without local support.

With respect to wildlife the value of parks is again clear, but the relative effectiveness of parks compared to other strategies, and the impact of different levels of hunting on conservation objectives is less so. We know that the answer to the question 'Do parks reduce mortality from hunting?' is 'Yes', but given that, several other questions become important:

- Precisely what impacts does hunting have on animal populations?
- How many and how large do parks need to be to protect wildlife?
- How will the impact of parks vary for different taxa according to their size and distribution across the landscape?
- What mosaic of parks and other strategies are required to advance conservation objectives?
- What hunting or other types of resource use could be allowed in parks?

We can sketch some broad geographical patterns dividing the world into temperate and tropical regions and the latter into forests and grassland. In temperate countries strong well-organized local sports hunting lobbies have campaigned vigorously and effectively for good hunting habitat. This form of hunting is often highly compatible with conservation objectives, as it means more land where wildlife can thrive. Parks are routinely hunted in the UK, and in many other countries that forbid hunting in protected areas, wildlife habitat extends far beyond park boundaries on private lands because of the lucrative revenues hunting on them can command.

There are some important exceptions to this rule. In Australia hunters want sustained populations of Sambar deer, and Brumbie runners want wild horses, both of which are large introduced species with problematic impacts on the ecosystem. In New Zealand large populations of deer, chamois, thar, goat and pig cause severe damage to vegetation (Mark, 1989). Hunting of these species is freely allowed in national parks, and again hunting lobbies desire sustained populations that other conservationists wish removed. Nor is this just a New World problem. In Scotland large deer populations inhibit the regrowth of forest (Toogood, 2003).

Hunting by indigenous people of indigenous fauna in temperate areas can be viewed with suspicion by some conservationists. Use within or near protected areas is often resented. In New Zealand Maori harvesting of mutton birds is a bone of contention with conservationists (Taiepa et al, 1997), as are Maori desires to hunt wildlife, such as the rare *kereru* (native pigeon) for traditional purposes (Galbreath, 2002; Young, 2004). Similar disputes are visible in Australia over hunting dugong (albeit not temperate) and the harvest of marine resources inside national parks, and in North America over indigenous whaling and seal kills.

In the tropics, the importance of parks for protecting wildlife is not disputed, but again the relative importance of parks to other strategies is not clear. In grasslands and open habitat, especially in Africa, parks are often inadequate to support many large species that migrate long distances and which depend on land outside their borders (Borner, 1985; Western, 1994). There are many attempts to sustain wildlife populations beyond park borders, which we will review in the next chapter. Improvements in village forest management have seen improvements in populations of many species, including large, slow breeding ones (Monela et al, 2004; Blomely and Ramadhani, 2006).

Commercial hunting operations outside national parks, and sometimes of village land can provide substantial sources of revenue, which if well distributed locally can make wildlife valuable (Novelli et al, 2006). In Africa it is a valuable industry and estimated to generate about $200 million a year, with half of that spent in South Africa (Lindsey et al, 2007). Sport and trophy hunting has increasingly become part of conservation argument and policies, and is promoted as a low-impact sustainable use approach, adding value to natural resources (Hofer, 2002; Novelli and Humavindu, 2005; Novelli et al, 2006). The studies show the central importance of sport hunting for wildlife to Namibian tourism economy. The ecological impact varies with the quality of control exerted over adherence to trophy quotas (Loveridge et al, 2007). Interestingly Novelli and colleagues argue that sport hunting should be defined as a form of ecotourism because although it depends on killing individual animals it has a lower overall impact on the environment and brings in a greater level of revenue than regular photographic tourism. Sport hunters do not require the levels of' infrastructure in the form of hotels, restaurants, bars and roads that non-consumptive tourism depends on (Smith and Duffy, 2003; Novelli et al, 2006).

Such 'consumptive' forms of wildlife tourism are highly controversial, either 'because they can kill charismatic animals such as elephants (Fortmann, 2005), or because they can restrict local access to valued resources (Dzingirai, 2003; Robbins and Luginbuhl, 2005). As a result community-based conservation and tourism programmes that are reliant on sport hunting have also been criticized; for example, Communal Areas Management Plan for Indigenous Resources (CAMPFIRE) in Zimbabwe was highly dependent on trophy hunting as a source of revenue and as such attracted criticism from the Humane Society of the US and International Fund for Animal Welfare, amongst others (Smith and Duffy, 2003, pp 145–158).

As to the relative importance of parks and commercial hunting operations for conservation, it is in fact often not realistic to compare the two. For viable commercial hunting often depends on nearby parks as a source of wildlife. Both are seen as complementary but the mosaics of land use resulting tend to reflect the willpower of governments, locals and donors rather than much systematic planning.

Hunting in tropical forests is particularly worrying for conservationists. Productivity of wild meat is an order of magnitude less than more open habitats (Milner-Gulland et al, 2003), and there is also often fewer domestic livestock to provide local needs for meat. Demands for protein (Brashares et al, 2004) and an urban preference for wild meat is driving substantial hunting. The impacts of changing animal abundance cascade through the ecosystem (affecting animal-dispersed seeds) and society (affecting income and diet, Stoner et al, 2007). Again there are clear geographical patterns in the consequences driven by population density (figures below are from Milner-Gulland et al, 2003). In Asia, where high population densities in forest (522/km2) combine with strong demands from prosperous urban areas, the effects are considerable, with numerous local and regional extirpations. One review suggested that commercially important species have disappeared or exist at low densities (Corlett, 2007). Bennett (2002) notes that diets have changed in order to cope with the lack of wild meat due to the combined effects of habitat loss and hunting.

In West Africa (population density 99/km2) substantial defaunation has already taken place with only resilient fast-breeding species remaining (Bennett et al, 2007) and offtake rates of many species are unsustainable in many parts of Central Africa. Wilkie and Carpenter (1999) report that hunting reduced species density by 43–100 percent, with the greatest effects on large slow-breeding animals. Oates documents empty forests in Ghana with hunters reduced to killing birds (Oates, 1999). Hunting combined with disease has resulted in the catastrophic decline of apes in western equatorial Africa (Walsh et al, 2003).

These problems are present but less severe in Latin American forests (population density 46/km^2). Hunting has a noticeable impact on population abundances and structure (Bodmer et al, 1997; Bodmer and Lozano, 2001). Kent Redford coined the term 'empty forest' to describe hunted forests in the neotropics (Redford, 1992). Indigenous hunters in the Amazon do not appear to hunt in order to conserve their prey populations, instead taking animals opportunistically, regardless of their gender and attempting to maximize return for effort rather than the long-term viability of prey populations (Alvard, 1993, 1995; Alvard et al, 1997). But people's impact is relatively slight because their numbers are few (Smith and Wishnie, 2000). In the Amazon there are large areas of land that are largely unhunted (Fa et al, 2002). These authors suggest that 60 percent of taxa in the Congo are exploited unsustainably but none in the Amazon.

What are the consequences of these patterns for the parks debate? In the Amazon, as in Australia and New Zealand, conservation concerns reflect desires to preserve fauna that do not reflect the presence of people. Wildlife is not generally threatened by hunting, but inhabited forest is simply less interesting to conservationists. Conservationists also fear repeating patterns of wildlife loss seen in Asia and Africa. As Redford and Sanderson observed of forest peoples and their representatives:

> They may speak for their version of a forest, but they do not speak for the forest we want to conserve.
>
> (Redford and Sanderson, 2000 p1364)

In West and Central Africa large areas free from hunting (parks) are indispensable to conservation objectives. But observers also recognize that a cornucopia of strategies to reduce hunting generally (more protein from other sources), changing the species taken (education campaigns, taxes, enforcement), and local conservation initiatives (no-take areas) will be necessary (Milner-Gulland et al, 2003; Bennett et al, 2007). The latter is particularly important for rural prosperity also. The decline in bushmeat availability due to sales to urban markets presents many problems to rural residents who then lose an important source of income and protein, especially in lean seasons (de Merode et al, 2004; Nielsen, 2006). Research by de Merode has shown that village chiefs have actively prevented the sale in local markets of slow-breeding species taken with heavy weaponry in the Democratic Republic of the Congo (DRC) even during the civil war. Urban markets in contrast showed a massive increase in wild meat availability in that period as controls broke down and hunting and weapons proliferated (de Merode and Cowlishaw, 2006).

The constant call in the literature is for a broader vision of a mosaic of land management—parks, no-take areas and diverse community-based strategies that will allow for larger healthier wildlife populations. What we lack are the data on the distribution and density of many hunted species would allow us to predict the consequences for wildlife of different mosaics (Milner-Gulland et al, 2003). Beyond securing a basic minimum of sites that might prevent extinction the appropriate configuration of parks and strategies for effective wildlife conservation is far from clear.

What do Parks do to People?

It is not as easy as it might seem to catalogue the way that parks distribute fortune and misfortune among different groups in society. In many cases a benefit to one group is a disadvantage to another. The loss of grazing for transhumant pastoralists and their removal elsewhere might result fewer cattle thefts for more sedentary neighbours. Lost income for women selling traditional medicines gathered in protected areas may be achieved through employment opportunities given to young men to act as forest guards. Prohibitions on hunting by elderly skilled hunters may be accompanied by distributions of cash or payments for local services by hunting revenues from wealthy tourists. Healthy forests on watersheds may benefit lowland irrigators, but could be accompanied by restrictions to the livelihoods of forest dwellers. When the Mkomazi Game Reserve in Tanzania was cleared of its pastoral occupants the cattle keepers lost prime grazing land, and a local cattle market collapsed. Nearby farmers in one village, however, benefited from new investments into schools and other infrastructure, which pastoralists were less able to enjoy because some had moved away and others were now earning less money and so could not send their children to school so easily (Brockington, 2002).

In spite of the difficulties in measuring the costs and benefits of conservation, and the lack of good data about them, debates about parks' impact on people are still often cast in terms of their costs and benefits. Studies have tended to focus either on simply the benefits, or on just the costs. Balanced evaluations of individual protected areas are rare, and on networks of protected areas even fewer. We will discuss each separately.

The benefits that advocates of parks list are legion. Parks safeguard ecosystem services. They act as water catchments, providing vegetation cover that aids infiltration of water into the ground and preventing soil erosion that would otherwise fill dams. They are sources of genetic diversity for food crops. They could house species that could be useful to medical science in its search for cures to human disease. Parks provide recreation and release for tired city dwellers; more than that, they focus tourists into a relatively few places, creating more space elsewhere. The tourist industries they sustain can make valuable contributions to the economy. They provide aesthetic pleasure, both to actual visitors, and through the industries of image making (film, painting, pictures and poetry), which they house. Parks are a focus of research activities, either on species only found easily within them, or because researchers wish to explore dynamics in ecosystems with relatively little human impact. Parks have become a focus of nation building and a focal point of development strategies. By providing people with the types of contact with nature that they lack in their daily lives they inspire them to become conservationists.

But the costs, which critics of parks decry, are also many. They cause eviction and physical displacement; they cause economic displacement, denying people access to fuelwood, thatching grass, water, lumber, meat and diverse other resources. The fact that they often do this to poor and weak rural groups, the better to create relaxing holidays and pleasing vistas for the world's wealthy is unpleasant, and often unjust. Parks also displace people symbolically. They write them out of landscape's history, proclaiming that they do not belong. Parks are a means by which states extend their bureaucratic powers over land use and lives. They can marginalize and disempower local resource management and fundamentally alter the livelihoods from which people derive their identities.

Parks rarely, if ever, do only one of these things, however. Instead they distribute fortune and misfortune at the same time. It is rarely meaningful to speak of benefits offsetting costs, or vice versa. In many cases the groups benefiting and those suffering are different. The benefits to one are a cost to another. 'Net' gain or loss is experienced only at the broad scale and rarely within the lives of those affected. Where individuals do experience both gains and costs they are often not particularly commensurable—it is simply a change, a new set of circumstances in which they now live. Quite often, however, costs are experienced in terms of access to natural resources, while benefits usually come in the form of training, technical development projects, and opportunities in the market economy (Igoe, 2006b). This basic pattern has two important implications for people living in and around protected areas: 1) technical development projects and trainings may indeed be benefits but they are not usually as direct and immediate as benefits from the environment—an especially important distinction in communities where many people are poor and food insecure; and 2) because the concept of development is premised on the idea that people will move to market-based livelihoods. In many cases, however, people displaced are not well absorbed by the market economy. This can be a common outcome whenever natural resources are appropriated from local people at the behest of more distant interests and agendas, whether this appropriation is for a park, a mine or a hydroelectric dam.

Criticisms of parks, however well founded, can still cause resentment among conservationists. One of us (Brockington) has attended high-level meetings to consider the social impacts of protected areas in which senior conservationists have said that conservationists simply need to communicate better the fact that parks are good things and win the argument again. But a more reasonable position is that there is a basic lack of data to make the assertion that parks are good. We have no comprehensive surveys of the social impacts of protected areas. There is still a considerable reluctance on behalf of some conservationists to collect basic data on, for example, evictions from protected areas or tourist revenues generated by them. Calls for systematic studies of the social impacts of protected areas (Brockington and Schmidt-Soltau, 2004) have largely gone unanswered (but see Wilkie et al, 2006 for an exception).

One of the more fundamental gaps in our current knowledge is that we do not even know how many people live in different types of protected area. The WDPA does not record whether or not people are found inside protected areas, or whether they would be allowed to live in them. We have to consult individual country case studies to examine this, and the best work is becoming increasingly dated. Work in India in the late 1980s found that 56 percent of national parks and 72 percent of sanctuaries had resident peoples (Kothari et al, 1989).[1] A survey of 70 percent of national parks in South America in 1991 found that 85 percent had people living inside them (Amend and Amend, 1995).[2] More recent studies also suggest that protected areas are characterized by high rates of occupancy. A study of 91 protected areas in well populated tropical areas found that 70 percent were occupied by people (Bruner et al, 2001a). Individual studies in Mongolia, East Kalimantan, Myanmar and the Central African Sub-region indicate use rates of 70–100 percent (Jepson et al, 2002; Rao et al, 2002; Bedunah and Schmidt, 2004; Cernea and Schmidt-Soltau, 2006).

Analyses of satellite data of agricultural activity within protected areas provide little extra guidance. The only global survey concluded that it is practised in 29 percent of the known area of protected areas (McNeely and Scherr, 2003; Molnar et al, 2004a). Unfortunately this research used an old version of the WDPA in which only 44,000 protected areas with adequate geographical information systems (GIS) data were available (Sebastian, pers. comm. 2005). Polygons or centre points are now available for more than 75,000 sites (Chape et al, 2005). However, there are also problems with the quality of the data. First, it is unable to detect agro-forestry, such as shade-grown coffee. It could also not distinguish between fallowed land growing trees, and unused land. Moreover since agricultural activity was defined as areas with at least 30 percent of land under crops it thus omits less intensive cultivation. It gives no indication of pastoral use of rangelands (present in 100 percent of Mongolia's protected areas). Finally the global 29 percent is a bald statistic. We do not have a breakdown of the extent of agricultural activity by geographic region, category of protected area or ecological potential.[3] It is difficult to say, therefore, how many protected areas are not cultivated because they are cold and inhospitable, or how much of the cultivation is an integral part of the conserved landscape (as in many British protected areas).

It is worth dwelling on one of the most contentious aspects of protected areas: their role in causing eviction of people (Brockington and Igoe, 2006; Redford and Fearn, 2007). Opinions about the natures and scale of this problem are divided. Borgerhoff Mulder and Coppolillo stated that the literature on evictions from protected areas offers 'a massive cataloguing of past, recent and ongoing abuses' (Borgerhoff Mulder and Coppolillo, 2005, p36). David Wilkie and his colleagues asserted, that 'to date little empirical evidence exists to substantiate the contention that parks are bad for local people' (Wilkie et al, 2006, p247). We believe that the truth lies somewhere between these two positions. There are many cases of displacement

Table 2. Establishment decades of protected area for which evictions have been reported

	Pre-1940	1940	1950	1960	1970	1980	1990	2000
S.E. Asia	–	–	–	1	3	3	3	–
South Asia	1	–	–	1	6	7	2	–
W. & C. Africa	2	–	4	6	2	2	3	7
E. & S. Africa	6	5	8	17	19	4	3	–
North Amer.	6	1	–	–	8	2	1	–
Cen. Amer.	–	–	–	–	5	3	2	–

that Wilkie and colleagues are ignoring. But Borgerhoff Mulder and Coppolillo are exaggerating the quality, extent and order of knowledge. Our grasp of the subject is simply not as good as they claim.

Brockington and Igoe (2006) carried out a global review of protected area evictions. The reports collected covered only 184 protected areas with many giving no details as to their actual impacts. It is highly likely that much has gone unreported. But we can get some inkling of the geography of evictions from these studies. Evictions have been most common in Africa, South and Southeast Asia and North America; relatively few are reported in this literature from South and Central America, Australia, Europe, the former Soviet Union and of the Caribbean and Pacific.

We also learnt something of the history of eviction. Most protected areas from which evictions have been reported were set up before 1980 (Table 2). This is not a global trend, but the consequence of the strong patterns in North America and sub-Saharan Africa that are well represented in the cases we have studied. In some regions (Central America, South and Southeast Asia) the opposite trend is apparent, with more protected areas for which evictions are reported established after 1980. Regardless of the trends in establishment, we should not infer the timing of evictions from the date of establishment. In many cases laws providing, for the removal of people from a protected area were not established until long after it was set up.

But there are remarkably few studies published on eviction before 1990, and a surge of publications thereafter (Table 3). The surge does not appear to have been driven by a spate of recent evictions. Rather they were mainly the result of a spate of historical investigations (Table 4). This has characterized research on protected areas in southern Africa (Carruthers, 1995; Koch, 1997; Ranger, 1999; Palmer et al, 2002; Bolaane, 2004a, b, 2005; Brooks, 2005) and eastern Africa (Neumann, 1998; Brockington, 2002). It has been a particularly strong feature of scholarship emerging from North America (Catton, 1997; Keller and Turek, 1998; Spence, 1999; Burnham, 2000; Jacoby, 2001; Igoe, 2004b; Nabakow and Lawrence, 2004). In other regions (such as South America) the relative lack of historical re-examination and the general paucity of eviction cases suggest that the practice has been relatively rare of late.

Table 3. The history of publication of eviction

Decade beginning	1970	1980	1990	2000
Number of studies	8	24	109	104

Table 4. Timing of removals reported in papers published after 1990

Timing of removals	Protected area established		
	Up to 1990	1990 to present	Total
Pre-1990	97	–	97
Post-1990	14	24	38
Unspec'd	16	1	17

Where eviction is still prevalent it is often bound up with other debates about environmental change or degradation (Tanzania—Usangu Game Reserve), ecosystem services (Thailand—the Karen people in the highlands) (Laungaramsri, 1999; Buergin and Kessler, 2000; Sato, 2000, 2002; Buergin, 2003), or the appropriate development strategy for undeveloped people who live in parks and who need to be moved out so that they can become proper citizens (Botswana) (Ikeya, 2001). Eviction is one of the techniques conservation requires to achieve its goals. The issue is how it is carried out, and with what consequences to local people (Schmidt-Soltau and Brockington, 2007). Unfortunately many of the important players in conservation circles have yet to come up with a coherent response over how to handle evictions (Winer et al, 2007). There are cases of relocation for conservation both increasing and intensifying inequality (McLean and Straede, 2003), and redressing it, providing once landless evictees with good land (Karanth, 2007).

But more importantly our review also showed that there were far more important things going on than just eviction. It remains the most dramatic and devastating impact, the most violent thing a state can do to its law-abiding citizens. But it is not the most prevalent problem that many people face and there is a real danger that a focus on eviction will divert attention away from more pressing issues.

One such pressing issue is the problem of empowerment and marginalization (which we examine in the following chapters). Another is the impacts of anti-poaching policies. Wildlife poaching is often identified as a key threat to the survival of some of the most high-profile species, including tigers, rhinos and elephants (Neumann, 2004). Poaching can range from subsistence hunting with snares and traps (for antelope, birds etc. for food) and commercial scale hunting for lucrative wildlife products (birds eggs, ivory and rhino horn etc.). But what is poaching exactly? In sub-Saharan Africa, the arrival of colonial rule was also accompanied by new stipulations on hunting. As Mackenzie's (1988) detailed study points out, 'hunting for the pot' by Africans was criminalized through laws banning the use of traps and snares. However, the newly declared reserves and parks were opened up for recreational hunting by Europeans. The colonial legal framework set the boundaries for defining poaching versus acceptable hunting, and also legitimated the ways that colonial authorities often used hunting for game to underpin and subsidize the costs of imperial expansion across Africa (Mackenzie, 1988; Mutwira, 1989).

In a sense this way of thinking about poachers versus hunters is present in current NGO campaigns about the need to prevent poaching. The view of commercial poachers in Africa that has been presented by NGOs and governments is that they are black, poverty-stricken and usually cross international borders to engage in commercial poaching. In the late 1980s the high-profile international campaigns about ivory poaching blamed illegal hunting in

Kenya on Somali *shifta* crossing the border to hunt and then sell ivory on the lucrative international black market. However, later analyses of poaching in East and southern Africa pointed the finger at government-level corruption and the role of national armies such as the South African Defence Force, which indicated that poaching was highly organized and interlinked with transnational organized criminal networks that traded ivory, rhino horn, drugs, stolen cars and engaged in people trafficking (Bonner, 1993; Ellis, 1994; Reeve and Ellis, 1995).

Following these high-profile campaigns, the issue of poaching has not gone away, although its profile is slightly different. In general, there have been two different types of response from authorities engaged in conservation including national governments and conservation NGOs. The first is related to the community conservation debates, and revolves around giving local communities a stake in conservation efforts. For example, programmes referred to as turning 'poachers into game guards' are focused on giving paid employment to former poachers as rangers for protected areas. These kinds of initiatives are discussed more fully in Chapter 5. The second kind of response is coercion. Peluso argues that a state's capacity to control and extract resources is a function of relations between state and society, but that the state's ability to enforce policy varies widely (Peluso, 1993). Extraction of resources has included allocation of land for tourism and rights of access to wildlife and this has led to the state and local people holding competing claims over national parks and wildlife. As a result, the state has used conservation as a means of coercing local people (Neumann, 1997, 1998). Successive governments have excluded local people from national parks and outlawed the use of wildlife in order to preserve a national asset for tourism, sport hunting and game viewing, which are mostly the realm of the wealthy.

Poachers cannot all be considered in the same way because there are different motivating reasons for poaching. But in a number of NGO campaigns in the 1980s all poachers were treated as equally culpable. The reasons for poaching were not generally explored since the fact that animals were being poached formed the basis of the campaigns (Peluso, 1993, pp205–209). In NGO campaigns poachers are often vilified as criminals or characterized as poverty stricken individuals driven to make money through illegal activity.

Coercive anti-poaching efforts are often reliant on an alliance between the state, donors and international green NGOs. For example, Bonner (1993) documents the use of a helicopter donated by Prince Phillip to the World Wildlife Fund for nature (WWF) for national government anti-poaching operations in Zimbabwe. After it was found that the helicopter had been authorized to engage in shoot-to-kill campaigns in the Zambezi Valley, WWF International withdrew the helicopter amidst claims by Amnesty International that the 'wildlife wars' in sub-Saharan Africa were responsible for massive human rights abuses (Bonner, 1993; Duffy, 2000). The use of various coercive methods, including violence and shoot-to-kill, raises questions about who gives authorization for the use of coercion and violence. These questions are all the more pertinent with the development of privately owned reserves and the use of private companies employed to carry out anti-poaching strategies.

Ferguson (2006) suggests that the commitment to privatized violence is visible in the realm of environmental politics because of the apparent 'need' to secure protected areas for internationally valuable ecotourism. States and international environmental NGOs have carved out spatial enclaves to protect biodiverse hotspots. In the zeal for protecting species, NGOs and states have presided over an expansion of use of mercenary forces to carry out anti-poaching patrols. Ferguson highlights the scheme by African Rainforest and River Conservation (cf. Shanahan, 2005) operating in Central African Republic where the sale of diamonds dug up in the area they control are used to fund the reserve; management of the reserve includes hiring ex-South African and Rhodesian mercenaries to organize anti-poaching patrols that attack groups of poachers operating from Sudan. As Ferguson suggests, these might seem like extreme measures but unfortunately they are not uncommon in conservation practice (Ferguson, 2006, pp42–47).

These schemes may begin with genuine goals of conserving species, but the commitment to the 'global good' of conservation can result not just in misfortune for certain groups and individuals, but can in fact end up legitimizing and justifying serious human rights abuses. This in turn reinforces the negative view (especially in Africa) that wildlife simply matters more than people. The development of private armies to protect reserves and species also raise complex ethical questions (Neumann, 2004): On whose authority do such private entities engage in violence against suspected poachers? Who legitimizes their use of shoot-to-kill policies? It is important not to forget that these private conservation armies generally deal with people who are only suspected of, and not convicted of, illegal hunting.

Poverty, Conservation and Local Support

The poverty and conservation debate is hotly contested between those who feel that conservation policy should address poverty issues, and those who do not. Among the latter a common theme is that conservation is not about reducing poverty but about saving habitat, wildness and biodiversity. Advocates of this position argue that conservation is not responsible for the high levels of inequality and poverty visible globally, and the conservation movement should not try to become responsible for addressing these ills. Many of the places that conservationists are interested in for biodiversity reasons just happen also to be poor, and conservationists should not seek to become responsible for tackling the thorny issues that cause this poverty. Rather they should recognize that development and poverty reduction is a hard and complex task, and they should accept the limitations to their expertise and restrict themselves to saving species and habitat (Sanderson and Redford, 2003).

This position was strengthened by the widely recognized problems with so-called 'Integrated Conservation with Development' Projects, which had tried to combine conservation with development goals. This idea had won widespread support among donor circles. Many projects had been attempted at the cost of millions of dollars, but few could show any tangible gains for conservation objectives; in many cases they may have disrupted them (Wels et al, 1999). Consequently many observers felt that it was better to 'decouple' the objectives of development and conservation, pursuing both separately (Barrett and Arcese, 1995).

In response critics of that proposed separation of duties observed that there were many cases where conservation, as we have seen above, was responsible for the impoverishment of rural people. It was quite wrong, they argued, to ignore the poverty for which conservation policies were responsible. Moreover it was self-defeating as poverty drove the environmentally damaging behaviour with which conservationists were struggling. Ignoring development, and 'decoupling' conservation from it denied the possibility of 'win–win' scenarios where conservation and development gains could both be realized. The failure of IDCPs was real, but these were large donor-driven initiatives that were unsustainable without aid. More locally driven community conservation initiatives, while complex and difficult, have already demonstrated that conservation and development goals can be realized together.

The poverty-conservation debate is fraught and often confused. It gets particularly heated because the centres of biodiversity conservationists value most are often also located in the poorest parts of the world where development needs are greatest. Bill Adams, with minor assistance from his colleagues, made a valuable contribution in *Science*, which distinguished two normative stances and two empirical arguments in the debate (Adams et al, 2004).

The normative stances were:

1. **Conservation and poverty reduction are separate policy realms**
   Conservation policy should not consider development goals directly. Any incidental benefits such as improved ecosystem services, or the development of local tourism industries could be welcomed but should not made explicit goals. Rather conservation policy should be evaluated according to its impact on species or landscape conservation.
2. **Conservation should not compromise poverty reduction**
   The success of conservation policy is measured by its impact on species and landscapes, but in the process it ought not to impoverish people. Where it causes local hardship this needs to be compensated, even if it is not strictly necessary to achieve conservation's goals.

The empirical claims were:

1. **Poverty impedes conservation**
   Poaching and environmental degradation is often pursued by the poor in short-sighted ways. When people become richer they are more amenable to accepting conservation policies. Addressing poverty is therefore a means of directly and indirectly promoting conservation.
2. **Poverty reduction depends on sustainable resource use**
   Where livelihoods depend on living resources their sustainable use will promote both the resource and the livelihood associated with it.

It is worth noting another position in this debate, specifically adopted with respect to protected areas, which is sometimes adopted in verbal debates, but which we have rarely seen in print. This holds that parks are just good things and generate wealth. This is implied in works that only examine the benefits of protected areas and not their cost. It is also implied in the performance indicators of the Millennium Development Goals. One of the indicators used to evaluate performance of goal 7 (ensure environmental sustainability) is the proportion of land held in protected areas (target 9). The implication is that more protected areas will result in less poverty.

As noted above, this has been a central premise of international development since the 1950s and the idea of growth poles, which are large-scale generators of wealth that are assumed to have amplifier effects to the local economy. From this perspective, then, parks are seen as a kind of growth pole. But the empirical basis for this claim is weak.

Conversely other observers have argued that poverty increases with protected area growth. Geisler and de Sousa (2001) have argued that in Africa the poorest countries had the largest protected area estate. Geisler (2003) also observed that between 1985 and 1997 poorer African countries gazetted many more protected areas than richer African countries. But this position too does not withstand close scrutiny. Upton and colleagues examined the relationship between diverse indices of poverty and compared them to more recent editions of the WDPA. They found no relationship between them at the national scale, concluding that the local impacts of protected areas are just that—local (Upton et al, 2008).

If we parse practical conservation problems according to the scheme Adams and colleagues outline we suspect much more constructive disagreements become possible. Few people will dispute that, if conservation objectives are about preventing extinction and reducing the threat of extinction, then its success and priorities are best measured in terms of relative abundance of rare species. In this respect its distinctness from poverty reduction policies are important. Equally few conservationists believe that it is acceptable for biodiversity reduction to cause or enhance poverty, particularly where the people affected are already disadvantaged. In terms of empirical positions, where it can be shown that conservation objectives are being threatened by poverty, or where they can be enhanced by diverse strategies of pursuing local prosperity, then few conservationists would object to strategies that reduce the one and promote the other.

This parsing does not necessarily make the decision making easy. For example, how can we determine how much poverty is caused by conservation? How closely do schemes to promote prosperity have to be tied to conservation outcomes for them to be valuable to conservation's remit? For example consider one of the first experiments in community-based conservation and ecotourism development in southern Belize: the Cockscomb Basin Jaguar Preserve. The preserve was initially designated as a forest reserve in 1984, and was later expanded and converted into the world's first jaguar sanctuary, supported by WWF International and Jaguar cars. In 2000 the EU agreed to a €1.28 million grant to support co-management of the Cockscomb Basin Jaguar Preserve and other protected areas by the Belize Audubon Society, in conjunction with local communities.[4]

Like many other protected areas the creation of the Jaguar Preserve required relocation of local communities to a new site: the Maya Centre Village. The initial rationale was that Cockscomb would be a community-managed conservation area, and that the people of Maya Centre Village would directly benefit from the ecotourism revenues generated by the scheme. These revenues would then be used to compensate them for loss of access to areas they had historically used for subsistence agriculture and hunting. This was intended to ensure that the local communities did not have to live with all the costs of creating and enforcing protected areas without any of the benefits.

The creation of Cockscomb meant that agriculture and hunting became illegal in the preserve, even though they were vital subsistence activities for local people. As a result, the establishment of the jaguar sanctuary led directly to a significant reduction in access to resources contained within the reserve, including locally important spiritual and religious sites. The preserve was managed by the Belize Audubon Society, while the community was supposed to develop the institutional capacity to take over running the preserve. This led to criticisms that the jaguar sanctuary merely replicated the traditional relationship between communities and state-run conservation agencies. Despite the promises that Cockscomb would constitute a significant departure in conservation policy local communities have failed to gain substantial economic benefits or genuine participation in the management of the preserve (Duffy, 2002, pp 105–107).

Such complex situations as these demonstrate how difficult it can be to see clearly with respect to the problems of conservation and poverty. Has the scheme made people poorer, or just failed to make them richer? Has it caused them any material harm, or has it marginalized them more, or has it merely failed to address, or worse intensified, existing inequalities of power? It might bring more economic benefit at some point in the future; else its market-guided alterations might not be associated with any meaningful changes.

A second area of confusion has arisen from the strongly held beliefs among advocates of community conservation that parks cannot survive without local support. This belief, called 'the principle of local support' (Brockington, 2004) is reiterated constantly in the conservation literature. It is one of the main reasons why strong approaches to conservation that impose protection laws (often called 'fortress conservation') have been criticized in recent years. David Western, once head of the Kenyan Wildlife Service, wrote that 'a fallacy of protectionism is that we can ignore costs locally' (Western, 2001, p202). The President of IUCN, opening the fourth World Parks Congress in Caracas, stated the importance in bald terms, claiming that 'quite simply, if local people do not support protected areas, then protected areas cannot last' (Ramphal, 1993, p57). Ed Barrow and Christo Fabricius, prominent conservationists in East and South Africa, stated that '[u]ltimately, conservation and protected areas in contemporary Africa must either contribute to national and local livelihoods, or fail in their biodiversity goals' (Barrow and Fabricius, 2002). Adrian Phillips, a leading figure in the IUCN, when asked to name one key lesson to be gleaned out of interactions between protected areas and their neighbours, found the answer 'very simple'; it was 'the iron rule that no protected area can succeed for long in the teeth of local opposition' (Borrini-Feyerabend et al, 2002).

Conservation undoubtedly becomes easier with the support of a sympathetic local population. There are many occasions when wildlife, vegetation and landscape have suffered because their conservation is unpopular locally. David Western recorded several instances when Maasai pastoralists expressed their antipathy to conservation policy by killing animals in and around the Amboseli National Park (Western, 1994). Saberwal and colleagues note that the heavy handed and exclusionist enforcing of conservation policy in India has created many local enemies of protected areas (Saberwal et al, 2001). The problems that conservation causes people have meant that, ironically, there are even a number of cases where parks have, unwittingly, initiated or enhanced nature's destruction. Fearing interference from governments and restriction on resource use, villagers have killed chimpanzees in Tanzania, diverse wildlife in Uganda and felled trees and forests in Nicaragua, Nepal, Norway and China (Walsh, 1997; Brandon, 1998; Harkness, 1998; Nygren, 2000; Murray, 1992, cited in Hulme and Infield, 2001).[5] Analysts of sustainable forestry have observed forest reserve creation can be made possible by increasing the intensity of production on other forest lands, with adverse results for biodiversity conservation (McAlpine et al, 2007).

But it is not true that parks will always fail in the face of local opposition. The principle of local support can, oddly, ignore the politics of protected areas. It fails to recognize that protected areas distribute fortune as well as misfortune, that they make allies as well as enemies. Often the local communities who oppose the existence and policies of their neighbouring protected areas tend to be politically weak rural groups. They can be opposed to powerful alliances of central and local government and rural groups, the police, park guards and paramilitary units, and national and international NGOs raising money and awareness for the cause of the protected areas. These are contests that the rural groups may be ill-equipped to win, especially when (as is often the case) the most powerful and educated members of a particular community are positioned to take advantage of economic opportunities presented by conservation and/or are being recruited as 'community representatives' by the powerful groups that other local people are resisting. Asserting the necessity of local cooperation, therefore, ignores the realities of power.

The principle of local support fails to recognize the power of the international biodiversity conservation movement and the important local power relations that sustain it. It can be, paradoxically, inimical to effective promotion of conservation policies that are fairer locally because it fails to recognize where the real power lies. If we are to understand the local impacts of conservation policy we require a much better grasp of its politics. If we want conservation practice that is more just then we have to understand what sustains injustice. Each local situation will have a different set of factors sustaining particular conservation policies.

To put it another way: there are countless examples throughout history of inequalities and injustices being perpetrated and perpetuated despite resistance to them, and despite the opposition and hatred they generated. The Roman Empire brought down by its slaves, enclosure in England and highland clearances in Scotland were not prevented by the people who lost their rights to the commons, nor were the iniquities of England's factory system overturned by a worker's revolt.[6] Indigenous peoples in Latin America, North America and Australia have been removed from their lands and violently treated for hundreds of years. Why should the injustices perpetrated by conservation be any different?

Conclusion

Protected areas have expanded rapidly in recent decades. They continue to proliferate. Many more are needed and will be needed in diverse regions and habitats that are not well protected. And as they spread they will have all sorts of consequences, both expected and surprising. As the reach of conservation areas expands, and the influence of parks grows, we can expect these changes to become more common. The issues we have examined above will become more pervasive.

But to understand their importance properly we must recognize, first, that protected areas are also just one type of conservation strategy. The reach of conservation policy is extending far beyond protected areas boundaries. It has to if its objectives are to be achieved. We must therefore examine more carefully what happens when rural groups become involved in implementing conservation policy. Second, we must realize that protected areas are being incorporated into new networks of international governance, and new development strategies and programmes, such as the growth of ecotourism.

References

Adams, W. M., R. Aveling, D. Brockington, B. Dickson, J. Elliott, J. Hutton, D. Roe, B. Vira, and W. Wolmer. 2004. "Biodiversity Conservation and the Eradication of Poverty." Science 306: 1146-49.

Alvard, M. S. 1995. "Shotguns and Sustainable Hunting in the Neotropics." Oryx 29: 58–66.

Alvard, M. S. 1993. "Testing the 'Ecologically Noble Savage' Hypothesis: Interspecific Prey Choice by Piro Hunters of Amazonian Peru." Human Ecology 21: 355–87.

Alvard, M. S., J. G. Robinson, K. H. Redford, and H. Kaplan. 1997. "The Sustainability of Subsistence Hunting in the Neotropics." Conservation Biology 11: 977–82.

Amend, S., and T. Amend. 1995. National Parks without People? The South American Experience. Quito, Ecuador: IUCN—the World Conservation Union.

Barrett, C. B., and P. Arcese. 1995. "Are Integrated Conservation-Development Projects (ICDPs) Sustainable? On the Conservation of Large Mammals in Sub-Saharan Africa." World Development 23: 1073–84.

Barrow, E., and C. Fabricius. 2002. "Do Rural People Really Benefit from Protected Areas—Rhetoric or Reality?" Parks 12: 67–79.

Bedunah, D. J., and S. M. Schmidt. 2004. "Pastoralism and Protected Area Management in Mongolia's Gobi Gurvansaikhan National Park." Development and Change 35: 167–91.

Bennett, E. L. 2002. "Is There a Link between Wild Meat and Food Security?" Conservation Biology 16(3): 590-92.

Bennett, E. L., E. Blencowe, K. Brandon, D. Brown, R. W. Burn, G. Cowlishaw, G. Davies, H. Dublin, J. E. Fa, and E. Milner-Gulland. 2007. "Hunting for Consensus: Reconciling Bushmeat Harvest, Conservation, and Development Policy in West and Central Africa." Conservation Biology 21: 884–87.

Blomely, T., and H. Ramadhani. 2006. "Going to Scale with Participatory Forest Management: Early Lessons from Tanzania 1." International Forestry Review 8: 93–100.

Bodmer, R. E., J. F. Eisenberg, and K. H. Redford. 1997. "Hunting and the Likelihood of Extinction of Amazonian Mammals." Conservation Biology 11: 460–66.

Bodmer, R. E., and E. P. Lozano. 2001. "Rural Development and Sustainable Wildlife Use in Peru." Conservation Biology 15: 1163–70.

Bolaane, M. 2004a. "The Impact of Game Reserve Policy on the River Basarwa/Bushmen of Botswana." Social Policy & Administration 38.

Bolaane, M. 2004b. "Wildlife Conservation and Local Management: The Establishment of the Moremi Park, Okavango, Botswana in the 1950s–1960s." Unpublished D. Phil. Dissertation, Oxford University.

Bolaane, M. 2005. "Chiefs, Hunters and Adventurers: The Foundation of the Okavango/Moremi National Park, Botswana." Journal of Historical Geography 31: 241–59.

Bonner, R. 1993. At the Hand of Man: Peril and Hope for Africa's Wildlife. London: Simon and Schuster.

Borgerhoff Mulder, M., and P. Coppolillo. 2005. Conservation: Linking Ecology, Economics, and Culture. Princeton: Princeton University Press.

Borner, M. 1985. "The Increasing Isolation of Tarangire National Park." Oryx 19: 91–96.

Borrini-Feyerabend, G., T. Banuri, T. Farvar, K. Miller, and A. Phillips. 2002. "Indigenous and Local Communities and Protected Areas: Rethinking the Relationship." Parks 12(2): 5-15.

Brandon, K. 1998. "Perils to Parks: The Social Context of Threats." In Parks in Peril: People, Politics, and Protected Areas, edited by K. Brandon, K.H. Redford and S.E. Sanderson. Washington, DC: Island Press.

Brockington, D. 2002. Fortress Conservation: The Preservation of the Mkomazi Game Reserve, Tanzania. Bloomington: Indiana University Press.

Brockington, D. 2004. "Community Conservation, Inequality and Injustice: Myths of Power in Protected Area Management." Conservation and Society 2: 411.

Brockington, D., and J. Igoe. 2006. "Eviction for Conservation: A Global Overview." Conservation and Society 4(3): 424-70.

Brockington, D., and K. Schmidt-Soltau. 2004. "The Social and Environmental Impacts of Wilderness and Development." Oryx 38: 140–42.

Brooks, S. 2005. "Images of 'Wild Africa': Nature Tourism and the (Re) Creation of Hluhluwe Game Reserve, 1930–1945." Journal of Historical Geography 31: 220–40.

Bruner, A. G., R. E. Gullison, R. E. Rice, and G. A. Da Fonseca. 2001. "Effectiveness of Parks in Protecting Tropical Biodiversity." Science 291: 125–28.

Buergin, R. 2003. "Shifting Frames for Local People and Forests in a Global Heritage: The Thung Yai Naresuan Wildlife Sanctuary in the Context of Thailand's Globalization and Modernization." Geoforum 34: 375–93.

Buergin, R., and C. Kessler. 2000. "Intrusions and Exclusions: Democratization in Thailand in the Context of Environmental Discourses and Resource Conflicts." GeoJournal 52: 71–80.

Burnham, P. 2000. Indian Country, God's Country: Native Americans and the National Parks. Washington, DC: Island Press.

Carruthers, J. 1995. The Kruger National Park: A Social and Political History. Durban: University of Natal Press.

Catton, T. 1997. Inhabited Wilderness: Indians, Eskimos, and National Parks in Alaska. Albuquerque: University of New Mexico Press.

Cernea, M. M., and K. Schmidt-Soltau. 2006. "Poverty Risks and National Parks: Policy Issues in Conservation and Resettlement." World Development 34: 1808–30.

Chape, S., J. Harrison, M. Spalding, and I. Lysenko. 2005. "Measuring the Extent and Effectiveness of Protected Areas as an Indicator for Meeting Global Biodiversity Targets." Philosophical Transactions of the Royal Society B: Biological Sciences 360: 443–55.

Corlett, R. T. 2007. "The Impact of Hunting on the Mammalian Fauna of Tropical Asian Forests." Biotropica 39: 292–303.

DeFries, R., A. Hansen, A. C. Newton, and M. C. Hansen. 2005. "Increasing Isolation of Protected Areas in Tropical Forests over the Past Twenty Years." Ecological Applications 15: 19–26.

de Merode, E., and G. Cowlishaw. 2006. "Species Protection, the Changing Informal Economy, and the Politics of Access to the Bushmeat Trade in the Democratic Republic of Congo." Conservation Biology 20: 1262–71.

de Merode, E., K. Homewood, and G. Cowlishaw. 2004. "The Value of Bushmeat and Other Wild Foods to Rural Households Living in Extreme Poverty in Democratic Republic of Congo." Biological Conservation 118: 573–81.

Duffy, R. 2000. Killing for Conservation: Wildlife Policy in Zimbabwe. Oxford and Bloomington: James Currey Ltd.

Duffy, R. 2002. A Trip Too Far: Ecotourism Politics and Exploitation. London: Earthscan.

Dzingirai, V. 2003. "The New Scramble for the African Countryside." Development and Change 34: 243–64.

Ellis, S. 1994. "Of Elephants and Men: Politics and Nature Conservation in South Africa." Journal of Southern African Studies 20: 53–69.

Fa, J. E., C. A. Peres, and J. Meeuwig. 2002. "Bushmeat Exploitation in Tropical Forests: An Intercontinental Comparison." Conservation Biology 16: 232–37.

Ferguson, J. 2006. Global Shadows: Africa in the Neoliberal World Order. Durham: Duke University Press.

Fortmann, L. 2005. "What We Need Is a Community Bambi: The Perils and Possibilities of Powerful Symbols." In Communities and Conservation: Histories and Politics of Community-Based Natural Resource Management, edited by J.P. Brosius, A.L. Tsing and C. Zerner. New York: Rowman and Littlefield.

Galbreath, R. 2002. "Displacement, Conservation and Customary Use of Native Plants and Animals in New Zealand." New Zealand Journal of History 36: 36–47.

Geisler, C., and R. De Sousa. 2001. "From Refuge to Refugee: The African Case." Public Administration and Development 21: 159–70.

Geisler, C. 2003. "A New Kind of Trouble: Evictions in Eden." International Social Science Journal 55: 69–78.

Gillies, C. A., M. R. Leach, N. B. Coad, S. W. Theobald, J. Campbell, T. Herbert, P. J. Graham, and R. J. Pierce. 2003. "Six Years of Intensive Pest Mammal Control at Trounson Kauri Park, a Department of Conservation 'Mainland Island,' June 1996–July 2002." New Zealand Journal of Zoology 30: 399–420.

Harkness, J. 1998. "Recent Trends in Forestry and Conservation of Biodiversity in China." The China Quarterly 156: 911–34.

Hofer, D. 2002. The Lion's Share of the Hunt: Trophy Hunting and Conservation: A Review of the Legal Eurasian Tourist Hunting Market and Trophy Trade under Cites. Brussels: Traffic Europe.

Hulme, D., and M. Infield. 2001. "Community Conservation, Reciprocity and Park-People Relationships: Lake Mburo National Park, Uganda." In African Wildlife and Livelihoods: The Promise and Performance of Community Conservation, edited by D. Hulme and M. Murphree. Portsmouth: Heinemann.

Igoe, J. 2004. Conservation and Globalization: A Study of National Parks and Indigenous Communities from East Africa to South Dakota. Belmont: Wadsworth Publishing Company.

Igoe, J. 2006. "Measuring the Costs and Benefits of Conservation to Local Communities." Journal of Ecological Anthropology 10: 72–77.

Ikeya, K. 2001. "Some Changes among the San under the Influence of Relocation Plan in Botswana." In Parks, Property and Power: Managing Hunting Practice and Identity within State Policy Regimes (Papers presented at the Eighth International Conference on Hunting and Gathering

Societies - CHAGS 8, National Museum of Ethnology, Osaka, October 1998) edited by D.G. Anderson and K. Ikeya. Osaka: National Museum of Ethnology, 183–98.

Jacoby, K. 2001. Crimes against Nature: Squatters, Poachers, Thieves, and the Hidden History of American Conservation. Berkeley and Los Angeles: University of California Press.

Jepson, P., F. Momberg, and H. van Noord. 2002. "A Review of the Efficacy of the Protected Area System of East Kalimantan Province, Indonesia." Natural Areas Journal 22(1): 28-42.

Karanth, K. K. 2007. "Making Resettlement Work: The Case of India's Bhadra Wildlife Sanctuary." Biological Conservation 139: 315–24.

Keller, R. H., and M. F. Turek. 1998. American Indians and National Parks. Tucson: University of Arizona Press.

Koch, E. 1997. "Ecotourism and Rural Reconstruction in South Africa: Reality or Rhetoric?" In Social Change and Conservation, edited by K.B. Ghimire and M.P. Pimbert. Abingdon and New York: Earthscan.

Kothari, A., P. Pande, S. Singh, and D. Variava. 1989. Management of National Parks and Sanctuaries in India: A Status Report. New Delhi: Indian Institute of Public Administration.

Kramer, R. A., C. von Schaik, and J. Johnson. 1997. Last Stand: Protected Areas and the Defense of Tropical Biodiversity. Oxford: Oxford University Press.

Laungaramsri, P. 1999. "The Ambiguity of 'Watershed': The Politics of People and Conservation in Northern Thailand. A Case Study of the Chom Thong Conflict." In Indigenous Peoples and Protected Areas in South and Southeast Asia: From Principles to Practice, edited by M. Colchester and C. Erni. Copenhagen: IWGIA.

Loveridge, A. J., A. W. Searle, F. Murindagomo, and D. W. Macdonald. 2007. "The Impact of Sport-Hunting on the Population Dynamics of an African Lion Population in a Protected Area." Biological Conservation 134: 548–58.

MacKenzie, J. M. 1988. The Empire of Nature: Hunting, Conservation and British Imperialism. Manchester: Manchester University Press.

Mark, A. F. 1989. "Responses of Indigenous Vegetation to Contrasting Trends in Utilization by Red Deer in Two South-Western New Zealand National Parks." New Zealand Journal of Ecology 12: 103–14.

McAlpine, C. A., T. A. Spies, P. Norman, and A. Peterson. 2007. "Conserving Forest Biodiversity across Multiple Land Ownerships: Lessons from the Northwest Forest Plan and the Southeast Queensland Regional Forests Agreement (Australia)." Biological Conservation 134: 548–58.

McLean, J., and S. Straede. 2003. "Conservation, Relocation, and the Paradigms of Park and People Management—A Case Study of Padampur Villages and the Royal Chitwan National Park, Nepal." Society & Natural Resources 16: 509–26.

McNeely, J. A., and S. J. Scherr. 2003. Ecoagriculture: Strategies to Feed the World and Save Wild Biodiversity. Washington, DC: Island Press.

Monela, G. C., S. A. O. Chamshama, R. Mwaipopo, and D. M. Gamassa. 2001. A Study on the Social, Economic, and Environmental Impacts of Forest Landscape Restoration in Shinyanga Region. Final Report to the Ministry of Natural Resources and Tourism Forestry and Beekeeping Division and IUCN-The World Conservation Union Eastern Africa Regional Office. Nairobi: IUCN.

Mutwira, R. 1989. "Southern Rhodesian Wildlife Policy (1890–1953): A Question of Condoning Game Slaughter?" Journal of Southern African Studies 15: 250–62.

Nabokov, P., and L. L. Loendorf. 2004. Restoring a Presence: American Indians and Yellowstone National Park. Norman: University of Oklahoma Press.

Naughton-Treves, L., M. B. Holland, and K. Brandon. 2005. "The Role of Protected Areas in Conserving Biodiversity and Sustaining Local Livelihoods." Annual Review of Environment and Resources 30(1): 219-52.

Neumann, R. P. 1997. "Primitive Ideas: Protected Area Buffer Zones and the Politics of Land in Africa." Development and Change 28: 559-82.

Neumann, R. P. 1998. Imposing Wilderness: Struggles over Livelihood and Nature Preservation in Africa. Berkeley and Los Angeles: University of California Press.

Neumann, R. P. 2004. "Moral and Discursive Geographies in the War for Biodiversity in Africa." Political Geography 23: 813–37.

Nielsen, M. R. 2006. "Importance, Cause and Effect of Bushmeat Hunting in the Udzungwa Mountains, Tanzania: Implications for Community Based Wildlife Management." Biological Conservation 128: 509–16.

Novelli, M., and M. Humavindu. 2005. "Wildlife Tourism: Wildlife Use Vs. Local Gain Trophy Hunting in Namibia." In Niche Tourism: Contemporary Issues, Trends and Cases, edited by M. Novelli. Oxford: Elsevier.

Nygren, A. 2000. "Environmental Narratives on Protection and Production: Nature-Based Conflicts in Río San Juan, Nicaragua." Development and Change 31: 807-30.

Oates, J. F. 1999. Myth and Reality in the Rain Forest: How Conservation Strategies Are Failing in West Africa. Berkeley: University of California Press.

Palmer, R. C. G., H. Timmermans, and D. Fay. 2002. From Conflict to Negotiation: Nature-Based Development on the South African Wild Coast. Pretoria: Human Sciences Research Council.

Peluso, N. L. 1993. "Coercing Conservation? The Politics of State Resource Control." Global Environmental Change 3: 199–217.

Ramphal, S. 1993. "Para Nostros La Patria Es El Planeta Tierra." In Parks for Life: Report of the IVth World Congress on National Parks and Protected Areas, edited by J. McNeely. Gland: IUCN.

Ranger, T. O. 1999. Voices from the Rocks: Nature, Culture & History in the Matopos Hills of Zimbabwe. Bloomington: Indiana University Press.

Rao, M., A. Rabinowitz, and S. T. Khaing. 2002. "Status Review of the Protected-Area System in Myanmar, with Recommendations for Conservation Planning." Conservation Biology 16: 360–68.

Redford, K. H. 1992. "The Empty Forest." BioScience 42: 412–22.

Redford, K. H., and E. Fearn. (eds.) 2007. Protected Areas and Human Displacement: A Conservation Perspective. Bronx: Wildlife Conservation Society.

Redford, K. H., and S. E. Sanderson. 2000. "Extracting Humans from Nature." Conservation Biology 14(5): 1362-64.

Reeve, R., and S. Ellis. 1995. "An Insider's Account of the South African Security Forces' Role in the Ivory Trade." Journal of Contemporary African Studies 13(2): 227-243.

Robbins, P., and A. Luginbuhl. 2005. "The Last Enclosure: Resisting Privatization of Wildlife in the Western United States." Capitalism Nature Socialism 16: 45–61.

Roe, D., J. Hutton, J. Elliott, M. Saruchera, and K. Chitepo. 2003. "In Pursuit of Pro-Poor Conservation—Changing Narratives...or More?" Section I: The Complexities of Governing Protected Areas 87.

Saberwal, V. K., M. Rangarajan, and A. Kothari. 2001. People, Parks, and Wildlife: Towards Coexistence. New Delhi: Orient Longman Private Limited.

Sanderson, S. E., and K. H. Redford. 2003. "Contested Relationships between Biodiversity Conservation and Poverty Alleviation." Oryx 37: 389–90.

Sato, J. 2000. "People in Between: Conversion and Conservation of Forest Lands in Thailand." Development and Change 31: 155–77.

Sato, J. 2002. "Karen and the Land in Between: Public and Private Enclosure of Forests in Thailand." In Conservation and Mobile Indigenous Peoples: Displacement, Forced Settlement, and Sustainable Development, edited by D. Chatty and M. Colchester, 277–95. New York: Berghahn Books.

Schmidt-Soltau, K., and D. Brockington. 2007. "Protected Areas and Resettlement: What Scope for Voluntary Relocation?" World Development 35: 2182–202.

Shanahan, C. L. 2005. "(No) Mercy Nary Patrols: A Controversial, Last-Ditch Effort to Salvage the Central African Republic's Chinko Basin." Thomas Jefferson Law Review 27(1): 223-54.

Smith, E. A., and M. Wishnie. 2000. "Conservation and Subsistence in Small-Scale Societies." Annual Review of Anthropology 29: 493-524.

Smith, M., and R. Duffy. 2003. The Ethics of Tourism Development. London and New York: Routledge.

Spence, M. D. 1999. Dispossessing the Wilderness: Indian Removal and the Making of the National Parks. Oxford: Oxford University Press.

Stoner, K. E., K. Vulinec, S. J. Wright, and C. A. Peres. 2007. "Hunting and Plant Community Dynamics in Tropical Forests: A Synthesis and Future Directions." Biotropica 39: 385–92.

Taiepa, T., P. Lyver, P. Horsley, J. Davis, M. Brag, and H. Moller. 1997. "Co-Management of New Zealand's Conservation Estate by Maori and Pakeha: A Review." Environmental Conservation 24: 236–50.

Toogood, M. 2003. "Decolonizing Highland Conservation." In Decolonizing Nature: Strategies for Conservation in a Post-Colonial Era, edited by W.M. Adams and M. Mulligan, 152-71. London: Earthscan.

Upton, C., R. Ladle, D. Hulme, T. Jiang, D. Brockington, and W. M. Adams. 2008. "Are Poverty and Protected Area Establishment Linked at a National Scale?" Oryx 42: 19–25.

Walsh, M. 1997. "Mammals in Mtanga: Notes on Ha and Bembe Ethnomammalogy in a Village Bordering Gombe Streams National Park, Western Tanzania." A report for the Lake Tanganyika Biodiversity Project, Kigoma, Tanzania.

Western, D. 1994. "Ecosystem Conservation and Rural Development: The Case of Amboseli." In Natural Connections: Perspectives in Community-Based Conservation, edited by D. Western and R.M. Wright (with S. Strum, Associate Editor). Washington, DC: Island Press.

Western, D. 2001. "Taking the Broad View of Conservation—A Response to Adams and Hulme." Oryx 35: 201–03.

Wilkie, D. S., and J. F. Carpenter. 1999. "Bushmeat Hunting in the Congo Basin: An Assessment of Impacts and Options for Mitigation." Biodiversity & Conservation 8: 927–55.

Wilkie, D. S., G. A. Morelli, J. Demmer, M. Starkey, P. Telfer, and M. Steil. 2006. "Parks and People: Assessing the Human Welfare Effects of Establishing Protected Areas for Biodiversity Conservation." Conservation Biology 20: 247–49.

Winer, N., D. Turton, and D. Brockington. 2007. "Conservation Principles and Humanitarian Practice." Policy Matters 15: 232–40.

Young, D. 2004. Our Islands, Our Selves. Dunedin: University of Otago Press.

Notes

1. This work is dated because over 120 protected areas of some 600 protected areas in India were established since that work was carried out. More are proposed (see Bhomia and Brockington, forthcoming).

2. This work too is dated as the extent of category 1 and 2 protected areas on the continent has increased by more than 10 percent since its publication.

3. Since that original analysis has also been lost (Sebastian, pers. comm. 2005), it will be impossible to improve on that statistic.

4. *Belize Audubon Society Newsletter,* January–April 2000, vol 32, p1.

5. Although in the Norwegian case, when a landowner felled his forest on receipt of a letter announcing it was to become protected, it later emerged that the letter was in fact a practical joke sent by a neighbour (Svarstad, pers. comm. 13 October 2004).

6. Polanyi states "The labouring people themselves were hardly a factor in this great movement [of social reform] the effect of which was, figuratively speaking, to allow them to survive the great Middle Passage. They had almost as little to say in the determination of their own fate as the black cargo of Hawkins ships' (Polanyi, 2001 (1944)). Their demands were relatively easily ignored. In the UK when millions of Chartists demanded the vote in the 1840s, they were refused by a parliament representing only a few hundred thousand.

CASE STUDY

The Encroaching Forest

Struggles Over Land and Resources on the Boundary of Bwindi Impenetrable National Park, Uganda

By Ann A. Laudati

Tukamuheibwa Ignatius[1] has been dealing with wildlife raiding his crops for a long time. In the past few years, instances of these attacks have gotten progressively worse, and farmers such as Ignatius are constantly seeking new strategies to combat the problem. Ignatius's latest plan involves an elaborate scheme using multiple vehicle tires laid out at approximately 5-foot intervals just outside the boundary that separates his land from the national park known as Bwindi. With the use of a detailed sketch, he describes how individuals will keep fires burning throughout the night with the use of kerosene, a well-known strategy that successfully deters raiding wildlife. While technologically sound, this requires huge amounts of capital and labor—resources that Ignatius is lucky enough to have. For the several hundred other impoverished households whose lands border the park, however, the only option available is the use of individual household members on all-night (and occasionally, all-day) vigils. For rural farmers who depend on human labor, the costs of such a strategy are prohibitively high.

Crop raiding is a common problem for rural farmers around the world, particularly for those whose land borders protected areas. What distinguishes Ignatius and the other farmers living adjacent to Bwindi Impenetrable National Park are the restrictions they face in dealing with the various wildlife that encroach onto their land, with particular emphasis on one—the mountain gorilla (*Gorilla beringei beringei*). Ecotourism policies, established to minimize the amount of stress endured by these endangered animals, not only require that farmers refrain

Ann A. Laudati, "The Encroaching Forest: Struggles Over Land and Resources on the Boundary of Bwindi Impenetrable National Park, Uganda," *Society & Natural Resources: An International Journal*, vol. 23, no. 8, pp. 776–789. Copyright © 2010 by Taylor & Francis Group LLC. Reprinted with permission.

from scaring gorillas away if they wander onto their land or destroy their crops, but prohibit farmers from entering areas that gorillas venture into, even if these areas happen to be their own land. With the recent growth of ecotourism in the region, this has meant that farmers are more vulnerable to raids against their banana plantations and are experiencing more time spent away from farmland frequented by gorillas—resulting in the loss of crops, occasionally full harvests, and increasingly, for those who do not have the financial resources like Ignatius to keep the land, the loss of their farms.

The study of conservation territories (Schroeder 1999; Zimmerer 2000) and the exclusionary and coercive policies that often accompany the creation of these conservation spaces has been well served by political ecology. Particular attention to local-level investigations documenting struggles over resources and "the violence of displacement" (Neumann 2004) within conservation spaces (e.g., Peluso 1993; Neumann 1998; Brockington 2002; Sundberg 2003; Young 2003) has invigorated protected area debates within the field, contributing to the rise of a paradigm shift toward alternative "nature–society hybrids" (Zimmerer 2000, 356) within conservation (see Jones 2006). Yet as Neumann (2005, 146) argues, "the typical … project of today has not moved biodiversity conservation very far beyond the fortress park model," precisely because it fails to challenge the fundamental source of conflict between conservation and local communities: land rights and resource access (Zerner 2000). Rather than leading to greater economic and social justice, conservation planning has actually contributed new layers of outside control to communities surrounding protected areas (e.g., Moore 1998; Murombedzi 2003). The expansion of outside, particularly state, control into rural areas through policies designed to protect and serve endangered wildlife has found increasing significance within studies on human–wildlife conflicts—particularly in reference to the movement of charismatic species such as elephants and tigers onto community land, and the restrictions placed on rural peasants in responding to such incidents (e.g., Neumann 2004). This article expands the scope of these investigations by showing how this control has taken new forms, namely, through the dispossession of private property via conservation policies that not only restrict rural farmers from responding to incidents of crop raiding but also prevent local communities from accessing their own land.

Drawing from recent theoretical discussions within political ecology on the politics of social justice and nature conservation (Zerner 2000) and the normalization of violence against rural Africans within protected areas, which privileges wild animals over human groups (Neumann 2004), I argue that the circumstances surrounding the loss of land in Bwindi suggest a new form of coercion and control by the conservation state. By examining the linkages between a gorilla tourism project, the dispossession of private land, and the loss of control over local land use decisions, this article shows how gorilla conservation, coupled with wildlife mobility, has enabled the conservation state to extend the territory of park land and outside control onto private land. Such forms of control, I argue, represent a new phase in a very long-term conservation policy toward rural communities adjacent to Bwindi, defined by the "voluntary" relinquishment of access to land and resources on the park boundary by communities living adjacent to conservation areas. The implication then, for rural farmers' food security, livelihoods, and self-sufficiency, necessitates that we broaden our current understanding of the violence of conservation within "the war for conservation in Africa" (Neumann 2004).

The research presented here draws upon a year of ethnographic-based fieldwork carried out by the author in Bwindi Impenetrable National Park, Uganda, between 2004 and 2005. The primary data for this research were provided by three extended village stays in geographically and economically distinct areas surrounding the park, utilizing in-depth, open-ended interviews and participant observation. Villages were selected based on the varying degrees of their interactions with tourists, their location around the park, and their distinct geographic characteristics. Interview subjects were selected to represent all of the main stakeholders involved with Bwindi, including members of the local Bakiga and Bafumbira communities, members of the ethnically marginalized Batwa group, and park staff and nongovernmental organization (NGO) personnel from various levels of authority. Differences in economic status, gender, proximate household distance to the park, participation in foreign funded projects, and participation in local government council or park committees were sought among local informants to ensure a wider representation of local concerns and issues. Particular effort was made to reach the poorest and most marginalized households. The 166 open-ended interviews were supplemented with 27 semistructured village meetings held in each of the Parishes bordering the park and approximately 400 household-level surveys conducted at two separate field sites. Secondary data gathered from park staff reports and NGO documents were then used as a means of triangulating data already received.

Background

Located in the Kigezi region in southwest Uganda, Bwindi Impenetrable National Park represents one of the oldest, most complex and biologically rich systems on earth (Blomley 2003). With a total area of 330.8 km^2, Bwindi represents an important epicenter within the Albertine Branch of East Africa's Great Rift Valley—an area listed in the top 20 of the Global 200 priority areas for biodiversity and ranked as the highest priority for the conservation of restricted-range animals in Africa (Hatfield 2004). Declared a UNESCO World Heritage Site in 1995 (Wild and Mutebi 1996), Bwindi remains one of the most highly profiled national parks in Africa. Key to its international renown is the presence of one of the world's rarest apes, the mountain gorilla, of which approximately half the world's total of 700 reside in Bwindi (McNeilage et al. 2006).

Listed as endangered on the International Union for Conservation of Nature's Red List (IUCN 2009), mountain gorillas stand for many as an exemplary case of successful in situ conservation, largely the result of high levels of protection combined with an ecotourism program that promotes the lucrative attention of the international community toward their plight. Despite lamentations of the steep decline of "all great ape populations" (Anonymous 2006) and a Red Listing citing a decreasing population trend (IUCN 2009), mountain gorilla numbers have actually increased over the past few decades. The most recent census of Bwindi's gorillas, undertaken in 2006, claims a current population of 340, a 12% increase in the gorilla population since 1997 (McNeilage et al. 2006). While the increase in mountain gorilla numbers certainly presents a cause for celebration, the "success" of conservation in Bwindi needs to be understood in the context of the wider sociopolitical conditions within which gorillas and humans continue to compete for limited resources.

The dominant land use activity surrounding the park is smallholder agriculture. Some 90% of the approximately 170,000 inhabitants belonging to the Bakiga, Bafumbira, Batwa, and Barwandan peoples (Hamilton et al. 2000) earn a living on the region's rich volcanic soils (Hatfield 2004), with the majority classified as living in extreme poverty (Lanjouw et al. 2001). Foreign claims that extensive cultivation combined with poor management and minimal protection was leading to massive deforestation and serious environmental degradation (Harcourt 1992) escalated in the 1980s. Baker (2004) writes, for example, that by 1984 there were signs of human activity across 84% of the reserve. The true extent of local encroachment into the forest during this time, however, is contested, and as Hamilton et al. (2000, 1723) state, "Where [encroachment] did occur, it was often because politicians or other influential people circumvented the laws, not because ordinary people took action on their own." Nevertheless, following recommendations made by Butynski (1984) and under pressure from a donor agency that Bwindi "must" become a national park (Agaba 2004), Bwindi was so designated in 1991, resulting in the introduction of stringent policing and the complete "depeopling" of the park. Use or extraction of any forest resources by community members was henceforth illegal and subject to high fines or imprisonment (Mutebi 2003).

The loss of access to resources and land through the creation of conservation spaces has led to intense conflict between rural communities and state agencies (Peluso 1993; Neumann 1998; Schroeder 1999; Sundberg 2003; Young 2003). Such was the case with the conversion of Bwindi to a national park. Strong opposition by the surrounding community to the loss of access to park resources and land manifested in a barrage of physical attacks against the park, including arson and incidents of stoning the park staff (Baker 2004). Attempts to overcome poor relations between local people and conservation agencies like those witnessed in Bwindi have been forged under the banner of integrated conservation and development programs (ICDPs) (see Adams 2004).

ICDPs seek to build community support for parks and improve local attitudes toward wildlife by offsetting the costs of living with wildlife through economic incentives such as community development and revenue sharing (Newmark and Hough 2000; Archabald and Naughton-Treves 2001). Although ICD strategies have been widely adopted over the past few decades as "a new orthodoxy" (Hulme and Murphree 2001, 2), an expanding body of literature has emerged critiquing the ability of these programs to reach the poorest and most marginalized segments of society (Gray 2002), while others argue that these programs neither increase local livelihoods nor enhance environmental conservation (Adams 2001). Rather, most scholars working in the area argue that the implementation of ICDPs such as revenue sharing favors state interests over local needs and serves as little more than deflective mechanisms against popular and local resistance to conservation polices (Namara and Nsabagasani 2003). While traditional "fortress"-style conservation (Wells and Brandon 1992) is widely rejected today among social scientists,[2] the current conflict unfolding on the border of Bwindi suggests the emergence of even greater control over rural people and their land—a situation made possible and, in fact, fostered by one of the most popular ICD approaches: ecotourism.

Since its inception in 1993, ecotourism within Bwindi has gained steadily throughout the years, increasing 260% since the activation of the program, with a total of 6,500 visitors in 2005 (UWA 2006). Sightseeing tours or treks to visit habituated gorillas account for the main source of revenue for the park, as well as the primary reason tourists come to Bwindi. Two gorilla groups (Mubare and Katendegyere) were initially habituated for tourism until the Katendegyere group disintegrated in 1997 and a separate group (Ibaare-Habinyanja) was formed and opened for tourism. Visitation to see the gorillas has become so popular over the past decade that the Uganda Wildlife Authority (UWA) has habituated a fourth gorilla group, which opened to tourists in October of 2004—a decision that, while risky for the overall health of Bwindi's gorilla population (see Butynski 2001; Steklis 2004), offers the state substantial financial gain. Providing the second largest foreign income earner for Uganda, the income generated from gorilla tourism provides 80% of the entire national park system budget, including a proportion designated explicitly for community revenue-sharing programs. Yet few individuals at the local level are able to capture such benefits (see Archabald and Naughton-Treves 2001; Sandbrook 2006). Rather, the oft-cited benefits associated with ecotourism contrast sharply with the reality of rural peasants in Bwindi. The employment opportunities actually made available to community members through ecotourism, for example, rarely extend beyond marginal gains as unskilled, low-waged service-sector work and are largely concentrated to residents of one of the 21 surrounding Parishes. Not only marginalized from the financial opportunities presented through ecotourism, most local actors find themselves literally on the periphery of the very planning process purported to engage and empower local communities, which decides where tourism takes place, who participates, and how benefits are distributed. As one local chairman explains, "people bordering the park don't have the chance to track the gorillas and we are [supposedly] the stakeholders!"

Against a backdrop of pressure from the international community combined with a weak national budget for conservation initiatives, greater control over the planning process is being put in the hands of more financially and technologically capable extraterritorial, namely, Western, organizations (see Duffy 2006). This shift toward global environmental governance (see Duffield 2001; MacDonald 2005) not only limits local people's participation in the decision-making process, as benefits are often channeled through selection committees that minimally involve local governments, but also it restricts the type of development communities may pursue. Unlike national endowments of social welfare programs provided through the state, the provision of similar infrastructure improvement grants financed through outside organizations is often based on the fulfillment of certain conditions. Community development projects in Bwindi, for example, must "meet agreed criteria of environmental soundness [and] have a demonstrable positive impact on conservation" (World Bank 1995, 4). The paramount danger for local people is that they must continuously demonstrate their commitment to these terms or risk losing access to the few economic benefits available. Organizations such as the World Wide Fund for Nature (WWF), International Gorilla Conservation Programme (IGCP), African Wildlife Federation (AWF), and Mgahinga Bwindi Impenetrable Forest Conservation Trust (MBIFCT) already wield powerful influence over general conservation guidelines for the park, including the extent to which communities benefit from and the level of community involvement within ecotourism. Against the interests of these larger stakeholders, local farmers hold little authority with which to challenge current conservation policies even as they threaten to diminish community rights and access to critical natural resources within protected areas and, increasingly, on surrounding farmlands. Through a critical examination of the conflict between residents of Nteko Parish and fugitive gorillas on the boundary of Bwindi

Impenetrable National park, this article argues that for many rural farmers, the promise of ecotourism conceals a much starker reality, namely, the appropriation of rights, the loss to livelihood, and the surrender of land.

Gorilla Warfare: The Implications of Crop Raiding, Conservation Policy, and Tourists on Local Land Tenure and Food Security

Named after the trading center located approximately a quarter mile from the park boundary, the newest gorilla group opened to tourists in Bwindi, the Nkuringo group, offers tourists and conservation agencies access into the western portion of the park, an area adjoining the most isolated and arguably the poorest sector of all human settlements living adjacent to Bwindi. Living on the border of the Democratic Republic of the Congo on the west, Bwindi National Park to the east and north, and Rubuguli trading center to the south, residents of Nteko Parish face more daily insecurity than populations living adjacent to Bwindi elsewhere. A crucial factor in that insecurity is the violence that occasionally spills over into the area from the ongoing civil unrest occurring in neighboring eastern Democratic Republic of Congo. Local insecurity is further complicated by the steep topography, creating difficult farming conditions as well as restricting good sanitation facilities in the area. The promise of economic development in this area with the opening of the Nkuringo group to ecotourism has already resulted in improved roads, greater law enforcement brought in to protect tourists visiting the area, and limited employment opportunities, as well as the building of community infrastructure, including a water tank and a clinic, and the investment of foreign capital in the area. Despite these developments, the majority of residents living alongside the park face increasing obstacles to self-sufficiency in the form of rural people's appropriation of rights, the surrender of farmland, and the loss of livelihoods. Instrumental in the creation of these new forms of local "suffering" is the very same institution responsible for the betterment of local livelihoods, ecotourism.

From Out of the Mist and Onto the Farm

There are reports that gorilla groups habituated to human visitors change their foraging in ways that increase confrontation with aggressive nonhabituated groups, leading the habituated gorillas to seek sanctuary in areas wild gorilla groups tend to avoid human-occupied lands. Despite continued debate about the extent to which habituation and conservation efforts are in fact influencing gorilla movement (Baker 2005), habituated gorilla groups are nevertheless spending greater amounts of time on land outside the park (Goldsmith 2005), whether to escape confrontation with a growing number of gorilla groups, as a result of expanded foraging patterns and the readily available food source of community gardens, or due to a loss of fear of humans. UWA policies (Uganda Government 1996), which prevent the harassment of gorillas by local human populations, are further enabling gorilla encroachment by reducing the barriers gorillas once faced in accessing human-occupied areas, while disempowering local people by denying individual farmers a key coping strategy.

Once on community lands, gorillas often take advantage of the local crops, including bananas and, increasingly, eucalyptus tree bark and sweet potato vines (Muyambi 2005).

From archival data recorded between 1989 and 2000 by Baker (2005), the annual number of banana crop raiding incidents ranged from a minimum of one to a maximum of six, with an average of three incidents per year.[3] While crop depredation by gorillas affects only a small number of farmers, between two to three per incident, largely along the western boundary of the park, the cost to an individual farmer is high, as banana plants represent an important food crop and source of local income (Tukahirwa and Pomeroy 1993; Kiiza, Abele, and Kalyebara 2004). Reports during 1995 and 1996, for example, documented between 16 and 35 banana plants lost to individual farmers. Taking into account the average production and life span of a single green banana plant, the cost of a gorilla raid for a farmer can be estimated at a total of US$472 for the 10 years of the banana plant (Baker 2005)—a significant loss for the poorest households, which average between US$60 and $300 annually (FAO 2005). As incidents of crop damage by gorillas increase (Mudakikwa et al. 2001; Guerrera et al. 2003), community complaints of household food shortages become more frequent, forcing some households to emigrate out of the area altogether (see also Namara 2000).

This situation is compounded by the minimal assistance UWA policies provide for affected farmers. Despite years of community opposition,[4] UWA continues to endorse a noncompensation policy that prohibits the provision of compensation when local crops are destroyed by park animals. Assistance to affected farmers is not only financially limited but logistically limited as well. Prior to Bwindi's gazettement as a national park, crop-raiding animals were controlled through vermin guards whose only duty was to protect against local excursions by park animals (Baker 2005). Under current UWA policies, no park animals are defined as "vermin" and thus the necessity for "vermin guards" has been eradicated. Rather, problem animal control represents a secondary duty for the rangers after law enforcement. Decisions about whether or not to assist farmers by scare shooting or chasing wild animals from agricultural fields fall to individual rangers already engaged in full time responsibilities (Baker 2005), and the lack of ranger assistance for crop raiding animals remains a principal charge against the park by affected communities. In the late 1990s in response to increasing incidents of human—gorilla conflicts, the Human—Gorilla Conflict resolution program (HUGO) was established with members from the community to chase gorillas back to the forest by ringing bells and beating drums (Makombo 2003). The effectiveness of HUGO teams, however, has been notably limited in areas of high gorilla visitation and continues to suffer from declining morale, particularly in instances of recurring or extended visits by gorilla groups. Local complaints about the effectiveness of HUGO teams and their limited capacity to scare gorillas, as well as member complaints about insufficient funds and derogatory treatment by UWA staff, call into question UWA's establishment of HUGO as a sincere effort to address local concerns (as opposed to an effort merely to deflect opposition—see Neumann 2000). HUGO members work on a voluntary basis without supplementary pay even as their responsibilities increase, raising further questions about the agencies' commitment to community welfare.

Several informants, when asked about personally investing in efforts to control crop raiding, such as fences, replied that unlike Ignatius, most farmers have very limited capital to invest in similar efforts. It is questionable whether farmers would seek out such a solution even if funds were available, because, as has been noted in prior literature, people view crop raiding as a primary responsibility of UWA (Adams and Hulme 1998; Namara and Nsabagasani 2003). In-depth conversations with several farmers living on the park boundary revealed that households were further reluctant to invest in preventative efforts because many fear that the land will become part of the park anyway. Comments taken from household surveys undertaken in Nteko Parish further substantiate such concerns. For example, direct references to the movement of "[park] animals coming and going into community lands," whereby "[community] land is becoming forest," have led to "fear[s] of being kicked off their land" in order to "expand the park."

In early 2002, African Wildlife Federation, an international conservation organization working with the park, entered into negotiations to buy land immediately adjacent to the park that was frequented by gorillas. Implicit in the land acquisition deal was a fair price paid for the real estate and the promise that these gorillas would bring economic development for the area through the construction of tourist infrastructure, the emergence of new markets, the potential for entrepreneurial opportunities, and charity/sponsorship possibilities. The sale of land by farmers during times of hardship is not a new phenomenon. Farms in the area have traditionally been fragmented into several smaller and widely spaced plots in order to take advantage of multiple altitudes for growing a variety of crops and as a coping mechanism for farmers experiencing temporary hardship (Blarel et al. 1992). During times of famine or crop failure, farmers may use the sale from one of their plots of land to purchase food they otherwise have failed to grow, and during times of bounty they could potentially buy back another piece of land. With the rise of ecotourism in the area, however, this strategy is becoming increasingly difficult, as farmers who have sold their land are finding that land located close to tourism activities and the promise of economic prosperity has become too expensive to buy back. Much of the land centrally located within Nkuringo trading center and better situated to take advantage of the flourishing tourist activity in the area, for example, is being bought up by wealthier patrons from areas outside Nteko Parish, including the capital city of Kampala. For the farmers situated between the park boundary and Nkuringo, the possibility of acquiring land near their recently sold plots is virtually impossible.

Recent work by Namara (2006) argues that these transactions heavily favored national and international interests, as "UWA and conservation NGO officials … determin[ed] the terms of purchase, with no real community participation. The peasants … did not have all the necessary information [for] getting value out of their land" (Namara 2006, 53). Many farmers who initially sold their land now regret the decision, while still others harbor serious feelings of ill-will toward the park because they felt they had no other option but to sell, given the restrictive UWA policies. One village elder from Mukono Parish expressed a growing sentiment among villagers surrounding the park: "We had a good relationship with the park but now the park is forcing communities to surrender their land." In some cases, the choice to sell was not even a farmer's to make. Tumuheirwe Gad owned a parcel of land that was bordered by the park on one side and by several other neighboring farms on the other sides. The only way to access his land was through a community path that led through adjacent farms from the main road to his own land. When UWA negotiated the land acquisitions, all of Tumuheirwe's neighbors decided to sell. This ultimately assured that his farm became an isolated island in the middle of what was now deemed national park land. Any attempt to move beyond the borders of his land would thus be considered encroachment into a national park—a criminal act punishable by severe fines and incarceration.

It is debatable whether or not the new land acquisition will even resolve the problems of fugitive gorillas on neighboring farms. A report undertaken by CARE (1996) states that the sale of land will only extend the range of problem animals, a common fear expressed by villagers who sometimes migrate far to avoid "animals following them." Recent findings by Goldsmith (2005) verify CARE's initial report and call into question the efforts by UWA to reconcile the gorilla/human border conflicts through the establishment of a buffer zone with the recently purchased land. In her article, she presents evidence of the Nkuringo group moving beyond the 400-m border of the newly parceled parkland to a distance greater than 1.2 km from the original park boundary and proximate to the community trading center's main road. The extended ranging patterns of the newly habituated group, she argues, are largely fueled by the failure of UWA to chase gorillas out of the buffer zone. Left in peace on the newly acquired buffer zone, gorillas have unrestricted access to the land and, perhaps more significantly, the remaining crops from the abandoned farms—a danger, Goldsmith warns, that could eventually lead to the raiding of farms even further from the park as the remaining crops are consumed. As some community members still harbor fear toward gorillas, the occupation by gorillas of community lands also prevents access to community resources such as water sources and footpaths. While infrequent, reports of physical injury to community members by male silverbacks continue to fortify such fears. The combination of the aforementioned circumstances testifies to an emergent reality in which, as one resident from Nkwenda village remarked, "the forest encroaches on the community," and for which farmers have little other recourse but the relinquishment of their labor, their food security, and increasingly their land.

Of Gorillas and Men

The extent to which ecotourism presents a real opportunity for farmers living adjacent to Bwindi needs to be reevaluated—particularly when the tourism from which local people are supposed to be benefiting is the very reason farmers are facing increased hardship, whether in the form of marauding animals or increased restrictions placed on their daily movements and activities. Originally intended to provide tourists a perceived "primitive and unspoiled" wilderness, and as deterrence to local entrepreneurs seeking to conduct private gorilla tours, a recent policy now restricts farmers from entering land occupied by gorillas. For farmers whose land is subject to frequent visitations by gorillas, a significant amount of time is spent away from valuable farmland, which, together with UWA's harassment policy, makes land directly adjacent to the park even more vulnerable to crop raiding. Data gathered starting in the year 2002 from UWA ranger guide records, for example, show that annually, approximately 11% of all gorilla treks occurred on land owned by members of the local community, with a monthly high in May 2002 of 38%. Even these statistics are deceivingly low, however, for they fail to account for the ranging patterns of the Nkuringo group prior to the land purchase when the majority of their time was spent outside the park (Lepp 2002). Furthermore, these statistics do not consider the movement of gorillas onto private land outside of tourist viewing periods, which—as demonstrated earlier—poses significant threats for local farmers. Yet individuals living adjacent to the park receive no additional monetary benefit for the sacrifice of their land and resources for the protection of a global good—the inequity of which is not lost to members of Bujengwe Parish. "Tourists come onto the private land of many people around and the park doesn't ask permission [to trek gorillas on community land] yet they don't give us any money and we are not allowed to scare gorillas off [community] land and now we must get off our land when gorillas are there or be arrested!"

To the contrary, farmers often face suspicion and in some cases physical force by park staff just for being on land near the park. A member of the Community-Protected Areas Committee (CPAC) from Kashasha Parish cited several incidents of unprovoked violence on the part of park staff, including one incident in 2001 in which a villager "was beaten by park rangers. [He] was sitting on his land and they thought he was waiting to kill animals coming out of the park." Once seemingly innocent daily activities, then, become potential criminal acts against nature, subject to increased park surveillance, and acts of violence perpetrated by a paramilitary-trained park staff are justified in the name of the global good (Forsyth 2003; Neumann 2004). "Instead of going to guard against wild animals," exclaimed a resident from Kitojo Parish, "they guard against local communities." The infiltration of state control into rural and previously remote areas is aided by ecotourism policies, which necessitate nature's separation from humankind, and, in the case of Bwindi, that farmers remain spatially segregated from park resources so tourists can experience a wild and primitive nature, untouched by people.

Traditional park policies that restrict locals from entering the park or accessing park resources are now being extended onto private land outside protected areas. "Even if a big tree falls from the park," a female resident of Nkwenda testified, "an individual is not allowed to cut even a branch from it without authorization from the park." By designating resources, such as fallen trees and fugitive wildlife found outside the boundary, as park property, nonlocal actors are able to gain control over local claims to land and resource access. As one informant from Kiyebe Parish stated, "People feel the park is the owner of the community."

Conclusion

Despite public assurances by park personnel that the park harbors no intentions to acquire more land, private land in Nteko Parish is currently being deeded over to an international organization on behalf of the park. The park publicly assumes a stance as a defender of both wildlife and local people—a position enhanced by a widely touted but mostly rhetorical commitment to assist farmers facing severe instances of crop raiding. This public stance denies the sociopolitical reality of conservation in Bwindi, which privileges the life and liberty of gorillas over their human neighbors and which pits farmers against conservation policies that exert increasing control over the behavior and the property of local households. Such a constriction of rights has led many locals, including one villager in Ruhija, to question their own worth: "Is one gorilla life equal to 10 human lives?" As this article presents, gorilla conservation has in reality contributed to restrictive policies, which diminish local people's individual rights to self-sufficiency and self-control by appropriating local land rights at the same time that it promises to promote economic development and prosperity.

For the world's poorest people, control over land is a vital concern. The alienation of peasant land rights and the increasing control over surrounding communities and their environs not only denies people the ability to secure their own food—it also excludes them from a source of power. Who controls the land and how they do so affects how land is used and to whom the benefits of its use accrue (Tansey and Worsley 1995). Questions of power over and access to land are increasingly shaped by global forces, often at the expense of fundamental human rights to land, livelihood, and food security. Even the generation of eco-friendly development policies, imposed and implemented by outside agencies, may come at great cost to rural farmers. Bwindi's presence on the ecotourism circuit severely restricts people's use of their own landscape (and even their own property) as their lives become objects of greater governmental and international surveillance and regulation. The hidden costs of gorilla tourism in the context of Bwindi have resulted in the relinquishment of property rights of farmers living adjacent to Bwindi to serve a global good—the conservation of gorilla habitat.

In light of Bwindi's biological resource wealth, land and natural resource policies will continue to be exceptionally vulnerable to interference—especially by outside donors for privatization. A changing political economic landscape has already resulted in a greater diversity of stakeholders since ecotourism began in the late 1980s, including entrepreneurs from outside the area and foreign donors. While such changes will undoubtedly result in greater economic security overall, the increases in wealth creation and income levels experienced at the meso and macro level must be considered in light of diminishing livelihood security for some of Uganda's poorest rural farmers.

Recently, two additional gorilla groups (Bitukura and Nsongi) opened up for tourism in the southern and eastern parts of the park, respectively (Kimer and Natabaalo 2009). The implications of this expansion for the multiplicity of actors in the surrounding communities remains uncertain. For some, the introduction of foreign visitors and revenue may translate into limited tangible benefits and perhaps even improved livelihoods. For others, the growth of ecotourism in these areas may prove to be yet another Trojan horse of initial promises and later loss of control, loss of livelihood and food security, and loss of land. This case study testifies to the need to continue challenging the apolitical and benign nature of conservation, as much in its implementation as in its creation. Particularly important is understanding and elucidating the complexities of what is lost through conservation programs, to whom, by whom, and toward what end. Such inquiry inevitably compels a wider discussion of the more fundamental question: Should the basic human rights of indigenous and local communities be (allowed to be) traded off for the benefit of biodiversity conservation? Consider the woman who is forced to stand idly by as her crops are destroyed by a gorilla group being visited by tourists on community land—for which she will receive no compensation for her lost crops nor any direct monetary income from the tourist visit. That her story is not unique for the people of Nkuringo Parish, and may perhaps be replicated in the new tourism areas, raises the critical question as to whether such a story is ever justified on behalf of conservation. At the very least, such critical reflection deserves our full attention.

Notes

1. Pseudonyms were applied to protect the privacy of each individual interviewed and thus all names used throughout this article have been changed.
2. However, protectionist arguments have seen a resurgence within the conservation biology and ecology literatures (e.g., Terborgh et al. 2002; for a comprehensive critical review see Wilshusen et al. 2002).

3. These numbers represent crop raiding by nonhabituated gorillas and consider the consumption of banana plants only. Nor do these numbers represent time spent in community land not consuming crops, which may indirectly result in decreased crop productivity by preventing farmers from accessing their farms. In 1989, for example, rangers reported that a group of six gorillas stayed in community land for a month (Baker 2005).

4. Failure to compensate for crops damaged by animals foraging from the park continues remains the greatest issue of discontentment communities voice toward the park (see also Archabald and Naughton-Treves 2001).

References

Adams, W. 2001. *Green development.* London: Routledge.

Adams, W. 2004. *Against extinction.* London: Earthscan.

Adams, W., and D. Hulme. 1998. *Conservation and communities.* Community Conservation in Africa: Principles and Comparative Practice, Discussion Paper No. 4. Manchester, UK: IDPM, University of Manchester.

Agaba, B. 2004. *Community resource utilization in BINP.* MA thesis, Geography Department, Makerere University, Kampala, Uganda.

Anon. 2006. On the survival of great apes and their habitat. *Population Dev. Rev.* 32(2): 393–396.

Archabald, K., and L. Naughton-Treves. 2001. Tourism revenue sharing around national parks in Western Uganda. *Environ. Conserv.* 28(2):135–149.

Baker, J. 2004. *Evaluating conservation policy: Examining the impact of ICDPs on protected areas.* PhD dissertation, Durrell Institute of Conservation and Ecology, University of Kent at Canterbury, Kent, UK.

Baker, J. 2005. Mountain gorillas: Crop raiding and conflict at BINP, Uganda. Unpublished report, Durrell Institute of Conservation and Ecology, University of Kent at Canterbury, Kent, United Kingdom.

Blarel, B., P. Hazell, F. Place, and J. Quiggin. 1992. The economics of farm fragmentation. *World Bank Econ. Rev.* 6:233–254.

Blomley, T. 2003. Natural resource conflict management: The case of BINP and MGNP. Unpublished report, CARE-International, Kampala, Uganda.

Brockington, D. 2002. *Fortress conservation: The preservation of the Mkomazi Game Reserve, Tanzania.* Oxford, UK: James Currey.

Butynski, T. 1984. Ecological survey of the Impenetrable Bwindi Forest, Uganda. Unpublished report for the Government of Uganda, New York Zoological Society, New York.

Cooperative for Assistance and Relief Everywhere, Inc. (CARE). 1996. Crop raiding workshop report for BINP and MGNP. Unpublished report, CARE-International, Kabale, Uganda.

Duffield, M. 2001. *Global governance and the new wars.* London: Zed Books.

Duffy, R. 2006. Global governance and environmental management. *Polit. Geogr.* 25(1): 89–112.

Food and Agriculture Organization. 2005. *Community-based enterprise development for the conservation of biodiversity in Bwindi.* Forestry Policy and Institutions, Working Paper No. 11. Rome, Italy: FAO.

Forsyth, T. 2003. *Critical political ecology.* New York: Routledge.

Goldsmith, M. 2005. Impacts of habituation for ecotourism on the gorillas of Nkuringo. *Gorilla J.* 30:11–14.

Gray, L. 2002. Environmental policy, land rights and conflict. *Environ. Plan. D* 20:167–182. Guerrera, W., J. Sleeman, S. Jasper, L. Pace, T. Ichinose, and J. Reif. 2003. Medical survey of the local human population to determine possible health risks to the mountain gorillas of BINP, Uganda. *Int. J. Primatol.* 24:197–207.

Hamilton, A., A. Cunningham, D. Byarugaba, and F. Kayanja. 2000. Conservation in a region of political instability: BINP, Uganda. *Conserv. Biol.* 14(6):1722–1725.

Harcourt, C. 1992. Uganda. In *The conservation atlas of tropical forests,* ed. J. Sayer, C. S. Harcourt, and N. M. Collins, 262–270. London: Macmillan.

Hatfield, R. 2004. The economic value of the mountain gorilla forests. Paper presented at the International Society of Tropical Foresters Spring 2004 Conference: People in Parks: Beyond the Debate, 2–3 April, Yale University, New Haven, CT.

Hulme, D., and M. Murphree. 2001. Community conservation in Africa. In *African wildlife and livelihoods,* ed. D. Hulme and M. Murphee, 1–18. Oxford, UK: James Currey. International Union for Conservation of Nature. 2009. 2009 IUCN red list of threatened species. International Union for Conservation of Nature. http://www.iucnredlist.org/ details/39994/0 (accessed 10 August 2009).

Jones, S. 2006. A political ecology of wildlife conservation in Africa. *Rev. African Polit. Econ.* 109:483–495.

Kiiza, B., S. Abele, and R. Kalyebara. 2004. Market opportunities for Ugandan banana products: National, regional, and global perspectives. *Uganda J. Agric. Sci.* 9:743–749.

Kimer, L., and G. Natabaalo. 2009. UWA invests more in the gorilla tourist industry. *Daily Monitor,* 25 February. http://www.bushdrums.com/news/index.php?shownews=2136

Lanjouw, A., A. Kayitare, H. Rainer, E. Rutagarama, M. Sivha, S. Asuma, and J. Kalpers. 2001. *Beyond boundaries: Transboundary natural resource management for mountain gorillas in the Virunga–Bwindi region.* Washington, DC: Biodiversity Support Program.

Lepp, A. 2002. Uganda's BINP: Meeting the challenges of conservation and community development through sustainable tourism. In *Sustainable tourism,* ed. R. Harris, T. Griffin, and P. Williams, 211–220. Oxford, UK: Elsevier Butterworth-Heinemann.

MacDonald, K. 2005. Global hunting grounds: Power, scale and ecology in the negotiation of conservation. *Cultural Geogr.* 12(3):259–291.

Makombo, J. 2003. *Responding to the challenge: How protected areas can best provide benefits beyond boundaries.* Unpublished report, UWA, Kampala, Uganda.

McNeilage, A., M. M. Robbins, M. Gray, W. Olupot, D. Babaasa, R. Bitariho, A. Kasangaki,

H. Rainer, S. Asuma, G. Mugiri, and J. Baker. 2006. Census of the mountain gorilla *Gorilla beringei beringei* population in BINP, Uganda. *Oryx* 40(4):419–427.

Moore, D. 1998. Clear waters and muddied histories. *J. Southern African Stud.* 24(2):377–403. Mudakikwa, A., M. Cranfield, J. Sleeman, and U. Eilenberger. 2001. Clinical medicine, preventive health care and research on mountain gorillas in the Virunga volcanoes region. In *Mountain gorillas,* ed. M. Robbins, P. Sicotte, and K. Stewart, 341–360. Cambridge, UK: Cambridge University Press.

Murombedzi, J. 2003. *Revisiting the principles of CBNRM in Southern Africa.* Paper presented at the Proceedings of the Regional Conference on CBNRM in Southern Africa, 3–7 March, in Windhoek, Namibia.

Mutebi, J. 2003. Co-managed protected areas: From conflict to collaboration. Unpublished report, CARE-International, Kampala, Uganda.

Muyambi, F. 2005. Crop raiding: Human gorilla conflicts and its implications for conservation. Paper presented at the International Tropical Forest Conservation Researchers Meeting, 10 March, in Buhoma, Uganda.

Namara, A. 2000. People and Bwindi forest. Unpublished report, ITFC, Ruhija, Uganda.

Namara, A., and X. Nsabagasani. 2003. *Decentralization and wildlife management: Devolving or shedding responsibilities?* Environmental Governance in Africa, Working Paper No. 9. Washington, DC: World Resources Institute.

Namara, A. 2006. From paternalism to real partnership with local communities? *Africa Dev.* 31(2):39–68.

Neumann, R. 1998. Imposing *wilderness.* Berkeley: University of California Press.

Neumann, R. 2000. Primitive ideas: Protected area buffer zones and the politics of land in Africa. In *Producing nature and poverty in Africa,* ed. V. Broch-Due and R. A. Shroeder, 220–242. Stockholm, Sweden: Nordiska Afrikainstitutet.

Neumann, R. 2004. Moral and discursive geographies in the war for biodiversity in Africa. *Polit. Geogr.* 23:813–837.

Neumann, R. 2005. *Making political ecology.* New York: Oxford University Press.

Newmark, W., and J. Hough. 2000. Conserving wildlife in Africa. *Bioscience* 50(7):585–593. Peluso, N. 1993. Coercing conservation? *Global Environ. Change* 3(2):199–217.

Sandbrook, C. 2006. *Tourism, conservation and livelihoods.* PhD dissertation, Department of Anthropology, University College, London.

Schroeder, R. 1999. Geographies of environmental intervention in Africa. *Prog. Hum. Geogr.* 23(3):359–378.

Steklis, H. D. 2004. The impact of tourism on mountain gorillas. *Folia Primatoloigica 75* (suppl. 1):40–41.

Sundberg, J. 2003. Strategies for authenticity and space in the Maya Biosphere Reserve.

In *Political ecology,* ed. K. Zimmerer and T. Bassett, 50–69. New York: Guilford Press. Tansey, G., and T. Worsley. 1995. *The food system.* London: Earthscan.

Terborgh, J., C. Van Schaik, L. Davenport, and M. Rao. 2002. *Making parks work.* Washington, DC: Island Press.

Tukahirwa, E., and D. Pomeroy. 1993. Bwindi Impenetrable Forest: Baseline study report. Unpublished report, Makerere University Institute of Environment and Natural Resources, Kampala, Uganda.

Uganda Government. 1996. The Uganda wildlife statute 1996. *Uganda Government Gazette* No. 321, vol. LXXXIX. Entebbe, Uganda: Government printer.

Uganda Wildlife Authority. 2006. *Tourist visitors to BINP and MGNP, 1994–2005.* http://data.mtti.go.ug/docs/UWA%20NEWS.pdf (accessed 22 July 2008).

Wells, M., and K. Brandon. 1992. *People and parks: Linking protected areas with local communities.* Washington, DC: World Bank.

Wild, R., and J. Mutebi. 1996. *Conservation through community use of plant resources.* People and Plants Working Paper No. 5. Paris: UNESCO.

Wilshusen, P., S. Brechin, C. Fortwangler, and P. West. 2002. Reinventing a square wheel. *Society Nat. Resources* 15:17–40.

World Bank. 1995. *Uganda: BINP and MGNP conservation.* Global Environment Facility Project document 12430–UG. Global Environment Coordination Division. Washington, DC: World Bank.

Young, E. 2003. Balancing conservation with development in marine-dependent communities. In *Political ecology,* ed. K. Zimmerer and T. Bassett, 29–49. New York: Guilford Press.

Zerner, C. 2000. Toward a broader vision of justice and nature conservation. In *People, plants, and justice,* ed. C. Zerner, 3–20. New York: Columbia University Press.

Zimmerer, K. 2000. The reworking of conservation geographies. *Ann. Assoc. Am. Geogr.* 90(2):356–370.

SECTION I CONCLUSION

Laudati's (2010) article illustrates one of the ways in which poverty and conservation practices intertwine in complex political and local realities. This case is one of many examples of the tensions between people with different levels of political and economic power, land rights, and ability to influence conservation practice in this region of Uganda. Conservation through protected areas is only one of many partial and problematic approaches to addressing extinction and loss of biodiversity, including models that involve community-based conservation, natural resource management, and market-based conservation strategies (see critical explanations of these approaches in Fabricius et al. 2004 and Chapter 9 of Brockington et al. 2008). As Brockington and colleagues remind readers (2008), protected areas generate many winners and losers, and it is important to identify these power imbalances in addition to raising the questions of whether or not biodiversity and habitat enrichment has occurred and to what effect.

Despite the extraordinary financial, scientific, and political investments in protected-area conservation, protected areas often fail to achieve their specific goals and result in human costs including land eviction, violence, and appropriation of communal natural resources. Private reserves have proliferated in recent years (Brockington et al. 2008), even as evidence on the ground persistently calls this idea and image of protected areas into question. Instead of conservation efforts in sub-Saharan Africa proceeding with more humility and more modest goals, the opposite has occurred with the rise of massive **trans-frontier conservation areas (TFCAs)** also known as "Peace Parks" (Büscher 2013). Such parks are pitched through media campaigns as "win-win" solutions to biodiversity loss, poverty reduction, *and* cross-border conflicts between sub-Saharan African countries. Researchers such as Büscher (2013) have found that despite all of the sobering lessons learned from fortress conservation and other models, the insistence on promoting the *idea* of parks as the optimal solution to biodiversity conservation is more prominent and larger in scale than ever.

Trans-Frontier Conservation Areas (TFCAs) are conservation areas (parks or reserves and linked corridors) that extend across international borders and require international collaboration and development of regulations specific to these territories.

Part of this emphasis on win-win scenarios links to broader debates and other environmental issues such as climate change denial (see Section 6) and denial of other complex processes, including biodiversity loss (Sutherland et al. 2011; Rands et al. 2010). Many people relate their personal lives to climate change through experiences with changes in local weather patterns.[1] But it is often difficult for people to comprehend how they affect and are impacted by even more abstract concepts such as biodiversity loss, which makes it challenging to involve people in conversation. This makes the continued insistence on finding and asserting big win-win solutions through TFCAs perhaps more likely in the future, posing great difficulties for those trying to experiment with innovative, more nuanced strategies that directly take power relations into account (including community-based and participatory conservation). The question is whether or not more modest and politically engaged approaches will be overshadowed by charismatic large parks with big promises and professionally crafted image campaigns, supported by National Geographic films and the likes of billionaires such as Sir Richard Branson, who boldly make statements such as, "… What is Africa? Africa is its animals" (see Büscher 2013).[2]

One of the assumptions of the protected area type of approach to conservation is that humans must be kept separate from nature or wilderness in order to achieve conservation goals. Maintaining so-called pristine ecosystems without human interference is problematic in that humans rely on the environment for survival and cultural sustenance in ways that do not necessarily threaten the health of the environment. Excluding communities from using local natural resources in a low-impact, sustainable way is a strategy that introduces conflict and likely undermines the effectiveness of conservation in the long term. Guatemala's national protected areas system is an example that reflects the variety of human uses of ecosystems and the need for different degrees of protection and management. The Guatemalan government has established 19 different categories of protection based on how critically threatened species are and how humans have typically interacted with these ecosystems, such as regional and national parks, biosphere reserves, wildlife sanctuaries, and cultural monuments.[3]

---

1   The links between climate change and weather patterns and events are complex and at times quite indirect because of the different time scales of processes involved in weather versus climate patterns.
2   Video posted 10 May 2011 on Pifworld.com:
(http://www.pifworld.com/en/projects/TheElephantCorridor/61/blog/1353)
3   Details at: (http://www.conap.gob.gt/)

Section I Discussion Questions: Biodiversity and Protected Areas Review

1. What specific tools (parks, conventions, lists, etc) have been enacted to protect biodiversity? What are the strengths and weaknesses of such protection tools?

2. What types of biodiversity exist, beyond just the charismatic megafauna that we tend to associate with wildlife protection (e.g. gorillas)?

3. What is the purpose of protected areas or parks? According to Brockington et al. (2008), what is 'fortress conservation'? What are the strengths and weaknesses of relying on a protected areas approach to biodiversity conservation?

4. Brockington et al. (2008) examine the claim that "parks without local support are bound to fail" (p.8). What evidence do they show throughout the chapter to support or refute this statement?

5. What was the purpose of Integrated Conservation and Development Programs (ICDPs)? In general, were they successful in reaching their goals? Why or why not?

6. What is the relationship between conservation organizations and local farmers in the Uganda case study? What are the goals of each of these groups? Whose goal is more valid, noble, or critical?

7. What potential is there for ecotourism to improve the livelihoods of local people while also protecting natural resources? In Laudati's case study of Bwindi Impenetrable National Park, what were the observed results of ecotourism?

References

Adams, W.M. (2004) *Against Extinction: The Story of Conservation*. London; Sterling, VA: Earthscan.

Brockington, D., Duffy, R., and J. Igoe (2008) "The Power of Parks." In *Nature Unbound: Conservation, Capitalism and the Future of Protected Areas*. Chapter 4 (63–86). London: Earthscan.

Büscher, B. (2013) *Transforming the Frontier: Peace Parks and the Politics of Neoliberal Conservation in Southern Africa*. Durham and London: Duke University Press.

Fabricius, C., E. Koch, H. Magome, and S. Turner. (2004) *Rights, Resources and Rural Development: Community-Based Natural Resource Management in Southern Africa*. London; Sterling, VA: Earthscan.

Guyer, J. and P. Richards (1996) "The Invention of Biodiversity: Social Perspectives on the Management of Biological Variety in Africa." *Africa* 66(1): 1–13.

Hellmann, J.J. and G.W. Fowler (1999) "Bias, Precision, and Accuracy of Four Measures of Species Richness." *Ecological Applications* 9(3): 824–834.

Laudati, A.A. (2010). "The Encroaching Forest: Struggles Over Land and Resources on the Boundary of Bwindi Impenetrable National Park, Uganda." *Society & Natural Resources* 23(8): 776–789.

MacDonald, K.I. (2010). "The Devil Is in the (Bio)Diversity: Private Sector 'Engagement' and the Restructuring of Biodiversity Conservation." *Antipode* 42(3): 513–50.

Méndez, V.E., C.M. Bacon, M. Olson, K.S. Morris, and A.K. Shattuck. (2010) "Agrobiodiversity and Shade Coffee Smallholder Livelihoods: A Review and Synthesis of Ten Years of Research in Central America." *Professional Geographer* 62:357–376.

Perfecto, I. and J. Vandermeer (2008) "Biodiversity Conservation in Tropical Agroecosystems: A New Conservation Paradigm." In *The Year in Ecology and Conservation Biology 2008*, eds. R.S. Ostfeld and W.H. Schlesinger, 173–200. Oxford: Blackwell Publishing.

Sutherland, W.J., Bardsley, S., Bennun, L., Clout, M., Cote, I.M., Depledge, M.H., Dicks, L.V., Dobson, A.P., Fellman, L., Fleishman, E., Gibbons, D.W., Impey, A.J., Lawton, J.H., Lickorish, F., Lindenmayer, D.B., Lovejoy, T.E., Nally, R.M., Madgwick, J., Peck, L.S., Pretty, J., Prior, S.V., Redford, K.H., Scharlemann, J.P., Spalding, M.D. and Watkinson, A.R. (2011) "A Horizon Scan of Global Conservation Issues for 2011." *Trends in Ecology & Evolution* 26(1): 10–16.

Wake, D.B. and Vredenburg V.T. (2008) "Are We in the Midst of the Sixth Mass Extinction? A View from the World of Amphibians." *Proceedings of the National Academy of Sciences (PNAS)-USA* 105: 11466–73.

Wilson, E.O. (1998). *Consilience: The Unity of Knowledge.* New York: Knopf.

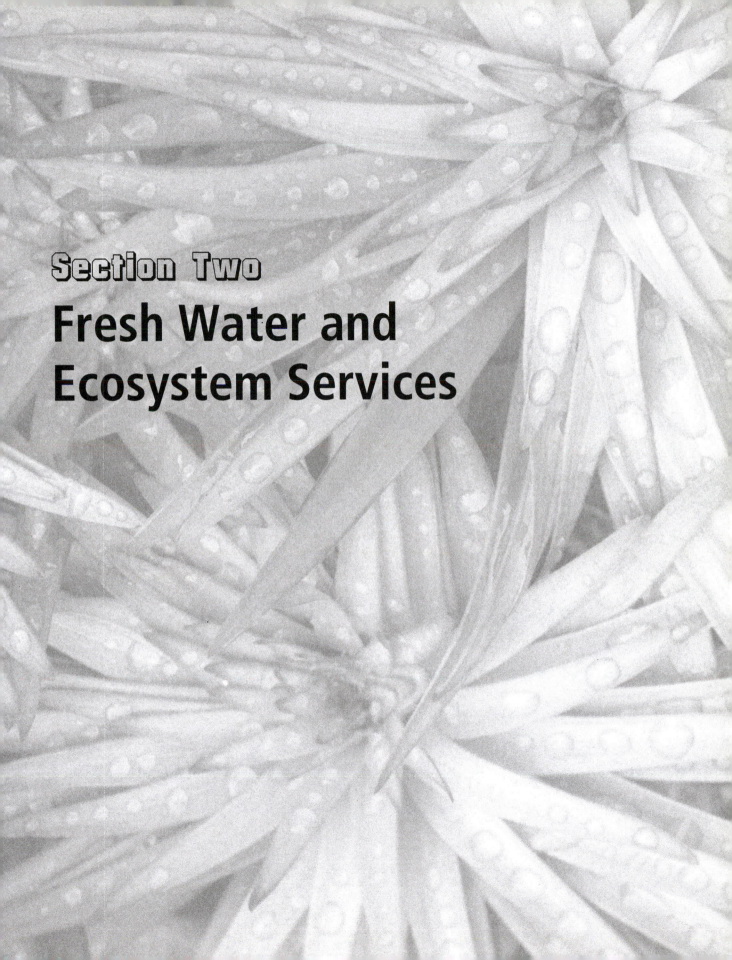

Section Two
Fresh Water and Ecosystem Services

INTRODUCTION TO CRITICAL GLOBAL FRESH WATER ISSUES

water scarcity integrated water resource management appropriate technology	ecosystem services payment for ecosystem services	**KEY TERMS**

C ritical water issues of the 21st century include fresh water scarcity, water quality degradation, and the effects of climate change on water resources. Fresh water resources are cross-cutting, linked to agriculture, climate change, waste and pollution, public health, and environmental justice.

Water Scarcity, Water Quality and Public Health

Today more than 40% of the world's population lives in conditions of **water scarcity**, including limited access to safe drinking water and sanitation (FAO 2013). As with many natural resource pressures, the poorest people are most vulnerable to water scarcity and poor water quality (Regassa, Givey, and Castillo 2010). Lack of access to clean drinking water and sanitation is a major public health concern in many developing countries, where 1.6 million people die each year from diarrheal diseases (WHO 2013). Experts expect the problem of fresh water scarcity to increase as global population continues to grow and climate change causes more unpredictable precipitation patterns, more severe and frequent floods and droughts, unequal rainfall distribution, and reduction in water availability in regions dependent on glacier ice and snow melt (Bates et al. 2008).

Increasing population pressure and climate change are also expected to exacerbate the number and intensity of water conflicts in the future (Gleick 2011). International water

Water Scarcity refers to insufficient water available to meet demand, as well as the degradation of groundwater and surface water quality, competition between different sectors of water use (e.g., industrial, agricultural and household), and regional and international conflicts for water resources (FAO 2013).

conflicts have longstanding historical precedents, including transboundary cases such as Egypt's and Sudan's conflict over Nile River rights (Pacific Institute 2009). More recently, indigenous groups in Cochabamba, Bolivia, have rioted over water privatization, the denial of their access to water and threats to their livelihoods, health, and food security. Predictions of future scenarios of limited water resources suggest an urgent need for **Integrated Water Resource Management** (IWRM) at national levels, as discussed later in this chapter (Liu et al. 2013) and international cooperation for clean water access and sanitation.

Integrated Water Resource Management (IWRM) refers to the strategic planning and management of activities that affect water resources. This often includes working at various scales and with the involvement of communities, conservation organizations, and governments.

Water Resource Management

Sound water resource management is needed to limit water waste and help ensure that populations have access to clean drinking water for the long term. Agriculture is an important sector in terms of water use, water waste, and water pollution, particularly in industrialized countries with large-scale irrigated agriculture. Agricultural use is responsible for 70% of the world's fresh water withdrawals (FAO 2008). Limiting fresh water waste by agricultural irrigation is essential, for example through the promotion of more efficient irrigation (i.e. drip versus spray) and soil-conservation practices. Agricultural policies and higher water pricing may be necessary for water efficiency practices to be adopted on a large scale.

Many international organizations including the Global Water Partnership, the United Nations, and the Food and Agriculture Organization (FAO), are dedicated to increasing clean water access where it is needed and promoting water resource management. This includes projects promoting **appropriate technology** in rural areas of developing countries, such as drilling wells for groundwater extraction and disseminating low-cost water filtration systems. In addition to development projects focused on clean water access for rural populations, water policy encouraging more efficient use of water is necessary. Sustainable water resource management requires balancing the needs of various uses, for example household drinking water and large-scale agricultural irrigation.

Appropriate Technology refers to small-scale, affordable, locally appropriate technologies aimed at reducing poverty and protecting natural resources. Examples of appropriate technology projects include solar cookstoves to replace wood-fired stoves, rain barrels to collect rainwater, and simple water purification systems. Appropriate technology relies on renewable resources (e.g., sun) and locally available materials so projects can be sustained by communities without the need for continued inputs.

Water and Ecosystem Services

Effective water policy also includes protection of wetland and forest ecosystems, which provide the essential ecosystem services of water purification and erosion control. **Ecosystem services** are the goods and services provided by natural resources that contribute to human welfare. There are four broad categories of ecosystem services: 1) provisioning services, such as food and timber production; 2) regulating services, including pest control, pollination, and water purification; 3) cultural services such as recreation; and 4) supporting services including soil formation and carbon sequestration (Costanza et al. 2011). Some ecosystem services have direct economic value through the provisioning of goods, such as food and timber. In these cases, a landowner has a direct economic incentive to provide goods and receives payment from a buyer for these goods. However, other services are more difficult to quantify and assign direct value, such as biodiversity and habitat and pollination. Those ecosystem services that are global in nature—biodiversity and carbon sequestration, for example—are perhaps most difficult to regulate, since the provider of the service is not likely to gain anything directly by the act of providing these services. Clean water is another challenging ecosystem service to control, since water resources are affected by many users who are generally not penalized sufficiently for polluting waterways through the dumping of waste or runoff of agrochemicals.

A variety of tools are available to encourage landowners to manage their natural resources in ways that support ecosystem service provisioning. Governmental policies are one option; for example, in order to limit deforestation of the Amazon and promote biodiversity, carbon sequestration, erosion control, and water purification, Brazil's environmental laws include a Forest Code. The law, originally established in 1965, requires rural landowners within the Amazon region to maintain 80% of their landholdings forested. Though Brazil's Forest Code has a mixed history of success, in part due to lack of law enforcement (Borner et al. 2007) and conflict between wealthy elites and small-scale farmers, international pressure to curb deforestation in recent years has resulted in the Brazilian government cracking down on illegal deforestation. This is an example of a policy-based tool focused on environmental protection and ecosystem services.

An additional tool for encouraging ecosystem service provisioning is a voluntary market-based mechanism, **Payment for Ecosystem Services** (PES). In PES projects, governments or private brokers identify service providers and connect them with "buyers" who are willing

---

Ecosystem Services are the goods and services provided by natural resources that contribute to human welfare. Categories of ecosystem services include provisioning/production services, such as food and timber, regulating and supporting services, including carbon sequestration and air and water purification, and cultural services such as recreation.

Payment for Ecosystem Services (PES) are financial incentives provided to landowners for practicing land management that protects specific ecosystem services. These voluntary, market-based transactions encourage landowners to conserve forest ecosystems by providing direct payments to landowners.

to pay for the service. Without such compensation landowners may have no incentive to maintain forests for ecosystem services such as water conservation, carbon sequestration, and biodiversity conservation (Scherr and McNeely 2008). One successful example of a PES project is the Quito Water Fund, in which the water-stressed region of Quito, Ecuador, benefited from forest protection through the fund. A partnership between Ecuadoran water and electric service providers and international environmental and development organizations (The Nature Conservancy and USAID) helped to develop a fund for protection of the Condor Biosphere Reserve. Water users pay fees for the service of clean water, which the municipal government and utility companies apply to biosphere protection to ensure a clean water supply in the future (Tallis et al. 2008). Costa Rican payments for water conservation represent another success, due to effective governance in identifying and quantifying ecosystem services, identifying beneficiaries, collecting and managing payment, and monitoring compliance (Pagiola 2004). The government developed an effective policy to generate income for payments; a sales tax on fuel pays for a large part of the PES program.

Challenges with PES projects have included inequitable distribution of compensation (Corbera et al. 2007); insufficient compensation (Rosa et al. 2003); barriers to entry for small-scale, poor farmers and those without land titles (Corbera et al. 2007; Tshakert 2007); and lack of project monitoring and evaluation (Wunder 2007). Critics of PES projects argue that natural resources should be preserved for their intrinsic value rather than attempting to quantify their monetary value (McCauley 2006). Others suggest that market-based approaches to environmental conservation, such as PES, should be coupled with policy-based mechanisms to ensure greatest effectiveness (Börner et al. 2010).

The following two sections outline the concept of ecosystem services (Costanza et al. 2011) and demonstrate the application of the ecosystem services approach through a case study in Australia's Murray-Darling Basin (Liu et al. 2013). The case study shows the potential for an ecosystem services approach to incorporate public interest in particular services, including water, in a regional plan for water resources management.

HIGHLIGHTED APPROACH: ECOSYSTEM SERVICES

Valuing Ecological Systems and Services

By Robert Costanza, Ida Kubiszewski, David Ervin, Randy Bluffstone, James Boyd, Darrell Brown, Heejun Chang, Veronica Dujon, Elise Granek, Stephen Polasky, Vivek Shandas, and Alan Yeakley

Ecosystem Services

"Ecosystem services" are the benefits people derive from functioning ecosystems, the ecological characteristics, functions, or processes that directly or indirectly contribute to human well-being [1,2]. Ecosystem processes and functions may contribute to ecosystem services, but they are not synonymous as they describe biophysical relationships (such as the carbon cycle) and exist regardless of whether or not humans benefit [3,4]. Ecosystem services, on the other hand, only exist if they contribute to human well-being and cannot be defined independently [5].

The ecosystems that provide the services are sometimes referred to as "natural capital," using the general definition of capital as a stock that yields a flow of services over time [6]. In order for these benefits to be realized, natural capital (natural ecosystems and their products that do not require human activity to build or maintain, such as fish stocks) must be combined with other forms of capital that *do* require human intervention to build and maintain. These include: built or manufactured capital (e.g., fishing boats); human capital (e.g., human labor and knowledge about how to fish); and social capital (e.g., fishing communities and cultures) [7].

These four general types of capital are all required in complex combinations to produce any and all human benefits. Ecosystem services can thus be defined as the relative contribution of natural capital to the production of human benefits, in combination with the three other forms of capital. These benefits can involve the use, option to use, or mere appreciation of the existence of natural capital.

The following categorization of ecosystem services has been used by the Millennium Ecosystem Assessment [2]:

a. **Provisioning services**—ecosystem services that combine with built, human, and social capital to produce food, timber, fiber, or other "provisioning" benefits. For example, fish delivered to people as food require fishing boats (built capital), fisherfolk (human capital), and fishing communities (social capital) to produce.

b. **Regulating services**—services that regulate different aspects of the integrated system. These are services that combine with the other three capitals to produce flood control, storm protection, water regulation, human disease regulation, water purification, air quality maintenance, pollination, pest control, and climate control. For example, the storm protection services of coastal wetlands require the wetlands and the built infrastructure, people, and communities to be protected. These services are generally not marketed but have clear value to society.

c. **Cultural services**—ecosystem services that combine with built, human, and social capital to produce recreation, aesthetic, scientific, cultural identity, or other "cultural" benefits. For example, to produce a recreational benefit requires a beautiful natural asset (a lake), in combination with built infrastructure (a road, trail, dock, and so on), human capital (people able to appreciate the lake experience), and social capital (family, friends, and institutions that make the lake accessible and safe).

d. **Supporting "services"**—services that maintain basic ecosystem processes and functions such as soil formation, carbon fixation, and habitat for animals. These services affect human well-being indirectly by maintaining processes necessary for provisioning, regulating, and cultural services. They also refer to the ecosystem services that have not yet been combined with built, human, and social capital to produce human benefits but nevertheless underlie these benefits. For example, net primary production is an ecosystem function that supports carbon sequestration and removal from the atmosphere, which combines with built, human, and social capital to provide the benefit of climate regulation. Some would argue that these "supporting" services should rightly be defined as ecosystem "functions", since they may not yet have interacted with the other three forms of capital to create benefits. We agree with this in principle, but recognize that supporting services/functions may sometimes be used as proxies for services in the other categories, such as when the benefits cannot be easily measured directly.

This categorization leads to a very broad definition of services, limited only by the requirement of a contribution to human well-being. Even without any subsequent valuation, explicitly listing the services derived from an ecosystem can help ensure appropriate recognition of their importance. This can help make the analysis of ecological systems more transparent and can help decision makers weigh up the relative merits of the different options before them.

Valuation

Many ecosystem services are public goods. This means that multiple users can simultaneously benefit from using them and it is difficult to exclude people from benefiting from them. This creates circumstances where analyzing individual choices is not the most appropriate way to assess an ecosystem's value and use. Instead, some form of community or group choice process is needed. As ecosystem services (being public goods) are generally not traded in markets, we need to develop other methods to assess their value.

There are a number of methods that can be used to estimate or measure benefits from ecosystems. Valuation can be expressed in several ways, including money, physical units, or indices. Economists have developed a number of valuation methods that typically use monetary units (see [8]) while ecologists and others have developed measures expressed in a variety of nonmonetary units such as biophysical trade-offs (cf. [9]) and qualitative analyses.

There are two main methods for estimating monetary values: revealed and stated preferences. Both of theses typically involve the use of sophisticated statistical methods to tease out the values [10]. Revealed preference methods involve analyzing individuals' choices in real-world settings and inferring value from those observed choices. Examples include production-oriented valuation that looks at changes in direct-use values from products actually extracted from the environment (e.g., fish trawled from the sea). This method may also be applicable to indirect-use values, such as the benefits forests provide to agricultural production by controlling soil erosion. Other revealed preference methods infer ecosystem service values from resulting changes in housing markets. For example, urban forest ecosystems and wetlands may improve water quality and that may be (partially) captured in property values [11]. The travel cost valuation method is used to value recreation ecosystem services based on the resources, money, and time visitors spend visiting recreation sites.

Stated preference methods rely on individuals' responses to hypothetical scenarios involving ecosystem services and include contingent valuation and structured choice experiments. Contingent valuation uses a highly structured survey methodology that asks respondents to value ecosystem improvements (e.g., better stream quality) and the ecosystem services they will generate (e.g., increased salmon stocks) [12].

Choice experiments present respondents with scenarios that embody combinations of ecosystem services and monetary costs and ask for the most preferred scenarios to infer ecosystem service values.

A key challenge in any valuation is imperfect information. Individuals might, for example, place no value on an ecosystem service if they do not know the role that the service is playing in their well-being [13]. Here is an analogy. If a tree falls in the forest and there is no one around to hear it, does it still make a sound? The answer to this old question obviously depends on how one defines "sound". If "sound" is defined as the perception of sound waves by people, then the answer is no. If "sound" is defined as the pattern of physical energy in the air, then the answer is yes. In this second case, choices in both revealed and stated preference models would not reflect the true benefit of ecosystem services. Another key challenge is accurately measuring the functioning of the system to correctly quantify the amount of a given service derived from that system (e.g., [14,15]).

But recognizing the importance of information does not obviate the limitations of obtaining it. As the tree analogy demonstrates, perceived value can be quite a limiting valuation criterion, because natural capital can provide positive contributions to human well-being that are either never or only vaguely perceived, or may only manifest themselves at a future time. A broader notion of value allows a more comprehensive view of value and benefits, including, for example, valuation relative to alternative goals, such as fairness and sustainability, within the broader goal of human well-being [16]. Whether these values are perceived or not and how well or accurately they can be measured are separate (and important) questions.

Case Studies

Early Valuation Syntheses

Scientists and economists have discussed the general concepts behind natural capital, ecosystem services, and their value for decades, with some early work dating as far back as the 1920s. However, the first explicit mention of the term "ecosystem services" in the peer-reviewed scientific literature was in a paper by Ehrlich and Mooney in 1983 [17]. More than 2,400 papers have been published on the topic of ecosystem services since then, according to a search of the Institute for Scientific Information's "Web of Science" database, accessed on February 22, 2011. This database includes only a subset of scientific journals and no books, so it represents only a subset of the literature on this topic. The first mention of the term "natural capital" in the scientific literature was in a paper by Costanza and Daly in 1992 [6].

One of the first studies to estimate the value of ecosystem services globally was published in *Nature* and entitled "The value of the world's ecosystem services and natural capital" [1]. This paper estimated the value of 17 ecosystem services for 16 biomes to be in the range of US\$16–54 trillion per year, with an average of US\$33 trillion per year, a figure larger than the annual gross domestic product (GDP) at the time. Some have argued that global society would not be able to pay more than their annual income for these services, so a value larger than global GDP does not make sense. However, not all benefits are picked up in GDP, so it should not represent a limit on real benefits [18].

In this study, estimates of global ecosystem services were derived from a synthesis of previous studies that utilized a wide variety of techniques, such as those mentioned above, to value specific ecosystem services in specific biomes (see [19] for a collection of commentaries and critiques of the methodology). This technique, called "benefit transfer", uses studies that have been done at other locations or in different contexts, but can be applied with some modification. Such a methodology, although useful as an initial estimate, is just a first cut and much progress has been made since then (cf. [20-22]).

Major World Reports on Ecosystem Services

More recently the concept of ecosystem services gained attention with a broader academic audience and the public when the Millennium Ecosystem Assessment was published [2]. The Millennium Ecosystem Assessment was a 4-year, 1,300-scientist study commissioned by the United Nations in 2005. The report analyzed the state of the world's ecosystem services and provided recommendations for policy makers. It determined that human actions have depleted the world's natural capital to the point that the ability of a majority of the globe's ecosystems to sustain future generations can no longer be taken for granted.

In 2008, a second international study was published on The Economics of Ecosystems and Biodiversity [23] hosted by United Nations Environment Programme. The Economics of Ecosystems and Biodiversity's primary purpose was to draw attention to the global economic benefits of biodiversity, to highlight the growing costs of biodiversity loss and ecosystem degradation, and to draw together expertise from the fields of science, economics, and policy to enable practical actions moving forward. The Economics of Ecosystems and Biodiversity report was picked up extensively by the mass media, bringing ecosystem services to a broad audience.

The Ecosystem Services Partnership and Ongoing Work

With such high profile reports being published, ecosystem services have entered not only the public media [24] but also into business. Just one example is the Dow Chemical Company's recently established US $10 million collaboration with The Nature Conservancy to tally up the ecosystem costs and benefits of every business decision [25]. Such collaborations will provide a significant addition to ecosystem services valuation knowledge and techniques. However, there is significant research that is still required (see below). Our scientific institutions can help lead this process through transdisciplinary graduate education, such as the Ecosystem Services for Urbanizing Regions program funded by the National Science Foundation's Integrative Graduate Education and Research Traineeship program [26].

Hundreds of projects and groups are currently working toward better understanding, modeling, valuation, and management of ecosystem services and natural capital. It would be impossible to list all of them here, but the new Ecosystem Services Partnership [27] is a global network that does just that and helps to coordinate the activities and build consensus. The following lays out the research agenda as agreed to by a group of 30 participants at a meeting in Salzau, Germany, in June 2010, at the launch of the Ecosystem Services Partnership.

Integrated Measurement, Modeling, Valuation, and Decision Science in Support of Ecosystem Services

The scientific community needs to continue to develop better methods to measure, monitor, map, model, and value ecosystem services at several scales [28]. Ideally, these efforts should take place using interdisciplinary teams and strategies and in close collaboration with ecosystem stakeholders. Moreover, this information must be provided to decision makers in an appropriate, transparent, and viable way, to clearly identify the different outcomes of different policies (i.e., [4]). At the same time, we cannot wait for high levels of certainty and precision to act when confronting significant irreversible and catastrophic consequences. We must synergistically continue to improve the measurements with evolving institutions and approaches that can effectively utilize these measurements.

Trade-Offs

Ecological conflicts arise from two sources: (a) scarcity and restrictions in the amount of ecosystem services that can be provided and (b) the distribution of the costs and benefits of the provisioning of the ecosystem services. Ecosystem services science makes trade-offs explicit and, thus, facilitates management and planning. It enables stakeholders to make sound value judgments. Ecosystem services science thus generates relevant socioecological knowledge for stakeholders and other decision makers and generates sets of planning options that can help resolve sociopolitical conflicts.

Accounting and Assessment

Accounting attempts to look at the flow of materials with relative objectivity, while assessment evaluates a system or process with a goal in mind and is more normative. Both are integrating frameworks with distinctive roles. Both ecosystem service accounting and assessment need to be developed and pursued using a broader lens that includes social, economic, and ecological components. Within the broader lens we also need to balance expert and local knowledge across scales.

Modeling

We need to improve modeling to synthesize and quantify our understanding of ecosystem services and to understand dynamic, nonlinear, spatially explicit trade-offs as part of the larger socioecological systems. Stakeholders should be active collaborators in this model development and testing process to assure relevancy. These models can incorporate and aid accounting and assessment exercises and link directly with the policy process at multiple time and space scales. In particular, modeling can quantify potential shifts in ecosystem services under different environmental and socioeconomic scenarios.

Bundling

Most ecosystem services are produced as joint products (or bundles) from intact ecosystems. The relative rates of production of each service vary from system to system, site to site, and time to time. We must consider the full range of services and the characteristics of their bundling in order to prevent creating dysfunctional incentives and to maximize the net benefits to society [29,30]. As an illustration, focusing only on the carbon sequestration service of ecosystems may in some instances reduce the overall value of the full range of ecosystem services; for example, by reducing biodiversity.

Scaling

Ecosystem services are relevant over a broad range of scales in space, time, governance, and complexity, including the legacy of past behavior. We need measurement, models, accounts, assessments, and policy discussions that address these multiple scales, as well as interactions, feedbacks, and hierarchies among them.

Adaptive Management and new Institutions for Ecosystem Services

Given that pervasive uncertainty always exists in ecosystem service measurement, monitoring, modeling, valuation, and management, we should continuously gather and integrate appropriate information regarding ecosystem services, with the goal of learning and adaptive improvement. To do this we should constantly evaluate the impacts of existing systems and, with stakeholder participation, design new systems to experiment with how we can more effectively quantify performance, and learn ways to better manage such complex systems to achieve social goals.

Property Rights

Given the public-goods nature of most ecosystem services, we need institutions that can effectively deal with this characteristic using a sophisticated suite of property-rights regimes. We need institutions that employ an appropriate combination of private, state, and common property-rights systems to establish clear property rights over ecosystems without privatizing them. Systems of payment for ecosystem services and common asset trusts can be effective elements in these institutions.

Scale-Matching

The scale of the institutions to manage ecosystem services must be matched with the scales of the services themselves. Mutually reinforcing institutions at local, regional, and global scales over short, medium, and long time scales will be required. Institutions should be designed to ensure the flow of information across scales, to take ownership regimes, cultures, and actors into account, and to fully internalize costs and benefits.

Distribution

Systems should be designed to ensure inclusion of the poor, since they are generally more dependent on common property assets like ecosystem services. Free-riding, especially by wealthier segments of society, should be deterred, and beneficiaries should pay for the services they receive from biodiverse and productive ecosystems.

Information Dissemination

One key limiting factor in sustaining natural capital is lack of knowledge of how ecosystems function and how they support human well-being. This can be overcome with targeted educational campaigns that are tailored to disseminate success and failures to both the general public and officials and through collaboration among public, private, and government entities.

Participation

Relevant stakeholders (local, regional, national, and global) should be engaged in the formulation and implementation of management decisions. Full stakeholder awareness and participation not only improves ecosystem services analyses, but contributes to credible, accepted rules that identify and assign the corresponding responsibilities appropriately, and that can be effectively enforced.

Science/Policy Interface

Ecosystem services concepts can be an effective link between science and policy by making the trade-offs more transparent [4]. An ecosystem services framework can therefore be a beneficial *addition* to policy-making institutions and frameworks and to integration of science and policy.

Conclusions

Natural capital and ecosystem services are key concepts that are changing the way we view, value, and manage the natural environment. They are changing the framing of the issue away from "jobs versus the environment" to a more balanced assessment of all the assets that contribute to human well-being and their interrelationships. Significant transdisciplinary research has been done in recent years on ecosystem services, but there is still much more to do and this will be an active and vibrant research area for the coming years, because better understanding of ecosystem services is critical for creating a sustainable and desirable future. Placing credible values on the full suite of ecosystem services is key to improving their sustainable management.

Abbreviation

GDP, gross domestic product.

Competing Interests

The authors declare that they have no competing interests.

Acknowledgements

We thank the Institute for Sustainable Solutions at Portland State University for supporting several of the coauthors during the preparation of this manuscript. We also thank the Ecosystem Services Partnership (www.es-partnership.org/) and the participants at the 2010

Salzau meeting for developing the research agenda included here. Parts of this paper benefited from discussions at a meeting in Vienna in November 2009 on Cultural Ecosystem Services organized by Terry Daniel.

References

1. Costanza R, d'Arge R, de Groot R, Farber S, Grasso M, Hannon B, Limburg K, Naeem S, O'Neill RV, Paruelo J, Raskin RG, Sutton P, van den Belt M: The value of the world's ecosystem services and natural capital. *Nature* 1997, 387:253–60.

2. Millennium Ecosystem Assessment Board: Living beyond our means–Natural assets and human well-being. United Nations; 2005. [http://www.maweb.org/documents/document.429.aspx.pdf]

3. Boyd J, Banzhaf S: What are ecosystem services? The need for standardized environmental accounting units. *Ecol Econ* 2007, 63:616–26.

4. Granek EF, Polasky S, Kappel CV, Reed DJ, Stoms DM, Koch EW, Kennedy CJ, Cramer LA, Hacker SD, Barbier EB, Aswani S, Ruckelshaus M, Perillo GM, Silliman BR, Muthiga N, Bael D, Wolanski E: Ecosystem services as a common language for coastal ecosystem-based management. *Conserv Biol* 2010, 24:207–16.

5. de Groot RS, Wilson MA, Boumans RMJ: A typology for the classification, description and valuation of ecosystem functions, goods and services. *Ecol Econ* 2002, 41:393–408.

6. Costanza R, Daly HE: Natural capital and sustainable development. *Conserv Biol* 1992, 6:37-46.

7. Costanza R, Cumberland JH, Daly H, Goodland R, Norgaard RB: *An Introduction to Ecological Economics*. Boca Raton, Florida: CRC Press; 1997.

8. Freeman AM 3rd: *The Measurement of Environmental and Resource Values: Theories and Methods*. 2nd edition. Washington, DC; RFF Press; 2003.

9. Costanza R: Value theory and energy. In *Encyclopedia of Energy. Volume 6.* Edited by Cleveland CJ. Amsterdam: Elsevier; 2004: 337–346.

10. Haab TC, McConnell KE: *Valuing Environmental and Natural Resources: The Econometrics of Non-Market Valuation*. Cheltenham, UK: Edward Elgar Publishing Ltd; 2002.

11. Phaneuf DJ, Smith VK, Palmquist RB, Pope JC: Integrating property value and local recreation models to value ecosystem services in urban watersheds. *Land Econ* 2008, 84:361–81.F1000 Factor 6. Evaluated by Robert Costanza 20 Jun 2011

12. Boardman AE, Greenberg DH, Vining AR, Weimer DL: *Cost-Benefit Analysis: Concepts and Practice*. 4th edition. Upper Saddle River, NJ: Prentice Hall; 2006.

13. Norton B, Costanza R, Bishop RC: The evolution of preferences: why 'sovereign' preferences may not lead to sustainable policies and what to do about it. *Ecol Econ* 1998, 24:193–211.

14. Barbier EB, Koch EW, Silliman BR, Hacker SD, Wolanski E, Primavera J, Granek EF, Polasky S, Aswani S, Cramer LA, Stoms DM, Kennedy CJ, Bael D, Kappel CV, Perillo GM, Reed DJ: Coastal ecosystem-based management with nonlinear ecological functions and values. *Science* 2008, 319:321–3. F1000 Factor 6. Evaluated by Garry Peterson 10 Jun 2008

15. Koch EW, Barbier EB, Silliman BR, Reed DJ, Perillo GME, Hacker SD, Granek EF, Primavera JH, Muthiga N, Polasky S, Halpern BS, Kennedy CJ, Kappel CV, Wolanski E: Non-linearity in ecosys-

tem services: temporal and spatial variability in coastal protection. Front Ecol Environ 2009, **7**:29–37. F1000 Factor 6. Evaluated by Elena Bennett 25 Mar 2009

16. Costanza R: Social goals and the valuation of ecosystem services. *Ecosystems* 2000, **3**:4–10.

17. Ehrlich PR, Mooney H: Extinction, substitution, and ecosystem services. *Bioscience* 1983, **33**:248-54. F1000 Factor 6. Evaluated by Robert Costanza xx Jun 2011

18. Costanza R, d'Arge R, de Groot R, Farber S, Grasso M, Hannon B, Limburg K, Naeem S, O'Neill RV, Paruelo J, Raskin R, Sutton P, van den Belt M: The value of ecosystem services: putting the issues in perspective. *Ecol Econ* 1998, **25**:67–72.

19. Costanza R: The value of ecosystem services. *Ecol Econ* 1998, **25**:1–2.

20. Boumans R, Costanza R, Farley J, Wilson MA, Portela R, Rotmans J, Villa F, Grasso M: Modeling the dynamics of the integrated earth system and the value of global ecosystem services using the GUMBO model. *Ecol Econ* 2002, **41**:529–60.

21. United States Environmental Protection Agency's Science Advisory Board: Valuing the Protection of Ecological Systems and Services: A Report of the EPA Science Advisory Board (EPASAB-09-012). Washington, DC: EPA; 2009.

22. Polasky S, Segerson K: Integrating Ecology and Economics in the Study of Ecosystem Services: Some Lessons Learned. *Annu Rev Resour Econ* 2009, **1**:409–34.

23. Sukhdev P, Wittmer H, Schröter-Schlaack C, Nesshöver C, Bishop J, ten Brink P, Gundimeda H, Kumar P, Simmons B: The Economics of Ecosystems & Biodiversity (TEEB): Mainstreaming the Economics of Nature: A synthesis of the approach, conclusions and recommendations of TEEB. United Nations Environment Programme; 2010. [http://www.teebweb.org/TEEBSynthesisReport/ tabid/29410/Default.aspx]

24. Schwartz JD: Should We Put A Dollar Value On Nature? Time Magazine (online edition). March 06, 2010. [http://www.time.com/ time/business/article/0,8599,1970173,00.html]

25. Walsh B: Paying for Nature. Time Magazine (online edition). February 21, 2011. [http://www.time.com/time/magazine/article/ 0,9171,2048324,00.html]

26. Ecosystem Services for Urbanizing Regions (ESUR)–Integrative Graduate Education and Research Traineeship (IGERT), Portland State University. [www.pdx.edu/esur-igert]

27. The Ecosystem Services Partnership (ESP) homepage. [http:// www.es-partnership.org/]

28. Daily GC, Polasky S, Goldstein J, Kareiva PM, Mooney HA, Pejchar L, Ricketts TH, Salzman J, Shallenberger R: Ecosystem services in decision making: time to deliver. *Front Ecol Environ* 2009, **7**:21–8.

29. Nelson E, Mendoza G, Regetz J, Polasky S, Tallis H, Cameron DR, Chan KMA, Daily GC, Goldstein J, Kareiva PM, Lonsdorf E, Naidoo R, Ricketts TH, Shaw MR: Modeling multiple ecosystem services, biodiversity conservation, commodity production, and tradeoffs at landscape scales. *Front Ecol Environ* 2009, **7**:4–11.

30. Polasky S, Nelson E, Pennington D, Johnson KA: The impact of land-use change on ecosystem services, biodiversity and returns to landowners: a case study in the State of Minnesota. *Environ Resourc Econ* 2011, **48**:219–42.

CASE STUDY

Bringing Ecosystem Services into Integrated Water Resources Management

By Shuang Liu, Neville D. Crossman, Martin Nolan, and Hiyoba Ghirmay

1. Introduction

Achieving an effective and sustainable balance between human and ecological needs for freshwater is a substantial challenge (Poff et al., 2003). Population growth and climate change impose constraints on both the spatial and temporal distribution of water, resulting in increased competition for declining water resources (UNEP, 2012). Integrated Water Resource Management (IWRM) (refer back to p. 50 for IWRM text box definition) has been developed to "promote the coordinated development and management of water, land and related resources in order to maximize the resultant economic and social welfare in an equitable manner without compromising the sustainability of vital ecosystems" (Lenton and Muller, 2009; The Global Water Partnership, 2012). Since the concept was formally shaped in 1992 (Snellen and Schrevel, 2004), 80% of countries have embarked on reforms to improve the enabling environment for water resources management based on the application of integrated approaches, and 65% have developed IWRM plans (UNEP, 2012).

The success of IWRM depends on striking a balance between ecosystem health and human demand (Bakker, 2012). Managing ecosystems for both goals depends on the effective integration of scientific information with an understanding of how ecosystems affect the welfare of the society, and ecosystem services addresses this integration (Granek et al., 2010).

The concept of ecosystem services has shifted the paradigm of how nature matters to human societies (Liu et al., 2010). Instead of viewing the preservation of nature as something for which human society has to sacrifice its well-being, we now perceive of the environment as natural capital, one of society's critical assets (Costanza and Daly, 1992; Millennium Ecosystem Assessment, 2005).

IWRM and ecosystem services both emphasize the critical role of integrating competing interests in environmental decision-making, and this similarity suggests an opportunity for adopting ecosystem service-based IWRM schemes (Cook and Spray, 2012). Yet, to our knowledge, there is no existing study that has developed an operational ecosystem services framework to support IWRM.

In this paper, we attempt to fill this gap in the literature by developing an ecosystem services framework to support IWRM. We apply the framework to the Murray-Darling Basin (MDB) in Australia, which is typical of many large river basins where the integrity of ecosystems is threatened by over allocating water resources to irrigation (Özerol et al., 2012). Using multi-criteria decision analysis (MCDA), we combined scientific information on regional potentials in supplying ecosystem services with stakeholders' preferences towards these services. The MCDA results rank the 19 sub-catchments at the basin scale to identify which sub-catchments are the top suppliers of ecosystem services.

MCDA has been widely used in the area of water resources management (Bryan and Crossman, 2008; Bryan et al., 2010; Gurocak and Whittlesey, 1998; Hajkowicz and Collins, 2007; Silva et al., 2010), and it was applied to support IWRM for the purpose of regional delineation (Coelho et al., 2012), identifying water management strategies (Calizaya et al., 2010), and ranking the desirability of different farming systems (Prato and Herath, 2007). In this paper, we contribute to the emerging MCDA literature that attempts to integrate the concept of ecosystem services and visualization maps (via Geographic Information Systems, GIS) (Jackson et al., 2013; Labiosa et al., 2013). This integration allows us to explore spatially explicit synergies and trade-offs amongst ecosystem services to support IWRM. To our knowledge, this is the first case study to apply the integrated framework in facilitating water resources management.

The framework developed in this paper can be used for at least two purposes: to communicate the importance of ecosystem services and spatial heterogeneity of ecosystem services supply to a broader audience; and to be used as a screening tool for the next level of analysis or to be further developed to support decisions in prioritizing water management and investment across MDB sub-catchments for supplying ecosystem services.

2. Methods

2.1. Study Area and Current IWRM Management

Extending over 1 million km², the MDB (Figure 1) is defined by the 19 sub-catchments of the Murray and Darling rivers and their many tributaries (Murray-Darling Basin Authority, 2010). Compared to most other river systems of similar size, the Murray-Darling Basin is characterized by low average rainfall with high variability. This variability has encouraged over-allocation

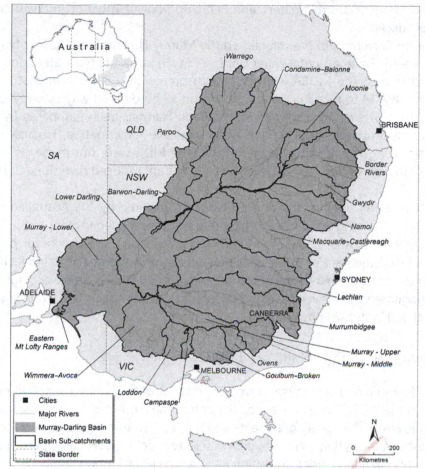

Figure 1. The sub-catchments in the Murray-Darling Basin (In our analysis, the original Murray was divided into the three sub-catchments of Murray-Lower, Murray-mid and Murray-upper because of its diverse biogeography, giving a total of 21 sub-catchments).

of irrigated water, leading to problems of unreliable supplies, low residual flows and conflicts between upstream and downstream water users (Quiggin, 2001).

The MDB is home to over two million people and supplies much of the water used by another million outside the Basin in the city of Adelaide. The three million people and various industrial activities use about 4% of the water diverted from the region's rivers, and the other 96% is used by irrigated agriculture (Connell, 2011). Water policy in the MDB has been dominated by the trade-offs between the two interests: an increase of water for the environment is thought to undermine the welfare of irrigation communities, on the other hand, extensive water diversions for irrigation threaten the integrity of ecosystems (Quiggin, 2001).

Recognizing the challenge in balancing the trade-offs between irrigation and the environmental needs, the Australian Government is reforming water resource management in the MDB with the aim of reducing the amount of water currently diverted for irrigation by 2750 GL/yr (approximately 25% of current diversions) (Murray-Darling Basin Authority, 2011). The two main instruments used by the Australian Government to reduce diversions are 1) the purchase of water use entitlements from irrigators, and 2) the upgrade of irrigation infrastructure for more efficient water supply.

The Australian Government has established the Murray-Darling Basin Authority (MDBA) and the Commonwealth Environmental Water Holder (CEWH) as part of the water reforms to ensure sustainable water use. The MDBA is charged with preparing a Basin Plan that borrows from the principles of IWRM to manage water resources in a coordinated way (Murray-Darling Basin Authority, 2010). However, development of the Basin Plan has been hampered by community concern over the proposed reductions in water available for irrigation, because the broader benefits of improving the health of ecosystems in the MDB were not made clear despite the potential for many ecosystem service benefits to result from reduced diversion (Crossman et al., 2010; CSIRO, 2012).

The CEWH is responsible for managing the water acquired by the Australian Government through the Basin Planning and broader water reform process (Department of the Environment Water Heritage and the Arts, 2009). The CEWH has developed a framework for prioritizing the acquisition and management of water, which includes qualitative ecological objectives that will change under different water availability scenarios and broad criteria on the ecological outcomes of water management. However, there is no coordinated approach to identifying investment priorities (National Water Commission, 2012).

2.2. Internet Survey on the Importance of Ecosystem Services

A survey was designed to assess the perceived importance of the benefits supplied by the natural environment in the MDB. The survey aimed to capture the current level of public understanding and attitudes towards the variety of benefits and services. To test the survey's clarity prior to its release, we tested it using two focus groups. We selected focus group participants to encompass a wide distribution of age, gender, education and income level. During the focus group sessions, participants filled out the survey individually and then participated in a discussion on the content and clarity of each question. We amended the trial survey based on the feedback from the focus group discussions.

The final survey was administered to the wider Australian public by Pureprofile, an online target marketing company. Pureprofile maintains a large membership database of people willing to complete surveys in return for a small payment. The survey was launched on 15 September 2011 and appropriate members of the database were invited to complete the survey. The survey closed on 25 September 2011 once the number of respondents reached our threshold of 500. Respondents had to be aged 18 or over, be approximately equally spread across age groups, gender and educational levels, had to be reasonably familiar with natural environments in the MDB by having used recreation facilities in the MDB, and they had to live in the States and Territory that have part or all of their territory in the MDB: South Australia, Victoria, New South Wales, Queensland, and the Australian Capital Territory.

When answering the survey, the participants stated their preferences towards ecosystem services referring to a Likert scale of 1 (not important) to 5 (extremely important) categories (Likert, 1932). They were also asked questions regarding their familiarity with the concept of ecosystem services and awareness of the benefits provided by nature, along with demographic questions. These survey questions are presented in the Online Supplementary Material (Appendix 1).

2.3. Sub-Catchments as Suppliers of Ecosystem Services

The foundation of an MCDA is a set of objectives and alternatives. Objectives are what matters or the criteria that are important for a decision, and the alternatives are ways for achieving those objectives (Keeney and Gregory, 2005). We treated ecosystem services as the objectives and the sub-catchments in the MDB as the alternatives. Each sub-catchment is an ecosystem services supplier that provides multiple benefits to Australian society.

In MCDA it is also necessary to identify a performance measure to describe the anticipated consequences of an alternative with respect to a particular objective, because objectives may sometimes be quite broad and a specific performance measure will define how an objective is to be interpreted and evaluated (Gregory et al., 2012). We adopted the ecosystem service framework developed by The Economics of Ecosystems and Biodiversity (TEEB, 2011) and selected our performance measures from a master list of potential ecosystem service indicators compiled from the Millennium Ecosystem Assessment (Layke, 2009; Layke et al., 2012), because these works are among the most recent and comprehensive assessment frameworks.

The identified set of performance measures was not designed to be comprehensive, but to provide a first set, based on available data, to describe the baseline of ecosystem service supply. The following four design principles also guided the selection of our performance measures:

1. We only reported data that meet high standards for quality and coverage across the whole basin. The resulting set of performance measures was based on the most up-to-date scientific knowledge.
2. We focused on performance measures of condition and trends. If we have data for more than one measure from the master list (Layke, 2009; Layke et al., 2012), we select the one that describes important characteristics and trends rather than identifying the causes or cures for a problem.
3. We excluded the performance measures that violate the rule of 'mutual independence of preferences' to avoid double counting in MCDA (Keeney and Raiffa, 1976).
4. We selected performance measures that are relatively easy to communicate to the public and decision-makers.

We presented the objectives and their corresponding performance measures in the format of a value tree (Figure 2). We also documented each performance measure's units, definition, and input data requirements (Table 1 in Online Supplementary Material). Due to gaps in the data, it was not possible to identify performance measures for all the ecosystem services included in the TEEB scheme. We calculated the value of performance measures for each of the eight services within a GIS for each of the 19 MDB sub-catchments. CSIRO (2012) should be consulted for a detailed description of each calculation. The original Murray sub-catchment was divided into three sub-catchments (Murray-Lower; Murray-Middle; Murray-Upper) because of its diverse biogeography, giving a total of 21 sub-catchments. Based on census data, we also calculated the average gross value of irrigated agricultural production (GVIAP) for each of the 21 sub-catchments (Australian Bureau of Statistics, 2010) to compare their capacities in providing ecosystem services with their production of conventional marketable goods.

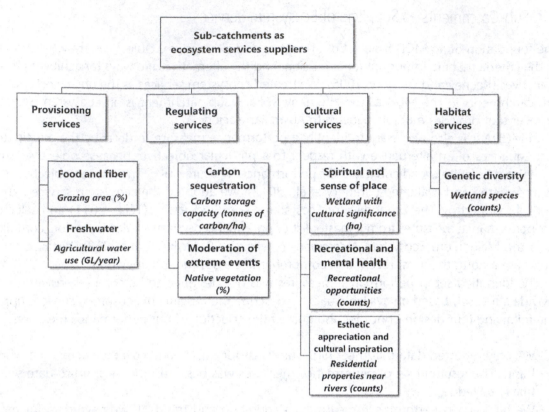

Figure 2. The value tree with ecosystem services as objectives for the MCDA and their corresponding performance measures.

We audited the capacity of the MDB sub-catchments to supply ecosystem services at the basin scale by creating a consequence table, a summary matrix in which the performance of each alternative is measured against the identified objectives. In our case, the objectives were the eight ecosystem services and the alternatives were the 21 sub-catchments.

In order to present the information in the consequence table in a spatially explicit manner, we produced maps for each ecosystem service by grouping the estimates of each performance measure into three classes of magnitude, using a method based on the Jenks Natural Breaks algorithm (Environmental Systems Research Institute, 2011). This algorithm identifies class breaks that best group similar values and that maximize the differences between classes. The Jenks Natural Breaks algorithm identifies the actual breaks observed in the data as opposed to some arbitrary classificatory scheme such as equal intervals. This preserves the actual clustering of data values subject to the arbitrary specification of k classes (in our case $k = 3$). We designated the three classes 'low', 'medium' and 'high'.

2.4. Ranking Sub-Catchments

Environmental management decisions usually involve conflicting objectives, so deciding among policy alternatives that are less than ideal is unavoidable (Liu et al., 2012). Often no one alternative will be obviously best in achieving all objectives, rather alternative A is more likely than alternative B to achieve some objectives but less likely to achieve others. One critical step of MCDA requires that one make explicit trade-offs about which alternative is preferred, with the goal of deriving an overall ordering of alternatives, from the most preferred to the least preferred alternative (UK Department for Communities and Local Government, 2009). We applied MCDA to rank the capability of the 21 sub-catchments as ecosystem service supply units, taking into account the best available scientific information and the opinions of stakeholders.

The ranking was based on a preference score calculated for each sub-catchment. To derive the scores, we integrated two sets of information—one evidence-based and the other preference-based. The former consisted of the values of performance measures in the consequence table. The latter was a set of weights converted from the results of the online survey using the method of Koschke et al. (2012). For each ecosystem service, we multiplied the number of survey respondents who selected a given level of importance on the Likert scale by the corresponding Likert value and then summed these up to derive a total weight for the ecosystem service.

The overall preference score for each sub-catchment is the weighted average of its performance values in the consequence table on all the objectives, according to a commonly applied linear additive model (Prato and Herath, 2007; UK Department for Communities and Local Government, 2009). Letting the preference score for option i and objective j be represented by Sij and the weight for each objective by Wj, then if there are n objectives the overall score for each option, Si, is given by Equation (1):

$$S_i = W_1 S_{i1} + W_2 S_{i2} + \ldots + W_n S_{in} = \sum_{j=1}^{n} W_i S_{ij} \qquad (1)$$

We used HiView 3 (Catalyze, 2008) to normalize the performance values, calculate the overall preference scores and conduct sensitivity analysis. The normalization process allows comparisons of value to be made between criteria with different units. We used linear functions to transform raw values to normalized ones (Catalyze, 2008). Given the complexity of ecosystems services at the basin scale, it should be noted that it is an extreme simplification to assume linear relationships, and non-linear ones such as a sigmoid functions might be more appropriate. For a stressed ecosystem like the MDB though, we argue that its capacity to deliver ecosystem services is far from reaching its maximum potential or the saturation point of the sigmoid function and the rising part of the sigmoid curve can be approximated by a linear function. For future development of the operational framework, the shape of the value functions is an area that requires in-depth investigation. As a starting point, however, the linear function has the advantage of being easy to communicate to decision-makers.

The sensitivity of the MCDA model was explored to test the robustness of the resulting ranking to changes in both the weights and performance values. We first investigated whether the ranking would be changed by using equal weights for the eight ecosystem services. We further examined the influence of changes in performance values on the ranking of the top two most preferred sub-catchments.

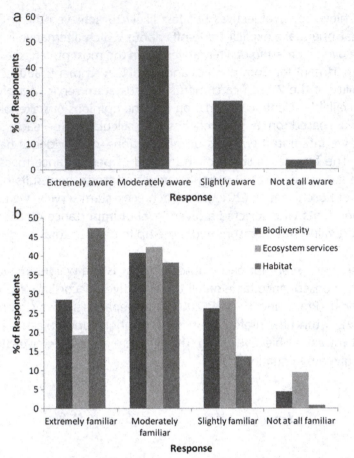

Figure 3. Survey results for the questions: a) "Have you ever thought of nature in regards to the benefits and services outlined? Please state your level of awareness prior to the survey"; b) "How familiar are you with the following terms?"

3. Results

3.1. The Importance of Ecosystem Services

A total of 503 members of the general public participated in the survey, distributed approximately equally across the States and Territory that encompass the MDB. A total of 125 survey respondents were from South Australia, 125 from Victoria, 125 from Queensland, and 128 from New South Wales including the Australian Capital Territory. We documented the socio-demographics of the respondents and the general population living in these States and Territory (Table 2 in Online Supplementary Material). The two groups are fairly close in terms of gender ratios and the distribution of age groups. However, the survey respondents are better educated than the general population.

Using the Internet survey, we investigated how important each of the ecosystem services is to the people who benefit from the MDB. Figure 3a demonstrates that people have a strong awareness of nature providing them with benefits, with a total of about 70% of respondents being either moderately aware or extremely aware that nature provides them with benefits. Figure 3b shows the familiarity of respondents with the relatively new concept of ecosystem services'

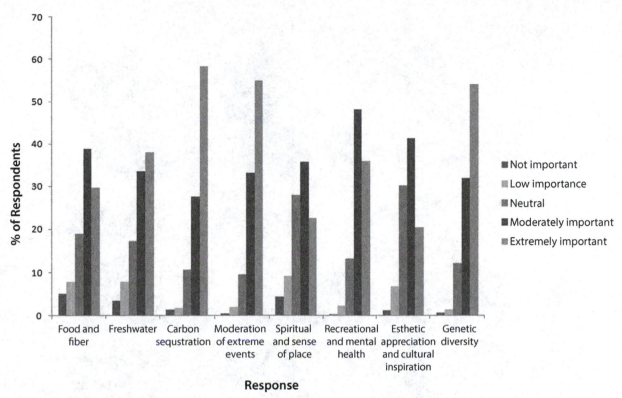

Figure 4. Survey results for the question: "please list the relative importance of each ecosystem services from extremely important to not important".

when compared to the other environmental concepts of 'habitat' and 'biodiversity'. 'Ecosystem services' is the concept that the smallest fraction of respondents is extremely familiar with. Only around 20% of the respondents were extremely familiar with the term and nearly 10% of the respondents were not at all familiar with the concept.

Figure 4 shows the relative importance of each of the eight ecosystem services elicited from the survey. The top three 'extremely important' ecosystem services were carbon sequestration, moderation of extreme events, and genetic diversity. Over 50% of the people believed these services were extremely important. The three ecosystem services which the most respondents claimed were "not important" were food and fiber (5%), spiritual and sense of place (4%), and freshwater for agricultural irrigation (3%). By comparison, only 0.2% of respondents chose "not important" for recreational and mental health.

3.2. Ecosystem Services Supply

Figure 5 shows the ecosystem service provisioning capacity for the 21 MDB sub-catchments in a spatially-explicit way. These maps are based on the best available scientific knowledge as documented in the consequence table (Table 2 in online Supplementary Material).

The number in each cell of the table is the performance value of each sub-catchment and ecosystem service pair.

The maps demonstrate the spatial heterogeneity of the sub-catchments' ability to supply ecosystem services (Figure 5a to h). 18 out of the 21 catchments supply at least one ecosystem

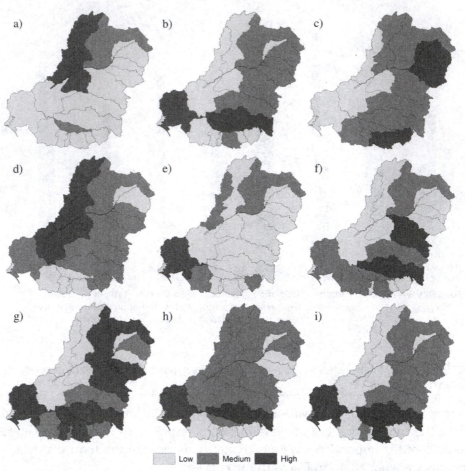

Figure 5. Ecosystem service supply across the 21 sub-catchments: a) Food and fiber; b) Freshwater; c) Carbon sequestration; d) Moderation of extreme events; e) Spiritual and sense of place; f) Recreational and mental health; g) Esthetic appreciation and cultural inspiration; h) Genetic diversity; i) Gross value of irrigated agricultural production (GVIAP).

service at a high level. With the exception of esthetic appreciation and cultural inspiration, high levels of supply of the other seven services are concentrated in a few sub-catchments though, as in the case of carbon sequestration, these may not be geographically contiguous. The Murray-Lower sub-catchment stands out, because not only has it the capacity to supply four out of the eight ecosystem services at a high level, it is also the only high-level provider of the service of spiritual and sense of place (Figure 5e).

Figure 5i shows the spatial heterogeneity of the GVIAP of the 21 sub-catchments. Murray-Lower, Murray-Middle, and Murrumbidgee produce conventional and marketable goods with high gross value. The spatial distribution of the high, medium, and low classes of this map is very different from the maps of ecosystem services except for the freshwater ecosystem service (Figure 5b). The similarity between Figure 5i and b is due to our use of agricultural water consumption as the performance measure for assessing the freshwater service.

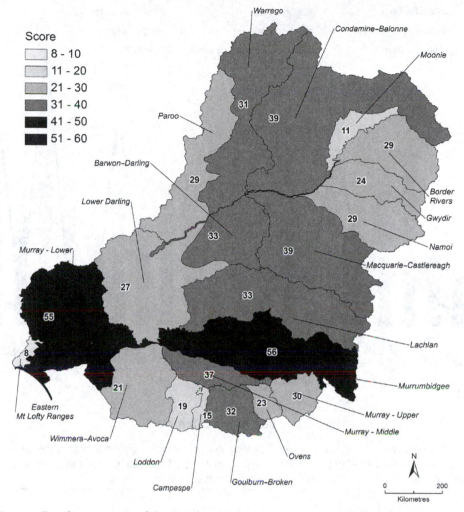

Figure 6. The overall preference scores of the 21 sub-catchments as ecosystem service supply units.

3.3. Ranking Sub-Catchments

Using the performance values in the consequence table (Table 3 in Online Supplementary Material) and the weights derived from the online survey as inputs (See Table 4 in Supplementary Material), we applied the additive linear model (Equation (1))to calculate the overall preference or weighted performance score for each of the 21 sub-catchments. The scores range between 1 and 100, where a higher score indicates a more preferred option for supplying ecosystem service benefits (Figure 6). The Murrumbidgee sub-catchment has the highest score—56—followed by Murray-Lower (55), Macquarie-Castlereagh (39), Condamine-Balonne (also 39), and Murray-Middle (37). The relative heights of each bar in Figure 6 demonstrates the ranking of the 21 sub-catchments' weighted scores in supplying ecosystem services, and this ranking is considerably different from that using GVIAP. Figure 7 provides a higher level of detail by breaking down the scores into specific scores related

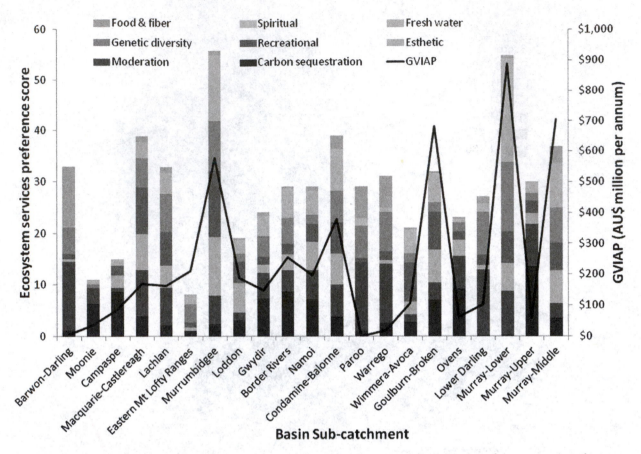

Figure 7. The ranking of overall performance scores of the sub-catchments compared to that of the gross value of irrigated agricultural production (GVIAP) (AU$ million per annum) of the 21 sub-catchments. The composition of each bar demonstrates performance scores contributed to each ecosystem services.

to each ecosystem service. For example, the high overall score for Murray-Lower is primarily explained by its high scores in both genetic diversity and spiritual services.

Using equal weights for all the services instead of the set of weights converted from the survey results, we found no significant changes in the ranking of the 21 catchments as ecosystem services suppliers. We then altered the performance value of recreational service provided by the Murrumbidgee sub-catchments and tested the influence of this change on its top ranking position. Figure 8 shows the difference in preference scores between Murrumbidgee and the second most preferred sub-catchment, Murray-Lower, as the recreational values change. When the performance value drops to about 80% of its current value, Murray-Lower becomes the most preferred option. By comparison, the top position of Murrumbidgee is more robust to changes to the performance value of spiritual services provided by the Murray-Lower. Murrumbidgee remains the top services provider even when the spiritual values for Murray-Lower increase or decrease by 50%.

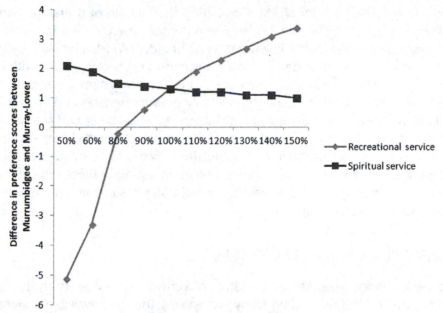

Figure 8. The difference in preference scores between Murrmbidgee and Murray-Lower with different values of performance measures.

4. Discussion

4.1. Policy Implication for IWRM Management

IWRM requires integration at multiple levels, including those between the natural and social sciences, between scientists and managers, and between stakeholders and policy makers (Holzkaemper et al., 2012). Presenting information that is understandable to all parties can increase transparency. As an interdisciplinary concept, framing the decision-making process in terms of ecosystem services provides a common set of facts and a common currency for quantifying trade-offs that help in the often difficult negotiations among groups with competing interests (Granek et al., 2010). The ecosystem service supply maps (Figure 5a to h) provide information on the broader benefits provided by the MDB, as compared to the conventional benefit of agricultural production demonstrated by the GVIAP map (Figure 5i). The presentation of both demonstrates the challenge of IWRM in the MDB. The historical focus on maximizing the supply of the freshwater service for irrigation use at the Murray-Lower, Murray-Middle, and Murrumbidgee might result in under-investment in the rest of the sub-catchments because they have high capacity to supply other services. This past focus on private benefits from irrigation use of freshwater has been challenged, given the demand for the MDB ecosystems to supply a broader range of ecosystem services such as carbon sequestration, genetic diversity, and moderation of extreme events in times of stress such as climate change. Over 50% of the respondents in our survey rated these three services as "extremely important."

For success in IWRM it is also critical to find a balance between human and environmental needs (Bakker, 2012). The concept of ecosystem services ends the traditional dichotomy of people or nature by promoting an integrated perspective. A clear mandate to sustain the delivery of ecosystem services and a framework for quantifying synergies and trade-offs among them can provide a new foundation for IWRM. Comparing the ranking of overall preference scores against the ranking by GVIAP (Figure 7) identifies potential synergies and trade-offs in current Australian Government water reform investments and broader IWRM. It would be advantageous to prioritize environmental water delivery and investment in sub-catchments with high values of agricultural production and high preference scores for ecosystem services, because such prioritization protects ecosystems' capacity to supply broader benefits and creates less impact on irrigated agriculture. These sub-catchments include Murray-Lower and Murray-Middle. On the other hand, it might be sub-optimal to invest in infrastructure efficiency improvements in sub-catchments with high agricultural value but relatively low ecosystem service supply capacity (e.g. Goulburn-Broken). In a world of scarce resources, investing in these sub-catchments may also reduce the opportunity to manage environmental water in sub-catchments with important natural capital such as Warrego and Paroo.

4.2. Limitations of the Performance Measures

Developing performance measures or indicators of ecosystem services is an iterative process (UNEP-WCMC, 2011). In this scoping study we applied the best available knowledge as an interim strategy. This practice is a necessary compromise in the short run but has two limitations.

First, our performance measures provide a one-time static view of ecosystem services supply in each sub-catchment. Tracking and communicating trends in the quantity and quality of ecosystem services are essential to understanding whether or not these services are being sustained or lost, and how policies should be designed to ensure the sustainable flow of services to support human welfare (Layke et al., 2012). A better approach is to link to biophysical process models of the supply of ecosystem services so that the outcomes of a management intervention can be quantified by models and then related back to the performance measures. In related work, we use a number of process models to understand the marginal change in ecosystem service supply following the return to the environment of 25% of water currently diverted for irrigation in the MDB (CSIRO, 2012).

Second, our single indicator approach inevitably masks the complexity of ecosystem processes and functions (de Groot et al., 2010). The design of indicators should be driven by the intended purpose or use of the indicator, and different audiences will require different indicators (Mace and Baillie, 2007). Our aim was to use the ecosystem services framework to support IWRM with an audience of decision-makers who were not familiar with the concept of ecosystem services. So we applied the single indicator approach for the purpose of easy communication as a starting point.

4.3. Challenges in Integrating Ecosystem Services and GIS with MCDA

The integration of ecosystem services and GIS with MCDA allows us to explore spatially explicit synergies and trade-offs of ecosystem services to support IWRM. We encountered two major challenges in making such an integrated framework operational: the first relates to adopting the ecosystem services of the TEEB scheme as the objectives for MCDA, and the second challenge arises from coupling the MCDA process with GIS.

The TEEB scheme divides ecosystem services into the four categories of provisioning, regulating, cultural, and habitat services (TEEB, 2011). While this typology is useful as a heuristic tool for communicating multiple benefits provided by the MDB, it can lead to double counting when we aggregate them using the linear additive model. For example, we probably would violate the rule of 'preferential independence' if we include the service of tourism in addition to esthetic, spiritual, and recreational services. We solved this problem by excluding tourism from our analysis. An alternative solution would be to adopt a scheme that clearly differentiates final and intermediate services (Fisher et al., 2008), and then a means-ends diagram (Gregory et al., 2012) can by jointly applied to build a value tree such as Figure 2 for the MCDA.

Three levels of integration between GIS and MCDA are possible: in the loose-coupling approach, one system uses data from the other as an input; a tight-coupling approach is based on a common user interface; and full integration can be achieved by adding user-specified routines to the standard commands of the GIS package (Malczewski, 2006). A more complete integration between the two systems would save time and labor, especially when a decision has to be made 'on the fly.' Yet the tighter the coupling process is, the more likely it is for researchers to inject their own value judgments into the MCDA process. For example, the Jenks Natural Breaks algorithm for clustering performance values carries an implicit value judgment. Therefore, we used the algorithm for the purpose of mapping the performance measures only, so the choice of the algorithm did not affect the MCDA ranking. Similarly, if we were to use a value function other than the linear function in our future work, it would be advisable to test the influence of alternative functions through a sensitivity analysis.

4.4. Pros and Cons of Using on-Line Survey for Weight Elicitation

Public participation is a key IWRM element that can be characterized by different levels of stakeholder engagement (De Stefano, 2010). We conducted the Internet survey of 503 members of the general public from the MDB States and Territory and translated the survey results into weights for the MCDA. Compared to other forms of participatory MCDA that typically involve a small group of 10–20 decision-makers, such as decision conferencing (Phillips and Phillips, 1993), deliberative multi-criteria evaluation (Proctor and Drechsler, 2003), and structured decision making (Gregory et al., 2012), this survey method canvases a broader and more representative sample of society. For a scoping study like ours, it also has other advantages such as reduced cost, shorter administration time, and provision of respondents with privacy (Marta-Pedroso et al., 2007). However, choosing weights via an online survey also has limitations.

The online format introduces selection bias into the results of the survey, because only people who have access to the Internet can respond. Some members of the general public may be excluded from completing an Internet survey through lack of Internet access (Olsen, 2009). This explains our survey result that the 503 respondents are better educated than the general public living in the MDB States and Territory. On the other hand, this selection bias does not necessarily influence the preferences elicited from online surveys, as demonstrated by recent environmental economics studies (Lindhjem and Navrud, 2011).

An arguably greater limitation is that online surveys do not involve stakeholders actively participating in any decision-making process via open discussion and social learning. Research has shown people do not have pre-existing preferences for novel concepts and they tend to be constructed during the decision making (Slovic, 1995). There are often shifts in preferences over the course of a deliberation process that allows participants to think and learn in new ways (Gregory et al., 2012). Without such a process, people tend to rely on "heuristic principles" to help them simplify the process of making judgments (Tversky and Kahneman, 1974). These heuristics might become psychological traps that lead them astray (Kahneman and Tversky, 1984). In our study, nearly 10% of the respondents were not familiar with the relatively new concept of ecosystem services. So it is likely that some of the respondents applied heuristic principles when responding to the survey. We asked eight Likert scale questions to directly elicit the importance of each service. Our intention was to reduce survey respondents' psychological burdens, as the Likert format works well in the context of a series of questions that seek to elicit attitudinal information about one specific subject matter (Rea and Parker, 2005). Yet such a method of weight elicitation termed "direct rating" is not recommended by decision analysts (Bouyssou et al., 2006), especially when there is a small range between the least-and most-preferred alternatives for each performance measure (Von Vinterfeldt and Edwards, 1986). This is not the case here though, because for all of the eight ecosystem services, the range between the best and the worst performance values is fairly large. Our sensitivity analysis also demonstrated that using equal weights in place of the survey derived weights did not change the ranking of the sub-catchments. In other words, the preferences of stakeholders for services did not affect the ranking. The performance values had a greater effect on the overall preference scores.

5. Conclusion

In a world undergoing climate change, high levels of past and current water extraction will likely remain the principal contributor to reduced flows in major freshwater ecosystems (Grafton et al., 2012), yet we need not face a water crisis if limited water resources are wisely managed (Lenton and Muller, 2009). The aim of this study was to bring the concept of ecosystem services into IWRM by developing an operational framework and trialing the methods in the MDB. Our paper demonstrates that the concept of ecosystem services can function as an effective way to communicate the interdependence of humans and nature, and MCDA can lead to better informed and more transparent decisions by integrating evidence-based and preference-based information.

We argue that the framework represents a significant leap forward compared to current practice, where the volume of water held for the environment has been used as the sole indicator of environmental benefits. Not only have we broadened the definition of environmental benefits by introducing the concept of ecosystem services, we also treat IWRM as a participatory process where stakeholders' values and preferences are taken into consideration in the decision-making process. Instead of analytically prescribing an optimal decision, we designed an operational framework to help inform the IWRM process by creating a shared understanding for quantifying trade-offs and engaging the public via an online survey.

Using well-established and high-quality data sets and a relatively cost-effective online survey, the results of this paper can be used as a first cut screening tool. Such rapid assessments are suitable solutions that show states and potentially trends of ecosystem services and help decision-makers to prioritize areas for further analysis to support IWRM. Our framework could be used to support the development of the Basin Plan and the investment activities of CEWH by identifying regional-scale synergies and trade-offs of reducing irrigation diversions. Jointly applied with the techniques of water resources optimization (Grundmann et al., 2013, 2012; Liu et al., 2011; Schreider, 2005; Tilmant et al., 2007; Zarghaami, 2006), this framework could also assist IWRM decision-making by prioritizing the sub-catchments where the water held for the environment should be acquired and then delivered to maximize the returns to a set of collective objectives such as ecosystem services.

Acknowledgments

This work was an output of the Multiple Benefits of the Basin Plan Project, funded by the Murray-Darling Basin Authority and CSIRO. We thank the help from Rosalind Bark, Sorada Tapsuwan, Lars Koschke and Carmen Carmona in conducting the research. We also thank two anonymous reviewers, Brett Bryan, and David Stern for comments on an earlier version of the paper.

Appendix A. Supplementary Data

Supplementary data related to this article can be found at http://dx.doi.org/10.1016/j.jenvman.2013.06.047.

References

Australian Bureau of Statistics, 2010. *Experimental Estimates of the Gross Value of Irrigated Agricultural Production, 2000–01 –; 2009–09.*

Bakker, K., 2012. Water security: research challenges and opportunities. *Science* 337, 914–915.

Bouyssou, D., Marchant, T., Pirlot, M., Tsoukias, A., Vincke, P., 2006. *Evaluation and Decision Models With Multiple Criteria: Stepping Stones for the Analyst.* Springer, New York.

Bryan, B.A., Crossman, N.D., 2008. Systematic regional planning for multiple objective natural resource management. *Journal of Environmental Management* 88, 1175–1189.

Bryan, B.A., Grandgirard, A., Ward, J.R., 2010. Quantifying and exploring strategic regional priorities for managing natural capital and ecosystem services given multiple stakeholder perspectives. *Ecosystems* 13, 539–555.

Calizaya, A., Meixner, O., Bengtsson, L., Berndtsson, R., 2010. Multi-criteria decision analysis (MCDA) for integrated water resources management (IWRM) in the lake Poopo Basin, Bolivia. *Water Resources Management* 24, 2267–2289.

Catalyze, 2008. *Hiview* 3.2.0.7.

Coelho, A.C., Labadie, J.W., Fontane, D.G., 2012. Multicriteria decision support system for regionalization of integrated water resources management. *Water Resources Management* 26, 1325–1346.

Connell, D., 2011. Water reform and the Federal system in the Murray-Darling Basin. *Water Resources Management* 25, 3993–4003.

Cook, B.R., Spray, C.J., 2012. Ecosystem services and integrated water resource management: different paths to the same end? *Journal of Environmental Management* 109, 93–100.

Costanza, R., Daly, H.E., 1992. Natural capital and sustainable development. *Conservation Biology* 6, 37–46.

Crossman, N.D., Connor, J.D., Bryan, B.A., Summers, D.M., Ginnivan, J., 2010. Reconfiguring an irrigation landscape to improve provision of ecosystem services. *Ecological Economics* 69, 1031–1042.

CSIRO, 2012. *Assessment of the Ecological and Economic Benefits of Environmental Water in the Murray-darling Basin.* CSIRO Water for a Healthy Country National Research Flagship, Canberra, Australia.

de Groot, R.S., Alkemade, R., Braat, L., Hein, L., Willemen, L., 2010. Challenges in integrating the concept of ecosystem services and values in landscape planning, management and decision making. *Ecological Complexity* 7, 260–272.

De Stefano, L., 2010. Facing the water framework directive challenges: a baseline of stakeholder participation in the European Union. *Journal of Environmental Management* 91, 1332–1340.

Department of the Environment Water Heritage and the Arts, 2009. *A Framework for Determining Commonwealth Environmental Watering Actions (Canberra).*

Environmental Systems Research Institute, 2011. *ArcGIS 10.0 Desktop Help* (Redlands, CA).

Fisher, B., Turner, K., Zylstra, M., Brouwer, R., de Groot, R., Farber, S., Ferraro, P., Green, R., Hadley, D., Harlow, J., Jefferiss, P., Kirkby, C., Morling, P., Mowatt, S., Naidoo, R., Paavola, J., Strassburg, B., Yu, D., Balmford, A., 2008. Ecosystem services and economic theory: integration for policy-relevant research. *Ecological Applications* 18, 2050–2067.

Grafton, R.Q., Pittock, J., Davis, R., Williams, J., G, Fu, Warburton, M., Udall, B., McKenzie, R., Yu, X., Che, N., Connell, D., Jiang, Q., Kompas, T., Lynch, A., Norris, R., Possingham, H., Quiggin, J., 2012. Global insights into water resources, climate change and governance. *Nature Climate Change.* Advance Online Publication.

Granek, E.F., Polasky, S., Kappel, C.V., Reed, D.J., Stoms, D.M., Koch, E.W., Kennedy, C.J., Cramer, L.A., Hacker, S.D., Barbier, E.B., Aswani, S., Ruckelshaus, M., Perillo, G.M.E., Silliman, B.R., Muthiga, N., Bael, D., Wolanski, E., 2010. Ecosystem services as a common language for coastal ecosystem-based management. *Conservation Biology* 24, 207–216.

Gregory, R., Failing, L., Harstone, M., Long, G., McDaniels, T., Ohlson, D., 2012. *Structured Decision Making: a Practical Guide to Environmental Management Choices.* Wiley-Blackwell, West Sussex, UK.

Grundmann, J., Schuetze, N., Lennartz, F., 2013. Sustainable management of a coupled groundwater-agriculture hydrosystem using multi-criteria simulation based optimisation. *Water Science and Technology* 67, 689–698.

Grundmann, J., Schuetze, N., Schmitz, G.H., Al-Shaqsi, S., 2012. Towards an integrated arid zone water management using simulation-based optimisation. *Environmental Earth Sciences* 65, 1381–1394.

Gurocak, E.R., Whittlesey, N.K., 1998. Multiple criteria decision making e a case study of the Columbia river salmon recovery plan. *Environmental & Resource Economics* 12, 479–495.

Hajkowicz, S., Collins, K., 2007. A review of multiple criteria analysis for water resource planning and management. *Water Resources Management* 21, 1553–1566.

Holzkaemper, A., Kumar, V., Surridge, B.W.J., Paetzold, A., Lerner, D.N., 2012. Bringing diverse knowledge sources together—a meta-model for supporting integrated catchment management. *Journal of Environmental Management* 96, 116–127.

Jackson, B., Pagella, T., Sinclair, F., Orellana, B., Henshaw, A., Reynolds, B., McIntyre, N., Wheater, H., Eycott, A., 2013. Polyscape: a GIS mapping framework providing efficient and spatially explicit landscape-scale valuation of multiple ecosystem services. *Landscape and Urban Planning* 112, 74–88.

Kahneman, D., Tversky, A., 1984. Choices, values, and frames. American Psychologist 39, 341–350.

Keeney, R.L., Gregory, R.S., 2005. Selecting attributes to measure the achievement of objectives. *Operations Research* 53, 1–11.

Keeney, R.L., Raiffa, H., 1976. *Decisions with Multiple Objectives: Preferences and Value Tradeoffs*. John Wiley & Sons Inc.

Koschke, L., Fürst, C., Frank, S., Makeschin, F., 2012. A multi-criteria approach for an integrated land-cover-based assessment of ecosystem services provision to support landscape planning. *Ecological Indicators* 21, 54–66.

Labiosa, W.B., Forney, W.M., Esnard, A.M., Mitsoya-Boneva, D., Bernknopf, R., Hearn, P., Hogan, D., Pearlstine, L., Strong, D., Gladwin, H., Swain, E., 2013. An integrated multi-criteria scenario evaluation web tool for participatory land-use planning in urbanized areas: the ecosystem portfolio model. *Environmental Modelling & Software* 41, 210–222.

Layke, C., 2009. Measuring Nature's Benefits: a Preliminary Roadmap for Improving Ecosystem Service Indicators. WRI working paper. Word Resources Institute.

Layke, C., Mapendembe, A., Brown, C., Walpole, M., Winn, J., 2012. Indicators from the global and sub-global millennium ecosystem assessments: an analysis and next steps. *Ecological Indicators* 17, 77–87.

Lenton, R., Muller, M., 2009. *Conclusions: lessons learned and final reflections*. In: Lenton, R., Muller, M. (Eds.), Integrated Water Resource Management in Practiceebetter Water Management for Development. Earthscan, London, pp. 205–219.

Likert, R., 1932. a technique for the measurement of attitudes. *Archives of Psychology* 140.

Lindhjem, H., Navrud, S., 2011. Are Internet surveys an alternative to face-to-face interviews in contingent valuation? *Ecological Economics* 70, 1628–1637.

Liu, S., Konstantopoulou, F., Gikas, P., Papageorgiou, L.G., 2011. A mixed integer optimisation approach for integrated water resources management. *Computers & Chemical Engineering* 35, 858–875.

Liu, S., Robert, C., Stephen, F., Austin, T., 2010. Valuing ecosystem services. *Annals of the New York Academy of Sciences* 1185, 54–78.

Liu, S., Walshe, T., Long, G., Cook, D., 2012. Evaluation of potential responses to invasive non-native species with structured decision making. *Conservation Biology* 26, 539–546.

Mace, G.M., Baillie, J.E.M., 2007. The 2010 biodiversity indicators: challenges for science and policy. *Conservation Biology* 21, 1406–1413.

Malczewski, J., 2006. GIS-based multicriteria decision analysis: a survey of the literature. *International Journal of Geographical Information Science* 20, 703–726.

Marta-Pedroso, C., Freitas, H., Domingos, T., 2007. Testing for the survey mode effect on contingent valuation data quality: a case study of web based versus in-person interviews. *Ecological Economics* 62, 388–398.

Millennium Ecosystem Assessment, 2005. In: Hassan, R., Scholes, R.J., Ash, N. (Eds.), Ecosystems and Human Well-being: Current State and Trends. Island Press, Washington, D.C.

Murray-Darling Basin Authority, 2010. *Guide to the Proposed Basin Plan: Technical Background.* Murray-Darling Basin Authority, Canberra.

Murray-Darling Basin Authority, 2011. *Plain English Summary of the Proposed Basin Plan—Including Explanatory Notes (Canberra).*

National Water Commission, 2012. *Australian Environmental Water Management: 2012 Review (Canberra).*

Olsen, S.B., 2009. Choosing between Internet and mail survey modes for choice experiment surveys considering non-market goods. *Environmental & Resource Economics* 44, 591–610.

Özerol, G., Bressers, H., Coenen, F., 2012. Irrigated agriculture and environmental sustainability: an alignment perspective. *Environmental Science & Policy* 23, 57–67.

Phillips, L.D., Phillips, M.C., 1993. Facilitated work groupsetheory and practice. *Journal of the Operational Research Society* 44, 533–549.

Poff, N.L., Allan, J.D., Palmer, M.A., Hart, D.D., Richter, B.D., Arthington, A.H., Rogers, K.H., Meyers, J.L., Stanford, J.A., 2003. River flows and water wars: emerging science for environmental decision making. *Frontiers in Ecology and the Environment* 1, 298–306.

Prato, T., Herath, G., 2007. Multiple-criteria decision analysis for integrated catchment management. *Ecological Economics* 63, 627–632.

Proctor, W., Drechsler, M., 2003. *Deliberative Multi-criteria Evaluation: a Case Study of Recreation and Tourism Options in Victoria.* European Society for Ecological Economics, Tenerife.

Quiggin, J., 2001. Environmental economics and the Murray-Darling river system. *Australian Journal of Agricultural and Resource Economics* 45, 67–94.

Rea, L.M., Parker, P.A., 2005. *Designing and Conducting Survey Research: a Comprehensive Guide, third ed.* Jossey-Bass, San Francisco, CA.

Schreider, S.Y., 2005. Special issue: integrative modelling for sustainable water allocation. *Journal of Environmental Management* 77, 267–325.

Silva, V.B.S., Morais, D.C., Almeida, A.T., 2010. A multicriteria group decision model to support watershed committees in Brazil. *Water Resources Management* 24, 4075–4091.

Slovic, P., 1995. The construction of preference. *American Psychologist* 50, 364–371.

Snellen, W.B., Schrevel, A., 2004. *IWRM: For Sustainable Use of Water 50 Years of International Experience with the Concept of Integrated Water Management.* Ministry of Agriculture, Nature, and Food Quality, Wageningen, the Netherlands.

TEEB, 2011. *The Economics of Ecosystem and Biodiversity for Local and Regional Policy Makers (London).*

The Global Water Partnership, 2012.

Tilmant, A., van der Zaag, P., Fortemps, P., 2007. Modeling and analysis of collective management of water resources. *Hydrology and Earth System Sciences* 11, 711–720.

Tversky, A., Kahneman, D., 1974. Judgment under uncertainty: heuristics and biases. *Science* 185, 1124–1131.

UK Department for Communities and Local Government, 2009. *Multi-criteria Analysis: a Manual (London).*

UNEP-WCMC, 2011. *Developing Ecosystem Service Indicators: Experiences and Lessons Learned from Sub-global Assessments and Other Initiatives.* Technical series No. 58. Secretariat of the Conention on Biological Diversity, Montreal, Canada.

UNEP, 2012. *Status Report on the Application of Integrated Approaches to Water Resources Management.*

Von Vinterfeldt, D., Edwards, W., 1986. *Decision Analysis and Behavioral Research.* Cambridge University Press, Cambridge, UK.

Zarghaami, M., 2006. Integrated water resources management in Poland's irrigation system. *Water Resources Management* 20, 215–225.

SECTION II CONCLUSION

E cosystem service valuation and ranking can be a useful tool to assess the potential for natural resource management through an ecosystem services approach. The case study of ecosystem service ranking in Australia's Murray-Darling Basin illustrates the potential for approaching an environmental problem—overuse of agricultural irrigation leading to fresh water shortages—through an assessment of ecosystem service priorities and tradeoffs. In addition, this case study illustrates the importance of community involvement in 1) discovering which services end users prioritize and should therefore receive project funding, and 2) informing the public about the human-derived benefits of natural resource use. Surveying community members about their priorities increases public awareness of the costs and benefits of various activities and the tradeoffs of natural resource use.

One of the strengths of an ecosystem services approach to environmental issues is that by encouraging resource users to consider and fully articulate the variety of benefits they receive from ecosystems, they may be more willing to participate in sustainable resource management and/or pay for ecosystem services. However, one limitation of an ecosystem services approach is that it may inadequately value certain services that have overlapping, sporadic, or highly varied uses and symbolic meaning. In addition, the valuation of ecosystem goods and services may exacerbate existing political and economic disparities. By assigning economic value to ecosystem services, certain groups may be denied access to these benefits due to economic class, race or ethnicity, or other factors. In particular with Payment for Ecosystem Service (PES) projects, the poorest people who stand to benefit the most from direct payments for conservation are the least likely to receive benefits if they do not have secure land tenure or have small landholdings. In such cases, incorporating political ecology and environmental justice approaches[1] can be useful in explicitly identifying winners and losers with different conservation scenarios and helping to remedy these disparities.

Section II Discussion Questions: Water and Ecosystem Services Review

1. What are the four types of 'capital' related to ecosystem services, as noted in Costanza et al. (2011)? What are the four categories of ecosystem services outlined in the Millennium Ecosystem Assessment?
2. Identify a specific ecosystem service from which you have benefitted.
3. Under what circumstances might Payment for Ecosystem Services (PES) be an effective tool for encouraging natural resource conservation? Briefly explain two successful cases of PES discussed in the introduction to this section.
4. What is the purpose of assigning value ('valuation') to ecosystem services? Is this the same thing as assigning value to nature? Why or why not? For whom might assigning value to ecosystem services be useful? For whom or what might it be problematic?
5. What are the inherent trade-offs associated with water use in the Murray-Darling Basin (MDB)?
6. When surveyed about the importance of various ecosystem services, which services did people in the Murray-Darling Basin case study value most? Which services did they value least? Why do you think this is the case?

References

Bates, B.C., Z.W. Kundzewicz, S. Wu and J.P. Palutikof (eds.) (2008) *Climate Change and Water.* IPCC Secretariat: Geneva, Switzerland.

Börner, J., Mendoza, A., and Vosti, S.A. (2007). "Ecosystem Services, Agriculture, and Rural Poverty in the Eastern Brazilian Amazon: Interrelationships and Policy Prescriptions." *Ecological Economics, 64*(2), 356–373.

Corbera, E., N. Kosoy, and M. Martínez Tuna. (2007) "Equity Implications of Marketing Ecosystem Services in Protected Areas and Rural Communities: Case Studies from Meso-America." *Global Environmental Change* 17:365–380.

---

1 See sections IV and V, this volume, for a discussion of these approaches

FAO (2008) "Coping with Water Scarcity: An Action Framework for Agriculture and Food Security." FAO Water Reports 38. (http://www.fao.org/docrep/016/i3015e/i3015e.pdf).

FAO (2013) "Water and Poverty, an Issue of Life and Livelihoods." FAO Natural Resources and Environment Department. (http://www.fao.org/nr/water/issues/topics_scarcity_poverty.html).

Gleick, P.H. (2011) "The World's Water: The Biennial Report on Freshwater Resources." Island Press/Center for Resource Economics.

McCauley, D.J. (2006). "Selling out on Nature." *Nature, 443*(7107), 27–28.

Pacific Institute (2009) "The World's Water: Water Conflict Chronology." Updated 11/09: (http://www.worldwater.org/conflict.html).

Pagiola, S. (2004) "Paying for Water Services in Central America: Learning from Costa Rica." In S. Pagiola, J. Bishop, and N. Landel-Mills, editors, *Selling Forest Environmental Services: Market-Based Mechanisms for Conservation and Development.* Earthscan Publications Ltd., Sterlin, VA.

Regassa, S., Givey, C. and Castillo, G.E. (2010). "The Rain Doesn't Come on Time Anymore: Poverty, Vulnerability, and Climate Variability in Ethiopia." Oxfam International.

Scherr, S.J. and J.A. McNeely. (2008) "Biodiversity Conservation and Agricultural Sustainability: Towards a New Paradigm of 'Ecoagriculture' Landscapes." *Philosophical Transactions of the Royal Society B-Biological Sciences* 363:477–494.

Tallis, H., Kareiva, P., Marvier, M., and Chang, A. (2008) "An Ecosystem Services Framework to Support Both Practical Conservation and Economic Development." *PNAS* 105(28), 9457–9464.

Tschakert, P. (2007) "Environmental Services and Poverty Reduction: Options for Smallholders in the Sahel." *Agricultural Systems* 94:75–86.

U.N. Water. "U.N. Water Statistics: Graphs and Maps, Water Resources." Accessed 21–09–13: (http://www.unwater.org/statistics.html).

WHO (2013) "Water, Sanitation and Health." Accessed 23-09-13: (http://www.who.int/water_sanitation_health/mdg1/en/).

Wunder, S.(2007) "The Efficiency of Payments for Environmental Services in Tropical Conservation." *Conservation Biology* 21:48–58.

Section Three
Agriculture, Food, and Agroecology

INTRODUCTION TO AGRICULTURE AND GLOBAL FOOD SYSTEMS

agrifood systems	food sovereignty	**KEY TERMS**
carbon footprint	agroecology	
life cycle assessment or analysis (lca)	livelihood	
food security	agroecosystem	

Agriculture, **agrifood systems**, and the environment interact in dynamic and complex ways. From an environmental perspective, agricultural production depends on the health of the natural resource base of our planet (i.e. soil, water, sunlight). In turn, agricultural activities can enhance and/or degrade the ecosystems and natural resources on which they are practiced. Examples of negative impacts from agriculture are soil erosion, agro-chemical contamination, and water depletion, which are widespread as a result of industrialized agriculture or conventional agriculture. This model of farming is characterized by large-scale monocultures (plantings of only one crop) and heavy reliance on agrochemicals and irrigation. In contrast, agricultural systems can also help to conserve soil (by including soil-conservation practices), biodiversity (by providing habitat), and water through the use of a variety of alternative agricultural models that avoid monocultures and excessive use of external inputs and irrigation.

However, the agricultural production process is only one stage of the totality of what we term here as "agrifood systems" which are the vehicles through which human populations access agricultural products for food, livestock feed, and other uses (e.g., cotton and hemp used for fiber). As a whole, an agrifood system includes all the steps that it takes for an agricultural product to go from farm to table, if it is edible, or final consumption if it is not for food (e.g. a cotton shirt). Each one of the stages of the agrifood system can have both negative and positive impacts on the environment and the people living near and laboring

Agrifood Systems are composed of land, agricultural systems, people, and animals, as well as the set of activities and relationships that interact to determine what and how much, by what method and for whom, food is produced, processed, distributed, and consumed (Pimbert et al. 2001).

Carbon Footprint is the total amount of greenhouse gases that are emitted into the atmosphere each year by a person, family, building, organization, or company (source: http://www.epa.gov/climatechange/glossary.html).

in the system. For example, product transportation and distribution can have a large **carbon footprint** if they occur over long distances, as this is usually dependent on petroleum-based fuels. Likewise, food products that require a high level of processing (e.g. instant foods such as macaroni and cheese) will need more energy expenditures than those that are produced locally and consumed fresh such as fruit and vegetables (see Freidberg 2009 for an in-depth analysis of the political economy, cultural production, and history of "freshness"). Beyond environmental impacts or benefits, agrifood systems are affected by intricately related social, cultural, and political-economic factors. For example, countries and regions can sometimes adhere to agricultural production and trade policy that directly determines how and what types of food may be grown and which foods will be imported. That is why it is so important to address agrifood systems from a comprehensive perspective, which includes ecological, socio-cultural, and political-economic dimensions (this is further addressed when discussing agroecology in the next sub-section).

The introductory chapter for this section by McDonald (2010) presents a historical overview of the environmental impacts of agricultural production. The author first discusses available statistics and evidence of how agricultural activities affect a range of environmental factors, including land and soil; water use and quality; habitats and biodiversity; energy use; and climate change. These first sections focus specifically on the agricultural production process and do not discuss other stages of agrifood systems (i.e., processing, distribution, retailing, consumption). Thus, in order to fully understand environmental impacts at the agrifood system level, we would have to assess them at each of these stages and for the full life of the product. A useful tool for calculating impacts at each stage is the **Life Cycle Analysis or Assessment (LCA)**, which involves calculating all the inputs (materials, energy, etc.) and outputs (waste, pollution, etc.) of the life of a product or activity (Heller and Keoleian, 2003). This can be estimated partially, up to any stage (e.g., distribution), or until the usable life of a product has expired, including the management of its final waste products. At the end of his chapter, McDonald introduces the concept of **sustainable intensification**, which broadly refers to an approach that increases agricultural production while minimizing or eliminating environmental impacts. Although this section explicitly discusses the global food system scale, it remains focused predominantly on technological and production aspects, such as

Life Cycle Assessment or Analysis (LCA) refers to a method or methods of analysis that evaluate the use of resources and environmental impacts associated with a product, process, or activity. This includes material and energy inputs and outputs (including waste) at all the stages of the life cycle of a particular product, process, or activity, and which can include acquisition of raw materials, production, processing, packaging, use, and retirement (Heller and Keoleian, 2003).

the potential benefits and limitations of genetically modified crops (the general term for all organisms that are modified genetically is "genetically modified organisms" or GMOs).

Extremely important factors related to agrifood systems and their interactions with ecosystems are human hunger and **food security**. Hunger represents one of the most pressing challenges of our time, with recent estimations of more than 870 million people going hungry in the world today (FAO et al. 2012). Food security and **food sovereignty**, which are fields that emerged as ways to study and address this issue, remain contentious. In general, food security tends to address how people will access food, without fully taking into account the social, cultural, or political nuances of how this is achieved in an increasingly globalized agrifood system (FAO et al. 2012). Food insecurity is not simply about the availability of food but also an issue of food access and distribution, persistent poverty (Singh and Gilman 1999), and even food preference and appropriateness (Pinstrup-Andersen 2009). Therefore any solution to food insecurity must not only address food availability through agricultural production but also food access and equal distribution of food in order to ensure food security for all. In contrast, food sovereignty focuses on people's rights to decide what kind of food and agricultural production system they would like their food to come from (Wittman et al. 2010). The interplay between food security and food sovereignty has become a contested issue in academic and international development policy debates. The resolution to the issue of global hunger may well lie in finding the right balance between providing a consistent food supply and ensuring populations have the political rights to decide the kind of food that they want to eat.

Food Security refers to people having food availability, access, quality, safety, and nutrition. The Rome Declaration on World Food Security stated in 1996 that "Food security exists when all people, at all times, have physical and economic access to sufficient, safe and nutritious food to meet their dietary needs and food preferences for an active and healthy lifestyle" (FAO, 1996; Pinstrup-Andersen, 2009).

Food Sovereignty is the right of peoples, communities, and countries to define their own agricultural, labor, fishing, food and land policies that are ecologically, socially, economically, and culturally appropriate to their unique circumstances. It views food as a fundamental human right rather than a marketable commodity, including that all people have the right to safe, nutritious, and culturally appropriate food and food-producing resources, and the ability to sustain themselves and their societies; also see (http://www.nyeleni.org/spip.php?article125); and (Patel, 2009).

Agroecology: A Transdisciplinary, Participatory Action Research Approach to Agrifood System Sustainability

Agroecology is one of several approaches that emerged as a response to the environmental and social impacts of industrialized or conventional agriculture. Industrial agriculture's focus on maximizing yields and profits has resulted in negative impacts on social and ecological systems around the world. Many of the practices associated with industrial agriculture (e.g., monocultures, soil tillage, excessive use of water, pesticides, and fertilizers) have led to

Agroecology is a transdisciplinary, participatory, and action-oriented approach that applies an ecological lens and integrates scientific and practical knowledge to study and develop more sustainable food systems (Méndez et al. 2013).

increasing degradation of the long-term productivity and health of agricultural land (Méndez, 2010). Other related approaches that seek similar goals as agroecology include natural systems agriculture (Cox et al. 2004), ecological agriculture (Magdoff 2007), ecoagriculture (McNeely and Scherr 2002), permaculture (Mollison and Slay, 1997), and organic agriculture (Willer and Kilcher, 2010). There are similarities and differences between agroecology and these other approaches, and for many students, researchers, and practitioners, selecting a particular approach for their work remains a matter of personal preference. However, agroecology aligns well with the transdisciplinary and global nature of an international environmental studies perspective, and we believe it to be the most adequate approach to present in this volume.

In its early stages, agroecology focused mostly on the "ecology" of agriculture, with an aim to improve the ecological performance and biophysical sustainability of agricultural systems (Altieri 1987; Gliessman 1990). This was followed by a desire to become more inter- and transdisciplinary, through the integration of concepts and methods from the social sciences (Guzmán-Casado et al. 1999; Hecht 1995). The conceptual article presented in this section discusses the current and future directions of the field of agroecology or the agroecological approach (Section III, Part C: Méndez, Bacon, and Cohen, 2013). It stresses the need to identify different perspectives within the field and discusses in detail a particular agroecological perspective. The authors argue that in order to address pressing agrifood system issues related to food security and environmental impacts, it is necessary to use a transdisciplinary approach that is also combined with participatory action research (PAR). The former is necessary to be able to take into account the entirety of dimensions that encompass agrifood systems (ecological, social, economic, political, cultural, etc.). The PAR approach allows for the inclusion of a broad stakeholder base in directing research and applications oriented to improve and design more sustainable agrifood systems. Of great importance here is the need to engage political-economic issues, such as the concentration of food distribution by transnational corporate actors and how they affect agriculture and food policy nationally and globally.

Agroecology and Food Sovereignty in Latin America

The case study presented in this section discusses the integration of agroecology and food sovereignty in Latin America. The author highlights some of the distinctive features of the agroecological approach in this region, including the following:

- An emphasis on credit and support for smallholder farmers in their role as important agricultural producers in the region.
- Acknowledging that smallholder agriculture has a strong agroecological basis and history, but that this sector also needs policies, research, and extension that further develops agroecological practices for enhanced production and **livelihoods**.

Livelihood is composed of the capabilities, skills, assets (including material and social resources) required for a means of living, including food production, meeting basic needs, and earning income (Chambers and Conway, 1992)

- The high resilience potential of smallholder agroecological farming.
- The importance of rural social movements and smallholder agriculture in developing an agroecological approach to attain food sovereignty.

This regional analysis presents lessons that may apply to other developing regions and touches on issues of global concern. However, it should be clear that some of these insights may not translate as well to North America and Europe, where industrial agriculture predominates.

MANAGING GLOBAL ENVIRONMENTAL CHANGE
The Environmental Impacts of Agriculture and Food Production

By Bryan L. McDonald

This chapter considers a core challenge to ensuring food security, environmental change, and specifically looks at how environmental change results from and can in turn cause changes in the agriculture, fishing, and food production practices that are the basis of the global food network. As discussions of global environmental change have increasingly entered popular discourse in recent years, commentators and advocates have focused on energy sources and usage and proposed solutions such as improving car fuel efficiency or shifting to energy-efficient light bulbs. As Maria Rodale writes, "the debate over the climate crisis and environmental destruction has been almost completely focused on energy usage ... We haven't yet made the full connection between how we grow our food and the impact it can have on the climate crisis and our health crisis" (Rodale 2010: 5). Though it is a prominent feature in the scientific literature on climate and environmental change, popular and political discussions of global environmental change rarely raise food as a generative factor, likely area of impact, or possible source of solutions to global environmental change. This absence is significant given that land use and food production practices account for more than 30 percent of human-induced greenhouse gas emissions (Scherr and Sthapit 2009). Agricultural and food production systems are linked in that food systems drive environmental changes which in turn impact food systems which leads to further environmental changes and so on.

The environmental impacts of food and agriculture continue to be significant drivers of related environmental issues such as soil and water degradation, which can further complicate efforts to address climate change. Global agriculture, according to FAO (2003a), consumes more water than any other industry, and is also the primary source of nitrate and ammonia pollution. Agricultural practices are closely linked to problems such as land clearance, degradation, and increased salinization of soils, increased stresses on water resources, impacts on water quality from agricultural runoff, and the development of antibiotic-resistant microbes. This chapter examines how this "vicious cycle" of food system-induced environmental degradation could be harmonized with imperatives of sustainable development to create a "virtuous cycle" that enhances environmental quality, promotes human security, and ensures food security (Gore 1999; UNEP 2002; FAO 2006).

Drawing on the great wealth of information that now exists on the causes and impacts of global environmental change, the chapter reviews the environmental impacts agriculture and food production practices have had on the environment. The chapter considers environmental impacts in five major sectors: land and soil; water use and water quality; habitat and biodiversity loss; energy use; and climate change. The chapter concludes with a discussion of ways to reduce the environmental impact of agriculture and food production. This discussion focuses particular attention on the need to develop food systems that provide for human needs while also aiding efforts to both mitigate and adapt to processes of global environmental change, a process that I argue can be harmonized with efforts to increase agricultural sustainability.

Impacts on Land and Soil

Covering only about one-third of the earth's surface, land is indispensable to agriculture and livestock production. These land resources, according to a definition by UNEP (2002) include soil, land cover, and landscapes. Land and soil provide a range of additional benefits, including regulating hydrological cycles and aiding in the preservation of biodiversity, carbon storage, and other ecosystem services (the resources and process provided by natural systems that are beneficial to human livelihoods and well-being). Though finite, the functional amounts of land and soil resources, along with water and nutrients, are, as Smil (2000) asserts, variable with management practices that considerably affect their quality and efficiency of use. Many current agricultural practices reduce the ability of ecosystems to provide goods and services such as carbon sequestration and soil retention and absorption of water. The amount of land under agricultural cultivation has increased steadily in developing regions while remaining largely constant in developed regions, with the largest gains in cultivable land made in the mid-twentieth century (UNEP 2008). Degradation and pollution of land resources, such as the overuse of fertilizers and other chemicals, has also occurred as a result of policy failures and unsustainable agricultural practices (UNEP 2002). Human induced land modification, largely related to agricultural activities, has impelled significant environmental changes (Smil 2000; UNEP 2002, 2008).

Changes in land and land use patterns have positive and negative effects on human well-being, the environment, and the provision of ecosystem services. "The enormous increase in the production of farm and forest products has brought greater wealth and more secure livelihoods for billions, but often at the cost of land degradation, biodiversity loss and disruption of biophysical cycles such as the water and nutrient cycles" (UNEP 2008: 86). Since the early

1970s, efforts to increase food production have been the main factor increasing pressure on land resources. Other pressures on land resources include increasing human population and population density (especially in urban and peri-urban areas), increased productivity, higher incomes and changing consumption patterns, climate change and variability, and changes in technology. Land resources provide the overwhelming majority of food including 98 percent of food energy and 93 percent of dietary protein (Smil 2000). Changes in land and land use patterns can have impacts on a range of factors relevant to human security including the environment, human livelihoods, human health and safety, and socioeconomic dimensions (UNEP 2002, 2008).

Soil loss is an especially key component of impacts of agriculture and food production on land resources. While soil erosion is a natural cycle, soil loss can become a problem when land management practices or activities such as mining, urban development, and infrastructure development accelerate rates of erosion. Jason Clay notes that since 1850 humans have "converted close to 1 billion hectares of forests, grasslands, and wetlands to farmlands," dramatically increasing soil erosion in the process (Clay 2004: 46–7). Soil erosion can lead to reduced productivity as soil loss means not just the loss of organic matter, but also the loss of nutrients, reduced water retention capacity, and the loss of biodiversity including species of bacteria and other organisms that can aid in water and nutrient retention. Although soil is a renewable resource, many current agricultural and food production practices use soil at nonrenewable rates. According to some estimates, around one-third of all cropland in the United States has been abandoned due to soil erosion since 1950 (Hawken et al. 1999). A 2007 study estimated that soil is being depleted at rates that are one to two orders of magnitude (between 10 and 100 times) greater than it is being replenished (Montgomery 2007). The very long time periods for soil formation have led to calls that soil be regarded as a nonrenewable resource. For instance, Wes Jackson writes that "soil is as much of a non-renewable resource as oil" (Jackson 1996: 83). While soil can be replaced, the processes involved in converting organic matter into topsoil take very long periods of time, which suggests the need for efforts to conserve as much soil as possible. Negative impacts on land and soil are not unavoidable. Cases of conversion to sustainable agricultural practices have demonstrated that losses to soil and soil nutrients can be reversed (Hawken et al. 1999). Even in the absence of full conversion to sustainable methods, a number of techniques exist to reduce erosion from agricultural activities such as no-till agriculture, use of shelterbelts to protect fields from wind and water, and methods that leave some forest and vegetation cover, or use cover crops such as clover, on fields (Jackson 1996; UNEP 2002, 2008).

Salinization, or salt buildup, in soil is another key threat to land resources. Salinization, when salt is present in agricultural land or water sources that humans wish to use, occurs due to inadequate rainfall, improper irrigation, and poor drainage. Salt appears naturally in soil, streams, rivers, and groundwater, and concentrations of salt increase as plants intake water but leave the salt it carried in the soil. In high concentrations, salt can cause a range of problems, from inhibiting water absorption in plants and animals to corroding metal. Build-up of salt can be caused through irrigation methods which apply more water than crops can use and more water than would be provided to an ecosystem through natural rainfall or flooding. Perhaps the most dramatic example of irrigation-induced salinization can be found in the Aral Sea. Extensive irrigation, using water from the lake, has caused the volume of the lake to fall by 90 percent since 1960, and the land irrigated with the water has lost fertility due to salt buildup. Salinization can also occur when seawater is introduced to depleted or overdrawn coastal aquifers or when water-intensive crops and pastures replace native vegetation. The latter process, also known as dryland salinity, means that, as less water is used by crops and pastures, more water infiltrates groundwater stores, which results in the rise of more saline water into streams and onto the surface through the evaporation processes. Eventually, this process may create a crust of salt on the surface of soils. More than 20 percent of the arable land in West Asia has been degraded by salinization of soil. Globally, studies indicate that as much as 20 percent of irrigated land has reduced productivity due to salinization (FAO 2003a; Clay 2004; UNEP 2008).

Soil nutrient depletion is another major environmental impact from agricultural practices. Soil nutrient depletion refers to a decline in soil fertility based on reductions in soil of the levels of plant nutrients, such as nitrogen, phosphorus, potassium, and organic matter. Healthy soil contains a great deal of biodiversity and biomass, sustaining varied life such as microbes and organisms like earthworms, millipedes, spiders, snails, beetles, and centipedes. Organic matter—the decaying remains of plants and animals, animal wastes, and microbes—is a key indicator of soil quality and health. Organic matter is crucial for maintaining soil fertility and soil structure. Soil structure allows water and plant roots to penetrate soil and soil that loses its structure can become hard, brittle, and very difficult for water and roots to penetrate. The depletion of nutrients in soil operates through a variety of mechanisms. The conversion of land from forests, wetlands, or other natural habitat can also lead to significant decreases in soil fertility, as just a few decades after turning to cropland, carbon rates in soil decline by 30 to 50 percent. Conversion to cropland disrupts fertility in a number of ways. By its very purpose, cropland is intended to produce crops which will be harvested and thus removed from the soil, rather than returned to the soil as plant matter is in forests and natural eco-systems. Cultivation of crops also involves tilling and aeration, processes which speed up decomposition rates of organic matter in soil. In attempting to understand soil nutrient loss, it is thus important to look holistically at the health not just of fields and farms, but of entire agricultural ecosystems, as losses or gains in nutrient composition of soil in one area can impact others. In addition to increasing capital costs for agricultural activities, the addition of inputs, combined with soil nutrient loss, can also affect water resources and water quality as nutrients that are leached out of or washed off soil enter into water systems (Smil 2000; Clay 2004; UNEP 2008).

Impacts on Water use and Water Quality

Agricultural practices have a range of impacts on water use rates and water quality. While three-quarters of the earth is covered by water, most of this water is not fresh. As Hawken et al. estimate, only a tiny percentage of fresh water is available for use, as the majority is frozen in glaciers and icecaps (Hawken et al. 1999). Limited freshwater sources have been tapped by an increasing global population and growing irrigated agriculture. Some observers estimate increases in water use as high as "sixfold in the last century (from 579 to 3,750 cubic kilometers per year)" (Clay 2004: 54). These massive increases in freshwater use reflect the centrality of irrigation as a method used in the twentieth century to increase food production; according to some estimates, irrigation alone bears responsibility for the majority of world food production increases in the middle decades of the twentieth century (Hawken et al. 1999). Use has not diminished in recent decades; currently, agriculture is responsible for almost 70 percent of global freshwater withdrawals (Smil 2000; FAO 2003a; UNEP 2008).

Rates of freshwater use have raised concerns about possible stress on water resources. At the present time, "1.6 billion people, or almost one quarter of the world's population, face economic water shortage (where countries lack the necessary infrastructure to take water from rivers and aquifers)" (UN Water 2007: 4). Trends such as global population growth as well as impacts from climate change are likely to increase pressure on water resources. UN Water reports that regional water shortages are the greatest concern, as "by 2025, 1.8 billion people will be living in countries or regions with absolute water scarcity, and two-thirds of the world population could be under conditions of water stress" (ibid.: 10). The impact of rising rates of water scarcity will be varied and will certainly interact with other trends. For example, one of the major ways that water is transported around the world is in food. In some circumstances, to circumvent localized water shortages, it is easier for countries to grow food in other places and transport it back to feed their populations. Pakistan has recently attempted to capitalize on this interest in overseas farmland by offering their farmland to water-strapped Gulf nations. While this strategy may bring financial benefits to Pakistan, it also has costs (including the need to develop a new 100,000 strong agricultural security force) and could lead to exacerbations of water scarcity in Pakistan and the prospect of food-insecure Pakistanis watching food grown and watered in Pakistan shipped to wealthy Gulf states (Kugelman 2009). This is but one example of the ways that water and food can interact in security-relevant ways. A large literature explores the possibility that water could act as both a cause of increased conflict and a driver of improved cooperation (Gleick 1993; Conca and Dabelko 2002; Wolf et al. 2005).

Agriculture uses a large portion of global freshwater. All freshwater comes from rainfall, most of which is captured by soil and returned to the atmosphere by evaporation. Only 11 percent of freshwater is available as stream flow and groundwater that can be used for agriculture, consumption, or urban and industrial uses. Of that small available percentage, almost 70 percent is used for agriculture. However, use of freshwater varies by region and ecosystem. Almost three-quarters of irrigated land is in developed countries where it is used to produce crops such as rice (34 percent of crops produced on irrigated land), wheat (17 percent) and cotton (7 percent). The efficiency of water use varies greatly depending on the region and whether water is being used to grow crops or raise livestock. In general, livestock and aquaculture require markedly more water than crops, perhaps as high as 80 times as much for livestock (ibid.). Improved management of water resources must not only address water stress threats, but also ensure that agricultural production keeps pace with population growth and changing consumption patterns (Smil 2000; FAO 2003a; Clay 2004; UNEP 2008).

Agriculture and food production, in addition to affecting water usage rates, also have significant impacts on water quality. Hawken, Lovins and Lovins assert that "agriculture is America's largest, most diffuse, and most anonymous water polluter" (Hawken et al. 1999: 197). Agricultural inputs such as pesticides and fertilizers frequently escape from their application site and flow onto other lands and into waterways. In addition to impacting water quality, agricultural runoff can harm human health and other organisms. Many studies have documented the negative impacts of agricultural pesticides on birds, insects, mammals, and amphibians (Carson 1962). Water quality can also be impacted by improper storage or disposal of agricultural and livestock waste products. For example, one estimate of the waste impacts of large-scale livestock production facilities, also known as concentrated animal feeding operations (CAFOs), found that while the vast majority of operations work to meet environmental and health standards, "heavy rains or accidents can cause lagoons where liquefied animal waste is stored to eventually break or leak into the surrounding soil and watersheds, releasing dangerous levels of trace heavy metals and bacteria into drinking water" (Ellis and Turner 2007: 23). In addition to the direct impacts that waste can have on water resources by asphyxiating fish and aquatic life, waste products also contain medicines and can contribute to problems such as the development of antibiotic resistance among microbes (Garrett 1994; FAO 2003a; Clay 2004).

Beyond impacts on fresh water and water quality, food production is also a significant driver of impacts on the world's oceans. Oceans represent 97 percent of all water on earth and are the source of much of the moisture that falls as precipitation. Oceans also perform a number of vital services through circulation of waters. Ocean circulation is driven by differences in seawater density (determined by water temperature and salinity) and moves warm water towards the poles and cold water towards the equator. This circulation process has a number of effects, including helping to sequester carbon dioxide (CO_2) from the atmosphere into the ocean, distributing heat and nutrients, and influencing the climates of areas, such as the United Kingdom, which would be much colder without the infusion of warm waters. Changes in the world's oceans are having a number of impacts including altering precipitation patterns, and negative effects on marine life and aquatic ecosystems. There is also concern that climate change could alter global circulation patterns and increase the acidity and amount of carbon in oceans which could affect marine life (UNEP 2006, 2008).

Food and agriculture are indirectly affecting oceans by accelerating global climate change, but they are also having many direct and significant impacts on the state of the world's oceans. Agricultural runoff and other pollutants are major contributors to the increase in the number and size of deoxygenated areas (also called dead zones) in the world's oceans. According to UNEP (2006), the number of such areas has risen rapidly, doubling every decade since the 1960s, and there are now an estimated 200 dead zones in the world, compared with 149 in 2004. Such areas are a major threat to fish stocks and the many people who depend on marine life for food and livelihood. Marine life is also being heavily affected by fishing and food production activities. Population growth, changes in consumption rates, and changes in technology have all helped fuel significant increases in global fish catch which rose to 141 million tons of seafood in 2005, a figure that represents an eightfold increase over global seafood harvests in 1950 (Halweil and Nierenberg 2008). Moreover, agricultural runoff contributes to the destruction of coastal wetland and coral reef areas; agricultural runoff is expected to rise 14 percent globally by 2030 compared with the mid-1990s (UNEP 2006).

As with soil and land resources, food, fishing and agricultural activities do not necessarily require unsustainable use of freshwater flows or unacceptable impacts on water quality and oceans. A range of methods, policies, and technologies can improve the efficiency and sustainability of water use. Some solutions involve the use of new varieties of crops that require less water to grow. Another solution is improving the efficiency of water use. In the United States, water use efficiency has been steadily increasing since the 1980s. Even with a growing population and economy, the efficiency of water use in the United States has been improving in recent decades. For example, "the amount of freshwater withdrawn per American fell by 21 percent during the years 1980–1995 ... over twice as fast as energy efficiency improved" (Hawken et al. 1999: 216). Improvements in water use efficiency can come through a variety of methods, such as drip irrigation systems or methods that allow for better information about soil moisture levels that can guide how much water is needed in a given area, or even sub-area, of a farm. Other ways to improve water use efficiency include better efforts to capture and use rainfall at the sites where it falls. Using catch basins, cover crops, and substances that can be mixed into soil to increase water intake all provide ways to increase water use efficiency and reduce runoff. Efforts to improve management of fisheries and develop sustainable aquaculture can provide ways to improve local livelihoods and attract foreign investment but also need strong action to reduce fishing practices that harm fish stocks and should identify species and techniques for aquaculture that do not require substantial inputs, such as fish meal, and do not produce new sources of waste and pollution (WCED 1987; Hawken et al. 1999; Clay 2004; UNEP 2006, 2008).

Impacts on Habitat and Biodiversity Loss

Agricultural activities are a major driver of land modification and deforestation activities that lead to habitat and biodiversity loss. Estimates from FAO concluded that as much as 13 million hectares of forest are lost to agriculture land expansion in developing countries each year. Forests serve a variety of functions, many of which have direct and indirect benefits for humans. "In addition to directly supporting industries such as timber, pulp, and biotechnology, all forests provide a range of ecosystems services. These services include prevention of soil erosion, maintenance of soil fertility, and fixing carbon from the atmosphere as biomass and soil organic carbon" (UNEP 2008: 88). Beyond providing economic uses and ecosystem services, "forests host a large proportion of terrestrial biodiversity, protect water catchments and moderate climate change. Forests also support local livelihoods, provide fuel, traditional medicines and food to local communities and underpin many cultures" (ibid.). Land modification activities also affect habitats other than forests, such as waterways and "edge habitats," or the areas close to human settlements and farms. The loss of woodlots, hedgerows, and windbreaks combined with the draining of wetlands and altering of the course of waterways encroaches on wildlife habitat, breeding grounds, and migration routes. The loss of such habitat also affects human populations. As Donald Worster (1979) describes, one of the most destructive and widespread impacts of efforts to increase cropland and increase productivity were the North American dust storms of the 1930s. In addition to loss of habitat, practices such as shorter fallow periods, soil erosion, and soil nutrient loss, as well as poor water management practices, contribute to degradation of habitats (FAO 2003a; Clay 2004; UNEP 2008).

Destruction of habitat, frequently for conversion into agricultural lands or livestock pasture, results in loss of biodiversity and the ecosystem functions provided by natural habitat and is a significant contributor to biodiversity loss. The 1992 Convention on Biological Diversity (CBD) defines biodiversity as, "the variability among living organisms from all sources including, inter alia, terrestrial, marine and other aquatic ecosystems and the ecological complexes of which they are part; this includes diversity within species, between species and of ecosystems" (Convention on Biological Diversity 1992). Other definitions of biodiversity stress that it includes all forms of life, but also includes diversity among human cultures (UNEP 2008). Biodiversity is a key component of human and nonhuman systems. "As the basis for all ecosystem services, and the foundation for truly sustainable development, biodiversity plays fundamental roles in maintaining and enhancing the well-being of the world's more than 6.7 billion people, rich and poor, rural and urban alike" (UNEP 2008: 160). The CBD asserts that biological diversity has a range of values, including the intrinsic value of biological diversity as well as ecological, genetic, social, economic, scientific, educational, cultural, recreational, and aesthetic values (UNEP 1992a). Agricultural practices play many roles in the loss of biodiversity, including conversion of natural habitat into agricultural lands, deliberate eradication of species that threaten livestock such as wolves, and reduction of competition among native species by creating habitats that favor some species over others (Clay 2004; UNEP 2008).

Loss of species and declines in biological diversity can have a range of impacts on humans, agriculture, and ecosystems. Species exist in complex relationships with their ecosystems and other organisms. Often, humans have attempted to improve on the functioning of ecosystems for human use, such as sport hunting or raising livestock, by removing predator species such as wolves, only to find that the removal of key species can have significant negative impacts on the health of an ecosystem. Aldo Leopold writes about one occasion where he was with a group that happened on a pack of wolves:

> In those days we had never heard of passing up a chance to kill a wolf. In a second we were pumping lead into the pack ... When our rifles were empty, the old wolf was down and a pup was dragging a leg into impassible slide-rocks. We reached the old wolf in time to watch a fierce green fire dying in her eyes. I realized then, and have known ever since, that there was something new to me in those eyes—something known only to her and to the mountain. I was young then, and full of trigger itch; I thought that because fewer wolves meant more deer, that no wolves would mean hunters' paradise (Leopold 1949: 130).

Leopold goes on to describe how over time he observed the ecological impacts of species removal. Without wolves, rather than a bountiful supply of deer for hunting and a range ideal for cattle grazing, deer populations boomed, leading to over-foraged vegetation and, eventually, to a significant starvation induced die-off among the deer population. For Leopold, the lesson was that people needed to learn to "think like mountains," considering how their activities impacted the health of ecosystems and thus the long-term health and prosperity of human and nonhuman communities, rather than just considering short-term human interests (Leopold 1949).

Biological diversity has also been reduced by changes in the culture and methods of agriculture and food production. The industrialization of agriculture has resulted in significant increases in global food production, but has also led to major declines in the biological diversity of key food sources. For example, out of the approximately 30,000 species of edible plants, only 7,000 of them have been used as food while just fifteen species produce more than 90 percent of all food. In the last century, more than 75 percent of biodiversity among crop species has been lost, including 80 percent of the varieties of corn that existed in the 1930s and 94 percent of pea varieties once grown in the US (*New York Times*, February 29, 2008). Recognition of the impact of biodiversity loss has prompted renewed effort to create a global network of plant and seed banks to store samples and information about genetic resources of plant species (Smil 2000; Clay 2004). Domesticated animal breeds also have reduced biological diversity, though not as dramatically as the reduced diversity of crop species. However, Clay (2004) estimates that in the last hundred years, one in six of the domestic animal breeds have gone extinct.

Biodiversity loss also affects insects such as spiders and ladybugs which are enemies of pests, and honeybees and song birds which play key roles as pollinators. The economic value of such species has gained attention as a result of recent dramatic declines in honeybee populations. Beginning in 2006, close to a quarter of beekeeping operations in many parts of the United States and other countries lost up to 50 percent of their bee populations to a mysterious condition called Colony Collapse Disorder (*Science*, March 16, 2007). The loss of key ecosystem and economic services provided by species such as pollinators can have significant effects such as the lost value of the services they provide as crop pollinators (a service estimated to be valued at $14–20 billion each year). The cost and difficulty of replicating the pollination role of honeybees demonstrates the importance of protecting habitat and biological diversity, especially with regards to key crops and species (Smil 2000; Clay 2004; UNEP 2008).

Impacts on Energy use

The many processes involved in producing, transporting, preserving, preparing, and consuming food utilize a great deal of energy. Figures related to the use of energy in agriculture and food production vary widely, often depending on whether they focus on direct and indirect uses in agricultural production or take a broader look at the total energy cost of food. One estimate of total energy consumption found that the food sector uses 10 to 15 percent of the energy consumed in developed countries (Hawken et al. 1999). Direct energy uses include farm-level uses, including energy use to run machinery and equipment. "In 2002, the US agricultural sector (encompassing both crops and livestock production) used an estimated 1.1 quadrillion Btu of total direct energy. This represents slightly more than 1% of total US energy consumption of 98 quadrillion Btu in 2002" (CRS 2004: 2). With regards to indirect energy uses, or energy used to manufacture fertilizers and pesticides, estimates are that "in 2002 agriculture accounted for about 56% (12 million out of about 21.4 million metric tons) of total US nitrogen use ... In addition, the US Environmental Protection Agency (EPA) estimates that US agriculture accounted for 67% of expenditures on pesticides in the United States in 2001" (ibid.: 4). In addition to energy use on farms and in production of pesticides and fertilizers, much of the energy used by the global food system is involved in processes related to processing, manufacturing, and distributing food.

Transportation is a major factor in food-related energy use and includes the energy used in producing food and transporting it to consumers, but also must take into account the energy that consumers use in trips to markets and restaurants. Jason Clay writes that a German study "suggests that the production of 0.24 liters (a typical cup) of strawberry yogurt entails 9,093 kilometers (5,650 miles) of transportation … In the United States, the food for a typical meal has traveled nearly 2,092 kilometers (1,300 miles)" (Clay 2004: 59). Travel distance is only one useful measure of the energy cost of food, however, as methods of transportation greatly impact the amount of energy used. Foods transported by rail or ship use far less energy than foods transported by air, truck, or car. For example, a 2009 lifecycle assessment of salmon found that frozen salmon had significantly lower environmental impact than fresh salmon; in some cases the impact of frozen salmon was almost half that of fresh salmon as fresh salmon is almost always transported by air (Pelletier et al. 2009). As this discussion suggests, understanding the energy impacts of food and identifying which sorts of foods are more sustainable than others is a complex endeavor (Hawken et al. 1999; CRS 2004).

Impacts from Climate Change

Food production and land use are important drivers of processes of global climate change and account for almost one-third of greenhouse gas emissions. Agriculture and food production contribute a substantial share of many countries' GHG emissions, including gases such as carbon dioxide from land clearance and deforestation, as well as methane, nitrous oxide, and ammonia that result from crop and livestock production (FAO 2003a). "Of the total human-induced GHG emissions in 2004 (49 billion tons of carbon dioxide equivalent), roughly 31 percent—15 billion tons—was from land use. By comparison, fossil fuel burning accounts for 27.7 billion tons of CO2-equivalent emissions annually" (Scherr and Sthapit 2009: 9). Greenhouse gas emissions from land use include contributions from sources such as soil fertilization, biomass burning, irrigated rice production and livestock manure. Though burning of fossil fuels for transportation and energy production are often a focus of significant attention in climate change discussions, it is important to recognize that land use GHG emissions represent an amount of annual emissions that is more than half of the amount provided by burning of fossil fuels (FAO 2003a; Scherr and Sthapit 2009).

The impacts of climate change on agriculture will vary significantly, and, at least in the near term, will likely be both positive and negative. Overall, the global food system will face significant impacts from climate change through, for example, extending growing seasons in some places and reducing them in others. FAO finds that "there are large uncertainties as to when and where climate change will impact agricultural production and food security" (FAO 2003a: 357). In general, the agricultural sector is extremely sensitive to climate variability and food security could be compromised by rising temperatures and more frequent droughts and floods (Chan 2008). Climate change could also have significant consequences on food security through increased frequency of heat stress, drought, fires, and flooding events which could decrease crop yields and have impacts on livestock. Climate change will have both direct and indirect impacts on food production and food security. Direct impacts of climate change on agriculture could include impacts on crops, forests, increased water scarcity, biodiversity losses to animal and fish populations that provide key sources of nutrition, and sea level rise. It is also important to recognize that climate change impacts will likely not be limited to human populations, but could also have impacts through increased biodiversity loss in plant and animal populations. Climate change impacts could accelerate other negative environmental consequences of agriculture and food production activities such as increased soil erosion, nutrient depletion, and impacts on water quality caused by increased rainfall and extreme weather events. Climate change could also have indirect impacts on food security such as through effects on the availability of resources such as oil, thereby increasing costs for transportation, and also the prices of inputs such as synthetic pesticides and fertilizers or through mechanisms such as exacerbation of global health challenges through mechanisms such as changing the range of pests and pathogens (FAO 2003a; Clay 2004; Easterling et al. 2007; IPCC 2007; Schmidhuber and Tubiello 2007).

While agriculture and food production are often discussed as drivers of climate change, they could also play an important role in efforts to mitigate climate change. The recognition that agriculture is both a driver and a means of addressing climate change is compatible with more general recognition that agricultural practices can have positive impacts on the environment. As Scherr and Sthapit (2009: 12) write, "we face a unique opportunity to achieve 'climate-friendly landscapes.' These include, for example, large expanses of agricultural land, interconnected with natural habitats that are managed to minimize greenhouse gas emissions and maximize the sequestration of carbon in soils and vegetation." Agriculture, land use, and forestry can, under certain conditions, help provide and enhance environmental services such as water storage and purification and the preservation of rural landscapes. In addition, using croplands both more sustainably and more intensively provides a means to reduce pressures to develop forests, grasslands, and other natural habitats. FAO finds "there is a growing appreciation of agriculture's positive contribution to climate change mitigation through carbon sequestration and the substitution of biofuels for fossil fuels" (FAO 2003a: 358). Using certain methods, crop and livestock production can play a significant role in sequestering carbon in soil organic matter. For example, in the United States, altering agricultural practices to reduce the impacts of tilling, improve management of crop residue and implementing land restoration, could sequester about 140 million tons of carbon or nearly 10 percent of total United States emission of all GHGs (FAO 2003a; Scherr and Sthapit 2009).

Aside from mitigation efforts, agriculture can also play an important role in efforts to adapt to the effects of climate change. Adaptations can be divided into two broad categories: "*autonomous adaptation,* which is the ongoing implementation of existing knowledge and technology in response to the changes in climate experienced, and *planned adaptation,* which is the increase in adaptive capacity by mobilising institutions and policies to establish or strengthen conditions favourable for effective adaptations" (Easterling et al. 2007: 294). Adaptation efforts will involve a range of activities at various levels of action. At the local level, activities focus on helping farmers adapt to changes and variations in weather conditions. Efforts could include systems to distribute better weather information, especially in areas of the developing world where weather forecasts can be difficult to access. Adaptation efforts could also include programs to transition to more ecologically appropriate forms of crop production and the development of agricultural production systems that are more resilient to impacts from climate change and variability. Programs to encourage adaptation also need to take into account the likely large-scale impacts of climate change, such as increased incidence of extreme weather events, drought, salinity, and aridity. Under such conditions, a range of adaptive measures may help lessen the impacts of climate change, including actions such as: maintenance of broad genetic diversity among crops; developing traits such as drought resistance, tolerance for greater temperature extremes, and salt tolerance in crop cultivar varieties and livestock breeds; encouraging use of agricultural practices such as sustainable agriculture and agroforestry that make use of and enhance genetic diversity; improving the efficiency of on-site freshwater use, especially capturing rainwater, which can both improve water management and reduce runoff; and developing systems to manage floodwaters and address sea level rise. Such actions could help reduce the effects of current climate variations, as well as providing resilience in the face of expected future changes (FAO 2003a; Easterling et al. 2007; Matthew and Hammill 2009).

Reducing Environmental Impacts Through Sustainable Intensification of Food Production

This chapter has discussed the ways food production activities have had significant, though often unintentional, impacts on the global environment. Activities intended to provide people with sufficient food have been, and continue to be, major drivers of environmental change including climate change (Steinfeld 2006). These changes are often localized, such as cutting down or burning forests to create croplands. The impacts of such changes are often local as well, such as increased erosion of topsoil, loss of soil nutrients, and reducing water quality when siltation and agricultural runoff enter waterways. However, local changes can have regional and national impacts that contribute to problems such as toxic dead zones in rivers and oceans, desertification, and global climate change. During the twentieth century, agricultural production came to increasingly rely on mechanization and chemical inputs including fertilizers, insecticides, and pesticides, as well as scientific techniques to measure soil fertility, acidity, and aid in making adjustments to the nutrition and care of livestock. These developments led to significant increases in crop yields but also resulted in a number of unintended consequences such as pests developing resistance to pesticides and herbicides and negative impacts on land, water, and habitat and biodiversity. In response to the negative unintended consequences of intensification and industrialization of agriculture as well as concerns about reductions in productivity, a number of efforts are underway to amplify the positive benefits of agricultural production while minimizing its negative impacts.

A global food system optimized around the goal of sustainability could help boost soil fertility and reduce erosion, improve local water quality, reduce runoff, and aid in efforts to mitigate and adapt to climate change by providing buffer zones, sinks to remove greenhouse gases (GHG) from the atmosphere, and energy from current biological sources in order to reduce fossil fuel GHG emissions. The concept of sustainable development provides a solution to the signs of crisis increasingly apparent in various sectors, including food and agricultural production. In 1987, the World Commission on Environment and Development released its report designed to formulate "a global agenda for change" (WCED 1987: ix). In the report, the WCED articulated the most commonly used definition of sustainable development: "Humanity has the ability to make development sustainable—to ensure that it meets the needs of the present without compromising the ability of future generations to meet their own needs" (ibid.: 8). The importance and significance of sustainable development were affirmed in the Agenda 21 program, approved by 179 nations at the 1992 United Nations Conference on Environment and Development in Rio de Janeiro, Brazil (UN 1992). In the intervening time, the importance of sustainable development has been confirmed by a great deal of policy, scholarly, development, and economic activities in a range of sectors—including water, energy, business; in many of these sectors, people are identifying sustainable goals and targets (Ingram and Ingram 2002; *Canada Gazette* 2006; USDA 2007b; NASAA 2008; NOP 2008; Matthew and Hammill 2009).

Improving agricultural sustainability has been recognized as a key component of sustainable development. The WCED recognized that "agricultural production can only be sustained on a long term basis if the land, water, and forests on which it is based are not degraded" (WCED 1987: 133). The understanding that agricultural production must be made sustainable to meet obligations to future generations and to accomplish its goals of providing food in both the short-, near- and long-term is central to the WCED's concept of sustainable agriculture, and explains the definition's broad appeal to scholars, policymakers, and activists. The conceptualization of sustainable agriculture articulated by the WCED, and expanded on by others, explicitly links concerns about sustainable food to sustainability in other areas. To be sustainable, food policies "must take into account all the policies that bear upon the threefold challenge of shifting production to where it is most needed, of securing the livelihoods of rural poor, and of conserving resources" (WCED 1987: 130). Other definitions of sustainable agriculture have enhanced the ideas set out by the WCED.

Sustainable agriculture has been conceptualized and codified under a number of different formulations including no-till agriculture, low-input agriculture, and organic agriculture, many of which share the spirit of sustainable agriculture. For example, FAO finds that the concept of sustainable agriculture refers to a range of techniques and practices intended to "meet the dual goals of increased productivity and reduced environmental impact. They do this through diversification and selection of inputs and management practices that foster positive ecological relationships and biological processes within the entire agro-ecosystem" (FAO 2003a: 304). According to the International Federation of Organic Agriculture Movements (IFOAM 2008), organic agriculture is based on four ethical principles that are designed to inspire action: the principle of health, the principle of ecology, the principle of fairness, and the principle of care. These principles "apply to agriculture in the broadest sense, including the way people tend soils, water, plants and animals in order to produce, prepare and distribute food and other goods. They concern the way people interact with living landscapes, relate to one another and shape the legacy of future generations" (ibid.). In the United States, organic agriculture is defined as "an ecological production management system that promotes and enhances biodiversity, biological cycles and soil biological activity. It is based on minimal use of off-farm inputs and on management practices that restore, maintain and enhance ecological harmony" (USDA 2007b). While there are differences between definitions of sustainable agriculture and the producers of sustainable agriculture, each of these formulations embraces the notion of sustainable agriculture as a set of practices that can both provide for human needs now and in the future while also nourishing and protecting the earth's living systems.

Recognition of the need to improve the sustainability of the global food system have come from a range of sectors and tend to focus on the need to develop appropriate social, political, and technological systems to enable the sustainable intensification of agriculture. After examining trends in global food system, the WCED concluded that "the agricultural resources and the technology needed to feed growing populations are available. Much has been achieved over the past few decades. Agriculture does not lack resources; it lacks policies to ensure that the food is produced where it is needed and in a manner that sustains the livelihoods of the rural poor" (WCED 1987: 118). Per Pinstrup-Andersen argues that, "at this time, the key question confronting us is not whether natural resources are sufficient to feed future generations, but whether appropriate policies and technologies are introduced. Continued degradation of natural resources may bring us to a situation where our current productive capacity will not be sufficient to meet the demand for food" (Pinstrup-Andersen 2002: 1). Jack Wilkinson comments, "We've got enough land, we've got enough resources and we've got enough farmers. We just don't have enough good agricultural policy or the political will to get on a path towards sustainable development" (IFAP 2008). These statements make clear not only the need to make agricultural and food production systems sustainable, but that developing sustainable global food systems will involve confronting the social, political, and technological limiting factors that often constrain discussions and prevent consideration of alternatives.

Sustainable food security also requires full consideration of the likely intended and unintended consequences of sustainability efforts. The global promotion of biofuels provides an excellent example of such unintended consequences. The substitution of fuels made from current biological sources could prove to be important components of strategies to reduce the greenhouse gas emissions of agriculture and food production while also promoting vibrant rural economies and reducing dependence on fossil fuel energy sources. However, such a substitution must be done in ways that are fully aware of total impacts. A key determinant of a biofuel's utility as a fossil fuel substitute is the crop or plants used as its basis and the manner in which fuel is produced. There is evidence that biofuels derived from crops such as switchgrass or forms of algae can lead to substantial reductions in GHG emission compared to fossil fuels (Schmer et al. 2008). However, in many cases recent studies have found that, especially with biofuels made from crops such as corn, the total impact of GHG emissions from biofuels can he higher than GHG emissions from fossil fuels (Begley 2008). Under certain conditions, efforts to promote biofuels could actually lead to greater environmental impacts from agricultural practices as subsidies combine with higher prices to encourage farmers to plant as many acres as possible in biofuel crops, thus increasing impacts on land resources. Biofuel production could also lead to increased impacts on water quality if farmers dramatically increase production of fertilizer-intensive crops such as corn (Donner and Kucharik 2008). Thus we see that failing to fully consider the consequences of environmental sustainability adaptations can amplify rather than ameliorate threats and vulnerabilities to human health, security, and well-being (FAO 2003a).

For decades, sustainable agricultural techniques were seen as impractical and incompatible with the need to intensify agricultural production to meet global food demands. Only in the last decade or so—driven by consumer demands for sustainably produced foods and increasing recognition of agriculture's role in climate change—have sustainable methods begun to be viewed as viable in accomplishing agricultural goals. Like other changes to the food system, such as genetic modification, the utility of sustainable methods remain controversial. In both cases, these sets of agricultural practices have struggled to achieve legitimacy with skeptical critics. In the case of GM foods, limited scientific understanding of the technology has increased the emotional resonance of "science gone astray" and images of "killer tomatoes." Sustainable agriculture, on the other hand, has struggled to be taken seriously as an alternative to conventional agriculture, particularly as critics questioned its ability to meet market needs at prices competitive with conventional agriculture.

Genetic modification is often seen as the antithesis of sustainable agriculture (in the United States for example, foods that are certified organic by the National Organic Standards Program cannot be produced using genetic modification) but GMO technology could make contributions to achieving sustainable intensification of agriculture and food production. Commenting on the eve of a release of a 2009 report by the Royal Society on the importance of considering GM techniques as part of the answer to food security questions, Professor Sir John Beddington, the chief scientific advisor to HM government, remarked, "a range of solutions will be needed if a world population set to pass 8 billion by 2030 is to be fed equitably and sustainably. Improved protection of crops from pests and diseases in the field and during storage will be critical to reducing crop losses and has a major contribution to make" (*The Times*, October 20, 2009). Paul Collier (2009) writes, "The debate over genetically modified crops and food has been contaminated by political and aesthetic prejudices: hostility to US corporations, fear of big science and romanticism about local, organic production ... genetic modification is analogous to nuclear power: nobody loves it, but climate change has made its adoption imperative." Per Pinstrup-Andersen (2009) also embraces the notion that, while the health and environmental risks of new technologies must be assessed, "such risks should be compared to the health and environmental risks of not releasing a technology. Status quo is not kind to millions of starving children and failure to act now will further deteriorate the environment and make food very expensive for future generations." As these comments suggest, a growing sense of crisis impelled by trends such as rising food prices, persistent inequalities between rich and poor, and concerns about the expected impacts of global climate change are motivating efforts to adopt new technologies like GMOs (Schmidhuber and Tubiello 2007; Beddington 2009).

Many scholars and policymakers have endorsed the notion that under the proper conditions, crops and methods developed using genetic modification have a range of benefits. According to FAO (2003), the benefits from GM crops could include higher crop and livestock yields, lower pesticide and fertilizer applications, less demanding production techniques, higher product quality, better storage and easier processing, and enhanced methods to monitor the health of plants and animals. Reviews by groups such as FAO (2003a), the Royal Society (2009) and the National Research Council (NRC 2010) recognize that there are significant questions about genetically modified foods that need to be addressed. Concerns include: market concentration in the seed industry; intellectual property rights; and biological security concerns about a range of topics including, but not limited to, transfer of modified genes into microbes or pest species, transfer of allergens, mutation of genes, transfer of traits such as sterility, and impacts on animal welfare and biodiversity. Moreover, considerable barriers exist among consumers and environmental activists. As writers such as Shiva (2009), Patel (2009), and Rodale (2010) point out, developing compelling political, scientific, technological, and ethical answers to questions related to genetic modification is an ongoing concern. However, if such concerns can be adequately addressed, genetic modification could provide an important set of methods in developing crops with traits like drought tolerance, salt tolerance, and lower water usage. Under certain conditions, these more resilient crops could make important contributions to a more sustainable agricultural system that could mitigate and adapt to changes in the global environment while also meeting rising demand for food supplies (Pinstrup-Andersen 2002; FAO 2003a; The Royal Society 2009; NRC 2010; Tester and Langridge 2010).

One of the great challenges of envisioning a sustainable food system is that it must be reconciled with the increasingly globalized, networked structure of our world. Some aspects of the development of a network of global food systems remain stark reminders of the need to consider the full environmental impact of actions in the food system. For example, cod caught in the waters off Norway is shipped to China for processing and then shipped back to Norway for sale and consumption, while Great Britain both imports and exports 15,000 tons of waffles each year and both sends Australia and receives from it 20 tons of bottled water each year (*New York Times*, April 26, 2008). The impact of such trade flows, which often only seem profitable by failing to consider the externalities that accrue from the costs of transportation, could be dramatically altered by efforts such as the European Union's 2008 announcement that it would begin requiring all freight-carrying flights to participate in emissions-trading programs by 2012 (ibid.). While global change processes may make the effort to develop a sustainable global food system more difficult in some ways, advances in technology and communication could also open new pathways through strategic decoupling from global networks and the creation of sustainable local food systems. Changes in technology, demographics, and desires to improve food safety and reduce the energy intensiveness and environmental impacts of agricultural and food production systems could coalesce in the development of more robust local food systems.

A particularly fruitful area for the development of local food systems is in urban areas. Although an increasing number of people live in urban areas, most food production continues to be based in rural areas. Already, there is a great deal of evidence that urban poor in many parts of the world use a variety of informal systems to access food supplies, including use of reciprocal trade agreements or short-distance migrations for hunting of animals for bush meat. Initial studies of the impact of urban agricultural efforts in countries such as Namibia, Togo, Zimbabwe, Botswana, and Cuba have demonstrated the many ways urban agricultural systems could help provide key sources of food in more affordable and safer ways (Mougeot 2005). Even in more developed countries, urban agricultural systems have played key roles in improving health and nutrition by increasing agricultural production. A classic example comes from the program of Victory Gardens begun in the United States and Britain during World War II. During this time, some 20 million people answered the US government's call to grow food for local consumption to aid the war effort. By some estimates, Victory Gardens provided up to 40 percent of the food consumed in the United States between 1944 and 1946 (Thone 1943; Hanna and Oh 2000; Victory Seed Company 2008). One result of recent rising food prices and interest in food sustainability and self-sufficiency has been a renewed interest in urban gardening. In San Francisco, the City Hall Lawn was replaced with an organic vegetable garden in 2008 (*Wall Street Journal*, August 8, 2008). In the spring of 2009, US First Lady Michelle Obama worked with Washington, DC schoolchildren to plant a vegetable garden on a 1,100-square-foot plot of the White House's South Lawn, a garden which is the first at the White House since Eleanor Roosevelt's World War II victory garden (*The New York Times*, March 19, 2009). There are also possibilities for the development of intensive, sustainable urban agricultural systems. For instance, Dickson Despommier, a professor of environmental sciences and microbiology at Columbia University, has worked with his students to develop designs for vertical farms housed in skyscrapers, powered by renewable energy sources (Chamberlain 2007; Vertical Farm Project 2008).

While the need to improve the sustainability of the global food system is great, meeting this challenge requires addressing a wide range of scientific, technical, political, economic, and ethical challenges. Neither global trends nor the pace of scientific and technological innovation suggest that the complications of the sustainable intensification of agriculture will become less complex in the future. Publics, activists, and policymakers that are struggling with the implications of climate change and technologies like genetic modification are also being confronted (or are soon to be confronted) by nutraceuticals, or foods that provide health and medical benefits, as well as foods developed, enhanced, or protected using nanotechnology. The challenge of creating a sustainable global food system that can provide all people with sufficient, safe, and nutritious food is by no means simple. Such efforts must be mindful of human needs, sensitive to current and future ecological conditions, and must navigate complex global political, economic, and social systems. However, the ways human societies meet the challenge of growing a sustainable global food system network will be a significant factor in responding to the challenge of climate change and addressing persistent sources of human insecurity.

References

Beddington, J. 2009. "Professor Sir John Beddington's Speech at SDUK 09." www.govnet.co.uk/news/govnet/professor-sir-john-beddingtons-speech-at-sduk-09 (December 24, 2009).

Begley, S. 2008. "Sounds good, but...: We can't afford to make any more mistakes in how to 'save the planet.' Start by ditching corn ethanol." *Newsweek* (April 14). www.newsweek.com/id/130628 (April 18, 2008).

Canada Gazette. 2006. "Organic Products Regulations." http://canadagazette.gc.ca/partII/2006/20061221-x6/html/extra-e.html (December 28, 2009).

Carson, R. 1962. *Silent Spring.* Boston: Houghton Mifflin.

Chamberlain, L. 2007. "Skyfarming." *New York Magazine.* http://nymag.com/news/features/30020/ (February 22, 2008).

Chan, M. 2008. "The impact of climate change on human health: Statement by WHO Director-General Dr. Margaret Chan." www.who.int/mediacentre/news/statements/2008/s05/en/index.html (April 18, 2008).

Clay, J. 2004. *World Agriculture and the Environment.* Washington: Island Press.

Collier, P. 2009. "Put Aside Prejudices," in "Room for Debate: Can Biotech Food Cure World Hunger?" *The New York Times*, October 26. http://roomfordebate.blogs.nytimes.com/2009/10/26/can-bio-tech-food-cure-world-hunger/ (April 30, 2010).

Conca, K. and G.D. Dabelko (eds). 2002. *Environmental Peacemaking*. Baltimore: Johns Hopkins University Press.

Convention on Biological Diversity. 1992. "The Convention on Biological Diversity." www.cbd.int/ (April 28, 2008).

CRS (Congressional Research Service). 2004. "Energy Use in Agriculture: Background and Issues." www.ncseonline.org/NLE/CRSreports/04nov/RL32677.pdf (April 19, 2008).

Donner, S.D. and C.J. Kucharik. 2008. "Corn-Based Ethanol Production Compromises Goal of Reducing Nitrogen Export by the Mississippi River." *Proceedings of the National Academy of Sciences* 105(11): 4513–18.

Easterling, W., et al. 2007. "Food, fibre and forest products," in M.L. Parry, O.F. Canziani, J.P. Palutikof, P.J. van der Linden and C.E. Hanson (eds), *Climate Change 2007: Impacts, Adaptation and Vulnerability. Contribution of Working Group II to the Fourth Assessment Report of the Intergovernmental Panel on Climate Change*. New York, NY: Cambridge University Press, pp. 273–313.

Ellis, L.J. and J.L. Turner. 2007. "Surf and Turf: Environmental and Food Safety Concerns of China's Aquaculture and Animal Husbandry." *China Environment Series* 9: 19–42.

FAO (Food and Agriculture Organization of the United Nations). 2003. *World Agriculture: Towards 2015/2030*. London: Earthscan.

FAO (Food and Agriculture Organization of the United Nations). 2006. *The State of Food Insecurity in the World 2006*. www.fao.org/docrep/009/a0750e/a0750e00.htm (April 28, 2008).

Garrett, L. 1994. *The Coming Plague: Newly Emerging Disease in a World Out of Balance*. New York: Penguin Books.

Gleick, P.H. 1993. *Water in Crisis: A Guide to the World's Fresh Water Resources*. New York: Oxford University Press.

Gore, A. 1999. "Remarks as Prepared for Delivery by Vice President Al Gore." World Economic Forum, Davos, Switzerland. January 29, 1999. http://clinton2.nara.gov/WH/EOP/OVP/speeches/davos.html (April 28, 2008).

Halweil, B. and D. Nierenberg. 2008. "Meat and Seafood: The Global Diet's Most Costly Ingredients," in Worldwatch Institute, *State of the World 2008: Innovations for a Sustainable Economy*. New York: W.W. Norton, pp. 61–74.

Hanna, A.K. and P. Oh. 2000. "Rethinking Urban Poverty: A Look at Community Gardens." *Bulletin of Science, Technology & Society* 20(3): 207–16.

Hawken, P., A. Lovins and H. Lovins. 1999. *Natural Capitalism: Creating the Next Industrial Revolution*. Boston: Little, Brown.

IFAP (International Federation of Agricultural Producers). 2008. Press release: "IFAP Calls for Support of Farmers at the CSD." www.ifap.org/en/newsroom/documents/IFAP_CSD16.pdf (April 28, 2008).

IFOAM (International Federation of Organic Agriculture Movements). 2008. "The Principle of Organic Agriculture." www.ifoam.org/about_ifoam/principles/index.html (April 25, 2008).

Ingram, M. and H. Ingram. 2002. "Creating Credible Edibles: The Alternative Agriculture Movement and Passage of US Federal Organic Standards." Paper presented at Social Movements and Public Policy Workshop, Laguna Beach, CA, January 11–12.

IPCC (Intergovernmental Panel on Climate Change). 2007. *Fourth Assessment Report. Climate Change 2007: Synthesis Report.* www.ipcc.ch/publications_and_data/ar4/syr/en/contents.html (April 30, 2010).

Jackson, W. 1996. *Becoming Native to this Place.* Washington, DC: Counterpoint.

Kugelman, M. 2009. "Going Gaga over Grain: Pakistan and the International Farms Race." http://newsecuritybeat.blogspot.com/2009/009/going-gaga-over-grain-pakistan-and.html (December 27, 2009).

Leopold, A. 1949. *A Sand County Almanac and Sketches Here and There.* New York: Oxford University Press.

Matthew, R.A. and A. Hammill. 2009. "Sustainable Development and Climate Change." *International Affairs* 85(6): 1117–28.

Montgomery, D.R. 2007. "Soil erosion and agricultural sustainability." *Proceedings of the Natural Academy of Sciences* 104(33): 13268–72.

Mougeot, L.J.A. 2005. *Agropolis: The Social, Political and Environmental Dimensions of Urban Agriculture.* London: Earthscan.

NASAA (National Association for Sustainable Agriculture, Australia). 2008. www.nasaa.com.au/ (April 25, 2008).

NOP (National Organic Program). 2008. "Organic Labeling and Marketing Information." www.ams.usda.gov/AMSv1.0/getfile?dDocName=STELDEV3004446&acct=nopgeninfo (April 25, 2008).

NRC (National Research Council). 2010. *Impact of Genetically Engineered Crops on Farm Sustainability in the United States.* Washington, DC: National Academies Press.

Patel, R. 2009. "When Cheap Water and Oil Disappear," in "Room for Debate: Can Biotech Food Cure World Hunger?" *The New York Times,* October 26. http://roomfordebate.blogs.nytimes.com/2009/10/26/can-biotech-food-cure-world-hunger/ (April 30, 2010).

Pelletier, N., P. Tyedmers, U. Sonesson, A. Scholz, F. Ziegler, A. Flysjo, S. Kruse, B. Cancino and H. Silverman. 2009. "Not All Salmon Are Created Equal: Life Cycle Assessment (LCA) of Global Salmon Farming Systems." *Environmental Science & Technology* 43(23): 8730–6.

Pinstrup-Andersen, P. 2002. "Towards a Sustainable Global Food System: What Will it Take?" Keynote presentation for the Annual John Pesek Colloquium in Sustainable Agriculture, Iowa State University, March 26-27, 2002.

Pinstrup-Andersen, P. 2009. "A Green Revolution Done Right," in "Room for Debate: Can Biotech Food Cure World Hunger?" *The New York Times,* October 26. http://roomfordebate.blogs.nytimes.com/2009/10/26/can-biotech-food-cure-world-hunger/ (April 30, 2010).

Rodale, M. 2010. *Organic Manifesto: How Organic Farming Can Heal our Planet, Feed the World and Keep us Safe.* New York: Rodale.

Royal Society, The. 2009. *Reaping the Benefits: Science and the Sustainable Intensification of Global Agriculture.* http://royalsociety.org/reapingthebenefits/ (December 27, 2009).

Scherr, S.J. and S. Sthapit. 2009. "Mitigating Climate Change through Food and Land Use. Worldwatch Report 179." Washington, DC: Worldwatch Institute.

Schmer, M.R., K.P. Vogel, R.B. Mitchell and R.K. Perrin. 2008. "Net Energy of Cellulosic Ethanol from Switchgrass." *Proceedings of the National Academy of Sciences* 105(50): 19703–8.

Schmidhuber, J. and F. Tubiello. 2007. "Global Food Security under Climate Change." *Proceedings of the National Academy of Sciences* 104(50): 19703–8.

Shiva, V. 2009. "The Failure of Gene-Altered Crops," in "Room for Debate: Can Biotech Food Cure World Hunger?" *The New York Times*, October 26. http://roomfordebate.blogs.nytimes.com/2009/10/26/can-biotech-food-cure-world-hunger/ (April 30, 2010).

Smil, V. 2000. *Feeding the World: A Challenge for the Twenty-First Century.* Cambridge, MA: MIT Press.

Steinfeld, H. 2006. *Livestock's Long Shadow: Environmental Issues and Options.* www.fao.org/docrep/010/a0701e/a0701e00. HTM (December 27, 2009).

Tester, M. and P. Langridge. 2010. "Breeding Technologies to Increase Crop Production in a Changing World." *Science* 327(5967): 818–22.

Thone, F. 1943. "Victory Gardens." *Science News Letter* (March 20): 186–8.

UN (United Nations). 1992. "Agenda 21." www.un.org/esa/sustdev/documents/agenda21/English/agenda21toc.htm (February 29, 2008).

UN Water. 2007. "Coping with Water Scarcity: Challenge of the Twenty-First Century." www.unwater.org/wwd07/downloads/documents/scarcity.pdf (April 18, 2008).

UNEP (United Nations Environment Programme). 1992. "Convention on Biological Diversity." www.cbd.int/convention/convention.shtml (April 19, 2008).

UNEP (United Nations Environment Programme). 2002. *Global Environmental Outlook 3: Past, Present and Future Perspectives.* London: Earthscan.

UNEP (United Nations Environment Programme). 2006. *The State of the Marine Environment: Trends and Processes.* www.gpa.unep.org/documents/global_soe_webversion_english.pdf (December 27, 2009).

UNEP (United Nations Environment Programme). 2008. *Global Environmental Outlook 4: Environment for Development.* ww.unep.org/geo/geo4/media/ (April 28, 2008).

USDA (United States Department of Agriculture). 2007. "Organic Production/Organic Food: Information Access Tools." www.nal.usda.gov/afsic/pubs/ofp/ofp.shtml (April 25, 2008).

Vertical Farm Project. 2008. www.verticalfarm.com/ (February 22, 2008).

Victory Seed Company. 2008. "The Victory Garden." www.victoryseeds.com/TheVictoryGarden/page3.html (April 18, 2008).

WCED (World Commission on Environment and Development). 1987. *Our Common Future: The World Commission on Environment and Development.* New York: Oxford University Press.

Wolf, A.T., A. Kramer and A. Carius. 2005. "Managing Water Conflict and Cooperation." *State of the World 2005: Redefining Global Security*: 80–95.

Worster, D. 1979. *Dust Bowl: The Southern Plains in the 1930s.* Oxford: Oxford University Press.

HIGHLIGHTED APPROACH: AGROECOLOGY

Agroecology as a Transdisciplinary, Participatory, and Action-Oriented Approach

By V. Ernesto Méndez, Christopher M. Bacon, and Roseann Cohen

Introduction

Agroecology emerged as an approach to better understand the ecology of traditional farming systems and respond to the mounting problems resulting from an increasingly globalized and industrialized agro-food system (Altieri 1987). In its early stages, agroecology mainly focused on applying ecological concepts and principles to the design of sustainable agricultural systems (Altieri 1987; Gliessman 1990). This was followed by a more explicit integration of concepts and methods from the social sciences, which were necessary to better understand the complexity of agriculture that emerges from unique sociocultural contexts (Guzmán-Casado et al. 1999; Hecht 1995). In the last decade, the number of publications and initiatives that people describe as agroecological has exponentially increased (Wezel and Soldat 2009). The result is the emergence of several distinct standpoints, which, in this article, we refer to as different agroecological perspectives or *agroecologies*. As can be expected in any field of science or knowledge, we can observe some important differences between specific agroecologies. Hence, the specific objectives of this introductory article were to: 1) discuss the implications of the increasing use and adoption of agroecology in unprecedented scientific, social and political spaces; 2) examine the evolution of the field of agroecology into distinct perspectives, or agroecologies; and 3) present conceptual and applied contributions of an agroecological perspective grounded in transdisciplinary, participatory, and action-oriented approaches. We finalize this article with a description of how the other contributions to the special issue complement each other to form a coherent and integrated agroecological approach.

Agroecological Mainstreaming

The last three decades have seen a proliferation in the use of the term "agroecology" in a diversity of academic, policy, and advocacy spaces worldwide (Guzmán-Casado et al. 1999; International Assessment of Agricultural Knowledge, Science and Technology for Development [IAASTD] 2009; Wezel and Soldat 2009). In some cases, this is the result of agroecologists' concrete, long-term efforts to establish the field in academic and policy spaces. An example of this is the establishment of a growing number of agroecology programs and degrees at universities of both developed and developing countries (Francis et al. 2003). Other integrations of agroecology are more recent, but no less important. These include the adoption of the field by policy-oriented actors, as well as a wider use of agroecology within rural social movements and farmer or peasant organizations.

The appearance of agroecology in international food and agricultural policy debates is not new. However, until recently, it was mostly used in the context of nongovernmental organizations focusing on sustainable agriculture and rural development topics, and, more specifically, those oriented toward empowering small-scale farmers and resource poor rural communities (e.g. Food First). The turning point for the inclusion of agroecology at higher policy circles probably came with the publication of the IAASTD, and its recognition that the field represented an "alternative" promising approach to resolve the interrelated global problems of hunger, rural poverty, and sustainable development (IAASTD 2009).[1] Subsequently, Oliver De Schutter, who was appointed as the United Nations Special Rapporteur on the Right to Food in 2008, has continually advocated for the use of an agroecological approach to confront global food insecurity and food sovereignty issues. De Schutter has done this through policy-oriented presentations and lectures, publications geared for a broad audience, and an interactive website (see De Schutter 2011; De Schutter and Vanloqueren 2011; http://www.srfood.org/).

An Examination of the Different Agroecologies

A recent comprehensive review by Wezel and colleagues (2009) interpreted agroecology as a field that has expressions as a science, a movement, a practice, or a combination of all three. The authors concluded that there is "certain confusion in the use of the term 'agroecology' (10), and that how different people use the term is affected by a variety of factors related to geography, scientific and contextual backgrounds. We disagree with the notion that there are no clear lines between existing agroecological perspectives. Rather, we argue that a persistent depiction of agroecology as unclear explicitly ignores important aspects of its evolution as a field of knowledge. In addition, presenting the agroecological approach as confusing, justifies the application of narrow definitions that may be better suited for particular perspectives. More concretely, it seems that this interpretation is favored by those that view agroecology solely as a new form of scientific endeavor, and with a stronger bent toward the natural sciences.

Although we agree that there is a wide diversity of interpretations and applications of an agroecological approach, we have identified two predominant perspectives. The first one tends to exclusively apply agroecology as a framework to reinforce, expand or develop scientific research, firmly grounded in the western tradition and the natural sciences (Wezel et al. 2009; Wezel and Soldat 2009). A European example of this is represented by the Agroecology Group led by Professor Teja Tscharntke at the Georg-August University Göttingen in Germany. The group's web page describes their approach as follows: "Agroecological analyses focus on plant and animal communities, food web interactions, and conservation biology in temperate as well as tropical agricultural landscape and agroe-cosystems" (http://www.uni-goettingen. de/en/74726.html). This statement is consistent with the publications list in journals with an ecological and agricultural ecology focus. Other examples of academic groups in the United States, which also focus on the analysis of ecological processes at the farm and landscape scales, include the Henry A. Wallace Chair for Sustainable Agriculture at Iowa State University (http://www.wallacechair.iastate.edu/ default.html) and the Agroecology Lab at the University of California, Davis (http://www.plantsciences.ucdavis.edu/Agroecology/). These agroecological approaches represent important endeavors for advancing findings on agronomic and ecological processes, and for improving the management of farms and landscapes. The information they generate could contribute to redirect agricultural production and management toward an ecologically based approach. However, although these standpoints may seek to impact broader agro-food systems, their approach remains largely grounded in natural science research with a primary focus on analyses at different scales (i.e., farm, landscape, region) of the agricultural production process, not of the agro-food system. If these perspectives are taken as the only agroecological approach to redesigning agro-food systems, they would miss seeing agriculture as a complex social-ecological system, obscure the social dimensions of agriculture, and silence the contributions of knowledge constructed outside of the western scientific paradigm. Nonetheless, research that follows this line of inquiry has resulted in important findings on the biophysical and environmental aspects of agricultural production. However, it leaves social and cultural issues of the dominant agro-food system mostly unexamined, and fails to engage the wider social science literature on food systems as part of its analysis.

In contrast, some agroecological scholars, often trained in natural science disciplines (e.g., entomology, ecology, and agronomy), have pursued a path that simultaneously deepens conceptual inquiry within specific sub-fields while expanding and redefining a broader agroecological perspective; one that engages with the social sciences and broader agro-food system issues. This agroecological approach developed from firm roots in the sciences of ecology and agronomy, into a framework that seeks to integrate transdisciplinary, participatory, and action-oriented approaches, as well as to critically engage with political-economic issues that affect agro-food systems (Gliessman 2007; Méndez 2010; Sevilla-Guzmán 2006b; Wezel et al. 2009). The use of terms such as "transdisciplinary," "participatory," and "action-oriented" may be interpreted as optimistic and vague by some observers. However, we perceive that the evolution of this particular form of agroecology has explicitly embraced these characteristics through an in-depth, and frequently challenging, process of reflection and action.

We are not arguing that all scientific endeavors should be transdisciplinary, participatory, and action-oriented. In fact, we believe that the best-case scenario would be to have basic, discipline-oriented science actively informing and interacting with this reflexive perspective that seeks to be more participatory (by including knowledge from multiple actors) and increasingly clear about the normative values, politics, and possibilities for transformative change that are at play in today's agro-food systems.

In the previous paragraphs, we described what we consider the two predominant agro-ecological perspectives. In this context, it is important to recognize that in between these two broader approaches exists a gradient of interpretations and applications that may lean more toward one or the other, or seek a relatively balanced position between the two (Figure 1). For a recent example of an agroecological perspective in between the two dominant ones see a recent review by Tomich et al. (2011).

Agroecology as a Transdisciplinarly, Participatory, and Action-Oriented Approach

In this section, we discuss an agroecological perspective with the following characteristics: 1) it originated from a predominantly ecological and agronomic interpretation of the field

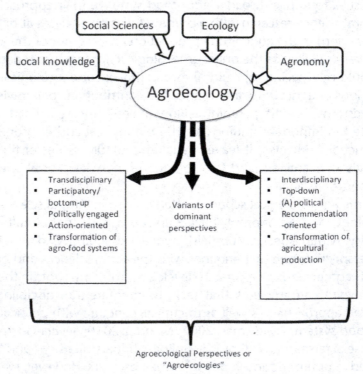

Figure 1. Schematic representation of the evolution of different types of agroecologies.

in the early 1970s; 2) it has evolved toward an approach grounded in transdisciplinary and participatory research through engagement with social scientists, agricultural communities and nonscientific knowledge systems; 3) it incorporates a critique of the role of prevalent political-economic structures in the construction of the current agro-food system; and 4) as an action-oriented effort, it seeks to directly contribute to redirect current agro-food systems toward sustainability. This particular agroecological perspective has been advanced by some of the most influential academics in the field, including Stephen R. Gliessman (Gliessman 2007), Miguel Altieri (Altieri and Toledo 2011), John Vandermeer (Vandermeer 2009), Ivette Perfecto (Perfecto et al. 2009) and Eduardo Sevilla-Guzmán (Sevilla-Guzmán 2006b). In this section, we undertake an in-depth examination of the key characteristics of this perspective.

Agroecology and Transdisciplinarity

We consider transdisciplinary approaches as those that value and integrate different types of knowledge systems, which can include scientific or academic disciplines, as well as different types of knowledge systems (i.e., experiential, local, indigenous, etc.), as well as adopt a problem-based focus (Aeberhard and Rist 2009; Belsky 2002; Francis et al. 2008; Godemann 2008). An appreciation for farmer-generated knowledge challenges conventional approaches to agricultural research and related policymaking that privileges Western epistemologies of knowledge production (Cuéllar-Padilla and Calle-Collado 2011). Since the 1980s, agroecologists have valued and sought to better understand the experiential agroecological knowledge of farmers as a necessary component to develop a more sustainable agriculture. This was clearly illustrated in Gliessman's (1978, 1980, 1982, this issue; Gliessman et al. 1981) work in the Mexican tropics in the 1970s and 80s, which focused on understanding the ecological bases of traditional Mexican agriculture, and which drew from the scholarship of Efraím Hernández-Xolocotzi. This empirical information, based on observation and practice, and which also integrates cultural aspects, was viewed as a source of knowledge to conceptualize and apply agroecology. More recently, the Universidad Intercultural Maya de Quintana Roo, Mexico, has institutionalized agroecological teaching and research through the concept of interculturality (http://www.uimqroo.edu.mx/). This approach is based on a platform for knowledge exchange and collaboration under conditions of mutual respect between cultures and knowledge systems (i.e., Maya and Western based), crucial for applying both participatory and transdisciplinary approaches. This incorporation of local or farmer-generated knowledge is an important component of this particular type of agroecological thought and practice.

Participatory and Principles-Based Approaches in Agroecology

An increasing interest in participatory and action-oriented research is evident in a variety of fields, such as ecology (Whitmer et al. 2010), several disciplines in the social sciences (Fals-Borda and Rahman 1991; Greenwood and Levin 1998; Stringer 1999) health (Minkler and Wallerstein 2008), natural resources (Castellanet and Jordan 2002; Fortmann 2008), geography (Kindon et al. 2007), and agroecology (Guzmán-Casado et al. 1999; Uphoff 2002; Snapp and Pound 2008). Participatory action research (PAR) and related approaches seek to involve a diversity of stakeholders as active participants of an iterative process that integrates research, reflection, and action, and which seeks to provide voice to actors that have been traditionally excluded from the research process (Bacon et al. 2005; Kindon et al. 2007).

Agroecological approaches that have sought to integrate farmer knowledge into research and outreach fit well with the PAR approach. In the last decade, an increasing number of studies have combined agroecology with participatory approaches in different ways. For example, graduate students and professors at the University of California at Santa Cruz collaborated in a participatory project involving coffee communities of Mexico and Central America, which yielded a variety of outcomes. These ranged from direct actions in coffee communities to research studies and academic publications. A key academic product of this work was an edited book on the coffee crisis (Bacon et al. 2008), while action-oriented projects and outreach were mostly channeled through the Community Agroecology Network (CAN; http://www. canunite.org/). A similar trajectory can be observed in Andalusia, Spain, where researchers, professors, and extensionists associated with the International University of Andalucia's graduate program in agroecology, have worked with a diversity of family farmers in southern Spain (Guzmán-Casado et al. 1999; Guzmán-Casado and Alonso-Mielgo 2007; Guzmán and Alonso 2008; Sevilla-Guzmán 2006a, 2006b; Cuéllar-Padilla and Calle-Collado 2011). In Brazil, agroecologists have worked with the Landless Rural Workers Movement (MST, in Portuguese) and La Via Campesina to support the incorporation of agroecology into these social movements (Altieri and Toledo 2011).

Participatory approaches in agroecology tend to adhere to a common set of principles associated with PAR. Not surprisingly, these principles share substantial overlap with an evolving set of agroecological principles that help define the field and unite different perspectives (Altieri 2000; Gliessman 2007). Table 1 summarizes selected and overlapping principles from both participatory action research and agroecology. A more complete list of the principles of agroecology and sustainability can be found at http://agroecology.org/Principles_List.html

Like agroecology, participatory action research approaches in agriculture involve farmers, community members, and partner organizations. The process values the collaborative definition, implementation, and interpretation of research, including different forms of knowledge, people's diverse aspirations in the design of research agendas and transitions toward collectively defined goals. Processes of empowerment are complex, uneven, and require attention to the formal and informal exercise of power, as well as critical reflections about the intersection of access to resources, privilege, and identity (Fox 2005; Minkler and Wallerstein 2008).

The final two principles listed for both agroecology and PAR concern approaches to temporal and diversity related issues. While researchers are aware of their own professional needs and pressing theoretical questions within their academic fields, these priorities do not often align with needs of farmers and other social actors (Fox 2005). Instead of predetermining a project and then asking non-research partners to sign off, PAR collaboration should begin at the earliest stages of the research process. Partners work through a mutual, iterative dialogue to arrive at a project proposal that harmonizes stakeholder needs, capacities, and methods. Through this dialogue, the researcher and other participants have a clear understanding of project expectations and potential challenges and benefits. The dialogue must also be linked to action, thus, creating a praxis—or an ongoing iterative process of reflection and action (Freire 2000). After an action is taken, the context shifts and this is when the longer-term partnership often becomes more important, as both the researcher and other partners have

Table 1. Comparison of selected participatory action research and agroecological principles

Participatory action research principles	Agroecology principles
PAR foregrounds empowerments as community partners play key roles in defining the research agenda.	Agroecologists work with farmers, food consumers, communities, agricultural ministries, food advocates and others to empower people.
PAR processes are context dependent as they bring together interdisciplinary teams responding to stakeholder aspirations.	Agroecology establishes farming and food systems that adjust to local environments.
PAR research processes inform action at multiple scales for positive social change.	Agroecology seeks to manage whole systems.
PAR processes deepen as long-term relationships are formed and multiple iterations of this cycle occur.	Agroecology develops strategies to maximize long-term benefits.
PAR processes listen to a diversity of voices and knowledge systems to democratize the research and social change processes.	Agroecology implies processes to diversify biota, landscapes and social institutions.

Sources. Modified from Bacon et al. (2005) and http://www.agroecology.org/Principles_List.html

learned from the first cycle and then continued with follow-up iterations. The agroecological principle of maximizing long-term benefits suggests multiple considerations, such as efforts to:

- maximize intergenerational benefits, not just annual profits;
- maximize livelihoods and quality of life in rural areas;
- facilitate intergenerational transfers;
- use long-term strategies, such as developing plans that can be adjusted and reevaluated through time;
- incorporate long-term sustainability into overall **agroecosystem** design and management;
- build soil fertility over the long-term.

The principle of recognizing, learning from, and engaging social and ecological diversity is among the most important for linking participatory action research with an action-oriented agroecology. The participatory action research approach calls for greater attention to a wider diversity of voices, especially those that are frequently marginalized by mainstream society (e.g., farm workers, smallholders, indigenous groups, and rural women). This suggests the need to create the time and space for deeper listening and identification of strategies that use human diversity as a source of innovation. The principle of diversity as seen through an agroecological lens is no less profound as it directs analytic attention to the domains of biota, landscape, and social institutions. Examples of farm and plot level management of

Agroecosystem is a term that represents an ecological characterization of an agricultural plot or farm. It implies the documentation and understanding of all of its living organisms (both agricultural and non-agricultural) and how they interact between themselves and their broader environment, including nutrient and energy flows within and outside of the agroecosystem's boundaries (modified from Gliessman, 2007).

diversity include intercrops, crop rotations, polycultures, and the integration of animals, cultivars, and genetic diversity. At the landscape scale, one must consider issues such as buffer zones, forest fragments, rotational grazing, and contour and strip tillage. The important point is not simply the presence of a wide diversity of species or agricultural practices, but the way they interact to provide critical ecosystem services (i.e., pollination, pest control, and nutrient cycling) that support agricultural production and farmer livelihoods (Kremen et al., forthcoming). The social domains of diversity encourage agroecologists to consider multiple forms of farmer organization, government regulation, and the many different types of markets and alternative agro-food networks that constitute agro-food systems (Goodman et al. 2011). The presence of alternative distribution systems and the diversity of social institutions and economic relations in agriculture, such as farmer's markets, community-supported agriculture, cooperatives, and production for both subsistence and sale, offer several important incentives that could be coupled with an enabling policy environment (Iles and Marsh, forthcoming). Together, these related strategies could contribute to a transformation of the current agro-food system into one that prioritizes ecological and human health at all stages, and integration among the interacting components of the system leading to greater long-term resilience.

Toward Transformative Agroecology

A transformative agroecology incorporates a critique of the political economic structures that shape the current agro-food system (see Holt-Giménez and Altieri, this issue, and González de Molina, this issue). It is explicitly committed to a more just and sustainable future by reshaping power relations from farm to table. This view requires that agroecologists move beyond the farm-scale to consider the broader forces—such as market and government institutions—that undermine farmers' cultural practices, economic self-sufficiency, and the ecological resource base. In part, agroecology as a field of study emerged in response to the social and ecological costs generated by agricultural industrialization and the implementation of Green Revolution technologies (Shiva 1989; Hecht 1995). Narrow approaches that reduce agroecology to an ecologically sensitive agronomic science have disregarded the influence of social concerns as part of the field's development. An agroecology-as-natural science perspective tends to privilege positivist science and Cartesian reductionism over other ways of knowing (e.g., indigenous or local knowledge), and, thus, risks producing research that is not appropriate to local contexts and which ignores the larger power structures that impact farmer livelihood strategies.

The transformative agroecology we propose has continued to develop a more holistic approach to the science and practice of agroecology in close dialogue with critiques of rural development put forth by academics, practitioners, and social movements. Political ecologists, in particular, have shown how external forces at the international, national, and regional level impact local practices. For instance, Blaikie and Brookefield's (1987) landmark study on soil degradation demonstrated how social marginalization, rather than maladaptation (i.e., in need of modernization), shaped farmers' land management practices. This was a crucial shift in perspective that emphasized a multi-scalar analysis to articulate local social and ecological phenomena to regional and global forces (Paulson et al. 2003). In short, political ecologists draw attention to the power relations that govern natural resources, often leaving farmers, due to their class, gender, or ethnic position, with a lack of access to productive resources (Rocheleau et al. 1996; Peet and Watts 2004). If farmers cannot access the resources they need, often dispersed within a surrounding territory and governed by overlapping power structures, they cannot continue to maintain or develop sustainable agroecosystems. A politically engaged agroecology considers the complex challenges, both social and ecological, that smallholders face in the transition toward sustainability (see González de Molina in this issue).

The connection between agroecological practice, equitable distribution of resources, and self-determination has been made explicit by marginalized communities demanding justice through food sovereignty (Holt-Giménez and Altieri, this issue). Ecological sustainability has become central to demands made in defense of rural livelihoods and culturally specific ways of life. These ways of living are increasingly at risk due to the deepening of capitalist relations that turn people into labor and nature into resources (Carruthers 1996; Grueso et al. 2003). Agroecologists are aptly positioned to contribute to these struggles by participating in a creative process of knowledge production with farmers. This requires a broader understanding of knowledge and learning as a community of practice that involves both farmer scientists and university-trained scientists (Kloppenburg 1991; Thomas-Slayter et al. 1996). Agroecology, through its parallel development as a science and social movement, is an apt site to construct relevant agroecologies that address asymmetrical power relations.

* * * *

Note

1. The IAASTD is a high-profile report commissioned by the World Bank, the United Nations, and the World Health Organization, sought to direct research and development policy solutions to the issues of global hunger, poverty, and sustainable agricultural development. It brought together hundreds of scientists and institutions from all regions of the world over a seven-year period. It is considered by many as the agricultural equivalent of the highly profiled International Panel for Climate Change (IPCC) reports.

References

Aeberhard, A., and S. Rist. 2009. Transdisciplinary co-production of knowledge in the development of organic agriculture in Switzerland. *Ecological Economics* 68: 1171–1181. DOI:10.1016/j.ecolecon.2008.08.008

Altieri, M. A. 2000. Agroecology: Principles and strategies for designing sustainable farming systems. http://nature.berkeley.edu/~miguel-alt/principles_ and_strategies (accessed January 20, 2012).

Altieri, M.A. 1987. *Agroecology: The scientific basis of alternative agriculture.* Boulder, CO: Westview Press.

Altieri, M. A., and V. M. Toledo. 2011. The agroecological revolution in Latin America: rescuing nature, ensuring food sovereignty and empowering peasants. *Journal of Peasant Studies* 38: 587–612. DOI:10.1080/03066150.2011.582947

Bacon, C., V. E. Méndez, and M. Brown. 2005. Participatory action-research and support for community development and conservation: Examples from shade coffee landscapes of Nicaragua and El Salvador. CASFS Research Brief 6. Santa Cruz, CA.: Center for Agroecology and Sustainable Food Systems (CASFS), University of California http://repositories.cdlib.org/casfs/rb/brief-n06/

Bacon, C. M., V. E. Méndez, S. R. Gliessman, D. Goodman, and J. A. Fox, eds. 2008. *Confronting the coffee crisis: Fair trade, sustainable livelihoods and ecosystems in Mexico and Central America*. Cambridge, MA: MIT Press.

Belsky, J. M. 2002. Beyond the natural resource and environmental sociology divide: Insights from a transdisciplinary perspective. *Society & Natural Resources* 15: 269–280.

Blaikie, P., and H. Brookfield. 1987. *Land degredation and society*. London: Longman.

Carruthers, D. V. 1996. Indigenous ecology and the politics of linkage in Mexican social movements. *Third World Quarterly* 17: 1007–1028.

Castellanet, C., and C. F. Jordan. 2002. *Participatory action research in natural resource management: A critique of the method based on five year's experience in the Transamazonica region of Brazil*. New York: Taylor and Francis.

Cuéllar-Padilla, M., and Á. Calle-Collado. 2011. Can we find solutions with people? Participatory action research with small organic producers in Andalusia. *Journal of Rural Studies* 27: 372–383. DOI:10.1016/j.jrurstud.2011.08.004

De Schutter, O. 2011. Agroecology and the right to food. Report presented at the 16th Session of the United Nations Human Rights Council [A/HRC/16/49]. March 8. United Nations Special Rapporteur on the Right to Food.

De Schutter, O., and G. Vanloqueren. 2011. The new green revolution: how twenty-first-century science can feed the world. *Solutions* 2(4): 33–44.

Fals-Borda, O., and M. A. Rahman, eds. 1991. *Action and knowledge: Breaking the monopoly with participatory action-research*. New York: Apex Press.

Fortmann, L., ed. 2008. *Participatory research in conservation and rural livelihoods: Doing science together*. Wiley-Blackwell.

Fox, J. A. 2005. Empowerment and institutional change: mapping 'virtuous circles' of state-society interaction. In *Power, rights and poverty: Concepts and connections*, ed. R. Alsop, 68–92. Washington, DC: The World Bank.

Francis, C. A., G. Lieblein, T. A. Breland, L. Salomonsson, U. Geber, N. Sriskandarajah, and V. Langer. 2008. Transdisciplinary research for a sustainable agriculture and food sector. *Agronomy Journal* 100(3): 771–776. DOI:10.2134/ agronj2007.0073

Francis, C., G. Lieblein, S. Gliessman, T. A. Breland, N. Creamer, R. Harwood, L. Salomonsson, J. Helenius, et al. 2003. Agroecology: The ecology of food systems. *Journal of Sustainable Agriculture* 22(3): 99–118.

Freire, P. 2000. *Pedagogy of the oppressed*. London: Continuum.

Gliessman, S. R., ed. 1978. *Seminarios regionales sobre agroecosistemas con enfasis en el estudio de tecnologia agricola tradicional*. H. Cardenas, Tabasco, Mexico: Colegio Superior de Agricultura Tropical.

Gliessman, S. R. 1980. Aspectos ecologicos de las practicas agricolas tradicionales en Tabasco, Mexico: aplicaciones para la produccion. *Biotica* 5: 93–101. Gliessman, S. R. 1982. Nitrogen distribution in several traditional agroecosystems in the humid tropical lowlands of southeastern Mexico. *Plant and Soil* 67 : 105–117.

Gliessman, S. R., ed. 1990. *Agroecology: Researching the ecological basis for sustainable agriculture.* New York: Springer-Verlag.

Gliessman, S. R. 2007. *Agroecology: The ecology of sustainable food systems* (2nd ed.). Boca Raton, FL: CRC Press/Taylor & Francis.

Gliessman, S. R., R. Garcia-Espinosa, and M. Amador. 1981. The ecological basis for the application of traditional agricultural technology in the management of tropical agro-ecosystems. *Agro-Ecosystems* 7: 173–185.

Godemann, J. 2008. Knowledge integration: A key challenge for transdisciplinary cooperation. *Environmental Education Research* 14: 625–641. DOI:10.1080/13504620802469188

Goodman, D., M. DuPuis, and M. K. Goodman. 2011. *Alternative food networks: Knowledge, place and politics.* London: Routledge.

Greenwood, D. J., and M. Levin. 1998. *Introduction to action research: Social research for social change.*Thousand Oaks, CA: Sage.

Grueso, L., C. Rosero, and A. Escobar. 2003. The process of black community organizing in the Southern Pacific coast region of Colombia. In *Perspectives on Las Américas: A reader in culture, history, and representation,* eds. M. C. Gutmann, F. V. Rodríguez, L. Stephen, and P. Zavella, 430–477. Malden, MA: Wiley-Blackwell.

Guzmán-Casado, G., M. Gonzáz de Molina, and E. Sevilla-Guzmán. 1999. *Introducción a la agroecología como desarrollo rural sostenible.* Madrid: Ediciones Mundi-Prensa.

Guzmán-Casado, G. I., and A. M. Alonso-Mielgo. 2007. La investigacion participativa en agroecologia: una herramienta para el desarrollo sustentable. *Ecosistemas* (Spain) 16: 24–36.

Guzmán, G. I., and A. M. Alonso. 2008. A comparison of energy use in conventional and organic olive oil production in Spain. *Agricultural Systems* 98(3): 167–176. DOI:10.1016/j.agsy.2008.06.004

Hecht, S. B. 1995. The evolution of agroecological thought. In *Agroecology: the science of sustainable agriculture,* ed. M. A. Altieri, 1–20. Boulder, CO: Westview Press.

International Assessment of Agricultural Knowledge, Science and Technology for Development. 2009. *Agriculture at a crossroads* [Global Report by the International Assessment of Agricultural Knowledge, Science and Technology for Development (IAASTD)].Washington, DC: Island Press.

Iles, A., and R. Marsh. forthcoming. Diversified farming systems and enabling policy frameworks. *Ecology and Society.*

Kindon, S., R. Pain, and M. Kesby, eds. 2007. *Participatory Action research approaches and methods.* Oxford, UK: Routledge.

Kloppenburg, J. 1991. Social theory and the reconstruction of agricultural science: local knowledge for an alternative agriculture. *Rural Sociology* 56: 519–548. Kremen, C., A. Iles, and C. M. Bacon. forthcoming. Diversified farming systems: An agroecological, systems-based alternative to modern industrial agriculture. *Ecology and Society.*

Méndez, V. E. 2010. Agroecology. In *Encyclopedia of geography,* ed. B. Warf, 55–59. Thousand Oaks, CA: Sage.

Minkler, M., and N. Wallerstein, eds. 2008. *Community-based participatory research for health: From process to outcomes.* San Francisco: Jossey-Bass.

Paulson, S., G. Lisa, and M. Watts. 2003. Locating the political in political ecology: an introduction. *Human Organization* 62: 205–217.

Peet, R., and M. J. Watts, eds. 2004. *Liberation ecologies: environment, development, social movements*. London: Routledge.

Perfecto, I., J. Vandermeer, and A. Wright. 2009. *Nature's matrix: Linking agriculture, conservation and food sovereignty.*London, UK: Earthscan.

Rocheleau, D., B. Thomas-Slayterm and E. Wangari, eds. 1996. *Feminist political ecology: global issues and local experiences.* London: Routledge.

Sevilla-Guzmán, E. 2006a. Agroecología y agricultural ecológica: hacia una "re" construcción de la soberanía alimentaria. *Agroecología* (Spain) 1: 7–18.

Sevilla-Guzmán, E. 2006b. *De la sociología rural a la agroecología.* Barcelona: Icaria Editorial.

Shiva, V. 1989. *The violence of the Green Revolution.* London: Zed.

Snapp, S., and B. Pound, eds. 2008. *Agricultural systems: Agroecology and rural innovation for development.* Amsterdam, the Netherlands: Academic Press.

Stringer, E. T. 1999. *Action research.*Thousand Oaks, CA: Sage.

Thomas-Slayter, B., E. Wangari, and D. Rocheleau. 1996. Feminist political ecology: crosscutting themes, theoretical insights, policy implications. In *Feminist political ecology: global issues and local experiences*, ed. D. Rocheleau, 287–307. London: Routledge.

Tomich, T. P., S. Brodt, H. Ferris, R. Galt, W. R. Horwath, E. Kebreab, J. H. J. Leveau, D. Liptzin, et al. 2011. Agroecology: A Review from a global-change perspective. *Annual Review of Environment and Resources* 36: 193–222. DOI:10.1146/annurev-environ-012110-121302

Uphoff, N., ed. 2002. *Agroecological innovations: Increasing food production with participatory development.* London, U.K.: Earthscan.

Vandermeer, J. H. 2009. *The ecology of agroecosystems.*Sudbury, MA: Jones & Bartlett Publishers.

Wezel, A., S. Bellon, T. Dore, C. Francis, D. Vallod, and C. David. 2009. Agroecology as a science, a movement and a practice. A review. *Agronomy for Sustainable Development* 29: 503–515. DOI:10.1051/agro/2009004

Wezel, A., and V. Soldat. 2009. A quantitative and qualitative historical analysis of the scientific discipline of agroecology. *International Journal of Agricultural Sustainability* 7: 3–18. DOI:10.3763/ijas.2009.0400

Whitmer, A., L. Ogden, J. Lawton, P. Sturner, P. M. Groffman, L. Schneider, D. Hart, B. Halpern, et al. 2010. The engaged university: providing a platform for research that transforms society. *Frontiers in Ecology and the Environment* 8: 314–321. DOI:10.1890/090241

CASE STUDY

Scaling Up Agroecological Approaches for Food Sovereignty in Latin America

By Miguel A. Altieri

G lobal and national forces are challenging the ability of Latin America to feed itself while also redefining the significance and the role of the agricultural sector, which has historically been of a dual nature. On the one side, there is a monocultural, competitive, export orientation, which makes a significant contribution to national economies while bringing a variety of economic, environmental and social problems. These problems include negative impacts on public health, ecosystem integrity and food quality, as well as disruption of traditional rural livelihoods and accelerating indebtedness among farmers (Uphoff 2002). The regional consequences of monoculture specialization are manyfold, including an array of environmental problems, worsening insect pest infestations and higher disease incidence linked to the high use of agro-chemicals and the simplification and genetic uniformity of modern crops. Moreover, the efficiency of applied inputs is decreasing, and yields in most key crops are leveling off. In some places, yields are actually in decline. Growing industrialization and globalization, with their emphasis on export crops (such as transgenic soybeans exported for cattle feed to countries such as China, Europe, the U.S. and others), and the rapidly increasing demand for biofuel crops (sugarcane, maize, soybean, oil palm, eucalyptus, etc.) are reshaping the region's agriculture and food supply, with yet unknown economic, social and ecological impacts and risks.

On the other hand, Latin America's peasant and small-farm sector is still significant, making up 63 percent of farmland (ECLAC 2009). Despite migration to urban areas, especially by young people, the situation has not changed much since the late 1980s, when the peasant population reached about 75 million people, representing almost two-thirds of Latin America's rural population (Ortega 1986). In Brazil alone, for example, more than 4.3 million traditional family farmers (about 85 percent of farmers) now occupy just 24.3 percent of the agricultural land of the country (IBGE 2009). In Ecuador, 91 percent of the 843,000 farms are smallholdings, and in Peru, smallholdings account for 80 percent of the 1.6 million farms (ECLAC 2009). Many of these peasants still use traditional farming systems, which represent microcosms of community-based agriculture, offering promising models for promoting biodiversity, sustaining yields without agro-chemicals and conserving ecological integrity while reaching food security (Altieri and Koohafkan 2008).

During the last two decades, the concepts of food sovereignty and agroecologically based production systems have gained much attention. New approaches and technologies blending modern agricultural science and indigenous knowledge systems, spearheaded by peasant organizations, NGOs and some government and academic institutions, are enhancing food security while conserving natural resources, agro-biodiversity and soil and water conservation throughout hundreds of rural communities in the region.

The science of agroecology—the application of ecological concepts and principles to the design and management of sustainable agroecosystems—provides a framework to assess the complexity of agroecosystems. The idea of agroecology is to develop a type of agriculture that does not depend on high chemical and energy inputs. The emphasis is on agricultural systems in which ecological interactions and synergisms between biological components provide the mechanisms for the system to sponsor its own soil fertility, productivity and crop protection (Altieri 1995). In addition to providing a scientific basis for sustainable and enhanced productivity, agroecology promotes the capability of local communities to innovate, evaluate and adapt themselves through farmer-to-farmer research and grassroots extension approaches. Technological approaches emphasizing diversity, synergy, recycling and integration, and social processes that value community involvement, point to the fact that human resource development is the cornerstone of any strategy aimed at increasing food production. In short, agroecology can have a significant effect on the region's food sovereignty.

Small Farmers are Key

In Latin America, the number of peasant farms reached about 16 million by the late 1980s and occupied close to 60.5 million hectares, or 34.5 percent of the cultivated land; the average size of these farms was about 1.8 hectares. The contribution of peasant agriculture to the general food supply in the region has been significant (DeGrandi 1996). In the 1980s, peasant farms produced approximately 41 percent of the agricultural output for domestic consumption: 5 percent of the maize, 77 percent of the beans and 61 percent of the potatoes. In Brazil, family farms control about 33 percent of the area sown to maize, 61 percent under beans and 64 percent planted to cassava, producing 84 percent of the total cassava and 67 percent of all beans. In Ecuador, the peasant sector occupies more than 50 percent of the area devoted to food crops such as maize, beans, barley and okra, and in Mexico, peasants occupy at least 70 percent of the area assigned to maize and 60 percent of the area under beans (FAO 2001). In addition to the peasant and family farm sector, there are about 50 million individuals belonging to some seven hundred different indigenous groups who live and utilize the humid tropical regions of the world. About two million of these live in the Amazon and Southern Mexico. In Mexico, as recently as the 1980s, half of the humid tropics was utilized by indigenous communities and *ejidos* (communally managed farms), featuring integrated agriculture-forestry systems with production aimed at subsistence and local-regional markets (Toledo et al. 1985).

Small Farms are More Productive and Resource Conserving

Although conventional wisdom claims that small family farms are backward and unproductive, research shows that small farms are much more productive than large farms if total output is considered rather than yield from a single crop (Rosset et al. 2006). Integrated farming systems, in which the small-scale farmer produces grains, fruits, vegetables, fodder and animal products, out-produce yields per unit of monoculture crops such as corn on large-scale farms (Funes-Monzote 2008). A large farm may produce more corn per hectare than a small farm in which the corn is grown as part of a polyculture that also includes beans, squash, potato and fodder. Yet, for smallholder polycultures, productivity in terms of harvestable products per unit area is higher than under large-scale sole cropping with the same level of management. Yield advantages can range from 20 to 60 percent, because polycultures reduce losses due to weeds, insects and diseases and make more efficient use of water, light and nutrients (Beets 1982; Funes-Monzote 2008). In Mexico, a 1.73 hectare plot of land has to be planted with maize monoculture to produce as much food as 1 hectare planted with a mixture of maize, squash and beans. In addition, the maize-squash-bean polyculture produces up to 4 tons per hectare of dry matter for plowing into the soil, compared with 2 tons in a maize monoculture. Likewise, in Brazil, polycultures containing 12,500 maize plants per hectare and 150,000 bean plants per hectare exhibited a yield advantage of 28 percent (Gliessman 1998).

In terms of overall output, the diversified farm produces much more food, even if measured in dollars. In the U.S., data show that 2-hectare farms produced $15,104 per hectare and netted about $2,902 per hectare; the largest farms, averaging 15,581 hectares, yielded $249 per hectare and netted about $52 per hectare (Rosset 2006). Not only do small to medium sized farms produce higher yields than large farms, but they do so with much lower negative impact on the environment. In this regard, small farms are multi-functional; they can be more productive, more efficient and contribute more to economic development than can large farms. Despite the fact that a proportion of medium- and small-scale farms are conventional, in many cases small farmers also take better care of natural resources, including reducing soil erosion and conserving biodiversity (Rosset et al. 2006).

The inverse relationship between farm size and output can be attributed to the more efficient use of land, water and other agricultural resources that usually results from the management of biodiverse farms by small farmers (Funes-Monzote 2008). In terms of converting inputs into outputs, then, on a per unit basis, food sovereignty is more likely to be achieved through the work of small-scale farmers. Building strong rural economies in the Global South based on productive small-scale farming will help stem the tide of out-migration and allow people to remain with their families. As population continues to grow and the amount of farmland and water available to each person continues to shrink, a small-farm structure may become central to feeding the planet, especially as large-scale agriculture increasingly devotes itself to feeding car tanks.

Diversified Farms as Models of Sustainability

In Latin America, the persistence of more than three million agricultural hectares under ancient, traditional management in the form of raised fields, terraces, polycultures, agro-forestry systems and so on demonstrates a successful indigenous agricultural strategy and comprises a tribute to the creativity of traditional farmers. These microcosms of traditional agriculture offer promising models for other areas as they promote biodiversity, thrive without agrochemicals and sustain year-round multicrop yields (Altieri 1999).

One such sustainable traditional system is the *frijol tapado,* used to produce beans in mid-elevation areas of Central America, on steep slopes with high amounts of rainfall, where most beans in the region are grown. To begin the process, farmers choose a fallow field that is two to three years old so that the woody vegetation dominates the grasses. If the fallow period is less than two years, the grasses will crowd out the emerging bean plants and soil fertility will not have been fully restored since the last harvest. Next, paths are cut through the field with machetes. Then, bean seeds are thrown, or broadcasted, into the fallow vegetation. Finally, the fallow vegetation is cut down into a mulch, which decays and provides nutrients to the maturing bean seedlings. Approximately twelve weeks after broadcasting, the beans are harvested. In Costa Rica, an estimated 60 to 70 percent of beans are produced by *frijol tapado.* Compared to the more labour- and chemical-intensive methods of bean production used by some smallholders, the *tapado* system has a higher rate of return because of lower labour and input costs (Buckles et al. 1998). The *tapado* system allows production of beans for both home consumption and cash to supplement meagre incomes. The cost-effective benefits include no need for expensive and potentially toxic chemicals such as fertilizers and pesticides and a relatively low labour requirement. Soil erosion is minimized because the continuous vegetation cover protects the bare ground from heavy rainfall.

The rationale of the *frijol tapado* has led to the use of green manures as an ecological pathway to the intensification of the maize-bean polyculture, or *milpa,* in areas where long fallows are no longer possible due to population growth or conversion of forest to pasture. After the maize is harvested, the field is abandoned to the previously broadcast *mucuna pruriens* (velvetbean, a leguminous cover crop), leaving a thick mulch layer year round. The velvetbean mulch layer results in improved mineral nutrition in the maize crop, cumulative soil fertility and reduced soil erosion (Altieri 2002). Experiences in Central America show that *mucuna*-based maize systems are fairly stable, allowing respectable yield levels (usually 2–4 tons per hectare) every year. In particular, the system appears to greatly diminish drought stress because the mulch layer helps conserve water in the soil profile. Adequate water in the soil allows nutrients to be readily available to the major crop. In addition, the *mucuna* system suppresses weeds, either because velvetbeans physically prevent them from emerging or surviving, or because a shallow rooting of weeds in the litter layer–soil interface makes them easier to control. Data show that this system, grounded in farmers' knowledge and involving the continuous annual rotation of velvetbean and maize, can be sustained for at least fifteen years at a reasonably high level of productivity without any apparent decline in the natural resource base (Flores 1989). As illustrated with the case of the *mucuna* system, an understanding of the agroecology of traditional farming systems can contribute to the development of contemporary systems. This awareness can only result from integrative studies that determine the myriad factors that condition how farmers perceive their environment and subsequently how they modify it.

In addition to mixing crops, many resource-poor farmers also exploit diversity by growing different varieties of the same crop at the same time and in the same field. In a worldwide survey of crop-varietal diversity on farms, involving twenty-seven crops, Jarvis et al. (2007) found that considerable crop genetic diversity continues to be maintained in traditional crop varieties, especially of major staple crops. In most cases, farmers maintain such diversity as insurance to meet future environmental change or social and economic needs. Many researchers conclude that variety richness enhances productivity and reduces yield variability (Brookfield and Padoch 1994).

Undoubtedly, the ensemble of traditional crop-management practices used by many resource-poor farmers represents a rich resource for modern workers seeking to create novel agroecosystems well adapted to the local agroecological and socioeconomic circumstances of peasants. Peasants use a diversity of techniques, many of which fit well to local conditions. The techniques tend to be knowledge intensive rather than input intensive, and many are site specific; if they are applied to other environments, modifications and adaptations may be necessary. It is vital to maintain the foundations of such modifications grounded in peasants' rationale and knowledge.

Small Farms are More Resilient to Climate Change

In traditional agroecosystems, the prevalence of complex and diverse cropping systems is of key importance to the stability of peasant farming systems, allowing crops to reach acceptable productivity levels even in the midst of environmentally stressful conditions. In general, traditional agroecosystems are less vulnerable to catastrophic loss because a wide variety of crops is grown in various spatial and temporal arrangements. Research suggests that many small farmers cope and even prepare for climate change, minimizing crop failure through increased use of drought-tolerant local varieties, water harvesting, mixed cropping, opportunistic weeding, agro-forestry and a series of other traditional techniques (Altieri and Koohafkan 2008).

Polycultures exhibit greater yield stability and lower productivity declines during a drought than do monocultures. Natarajan and Willey (1986) examined the effect of drought on enhanced yields with polycultures by manipulating water stress on combinations of sorghum, peanut and millet and on mono-crops of peanut, sorghum and millet. All the polycultures yielded consistently more than corresponding monocultures at five levels of moisture availability, ranging from 297 to 584 mm of water applied over the cropping season. Interestingly, the rate of overyielding actually increased with water stress, such that the relative differences in productivity between monocultures and polycultures became more accentuated as stress increased. Polycultures thus exhibited greater yield stability and lower productivity declines during a drought.

Many farmers grow crops in agro-forestry designs, where shade tree cover protects crop plants against extremes in micro-climate and soil moisture fluctuation. Farmers also influence micro-climate by retaining and planting trees, which reduce temperature, wind velocity, evaporation and direct exposure to sunlight and intercept hail and rain. Lin (2007) found that in coffee agroecosystems in Chiapas, Mexico, temperature, humidity and solar radiation fluctuations increased significantly as shade cover decreased. She concluded that shade cover was directly related to the mitigation of variability in micro-climate and soil moisture for the coffee crop.

Surveys conducted on hillsides after Hurricane Mitch in Central America showed that farmers using sustainable practices such as *mucuna* cover crops, intercropping and agro-forestry suffered less from mudslides than their conventional neighbours. A study spanning 360 communities and twenty-four departments in Nicaragua, Honduras and Guatemala showed that diversified plots had 20 to 40 percent more topsoil, greater soil moisture, less erosion and experienced lower economic losses than neighbours using monocultures (Holt-Gimenez 2001). Thus, a re-evaluation of indigenous technology can serve as a key source of information on adaptive capacity and resilient capabilities of small farms, features of strategic importance for world farmers in the face of climatic change. Indigenous technologies often reflect a worldview and an understanding of our relationship to the natural world that is more realistic and sustainable than those of western European heritage.

Enhancing the Productivity of Small-Farm Systems through Agroecology

Despite the evidence of the resiliency and productivity advantages of small-scale and traditional farming systems, many scientists and development officials argue that the performance of subsistence agriculture is unsatisfactory and that intensification of production is essential for the transition from subsistence to commercial production. While subsistence farming has not generally produced a meaningful marketable surplus due to land and labour constraints, subsistence farming has the potential to ensure food security (Altieri 1999). Many people wrongly believe that traditional systems do not produce more because hand tools and draft animals put a ceiling on productivity. Productivity may be low, but the cause appears to be social, not technical. When the farmer succeeds in providing enough food for subsistence; there is no pressure to innovate or to enhance yields. However, research shows that traditional crop and animal combinations can often be adapted to increase productivity when the agroecological structuring of the farm via crop combinations and/or animal integration is improved and when the use of labour and local resources is efficient (Altieri 2002). This approach contrasts strongly with many modern agricultural development projects, characterized by broad-scale technological recommendations, which have ignored the heterogeneity of traditional agriculture, resulting in an inevitable mismatching between agricultural development and the needs and potentials of local people and localities (Altieri 1995).

The failure of top-down development has become even more alarming as economic change, fueled by capital and market penetration, are leading to an ecological breakdown that is starting to destroy the sustainability of traditional agriculture. After creating resource-conserving systems for centuries, traditional cultures in areas such as Mesoamerica and the Andes are now being undermined by external political and economic forces. Biodiversity is decreasing on farms, soil degradation is accelerating, community and social organization is breaking down, genetic resources are being eroded and traditions are being lost. Under this scenario and given commercial pressures and urban demands, the challenge is how to guide such transitions in a way that yields and income are increased without raising the debt of peasants and further exacerbating environmental degradation. We contend that this can be done by generating and promoting agroecologically based resource-conserving technologies, a source of which are the very traditional systems that global, industrial monocultural farming is destroying.

Ecological Potential of Traditional Systems

As the inability of the Green Revolution to improve production and farm incomes for the very poor became apparent, the new enthusiasm for ancient technologies spearheaded a quest in Latin America for affordable, productive and ecologically sound technologies that enhance small-farm productivity while conserving resources. One of the early projects advocating this agroecological approach occurred in the mid 1970s, when the former Mexican National Research Institute on Biotic Resources (INIREB by its Spanish acronym) unveiled a plan to build *chinampas* in the swampy region of Veracruz and Tabasco. Perfected by the Aztec inhabitants of the Valley of Mexico prior to the Spanish Conquest, *chinampa* agriculture, a self-sustaining system of raised farming beds in shallow lakes or marshes that has operated for centuries, is one of the most intensive and productive ever devised humans. It demanded no significant capital inputs yet maintained extraordinary high yields year after year. A wide variety of staple crops, vegetables and flowers were mixed with an array of fruit from small trees and bushes. In addition, abundant aquatic life in the canals provided valuable sources of protein for the loc diet (Gliessman 1998).

According to Sanders (1957), in the mid 1950s, *chinampas* exhibited maize yields of 3.5–6.3 tons per hectare. At that time, these were the highest long-term yields achieved anywhere in Mexico. (In comparison, average maize yields in the U.S. in 1955 were 2.6 tons per hectare and did not pass the 4 tons per hectare map until 1965). Each hectare *of chinampa* could produce enough food for fifteen to twenty persons per year at modern subsistence levels. Later research indicated that each *chinampero* could work about three quarters of a hectare per year (Jimenez Osornio and del Amo 1986), meaning that each farmer can support twelve to fifteen people.

Threatened by the growth of Mexico City, *chinampas* nearly vanished except in a few isolated areas. Noting that this system offered a promising model for other areas as it promotes biological diversity, thrives without chemical inputs and sustains year-round yields, INIREB began to promote *chinampas* in the lowland tropics of Mexico. Although implementation and adoption of *chinampas* in Tabasco was somewhat successful, one criticism of the project was that no market outlets were explored for the outputs produced by the community. Nonetheless, the raised beds of Tabasco (or *camellones chontales*) are still in full operation in the swamps of this region, under full control of the Chontal Nation. These "swamp farmers" use traditional agriculture, and the new raised beds produce a great variety of products that provide income and food security.

In the totally different ecoregion of the Andes, several institutions have engaged in programs to restore abandoned terraces and build new ones. In the Colca Valley of Southern Peru, the Programa de Acondicionamiento Territorial y Vivienda Rural (Rural Housing and Territorial Development Program) sponsors terrace reconstruction by offering peasant communities low-interest loans, seeds and other inputs to restore large areas of abandoned terraces. The main advantages of terraces are that they minimize risks in times of frost and/or drought, reduce soil loss, amplify the cropping options because of the micro-climate and hydraulic advantages and improve crop yields. Yield data from new bench terraces showed a 43–65 percent yield increase in potatoes, maize and barley compared to yields of these crops grown on sloping fields (Browder 1989). One of the main constraints of this technology is that it is highly labour intensive, requiring about 350–500 worker days per hectare in a given year. Such demands, however, can be buffered when communities organize and share tasks (Altieri 1995).

In Peru, in search of solutions to contemporary problems of high altitude farming, researchers have uncovered remnants of thousands of hectares of "ridged fields." One fascinating farming effort is the revival of an ingenious system of raised fields that evolved on the high plains of the Peruvian Andes about 3,000 years ago. According to archaeological evidence; these *waru-warus,* platforms of soil surrounded by ditches filled with water, were able to produce bumper crops despite floods, droughts and the killing frost common at altitudes of nearly 4000 metres (Denevan 1995). The *waru-waru* combination of raised beds and canals has proven to have important temperature-moderation effects, extending the growing season and leading to higher productivity compared to chemically fertilized, but normally cultivated, pampa soils. In Camjata, the potato fields reached 13 tons per hectare per year in *waru-warus.* In the Huatta district, reconstructed raised fields also produced impressive harvests, exhibiting a sustained potato yield of 8–14 tons per hectare per year (Browder 1989). These figures contrast favourably with the average potato yields of 1–4 tons per hectare per year produced by other small farmers on the Puna. It is estimated that the initial construction, rebuilding every ten years and annual planting, weeding, harvest and maintenance of raised fields require 270 person-days per hectare per year.

On Chiloe Island in Southern Chile, a secondary centre of origin of potatoes, NGO development workers are tapping the ethno-botanical knowledge of female elders of the Huilliche Nation in an effort to slow genetic erosion and recover some of the original native potato germplasm (Altieri 1995). They intend to make it available to contemporary impoverished farmers, desperately in need of locally adapted varieties that can produce without agrochemicals. After surveying several agroecosystems of Chiloe, technicians collected hundreds of samples of native potatoes still grown by indigenous farmers. With this material and in collaboration with farmers they established community seed banks where more than 120 traditional varieties are grown year after year and are subjected to selection and seed enhancement. In this way, an *in situ* conservation program was initiated involving several farmers from various rural communities, ensuring the active conservation and exchange of varieties among participating farmers. As more farmers became involved, this strategy allowed a continuous supply of seeds of value to resource-poor farmers for subsistence and also provided a repository of vital genetic diversity for future regional crop-improvement programs (Altieri 2002).

Rural Social Movements & Agroecology

The development of sustainable agriculture requires significant structural changes in addition to technological innovation and farmer-to-farmer solidarity. This is impossible without social movements that create the political will among decision makers to dismantle and transform the institutions and regulations that presently hold back sustainable agricultural development. For this reason, many argue that a more radical transformation of agriculture is needed, one guided by the notion that ecological change in agriculture cannot be promoted without comparable changes in the social, political, cultural and economic arenas that conform and determine agriculture. The organized peasant- and indigenous-based agrarian movements like La Vía Campesina have long contended that peasants and small-scale farmers need land to produce food for their own communities and for their country. For this reason, they have advocated for genuine agrarian reforms to improve access to and control over land, water, agro-biodiversity and so on, which are of central importance for communities to be able to meet growing food demands. La Vía Campesina believes that in order to protect livelihoods, jobs, people's food security and health as well as the environment, food production has to remain in the hands of peasants and small-scale sustainable farmers and cannot be left under the control of large agri-business companies and supermarket chains. Only by changing the export-led, free-trade-based, industrial agriculture model of large farms can the downward spiral of poverty, low wages, rural-urban migration, hunger and environmental degradation be halted (La Vía Campesina 2008; Rosset 2006). Rural social movements embrace the concept of food sovereignty as an alternative to the neoliberal approach, which puts its faith in an inequitable international trade to solve the world's food problem. Instead, food sovereignty focuses on local autonomy, local markets, local production-consumption cycles, energy and technological sovereignty and farmer-to-farmer networks.

Today's peasant movements understand that dismantling the industrial agrifoods complex and restoring local food systems must be accompanied by the construction of technical and material alternatives that suit the needs of small-scale producers and low-income consumers, while acknowledging geographic and cultural diversity. Researchers can help farmers movements reach food-sovereignty and sustainable agriculture by documenting succesful agroecological experiences and sharing such alternative agricultural practices among broad sectors of the rural population via farmer-to-farmer networks (Holt-Gimenez 2006).

Outlook & Prospects

There is no question that small farmers in Latin America can produce much of the needed food for rural and urban communities in the midst of climate change and burgeoning energy costs (Uphoff and Altieri 1999; Pretty et al. 2003). The evidence is conclusive: new agroecological approaches and technologies spearheaded by farmers, NGOs and some local governments around the region are already making a sufficient contribution to food security at the household, national and regional levels. A variety of agroecological and participatory approaches in many countries show very positive outcomes even under adverse environmental conditions. Potentials include raising cereal yields from 50 to 200 percent, increasing stability of production through diversification, improving diets and income, contributing to national food security and even to exports, conservation of the natural-resource base and agro-biodiversity (Uphoff and Altieri 1999). As demonstrated above, many studies show that small, diversified farms can produce from two to ten times more per unit area than can large corporate farms (Funes-Monzote 2008).

Whether the potential and spread of thousands of local agroecological innovations is realized depends on several factors and actions. Proposed agroecological strategies have to deliberately target the poor and not only aim to increase production and conserve natural resources but also to create employment and provide access to local inputs and output markets. New strategies must focus on the facilitation of farmer learning to become experts on agroecology and at capturing the opportunities in their diverse environments (Uphoff 2002).

Researchers and rural development practitioners need to translate general ecological principles and natural resource management concepts into practical advice directly relevant to the needs and circumstances of smallholders. A focus on resource-conserving technologies that use labour efficiently and on diversified farming systems based on natural ecosystem processes is essential. This requires a clear understanding of the relationship between biodiversity and agroecosystem function and identifying management practices and designs that enhance the right kind of biodiversity, which in turn contributes to the maintenance and productivity of agroecosystems (Altieri 1995; Gliessman 1998). Any serious attempt at developing sustainable agricultural technologies must bring to bear local knowledge and skills on the research process (Toledo and Solís 2001). Particular emphasis must be given to involving farmers directly in the formulation of the research agenda and on their active participation in the process of technological innovation and dissemination through *campesino a campesino* (farmer-to-farmer) models that focus on sharing experiences and strengthening local research and problem-solving capacities.

Major changes must be made in policies, institutions and research and development to make sure that agroecological alternatives are adopted, made equitably and broadly accessible and multiplied so that their full benefit for sustainable food security can be realized. Existing subsidies and policy incentives for conventional chemical approaches must be dismantled. Corporate control over the food system must also he challenged. Governments and international public organizations must encourage and support effective partnerships between NGOs, local universities and farmer organizations in order to assist and empower poor farmers to achieve food security, income generation and natural resource conservation.

There is also a need to increase rural incomes through interventions other than enhancing yields, such as complementary marketing and processing activities. Therefore, equitable market opportunities should also be developed that emphasize fair trade, local commercialization and distribution schemes, fair prices and other mechanisms that link farmers and consumers more directly and in solidarity. However, simply opening niche markets for peasant produce among the rich in the North exhibits the same problems of any agro-export scheme that does not prioritize food sovereignty, thus perpetuating dependence and hunger. The ultimate challenge is to increase investment and research in agroecology and scale up projects that have already proven successful to thousands of other farmers. This will generate a meaningful impact on the income, food security and environmental wellbeing of the world's population, especially the millions of poor farmers yet untouched by modern agricultural technology.

Agrarian movements must continue to pressure multinational companies and government officials to ensure that all countries achieve food sovereignty by developing their own domestic farm and food policies that respond to the true needs of their farmers and all consumers, especially the poor. The need to rapidly foster sustainable agriculture requires coalitions among farmers, civil-society organizations (including consumers) and research organizations. Moving towards a more socially just, economically viable and environmentally sound agriculture will be the result of the coordinated action of emerging social movements in the rural sector in alliance with civil-society organizations that are committed to supporting the goals of these farmers movements. The expectation is that, through constant political pressure from organized farmers and members of civil-society, politicians will be pushed to develop and launch policies conducive to enhancing food sovereignty, preserving the natural resource base and ensuring social equity and economic viability.

The new research agenda requires institutional realignments and, if it is to be relevant to peasants and the small- and medium-scale farmers, it must be influenced by agroecology, with its emphasis on complex farming systems, labour demanding techniques and use of organic and local resources. This means that technological solutions have to be location specific and much more information intensive rather than capital intensive. In turn this implies using more farmer knowledge but also providing support to farmers to increase their management skills. Importantly, the agroecological process requires participation and enhancement of farmers' ecological literacy about their farms and resources, laying the foundation for empowerment and continuous innovation by rural communities.

Whether the potential and spread of local agroecological innovations is realized depends on investments, policies and attitude changes on the part of researchers and policymakers. "Greening" the Green Revolution will not be sufficient to reduce hunger and poverty and conserve biodiversity. If the root causes of hunger, poverty and inequity are not confronted head-on, tensions between socially equitable development and ecologically sound conservation are bound to accentuate. Organic farming systems that do not challenge the monocultural nature of plantations and that rely on external inputs and expensive foreign certification seals and fair-trade systems destined only for agro-export offer very little to peasants and small farmers, who become dependent on external inputs and foreign and volatile markets. The fine-tuning of the input-substitution approach will do little to move farmers towards the productive redesign of agroecosystems that would move them away from dependence on external inputs.

References

Altieri, M.A. 1995. *Agroecology: The Science of Sustainable Agriculture*. Boulder, CO: Westview Press.

_____. 1999. "Applying Agroecology to Enhance Productivity of Peasant Farming Systems in Latin America." *Environment, Development and Sustainability* 1.

_____. 2002. "Agroecology: The Science of Natural Resource Management for Poor Farmers in Marginal Environments." *Agriculture, Ecosystems and Environment* 93.

Altieri, M.A., and P. Koohafkan. 2008. *Enduring Farms: Climate Change, Smallholders and Traditional Farming Communities*. Environment and Development Series 6. Malaysia: Third World Network.

Beets, W.G. 1982. *Multiple Cropping and Tropical Farming Systems*. Boulder, CO: Westview Press.

Brookfield, H., and C. Padoch. 1994. "Appreciating Agrobiodiversity: A Look at the Dynamism and Diversity of Indigenous Farming Practices." *Environment* 36.

Browder, J.O. 1989. *Fragile Lands in Latin America: Strategies for Sustainable Development*. Boulder CO: Westview Press.

Buckles, D., B. Triomphe and G. Sain. 1998. *Cover Crops in Hillside Agriculture: Farmer Innovation with Mucuna*. Ottawa: International Development Research Center.

DeGrandi, J.C. 1996. *El Desarrollo de los Sistemas de Agricultura Campesina en America Latina: Un Analisis de la Influencia del Contexto Socio-Economico*. Rome: Food and Agriculture Organization.

Denevan, W.M. 1995. "Prehistoric Agricultural Methods as Models for Sustainability." *Advanced Plant Pathology* 11.

ECLAC (Economic Commission for Latin America and the Caribbean). 2009. The Outlook for Agriculture and Rural Development in the Americas: A Perspective on Latin America and the Caribbean. Santiago, Chile: ECLAC-IICA-FAO.

Flores, M. 1989. "Velvetbeans: An Alternative to Improve Small Farmers' Agriculture." *ILEIA Newsletter* 5.

FAO (Food and Agriculture Organization of the United Nations). 2001. FAOSTAT: FAO Statistical Databases. Available at apps.fao.org.

Funes-Monzote, F.R. 2008. "Farming Like We're Here to Stay: The Mixed Farming Alternative for Cuba." Ph.D. thesis, Wageningen University, Netherlands.

Gliessman, S.R. 1998. *Agro-ecology: Ecological Process in Sustainable Agriculture*. Michigan: Ann Arbor Press.

Holt-Gimenez, E. 2001. "Measuring Farms' Agroecological Resistance to Hurricane Mitch." *LEISA* 17.

_____. 2006. *Campesino a Campesino: Voices from Latin America's Farmer to Farmer Movement for Sustainable Agriculture*. Oakland: Food First Books.

IBGE (Instituto Brasileiro de Geografia e Estadistica). 2009. "Censo Agropecuario 2006" Available at ibge.gov.br/home/estatistica/economia/agropecuaria/censoagro/agri_familiar_2006/default.shtm.

Jimenez-Osornio, J., and S. del Amo. 1986. "An Intensive Mexican Traditional Agro-ecosystem: The Chinampa." Proceedings of 6th International Scientific Conference IFOAM. Santa Cruz, CA.

Jarvis. D.I., C. Padoch and H.D. Cooper. 2007. *Managing Biodiversity in Agricultural Ecosystems.* New York: Columbia University Press.

La Vía Campesina. 2008. "An Answer to the Global Food Crisis: Peasants and Small Farmers Can Feed the World!" Available at viacampesina.org.

Lin, B.B. 2007. "Agro-forestry Management as an Adaptive Strategy Against Potential Microclimate Extremes in Coffee Agriculture." *Agricultural and Forest Meteorology* 144.

Natarajan, M., and R.W. Willey. 1986. "The Effects of Water Stress on Yield Advantages of Intercropping Systems." *Field Crops Research* 13.

Ortega, E. 1986. *Peasant Agriculture in Latin America.* Santiago: Joint ECLAC/FAO Agriculture Division.

Pretty, J., J.I.L. Morrison and R.E. Hine. 2003. "Reducing Food Poverty by Increasing Agricultural Sustainability in Developing Countries." *Agriculture, Ecosystems and Environment* 95.

Rosset, P.M. 2006. *Food is Different: Why We Must Get the WTO Out of Agriculture.* Black Point, NS: Fernwood Publishing.

Rosset, P.M., R. Patel and M. Courville. 2006. *Promised Land: Competing Visions of Agrarian Reform.* Oakland, CA: Food First Books.

Sanders, W.T. 1957. "Tierra y Agua: A Study of the Ecological Factors in the Development of Meso-American Civilizations." PhD dissertation, Harvard University.

Toledo, V.M., J. Carabias, C. Mapes and C. Toledo. 1985. *Ecologia y Autosuficiencia Alimentaria.* Mexico City: Siglo Veintiuno Editores.

Toledo, V.M., and L. Solís. 2001. "Ciencia para los Pobres: El Programa 'Agua para Siempre' de la Regiòn Mixteca." *Ciencias* 64.

Uphoff, N. 2002. *Agroecological Innovations: Increasing Food Production with Participatory Development.* London: Earthscan.

Uphoff, N., and M.A. Altieri. 1999. *Alternatives to Conventional Modern Agriculture for Meeting World Food Needs in the Next Century.* Ithaca, NY: Cornell International Institute for Food, Agriculture and Development.

SECTION III CONCLUSION

This section discussed the interactions between agrifood systems and natural resources. Historically, agriculture has both impacted and enhanced natural resources. In the future, earth's ecosystems are expected to have a decreasing capacity to assimilate these impacts. Our current production, consumption, and pollution patterns have resulted in significant environmental impacts, including a changed climate, agricultural land degradation, and widespread hunger and poverty. For this reason, the development of agriculture has shifted towards approaches that are ecologically based, with the goals of not only minimizing environmental impacts, but also actively conserving and enhancing natural resources and supporting farmer livelihoods. To face these challenges, a diversity of both academic and practical approaches, with both similarities and differences, have been developed. These frameworks range from very publicly known fields, such as organic agriculture, to those that may be more academic, such as agroecology. Agrifood systems touch almost all aspects of human existence and wellbeing, from human health to multifaceted transnational industries. To understand this complexity it is necessary to address food and agriculture from a holistic perspective that includes social, cultural, political, economic, and ecological dimensions. In addition, since eating is a universal human need, it is important that all people participate in the decisions made about the food we eat. This necessitates an explicit effort for agrifood system policies and practices to stem, as much as possible, from participatory and democratic processes. We chose to present agroecology as an approach to address food and environment interactions because it integrates transdisciplinarity, participation, and action orientation in its perspective, which is promising to better understand and redirect our current agrifood systems (the need for transdisciplinary approaches is well argued by Méndez and colleagues). This also aligns well with the interdisciplinary and broad-reaching vision of environmental studies that we have adopted for this book.

There are, however, limitations to the agroecological approach. First, by seeking to be broad, there is the risk of losing depth in each of the dimensions that constitute agrifood systems. For example, addressing agricultural policy could result in less work at the farm level, which focuses on understanding how to increase production with fewer negative environmental and social impacts. In addition, achieving and operationalizing transdisciplinarity can be challenging, as it requires not only open minds, but also the commitment and ability to work in teams and with people from different disciplines and backgrounds. In a truly participatory process, the involvement of different actors can also be difficult, as each usually has their own agenda and timeline. Others have posed that it may be better to separate science and research from practice and policies (Wezel et al. 2009). In response to these critiques, we believe that transdisciplinary and participatory action research processes are not only possible, they are necessary. In addition, and as presented by Altieri in his chapter, there are interesting case studies that can provide important lessons for the redirection of our agrifood systems. The stakes are human wellbeing (i.e., eradicating hunger) and the integrity of the ecosystems we live in and depend on. Approaches such as agroecology and others with similar perspectives (e.g., socio-ecological systems) are not perfect, but they are flexible and adaptable to the dynamic realities that human agrifood systems face. They also require a great deal of effort and cooperation. Perhaps in the past scientists and policymakers had the luxury of avoiding engaging in such levels of complexity, but at present it seems as though dialogue and cooperation are needed to build healthier, more resilient food systems.

Section III Discussion Questions: Food and Agroecology Review

1. Why might it be important to consider 'agrifood systems', rather than simply agricultural production?
2. Explain four key environmental impacts of agriculture discussed in McDonald's chapter.
3. In what ways can agriculture contribute to the problem of climate change? In what ways can agriculture play a role in mitigating climate change?
4. What is PAR, as discussed in Mendez et al. (2013), and why is PAR promoted as an approach to sustainable agriculture and development?
5. How has agroecology evolved over time as a movement and practice?
6. How do food security and food sovereignty differ? (see section Introduction and Altieri, 2008)
7. What are some of the benefits of small-scale, diversified agriculture?
8. What factors are limiting the widespread adoption of agroecology, and what would be needed to promote agroecology at a large scale?

References

Altieri, M.A. (1987) *Agroecology: The Scientific Basis of Alternative Agriculture.* Westview Press: Boulder, CO.

Chambers, R. and G. Conway (1992) "Sustainable Rural Livelihoods: Practical Concepts for the 21st Century." Discussion Paper. 220. IDS-University of Sussex: Brighton.

Cox, T.S., C. Picone, and W. Jackson (2004) "Research Priorities in Natural Systems Agriculture." *Journal of Crop Improvement* 12(1-2): 511–531.

FAO (1996) "Rome Declaration on World Food Security." FAO World Food Summit. 13–17 November. Food & Agriculture Organization of the United Nations (FAO): Rome.

FAO, WFP and IFAD (2012) "The State of Food Insecurity in the World: Economic Growth Is Necessary but Not Sufficient to Accelerate Reduction of Hunger and Malnutrition." FAO: Rome.

Freidberg, S. (2009) *Fresh: A Perishable History.* Cambridge, MA: Belknap Press of Harvard University Press.

Gliessman, S.R. (Ed.) (1990) "Agroecology: Researching the Ecological Basis for Sustainable Agriculture." *Ecological Series.* Springer-Verlag: 78. New York.

Gliessman, S.R. (2007) *Agroecology: The Ecology of Sustainable Food Systems.* CRC Press/Taylor & Francis: Boca Raton, FL.

Guzmán-Casado, G., M. González de Molina, and E. Sevilla-Guzmán (1999) *Introducción a la agroecología como desarrollo rural sostenible.* Ediciones Mundi-Prensa: Madrid.

Hecht, S.B. (1995) "The Evolution of Agroecological Thought." In M.A. Altieri (Ed.) *Agroecology: The Science of Sustainable Agriculture.* Westview Press: Boulder, pp. 1–20.

Heller, M.C. and G.A. Keoleian (2003) "Assessing the Sustainability of the US Food System: A Life Cycle Perspective." *Agricultural Systems* 76(3): 1007–1041.

Magdoff, F. (2007) "Ecological Agriculture: Principles, Practices, and Constraints." *Renewable Agriculture and Food Systems* 22(02): 109–117.

McNeely, J.A. and S.J. Scherr (2002) *Ecoagriculture: Strategies to Feed the World and Save Wild Biodiversity.* Island Press: Washington, D.C.

Méndez, V.E. (2010) "Agroecology." In B. Warf (Ed.) *Encyclopedia of Geography.* Sage Publications: Thousand Oaks, CA, pp. 55–59

Méndez, V.E., C.M. Bacon, and R. Cohen (2013) "Agroecology as a Transdisciplinary, Participatory, and Action-Oriented Approach." *Agroecology and Sustainable Food Systems* 37(1): 3–18.

Mollison, B. and R.M. Slay (1997) *An Introduction to Permaculture.* Tagari Publications: Sisters Creek, Australia.

Patel, R. (2009) "Food Sovereignty." *Journal of Peasant Studies* 36(3): 663–673.

Pimbert, M.P., J. Thompson, W.T. Vorley, T. Fox, N. Kanji, and C. Tacoli (2001) "Global Restructuring, Agri-Food Systems and Livelihoods." Gatekeeper Series 100. International Institute for Environment and Development (IIED): London.

Pinstrup-Andersen, P. (2009) "Food Security: Definition and Measurement." *Food Security* 1: 5–7.

Singh, N. and J. Gilman (1999) "Making Livelihoods More Sustainable." *International Social Science Journal*/UNESCO 51.

Wezel, A., S. Bellon, T. Dore, C. Francis, D. Vallod, and C. David (2009) "Agroecology as a Science, a Movement and a Practice: A Review." *Agronomy for Sustainable Development* 29(4): 503–515.

Willer, H. and L. Kilcher (Eds.) (2010) "The World of Organic Agriculture: Statistics and Trends." IFOAM and FiBL. Bonn and Frick.

Wittman, H., A. Desmarais, and N. Wiebe (Eds.) (2010) *Food Sovereignty: Reconnecting Food, Nature and Community*. Fernwood Publishing: Halifax; Winnipeg/Food First Books: Oakland, CA/Pambazuka Press: Oxford.

Section Four
Energy and Environmental Justice

INTRODUCTION TO ENERGY PRODUCTION AND ENERGY POLITICS

renewable energy	hydropower	**KEY TERMS**
fossil fuels	greenhouse gas (ghg)	
energy poverty	emissions	
natural resource endowments	virgin biofuels	

Today's most pressing global energy issues include the depletion of easily accessible hydrocarbons (oil, natural gas, coal), and air pollution and climate change resulting from energy use. To continue to meet demand for heating and transportation fuels, energy firms are investing in more costly and environmentally damaging extraction techniques (Klare 2012). In recent years, extraction techniques with significant environmental and social impacts, including hydraulic fracturing or "fracking" for gas deposits and extracting oil from tar sands, have become more prevalent, spurring major debate on environmental justice in the United States, Canada, France, South Africa, and other countries. This section provides a brief introduction to key international energy issues, highlighting the inherent environmental, economic, and social tradeoffs of different energy sources. While many environmentalists consider **renewable energy** sources to be preferable to fossil fuels, both from the standpoint of resource extraction and pollution emissions, this section demonstrates that even renewable energy generation negatively impacts ecosystems and human populations. We hope to encourage deeper thought on the complex considerations and implications of different energy sources so that readers are better able to understand the real dilemmas involved in energy production and energy policy.

Renewable Energy includes energy derived from natural resources that are continually replenished, including solar, water, wind, and geothermal power.

Major global energy sources include oil, natural gas, coal, biofuels, wind, solar energy, hydropower, and nuclear energy. Of these, **fossil fuels** account for the majority of world energy supply and are projected to continue to supply nearly 80% of global energy through the next several decades (EIA 2013). Despite continued growth in renewable energy installations in many regions, renewable energy is likely to remain a small percentage of global energy production in the near future. In many developing countries, biomass including wood, animal dung, and charcoal is the primary energy source, particularly in rural areas where refined fuels are more difficult or expensive to access. Worldwide 1.3 billion people, 95% of whom are located in sub-Saharan Africa or Asia (IEA 2012), do not have access to electricity and basic energy applications such as household lighting and refrigeration. Such **energy poverty** is often associated with economic poverty and rural regions, but the urban poor also face high per-kilowatt energy costs and in some cases turn to "theft" and other means of acquiring energy. Lack of access to affordable energy is a major inhibitor to individual and broader economic development goals.

Fossil Fuels, also called hydrocarbons for their carbon content, are combustible materials derived from geologic deposits of organic matter. Fossil fuels include coal, oil, and natural gas.

Energy Poverty refers to a lack of access to modern energy services, including electricity and clean cooking fuels.

Energy Politics

Energy policies in different countries differ dramatically, based on unique **natural resource endowments**, social and cultural factors, and varying degrees of commitment to environmental issues. Government policies determining which energy sources to support with research and development funds and subsidies reflect considerable economic, environmental, and social tradeoffs. Every energy source comes with costs and risks, from extraction techniques such as mountaintop removal coal mining, to the radiation exposure risks of nuclear power plant accidents, or the displacement of human and animal populations for

Natural Resource Endowments include the natural resources available to people, including renewable resources such as sun and wind and non-renewable fossil fuel resources (in this context, natural resources available for energy production).

Hydropower entails damming rivers to harness water flows for electric power production for human use. Hydropower projects may be very small-scale ("micro-hydropower"), sometimes used to generate electricity in rural developing country settings where river power can be harnessed, or massive scale ("mega-hydropower"). Mega-power installations with capacity greater than 10 gigawatts include China's Three Gorges Dam, the Itaipu Dam across the Brazil/Paraguay border, and Venezuela's Guri Dam.

large-scale **hydropower** installations. Policymakers face challenges in developing an energy portfolio that meets energy demands while minimizing negative environmental and social impacts. Another priority reflected in energy policy is the diversification of energy sources in order to maintain a secure and affordable energy supply with domestically available sources of energy. Specific laws or policies are only a very narrow part of the broader *politics* of who has the right or opportunity to influence or decide where and how to source energy from local to global trade contexts.

Renewable Energy

A variety of factors influence government support for renewable energy, including economic motives, endowment of renewable resources, and political and cultural factors (Gallagher 2013). One of the most important environmental considerations related to energy is the quantity of **greenhouse gas (GHG) emissions** produced by different energy sources. Environmentalists and policymakers whose primary concern is climate change mitigation may promote renewable sources of energy as a means to reduce GHG emissions. However, renewable energy is not a panacea for meeting all energy needs across diverse geographies or for combating climate change. In terms of renewable energy endowments, only certain regions have sufficient and reliable solar radiation or wind to meet local or regional electricity demands. Despite the attractiveness of renewable energy from an environmental perspective—carbon-free electricity generation without long-term waste production—renewable energy faces challenges, including public resistance. For example, wind power projects have met with significant resistance, often for their effect on reshaping the landscape, including in Scotland, China, the United States, and Mexico (Pasqualetti 2011). Large-scale hydropower projects also produce significant social and environmental impacts (discussed in Barrington et al. 2012, this chapter, and Scudder 2005).

Though nuclear power generation produces little to no greenhouse gas emissions, it has long been contentious due to safety and security concerns and the lack of long-term storage

Greenhouse Gas (GHG) Emissions refers to the release of gases that trap and re-radiate heat in the atmosphere, including carbon dioxide, methane, nitrous oxide, and fluorinated gases (e.g., hydrofluorocarbons). Today's levels of GHG emissions are unprecedented, resulting from anthropogenic (human-caused) activities including industrial processes, energy generation, vehicle transportation, and agriculture.

options for spent fuel. Japan's Fukushima nuclear accident in 2011 and the Chernobyl accident in 1986 in Ukraine (then part of the Soviet Union), cast doubts on the safety of nuclear power for human and environmental health. Some countries, such as Austria, Denmark, and Ireland, are committed to national energy strategies that do not include nuclear power. The United States, France, Japan, and Russia, on the other hand, include nuclear power in their electricity-generating portfolios in order to address climate change, declining stocks of fossil fuels, and domestic energy security (McDonald 2008). Biofuels too have been promoted as a renewable, environmentally preferable transportation fuel. However, the production of **virgin biofuels** on farmland (e.g., corn ethanol in the United States or sugar ethanol in Mozambique) diverts substantial agricultural land and water resources away from food production, and may require synthetic fertilizer inputs (derived from fossil fuels) and result in agrochemical runoff. The net energy value of ethanol depends on the crop source (e.g., corn, sugarcane, switchgrass) and the specific production system (Shapouri et al. 2002). In addition, the amount of greenhouse gases displaced by ethanol versus oil is negligible if land is converted from rainforest or grass-land in order to grow biofuel crops (Fargione et al. 2008). A number of countries including Austria, Finland, Sweden, and India have addressed some of these environmental challenges by obtaining substantial renewable energy capacity from agricultural and forestry wastes rather than virgin biomass grown for energy production (Yee 2013).

Virgin Biofuels are liquid fuels produced from crops grown specifically for the purpose of fuel production, as opposed to biofuels produced from waste products such as agricultural crop residues or used vegetable oil.

China and Energy

Any discussion of global-scale comparative energy consumption, including its environmental impacts and socio-economic implications, must address the importance of China. China surpassed the United States for total greenhouse gas emissions in 2006 and total energy consumption in 2009, resulting in part from rapid industrialization (EIA 2012). China now rivals the entire rest of the world combined in its coal consumption, having more than doubled coal use in one decade from 2000 to 2010 (EIA 2013). Coal burning to fuel China's industrial sector is considered the leading cause of choking smog in Chinese cities; in 2010, outdoor air pollution led to 1.2 million premature deaths in China (Wong 2013). In recent years, the Chinese government pledged to reduce air pollution and carbon emissions by promoting energy efficiency and increasing renewable energy installations, including large-scale wind, hydro, and nuclear power (Qiu 2011).

One of China's most notable renewable energy projects is the Three Gorges Dam. Fully operational since 2012, Three Gorges is now the world's largest hydropower installation, producing the energy equivalent of burning 50 million tons of coal per year (Cleveland 2013). Construction of the Three Gorges Dam was highly contentious. The dam displaced 1.2 million people, flooded 1000 archaeological and cultural sites, and threatened dolphin, porpoise, sturgeon, and crane habitat. Despite China's research and funding for large renewable energy installations, the environmental impacts of energy use will remain significant due to China's massive industrial sector and the increasing energy demands of the country's growing middle class.

Energy and Environmental Justice

Rather than focus this energy chapter on the ecological impacts of energy production and consumption[1], we highlight the importance of a social, cultural, and political approach to global energy issues. Energy corporations and national governments far too often overlook important considerations of how people will be affected by the construction and operation of energy facilities, particularly for populations with limited political influence. One important tradeoff with different energy sources is identifying who will be affected by the extraction of fossil fuels, the placement of power plants, and the emission of pollutants. Recognizing the winners and losers and determining appropriate compensation or reparations for affected populations is important in terms of social and environmental justice. The section on environmental justice that follows (Claudio 2007) demonstrates how the environmental justice approach can apply to a variety of environmental problems. Common examples of environmental justice cases include conflicts over oil, natural gas, and mineral extraction by multinational corporations, and the siting of waste facilities or large-scale energy production facilities (including coal and nuclear power plants, and hydropower as discussed in the Barrington et al. 2012 case study). Many of these environmental justice cases exemplify environmental health issues that place a heavier burden on disadvantaged populations, including indigenous people, ethnic and racial minorities, women, children, and the poor.

The case study that follows (Barrington et al. 2012) highlights the complex impacts of large-scale hydropower projects, including human displacement and threats to food security. The authors approach hydropower from an engineering perspective, focusing on the impacts of the construction of large dams and the responsibilities of engineers to consider the long-term effects of dams on humans and the environment. The case shows the importance of the Mekong River to food security in Southeast Asia—for both rice farming and fishing—and the article discusses the social and ecological impacts of damming the river. Included is the commitment to environmental and social justice and the recommendation that communities affected by hydropower projects be consulted in project planning and considered in the long-term effects of the project. The case touches on important themes within transboundary environmental resource conflicts, including key ecosystem goods and services of water, food, energy, and socio-cultural significance.

---

1   See Cleveland and Morris 2013 for a thorough analysis of the environmental impacts of different energy sources.

HIGHLIGHTED APPROACH: ENVIRONMENTAL JUSTICE

Standing on Principle

The Global Push for Environmental Justice

By Luz Claudio

C limate change, acid rain, depletion of the ozone layer, species extinction—all of these issues point to one thing: environmental health is a global issue that concerns all nations of the world. Now add environmental justice to the list. From South Bronx to Soweto, from Penang to El Paso, communities all over the world are finding commonality in their experiences and goals in seeking environmental justice.

Environmental justice was defined by Robert Bullard, director of the Environmental Justice Resource Center at Clark Atlanta University, in his seminal 1990 work *Dumping in Dixie: Race, Class, and Environmental Quality* as "the principle that all people and communities are entitled to equal protection of environmental and public health laws and regulations." In countries around the world, the concept of environmental justice can apply to communities where those at a perceived disadvantage—whether due to their race, ethnicity, socioeconomic status, immigration status, lack of land ownership, geographic isolation, formal education, occupational characteristics, political power, gender, or other characteristics—puts them at disproportionate risk for being exposed to environmental hazards. At a global scale, environmental justice can also be applied to scenarios such as industrialized countries exporting their wastes to developing nations.

In either case, "environmental and human rights have no boundaries, because pollution has no boundaries," says Heeten Kalan, senior program officer of the Global Environmental

Health and Justice Fund of the New World Foundation in New York City. "Environmental justice organizations are starting to understand that they are working in a global context."

Global Awareness

The history of international efforts in environmental justice parallels the series of agreements and conventions held around the globe to address environmental issues. Bullard recounts that during the 1992 Earth Summit in Rio de Janeiro, Brazil, there was not much official discussion about environmental justice in the context of human health. "Most of the official discussion centered around saving the Amazon and other ecosystems. Human health and urban centers were not considered part of the 'environment,'" he says.

However, Bullard and other U.S. environmental justice leaders had already met in Washington, DC, at the First National People of Color Environmental Leadership Summit a year earlier, where they drafted the *Principles of Environmental Justice*, a document to guide grassroots organizing. "When we went to Rio in 1992 we found that some groups had translated the *Principles* into Portuguese and were circulating the document to local community leaders at the summit," remembers Bullard.

Ten years later, during the World Summit on Sustainable Development held in Johannesburg, South Africa, the issue of environmental inequity was formally recognized by the leadership of the summit. "By the time we went to Johannesburg, environmental justice had really caught on across borders as part of the whole idea of sustainable development," says Bullard. Just two years earlier, the eight UN Millennium Development Goals that resulted from the UN Millennium Summit held in New York City had encompassed environmental sustainability as a goal that would require a reduction in inequality.

International organization around environmental justice issues takes several different forms. Broad networks of community-based organizations can work on different issues affecting the disenfranchised and come together on matters related to the environment. Other groups may organize a particular labor sector to improve worker health. On an international scale, community-based groups in different countries who find themselves fighting similar environmental problems can unite in order to synergize their efforts.

"The issue of globalization is one of common concern to the environmental justice movement in many developing countries," says Michelle DePass, program officer of the Environmental Justice and Healthy Communities Program at the Ford Foundation. Concerns about globalization can bring together a wide range of stakeholders including workers, academics, and community leaders for whom increased industrial development is a common denominator.

Into Action

The Brazilian Network on Environmental Justice is an example of how groups can come together to address common concerns. This network brings together about 100 varied organizations including unions, academic centers, associations, ethics groups, community-based organizations of indigenous peoples, and descendants of enslaved Africans brought to Brazil, all with the common goal of improving the conditions for vulnerable populations in that nation.

Utilizing the *Principles of Environmental Justice*, the Brazilian network serves as a forum for debate, strategic planning, and mobilization by organizations and affected populations. Network meetings include members from other South American countries with common interests.

Marcelo Firpo, a network organizer and senior researcher at the Oswaldo Cruz Foundation in Rio de Janeiro, sees that what unites these varied organizations is their concern for issues of human rights and the effects of globalization on health and the environment. He offers the example of Petrobras, a Brazilian oil company that has become a major player in the global market. Because the current government in Brazil does not permit oil exploration in the Amazonian native reservations, Petrobras has begun exploration in Ecuador, where there are no such restrictions. "This kind of situation necessitates international collaboration," says Firpo.

Throughout the world, disadvantaged communities typically suffer the highest burdens of environmental degradation. One group that is often threatened by environmental hazards in developed and developing countries alike is rural farmworkers. These workers often suffer from the effects of disproportionate exposure to pesticides and other chemical agents as well as lack of access to health and education services, among other hindrances.

In Brazil, for example, 10% of the urban population over 5 years of age is illiterate whereas in the rural population this rate is as high as 30%, according to Frederico Peres, a researcher at the Center for Workers' Health and Human Ecology at the Oswaldo Cruz Foundation. So workers often cannot understand the written technical information about pesticides provided by chemical manufacturers. Protective gear is often ineffective or nonexistent, and government protections regulating use and disposal of pesticides may not be consistently applied to these vulnerable populations.

Peres has mobilized farmworkers and created educational materials on the safe use of pesticides that do not require literacy to be understood by the workers. In conducting this work, Peres connected with similar organizations in Mexico, Chile, Ecuador, Panama, and Argentina and observed that comparable situations take place in these countries. "The problems are the same: illiteracy, lack of government support, the strong influence of chemical industries to promote pesticide use—all of these are the same throughout Latin America," says Peres.

Farmworkers in South Africa face similar situations as those in Brazil. Labor conditions on South African farms are among the poorest of all employment sectors in that country, and until recently farm work was effectively unregulated. Similar to Brazil for Latin America, South Africa is the largest importer of pesticides in sub-Saharan Africa, so pesticide exposure is a significant hazard for South African farmworkers. Leslie London, a professor of public health at the University of Cape Town, has collaborated with South African farmworkers for many years to address their environmental justice concerns. But as he noted in the January/March 2003 issue of the *International Journal of Occupational and Environmental Health*, "The legacy of apartheid for the health and the dignity of farm workers has proved to be so deep-rooted that efforts towards redress in the new democracy have had only limited success. ... [I]t is the underlying powerlessness of farm workers that is both at the root of violations of farm workers' human rights and also responsible for the substantial burden of mortality and morbidity suffered by farm workers and their families."

Going International

Upon interacting with each other, some organizations in the environmental justice movement across the globe are discovering that although each case has its own particular circumstances, there are many common experiences that can inform each other's struggles for environmental justice. For example, members of the Farmworker Association of Florida have been exchanging visits with citrus farmers in Brazil to trade ideas on how to address environmental justice issues. They found that some of their local circumstances were different, primarily the fact that in the United States most of the farmworkers are immigrants, whereas in Brazil they are mostly nationals. "This makes a huge difference since in Brazil [workers] have the right to unionize to seek better working conditions," says Tirso Moreno, general coordinator of the Farmworker Association of Florida.

Yet, during these exchanges, the workers from both countries discovered that they had been facing similar working conditions established by the same multinational agrobusiness companies. "Some of the information that we had [was of use to] the Brazilians and vice versa because many of these multinational companies are the same ones with different names," says Moreno. "That is why there is a lot more interest in collaborating internationally. While the details may be different in each country, the struggles are the same."

Organizations like Via Campesina, an international organization of small and medium-sized agricultural producers based in Indonesia with members in 56 countries, aim to organize farm workers throughout the world who are affected by similar issues. Jose Adilson de Medeiros, president of the São Lourenço [Brazil] Rural Producers Association, says of these groups, "If [other environmental justice groups] know how to solve a problem, they can tell us how they did it. We learn from each other's mistakes so we don't have to make a mistake again to get there."

Another issue-based environmental justice network is the Global Alliance for Incinerator Alternatives (GAIA). This organization, headquartered in the Philippines, aims to coordinate efforts to reduce waste and stop incineration around the world with a particular focus on representing disadvantaged communities in both developed and developing countries.

With members from 77 countries and expanding, GAIA can mobilize quickly and globally to take coordinated actions. Its approach includes sharing information electronically, coordinating regional meetings, developing joint strategies for community organizing, and hosting international training sessions where skills can be shared. One effective strategy the group has used is letter-writing campaigns that include signatories representing organizations from many countries. GAIA is current mobilizing Asian members in opposition to an effort by the Japanese government to enter into bilateral agreements allowing the export of waste for burning in less-developed countries in the region.

Another approach taken by the environmental justice movement is to address the international bodies that support projects that may affect disadvantaged populations. For example, GAIA has launched a campaign to stop the World Bank from funding incinerators around the world. To achieve this goal, GAIA locates expert researchers who can share needed information on the health effects of incineration with members near the proposed incinerator where the information may not be readily available. They also facilitate linkages between members who may be campaigning against similar technologies or against the same incinerator vendor. In this way, environmental justice organizations can share strategies and information quickly and effectively.

The flow of information is highly bidirectional in the international environmental justice movement, providing models for both North-to-South as well as South-to-North exchange. For example, community-based organizations in the Philippines, where the government passed a national ban on incineration in 1999, are able to share with others around the world how they were able to achieve this in their country. And in Kenya, lawyers are required to train in environmental law through continuing education programs such as those managed by the Institute for Law and Environmental Governance (ILEG). "In the United States, we can learn a lot from organizations like ILEG," says DePass, who is herself an environmental lawyer who will be leading a delegation of U.S. lawyers to visit ILEG for consultation on environmental justice strategies.

A Common Cause

Increasingly, due to globalization and the advance of multinational corporations, communities around the world find they are fighting the same battles. One such example began in Diamond, a black community in Norco, Louisiana, which is home to 130 petrochemical facilities, incinerators, and landfills in what is known by some as the Chemical Corridor and by others as Cancer Alley. There, a local school teacher named Margie Richard and other neighbors founded Concerned Citizens of Norco in 1990 and began demanding that Shell Corporation, the owner of the nearby petrochemical facilities, take responsibility for its pollution by relocating affected residents to a cleaner area.

To achieve this, the group engaged in highly visible campaigns at the state, national, and international levels, culminating with Richard's presentation in 2001 at the international headquarters of Royal/Dutch Shell in the Netherlands. Shell agreed to relocate those in the community who wished to leave the area and to reduce its emissions by 30%. This unprecedented victory won Richard the 2004 Goldman Environmental Prize (considered the Nobel Prize for environmental activism). With this increased visibility and recognition, Richard began traveling abroad to talk about the environmental justice movement and likening this experience to the wider issue of international human rights.

Communities in other parts of the world are now utilizing tactics similar to those used by Concerned Citizens of Norco. For example, Desmond D'Sa, a resident of South Durban, South Africa, and chairperson of the South Durban Community Environmental Alliance, has engaged the leadership of Shell Corporation directly to deal with environmental issues similar to those in Norco. Other communities in Texas, the Philippines, Nigeria, Brazil, Curaçao, and Russia have brought similar complaints to Shell's annual General Meetings.

Friends of the Earth International, described as the world's largest grassroots environmental network with 70 national member groups and approximately 5,000 local activist groups, serves as an umbrella organization under which many of the communities organizing for environmental justice can find common ground for action. In a 2003 report titled *Behind the Shine*, Tony Juniper, executive director of Friends of the Earth in the UK, states that shareholders and investors in large corporations have rights established in law through which they can hold companies accountable; however, this cannot be said for the people who live next door to polluting facilities. Joining forces therefore helps these communities have their voices heard at the corporate table.

In recent months, attention has been focused on environmental justice issues within Europe, where poor and ethnically marginalized peoples in Central and Eastern Europe often face harsh environmental health conditions. "With the recent enlargement of the European Union to include countries of Central and Eastern Europe, the need for environmental justice across a more stratified society, especially as it relates to the promotion of human health, is increasingly evident," says Diana Smith, director of communications at the Health and Environment Alliance (HEAL), headquartered in Brussels. The alliance mainly addresses environmental justice within the context of the 1998 Aarhus Convention, which specifically links environmental rights and human rights.

HEAL and its member organization, the Centre for Environmental Policy and Law, produced the groundbreaking August 2007 report *Making the Case for Environmental Justice in Central and Eastern Europe* to raise awareness and advocate policy action against the deleterious environmental and human health conditions of poor and otherwise marginalized groups in Central and Eastern Europe. The report cites the case of a displaced persons camp sited near a mine complex in Northern Mitrovica, Kosovo. A 2005 WHO study visit to the camp showed that 88% of the children aged 6 years and younger had lead poisoning severe enough to require immediate medical intervention.

The global push for environmental justice can only be expected to grow—and the time for action is ripe. As Bullard summarizes, "if you live on the wrong side of the tracks and you are denied a good environment, then you need environmental justice. It is the same struggle everywhere."

CASE STUDY
Social and Environmental Justice for Communities of the Mekong River

By Dani J. Barrington, Stephen Dobbs, and Daniel I. Loden

Introduction

The Mekong River is the twelfth longest waterway in the world, stretching to well over 4000 kilometres in length (Jacobs, 2002). It begins its course in the high reaches of eastern Tibet before winding its way through the modern Southeast Asian states of Myanmar, Laos, Thailand, Cambodia and Vietnam. For a little less than half its total length, the Mekong runs through China's southern province of Yunnan and is known as the Lancang River (Figure 1).

The waters of the Mekong sustain a population of more than 70 million people (which is expected to keep growing) who are heavily dependent on the river for their livelihoods in fishing and agriculture (Jacobs, 2002). The river is the basin's main source of protein and sustenance through these occupations. Historically, it has sustained people and cultures of great diversity, as well as having provided the hydrological basis for some of the world's most impressive civilizational undertakings, such as the great Cambodian empire founded at Angkor near modern day Siem Reap. The Mekong and its environs are undergoing rapid change and transformation, as the modern nation states through which it courses look to it as a national resource to be exploited. The Mekong Basin is one of Southeast Asia's most contested political, social and environmental arenas. Whist there are many issues relating to various development projects that are cause for concern, the damming of the river to

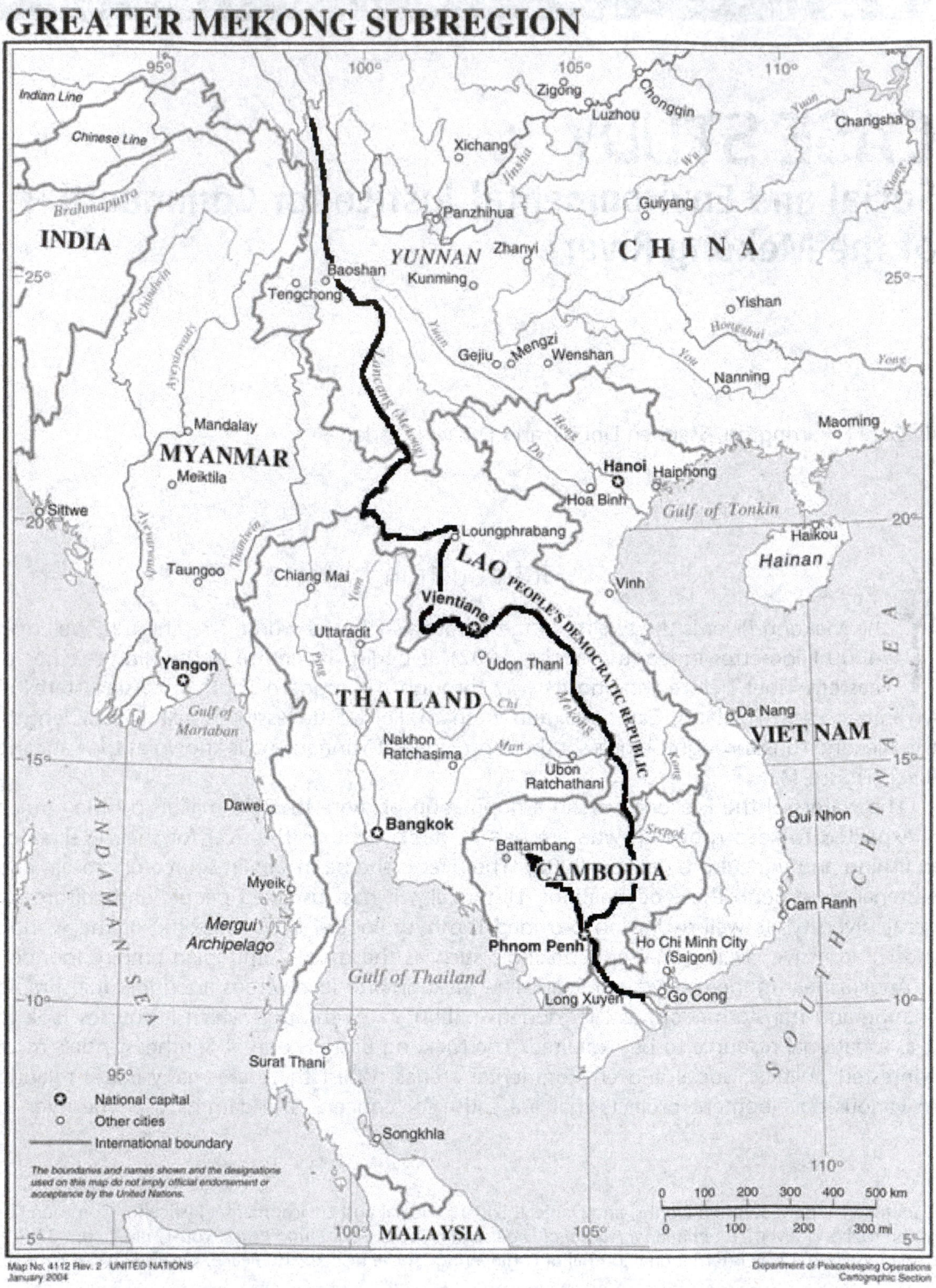

GREATER MEKONG SUBREGION

Figure 1: Map of South East Asia showing the route of the Mekong River (United Nations Department of Peacekeeping Operations Cartographic Section, 2004).

harness its potential as a source of hydroelectricity looms as a major threat to the riparian communities of the Mekong. Communities who are often already "impoverished" are further threatened by decisions about "large scale transformations designed and decided in other spheres, often without their knowledge" (Molle, Foran, & Kakonen, 2010, p. 2). Broadly speaking, the building of dams threatens domestic stability through displacement of people and loss of livelihoods, and threatens regional political stability as development projects in one national jurisdiction impact on neighbouring national jurisdictions.

The purpose of this paper is to explain the role that engineers can play in supporting social and environmental justice for the communities of the Mekong River system. The paper starts by discussing a theoretical framework the authors believe can be utilised for understanding what they mean by social and environmental justice in the context of the culturally, politically and ecologically sensitive Mekong Basin. This is followed by a short history of the Mekong River, highlighting its life- and culture-supporting roles within the societies and communities of the region. Due to the significance of the river to riparian communities, the paper explores the impacts of dams on natural resource management and the mechanisms which exist to protect the rights of traditionally under-represented groups. The impact of existing dams on the Mekong River is outlined focusing on the social justice impacts of their construction. The role of engineers in conceptualisation, design and delivery of large-scale dam projects is then explored to highlight the role that these individuals and the engineering profession can play in helping to ensure social justice for the developing communities of the Mekong River system, as well as the tools available to support this work. The paper concludes by outlining the role that engineers and organisations need to play in the future to ensure social and environmental justice for communities along the Mekong River.

This paper highlights the complexity of issues involved with major engineering projects such as dam building in a region of such social, cultural, economic and political diversity. In contextualising the impacts of dam building along the Mekong within a discourse of social and environmental justice, the authors are aware of the multiple meanings and vagaries such terms conjure up. Both are, as Nussbaum stresses for social justice, "profoundly normative" concepts (Nussbaum, 2003), heavily dependent on the context and background of the user. The starting position of the authors is that "social and environmental justice" needs to be viewed as intertwined with other elements of basic human rights as set out in the Universal Declaration of Human Rights (United Nations, 1948). While there are staunch debates about whether or not the framework for international human rights is too closely aligned with western liberalism and its focus on the rights of the individual over the group, a concern that has been taken up by academics and other critics, particularly from the Asian region, the authors feel a rights-based approach is appropriate for establishing a framework for assessing the impacts of large hydraulic projects and the role of engineers in the Mekong region. Whilst recognising a degree of genuine concern by some observers in the critique of human rights discourse, most states have "explicitly endorsed" the rights encapsulated by the Universal Declaration whether or not in practice they adhere to them (Donnelly, 2006). Arguments against a rights-based approach to issues of national interest in the Asian region by states are often what Donnelly has called "weak based relativism" which attempts to provide an "antiquarian" justification for modern abuses (Donnelly, 2006).

Environmental and Social Justice and the Rights-Based Approach

Environmental and social rights or justice, in the view of the authors, can clearly be framed within the broader context of human rights discourse, as Adeola (2000, p. 689) notes, "because human rights involve the assurance of people's means of livelihood, any threats to the environmental bases of livelihood could be considered a violation of basic human rights". It also seems to the authors that the links between social and environmental justice and human rights are often specific and immediate as in many developing regions of the world "environmental injustice and human rights violations are inextricably interwoven" as states appropriate the resources of minority groups, ethno classes and people of lower socio-economic status in the name of economic and national development (Adeola, 2000, p. 687). In almost all the hydraulic projects in the Mekong Basin, it is more marginalised groups who will feel the immediate social, cultural and economic impacts. Within the context of Southeast Asia, it is also worth noting that despite a long period of rapid economic growth and industrialisation in almost all countries along the Mekong, a majority of people "live in rural areas and depend in greater or lesser degree for their livelihood on their immediate physical environment … any encroachment on forest, land, and water resources on which people depend is also a claim on their sustenance, hence the inseparability of social impact and environmental degradation" (Hirsch, 1998, p. 56).

China, as a staunch opponent of any rights-based criticisms of its policies and a major player in terms of the future of the Mekong River, is increasingly being forced to deal with the negative environmental consequences of its rapid development (see for example Economy, 2005; Smil, 2004). The authors believe these consequences are forcing China to acknowledge the rights of minority and community groups affected by development. Recent state rhetoric suggests that within official communist party circles there is a growing recognition of the need for new approaches to economic development which factor in environmental and social/cultural elements. McLaren (2011) suggests that Hu Jintao's call in 2007 for an "ecological civilization" followed up by discussion of "scientific development" rather than "economic construction" was tied to the growing "plurality discourses" on the environment in China, and official recognition that development at any cost is unsustainable. McLaren also notes that within the context of China there is seen to be a close relationship between culture and the "eco-site" that nurtured it, thus a growing concern about the "sustainability of China's unique 'ecological civilization'" (2011, p. 431) as the environment is degraded. Not inconsequentially for this paper, McLaren highlights the importance of the Southeast Asian massif (which includes much of the Mekong Basin area) with regard to these dual concerns with "bio and cultural diversity" (2011). Hence, the authors hold the view that whilst refraining from discussing these issues in a discourse of rights, even the Chinese state is acknowledging the rights of ethnic and other communities to greater participation and determination of their futures.

Engineers are not neutral bystanders in these political, economic and environmental struggles but rather—such as with damming projects along the Mekong—active players. Whether they recognise it or not, the decisions they make with respect to projects they work on means they are political players and complicit in outcomes that lead to the curtailment or infringement of affected people's rights. This paper accepts the proposition put forward by Riley that the Marxian concept of *praxis* "is at the heart of what engineering and social justice must be about" (Riley, 2008, p. 108). To achieve what Rawls has termed "justice as fairness" (Rawls & Kelly, 2001), in the context of Mekong projects *praxis* means that local communities and engineers should be fully and meaningfully involved in the processes that lead to decisions being made on whether or not particular developments proceed. Similarly, mechanisms need to be in place to ensure that parties adversely affected by projects such as dams are appropriately and adequately compensated for social, cultural and economic dislocation where this cannot be avoided. It is the view of this paper that engineers and companies involved in major projects such as dam construction (often these are large foreign commercial interests) should be active in ensuring that they not only meet high technical standards but also high standards in public consultation and social/environmental impact assessment. Individually, the authors would argue, *praxis* can enable engineers to play a crucial role in ensuring just social and environmental outcomes—whether through application of their technical skills or through withdrawal of these same skills and expertise. The lessons that might be learned from the hydroelectric development schemes in this politically, culturally, demographically and economically complex region have potentially universal applicability.

Historical Setting

The rich and diverse waters of the Mekong have historically made possible the establishment of communities and polities of immense size and complexity. One of the earliest such kingdoms, Funan, located on the eastern side of the Gulf of Thailand, was chronicled by Chinese emissaries. According to the Chinese accounts, Funan was a major port where silk and various sorts of highly valued resins, aromatic woods and other produce of the Southeast Asian region found their way into the lucrative east/west trade system (Shaffer, 1996). The waters of the Mekong and fertile delta supported the development and population of this kingdom (Vickery, 1998) as well as a large number of traders and visitors who would sometimes have to spend months there waiting on the change of monsoon to begin their outward voyages (Hall, 1992). Whilst knowledge of this early Mekong-based kingdom is scant, another great Cambodian kingdom of the Mekong, Angkor, has numerous monuments to its greatness. The Angkorian period from the ninth to fifteenth century witnessed the flourishing of an empire that extended its reach into the modern states of Vietnam, Laos and Thailand.

Perhaps most remarkable was the extent of the population that lived at Angkor. At its centre it supported in excess of one million people (Osborne, 2000a). It is in this respect that the Mekong was so important to this great civilizational achievement. Water was crucial to the Angkorian kingdom, as it provided the ability to farm rice and harvest protein rich fish. Angkor was located near the northeastern shore of Southeast Asia's largest fresh water lake, Tonle Sap, and it was the Mekong that sustained the great lake then as it does now. During the monsoon season, the Mekong forces water to rush up its tributary, the Tonle Sap River, into the lake, and the water retreats as rainfall decreases (Keay, 2005). The great Tonle Sap only exists as a consequence of these annual reverse flows, and its role as the major source of protein in Cambodia hinges critically on this natural annual cycle. The quantity of fish supported in this ecosystem makes the lake one of the world's biggest freshwater fisheries (Keay, 2005), a role that marked its importance to both Angkor and the modern Cambodian state. Chou Ta-kuan, a Chinese envoy, who visited Angkor for a period of more than a year, arriving in April 1296, has provided the only contemporary eyewitness account of the role of water flows into and out of Tonle Sap in Angkorian agriculture. According to his account, three rice crops were grown each year by following a natural irrigation pattern based on the rise and fall of the great lake as governed by the flow of the Mekong River (Osborne, 2000a). As the lake rose and fell by as much as twelve metres, Chou's account describes Angkoreans moving with the water to plant their rice crops (Osborne, 2000a). Historically this Mekong based ecosystem has sustained a vast wealth of ecological diversity and great cultural achievements, and its ability to nurture this diversity has outlasted these earlier human political, social and economic constructions. The system now faces new and arguably much greater forces

Figure 2: Map showing approximate location of dams discussed in paper. (O) Indicates dams already operational.

of human intervention where for the first time the entire ecology of the Mekong, its environs and those people whose lives depend on it are at risk.

The Mekong Dams and Resource Management

The building of large dams, as noted by Hirsch, has resulted in "environmental degradation and marginalization of affected people as a general, if not universal, experience" (1998, p. 56). Dam building along the Mekong has occurred since the 1980s, with China leading the way. The Mekong begins its long meander to the coast from the Tibetan Plateau as the Lancang River. Currently China has four hydroelectric dams operating along this reach of the river. Three of these dams, the Jinghong, Manwan and Dachaoshan, have a generating capacity of 4,350 MW each. The most recently operational dam Xiaoman is the second largest hydroelectric dam in China with a capacity of 4,200 MW (Osborne, 2009). An even larger capacity dam, the Nuozhado (5,850 MW), is currently being constructed (Chinese National Committee on Large Dams, 2011). As China continues to push ahead with its program of economic transformation, a further three dams are proposed by 2030 (Osborne, 2011), the Gongguoqiao, Ganlanba and Mengsong dams, which when complete will bring the total number of dams along the Lancang to eight (Figure 2).

Many analysts have growing concerns about the impact of these dams on communities and states along the water course, with long time Mekong watcher Milton Osborne noting "it may be some years before the full effects of China's dams are apparent, there is no doubt many will be negative" (Osborne, 2011). Concerns have been exacerbated by plans by some Mekong riparian states to build even more dams along the main body of the river, the impacts of which Osborne notes will be almost "immediate and dangerous" (Osborne, 2011). Whilst many such plans have been discussed and examined over the past half century, there has been little action until recently, with the Laos government (as of 2011) proceeding with plans to build a 1,260 MW hydroelectric dam at Xayaburi despite the protestations of Cambodia and Vietnam (Vietnam Business and Economy News, 2011). As debate and concern continues over the impact of damming along various tributaries of the Mekong, the Xayaburi dam, if it is built, will be the first outside of China to interrupt the flow of the Mekong. With various proposals for up to ten more dams along the Mekong (Bangkok Post, 2011b), there has to be concern that if Laos pushes ahead with the Xayaburi project despite the concerns of its neighbours, more of these other "proposed" projects will become reality.

Issues relating to the Mekong as a resource and region of development are currently under the perusal of two regional bodies, the Mekong Committee/Mekong River Commission (MRC) (1957/1995) (Mekong River Commission, 2010) and the Greater Mekong Sub-Region (GMSR) (1992) (Asian Development Bank, 2011). This is a very important issue because of the number of riparian states involved and the potential for conflict. Both of these organisations interest themselves in the development and sustainability of the Mekong environment and environs. The idea of development in the Mekong region, as Osborne notes, started out very much as a product of Cold War politics supported by the United States, which has seen the river basin's development as closely linked to their war against communism in Southeast Asia (2000b).

These formal organisations (MRC and GMSR) seemingly have at the forefront of their deliberations concerns about the sustainability of the region and preservation or improvement of people's standards of living. However, they can only act in an advisory capacity and have no ability to regulate, so they are not responsible for ultimate outcomes. The public faces of the MRC and GMSR promote the desirable goals of protecting diversity and the environment whilst promoting development that is sustainable and "socially just" (Mekong River Commission, 2010). Clearly, however, there is cause for serious concern when it comes to the issue of how achievable these goals are in the context of national interests being given priority. The MRC is an international, country-driven river basin organisation that provides the institutional framework to promote regional cooperation (Mekong River Commission, 2010). The commission has done excellent work in publicising the impacts of activities along the Mekong, but has had a limited impact on policy. This is attributed to a lack of political power of the organisation, and the fact that China and Myanmar, two nations that significantly impact the Mekong, are not part of the Commission. As these organisations have no political authority, they have limited ability to influence decisions being made about the river's future at the national level within particular countries. The lack of dialogue and influence of these regional bodies within the countries of Southeast Asia effectively silences the voice of Mekong communities at the discussion table.

Without effective political leadership, downstream nations will continue to feel the impacts of upstream activities. With an ever-increasing population and demand for natural resources, this has significant potential to lead to conflict over water access (Cambodia Engineers Without Borders Returned Volunteer, interviewed 10Nov2010; Cambodia Engineers Without Borders Community Partner, interviewed 2Nov2010). Nothing highlights better the weakness of these bodies than Laos proceeding with the Xayaburi dam against the advice of the MRC (Bangkok Post, 2011a). Likewise, the vested interests of different states seem to dictate how they respond. In the case of Xayaburi, Cambodia and Vietnam have raised their concerns whilst Thailand, set to be a major beneficiary via the purchase of the generated electricity, officially remains largely silent about the issue.

It would seem logical that nations would want to recognise that they have a shared benefit from, and shared responsibility to protect, the Mekong River system. Yet whilst countries are not required to identify the social, economic and environmental consequences of dam building both within and outside their national borders, economic interests of individual states trump all other concerns. The risks involved in states taking a "go it alone" approach are not simply about possible national conflicts. There are very clear threats to entire ecosystems outside the borders of the go-it-alone state which could see impacted communities displaced and an enormous humanitarian crisis develop.

Impacts of Damming the Mekong

It is in the assessment of potential benefits and costs that effective *praxis* is crucial for all parties involved, including those individual engineers involved in design and implementation. Meaningful *praxis* in this context involves engagement with all stakeholders. Most importantly, local communities, where impacts of dams will be most immediately felt, need to be active participants in decision making to ensure that their rights to just social and environmental outcomes are met. It is without question, with regard to damming in the Mekong Basin, that the process of decision making continues to be a "top-down" one with decision makers far removed from the lives of affected peoples (Mitchell, 1998). The following discussion suggests that support for dam construction in the national interest is at the very least highly problematic when potential benefits and costs are compared.

Benefits of Dam Construction

All countries along the Mekong River system believe that dams are necessary to meet the growing domestic demand for energy, and to provide income. Hydroelectricity dams generate income from the sale of electricity to neighbouring communities and countries and provide benefits to both recipients and producers. The Xayaburi dam, for example, will supply 1,285 MW (close to its entire capacity) of electricity to the Electricity Generating Authority of Thailand (Bangkok Post, 2011a). Stimulation of the local economy can be considered socially just on a national scale, particularly in low-income countries, where this new market may help to increase the per capita GDP above poverty levels (Bakker, 1999). Dams allow for greater control of river flow, which during the dry season can assist in increasing water availability (Lu & Siew, 2006), and decrease saline intrusion (Kummu & Varis, 2007), resulting in better irrigation of crops. Dams also allow for greater navigation of the river from the addition of locks and the slowing of river flow (Kummu & Varis, 2007). The feedback from some Vietnamese communities along the river has been that these developments are beneficial as they enable the provision of services to the community that would be otherwise unobtainable (Vietnam Engineers Without Borders Volunteer, interviewed 4Nov2010).

Negative Consequences of Dam Construction

Despite the potential benefits, independent studies, details of which are outlined below, have observed that there are many negative social and environmental impacts associated with hydroelectricity dams, particularly along the complex Mekong River system. These include:

- Loss of migratory fish species
- Loss of protein source and income for communities
- Loss of nutrient rich soil deposits
- Reduced hydroelectric capacity over time
- Eco-system shifts
- Salt intrusion
- Loss of fish spawning grounds
- Loss of livelihoods and homes

The following sections examine in more detail these impacts and how they are already affecting the Mekong River system. Further hydropower project developments will only exacerbate existing problems.

Loss of Migratory Fish Species

A major detrimental effect of dams is the alteration of fish migration patterns through river systems (Dugan et al., 2010; Kang et al., 2009). These animals play a crucial role in the biodiversity of the Mekong system, as well as providing a source of food and income to communities along the river. Although it is possible for engineers to design systems such that fish can pass through hydroelectric turbines (Coutant & Whitney, 2000; Schilt, 2007), this has not been seen on any of the existing designs and constructions along the Mekong, and is not considered to be a viable solution to the massive fish migration along the Mekong system (Kang et al., 2009). The loss of migratory fish presents both an environmental and social issue within the Mekong system. The biodiversity of the Mekong is second only to the Amazon, and many endangered species, such as the Mekong giant catfish and the Irrawaddy dolphin, may become extinct if they are eradicated from the river system (Baird & Beasley, 2005; Ngamsiri et al., 2007). As Dugan et al. note, unless investment and innovative ways of dealing with these issues in the context of the Mekong are found, "current best evidence suggests significant and rapid loss of natural ecosystems and their services in the basin, leading to major social and economic impacts" (2010, p. 346).

Loss of Protein Source to Communities

Fishing as an income source and the dependence on fish for food have long been a central part of the human/river interface along the Mekong. The loss of migratory fish species as a result of hydroelectricity dams poses a direct threat to the food and income security of Mekong River communities. It is estimated that no less than 80% of Cambodia's protein comes from the Tonle Sap basin (Live & Learn Environmental Education, 2007), making it particularly vulnerable to any change in fish stocks. Recent years have seen a significant shift in the fish stocks in the river, with many of the larger fish disappearing from the system. This is attributed to climatic shifts and the impacts of upstream activities such as dams. A decrease in fish biomass means a dramatic decrease in food sources for communities, as well as a significant loss of income for the many families who rely on catching and selling fish as a means of employment (reviewed in Lamberts, 2006). The impacts of decreasing fish biomass have already been observed by communities along the Mekong system. To ensure the environmental and social wellbeing of animals and communities that depend upon the biomass provided by the Mekong, it is essential that dam engineers and designers determine ways of increasing fish migration through existing dams, and consider the impacts of future dams on the migration of river species.

Loss of Fish Spawning Grounds

In Cambodia, it has been observed that the dry seasons are dryer and that there is more water during the monsoon. The changes in monsoon and dry-season water levels, as with other areas in the region, are attributed to two main factors, namely shifts in climatic patterns and the reduction in flow down the Mekong caused by upstream damming. This is beginning to cause problems between the fishing communities, who produce so much of Cambodia's protein, and the farming communities, who produce approximately ten percent of Cambodia's rice. These communities are now competing over the same resource area. The rice farmers are clearing more forest during dry periods, as these locations are now viable for farming. But these forests are a key breeding ground for the fish that stock the river, which if removed risk decimating the future fish stocks of the lake (Cambodia Engineers Without Borders Returned Volunteer, interviewed 10 Nov 2010; Cambodia Engineers Without Borders Community Partner, interviewed 2 Nov 2010). Whilst Cambodia may be able to slightly increase their rice production, they will lose the fish protein which has come from Tonle Sap and the Mekong River.

Loss of Nutrient Rich Soil Deposits

The alteration of flow regime, resulting in sedimentation and erosion, is also important when considering both the upstream and downstream physical impacts of dams. By slowing river flow, and blocking solids transport, dams greatly decrease the sediment load able to flow through the system. This has many effects, including bed scouring, lateral expansion due to bank erosion, and a loss of nutrients to seasonally flooded plains downstream (Kummu & Varis, 2007; Lu & Siew, 2006; Zhai, Cui, Hu, & Zhang). It is estimated that approximately 50 percent of suspended sediments in the Mekong system originate in China, and this is decreasing with the construction of dams in the Upper Mekong (Fu & He, 2007). With dams proposed along the lower stretches of the Mekong, this situation is set to become even more dramatic, with Vietnam estimating that the Xayaburi dam will reduce nutrient-rich alluvial deposits in the Mekong Delta from 26 million tonnes to 7 million tonnes (Vietnam Business and Economy News, 2011). This loss of soil nutrients for downstream farmers will result in reduced soil fertility, yields and incomes.

Ecosystem Shifts

In a seasonally flooded ecosystem, permanent inundation behind dam walls will heavily impact the biodiversity and the ecosystem balance, with potentially unforeseen environmental and social consequences, including a shift in ecosystem function and a reduction in agriculture (discussed in Benger, 2007; Kummu & Varis, 2007; Lu & Siew, 2006). It has been suggested that a positive impact of damming the Mekong is that it allows the flow of water to be controlled, and hence will enable a higher than average dry season flow (Lu & Siew, 2006), improving agricultural production downstream from dams. However, this optimistic view fails to consider the ecological adjustments that the environment will need to make to conform to this new mode of operation.

Reduced Hydroelectric Capacity

Deposition of sediments behind dam walls leads to accretion of sediments upstream of dams, which raises basin levels, further changing the flow pattern and efficiency of electricity generation. To maintain the dam's capacity, expensive and potentially damaging dredging activities are required (Fu, He, & Lu, 2008). Several engineering models exist for estimating and minimising the negative impacts of dams on hydrological regimes. It is important that these models be considered in current design proposals for the Mekong, and that modelling of existing dams is used to assist engineers and designers in assessing and correcting problems associated with dam construction. This will benefit the country operating the dam as well as the downstream communities who rely on the annual nutrient flows for their harvests.

Salt Intrusion

In Vietnam there is an emerging issue of salt intrusion into the lower regions of the Mekong due to a change in flow regime. Currently the last ten to 20 kilometres of the river experience salt intrusion, which is impacting farmers in the area. Traditionally these lower Mekong communities utilised irrigation canals to divert water from the Mekong to their farmland; however, with the water becoming saline, this is no longer viable. These farmers, who represent the poorest members of Vietnamese society, are being forced either to move to other areas or to suffer the reduced land productivity that is resulting. This phenomenon of salinization has been attributed by the locals to a combination of reduced rainfall and lower flows down the Mekong River (Vietnam Engineers Without Borders Volunteer, interviewed 4Nov2010). Further dams may worsen the issue of saline intrusion in Vietnam. This situation presents clear social injustices, as the poorest members of the last country on the Mekong are seeing the consequences, whilst the benefits of these projects are flowing to people thousands of kilometres upstream.

Loss of Livelihood and Homes

Dams have also been shown to heavily impact the communities immediately around them (reviewed in Tilt, Braun, & He, 2009). The flooding of valleys to form dams often submerges cultural monuments, pastures and homes, resulting in displaced communities and economic restructuring. These are issues that have been well documented with large-scale dam projects such as the Three Gorges Dam (China) and the Sadar Sarovar Dam (India). In many communities, a shift away from traditional income generating activities has led to an increase in remittance work, meaning that in communities where males and females once worked alongside one another, males now work away from the family unit. In some areas, the price of electricity actually increases following dam construction, due to the increased cost of generation for large-scale hydroelectricity schemes compared to those traditionally used by small communities (Tilt et al., 2009). These changes to local economies and traditional livelihood patterns invariably impact those people with the least voice in planning discussions. In addition, the psycho-social effects of this economic restructuring on these communities has not been addressed well by engineers and designers (Scudder, 2005).

Magnitude of the Consequences

There is continued and growing community concern about the impacts of damming the Mekong River. Many believe that damming along with the impacts of climate change will directly and negatively affect livelihoods. Communities, for example in Cambodia, are concerned that reduced water flow will result in damage to the Tonle Sap and Mekong River ecospheres that they are so dependent upon (Cambodia Engineers Without Borders Volunteer, interviewed 5Nov2010). There is also concern that the change in flow regime, fish biomass and social impacts may lead to water conflict. This is an important factor for consideration of a river system which traverses six countries, and where the benefits of hydroelectricity are often being shared between neighbouring countries. Resource conflicts can be a cause of political and social unrest, and it is expected that conflicts over water are set to increase in coming years. Ismail Serageldin, Vice President of the World Bank in 1995, famously stated that wars of the twenty-first century "will be fought over water" (Shiva, 2002, p. 1). The most pressing of these issues identified is the loss of fish protein and salt intrusion on the lower Mekong. Protein forms an essential part of a balanced diet. If Mekong communities are forced to survive on decreasing protein in their diets, then the risk of infection and disease in an already marginal community will increase significantly. This is also true for the Vietnamese farmers who are being forced off their land. This process is concentrating the nation's productive land into a smaller area. Both these processes (decreasing protein in diets and loss of farmland) are very slow and could go unnoticed until it is too late to mitigate the consequences.

Current Regional Development Approach

Jacobs (1995) suggests that the relatively slow pace of developments along the river (until the mid-1990s at least) might be seen as a positive outcome of the Mekong Committee, in that no big mistakes were made in terms of damming and other water projects. More recently though, major dams and other large projects have been constructed that fail to take into consideration the significant impacts of their construction for downstream communities. Without political authority, the Mekong Committee is unlikely to be able to force dam constructors to make these impact assessments in the future either. It would seem that the current framework for handling these developments is not satisfactory. Even with the best intentions the MRC has no control over what states might decide to do in what they see as their own best interest. Long-time Mekong researcher Milton Osborne notes that:

> With China holding to a firm position that what it does within its own territorial boundaries is its own business, there seems no reason to expect that the projected dams on the Mekong will not be built. Since this is so, it does not seem alarmist to conclude that there is a very real possibility that in the relatively near future there could be major environmental problems for the countries on the lower Mekong. These will be problems that will be impossible to reverse short of demolishing the dams China has built. (Osborne, 2000b, p. 439)

China's reluctance to commit to water agreements is highlighted no better than by its voting against a 1997 United Nations convention which established a framework and "principles for the use of international rivers" (Wolf, 2003, p. 120). China will within the next decade be in a position to control the "flood pulse" of the Mekong, giving it considerable political leverage over other riparian states (Osborne, 2009). Equally alarming are recently revealed plans to build up to 11 dams along the main course of the Mekong below the border with China. Laos alone is considering the construction of dams at seven sites (Osborne, 2009).

Clearly development and management of the Mekong region is not something that should be simply left to relatively powerless regional groupings such as the MRC and GMSR. However well-intentioned these groups are, they are bound by the demands of their political masters. As Osborne observes, the only chance of meaningful changes in policy with respect to dams and other development projects is through influencing the states involved (Osborne, 2009).

It is essential that states explore all possible avenues to develop the Mekong region and provide better living conditions for citizens in the area. However, the rather secretive and arbitrary nature of the way in which various projects have been undertaken (with respect to dam proposals and developments along the Mekong) suggests that meaningful consultation is often lacking or ignored. International pressure is being exerted through the International Declaration of Human Rights, the Rio Declaration of Environmental and Development principles and the work of the World Commissions on Dams; however, a tangible shift in national approaches has yet to be observed. The World Commission on Dams in 2000 noted that the appropriate consultative framework for such large dam projects was one already clearly set out by the United Nations Charter (1945) and International Declaration of Human Rights (1947) (World Commission on Dams, 2000). These rights include being consulted and the right not to have property arbitrarily taken. Later UN declarations, such as the Declaration on the Right to Development (1986) and the Rio Declaration on Environment and Development Principles (1992), have further strengthened the notion that any assessment of such projects incorporate a "rights and risk" approach where all stakeholders are involved (Tilt et al., 2009). Clearly the issue of sovereignty and rights is a much more complex one in the context of the Mekong Basin where more than one state share the resource. A 1970 study by the UN made the following observation which is as relevant today as when it was made:

> Even in the best of circumstances joint use of international waters can give rise to ill feeling and political tension. Although there may be on all sides a sincere will to co-operate, questions of accuracy of flow measurements and of the justice of water allocations may lead to difficulties. … These factors, combined with the usual political differences arising in any international basin, tend to aggravate rather than ease the problem of integrated planning; in this respect it often differs from the planning involved in a national basin under the rule of a single Government. (Jacobs, 1995, p. 146)

Where policy alterations to improve the environmental and social outcomes of dams are failing, it is important that engineering designs for dams attempt to minimise the negative outcomes for communities and the environment. Nations need to recognise that the benefits to their neighbour are also benefits to themselves. After World War 2 the United States gave extensive aid to Europe for their own benefit, to ensure they had someone to trade with. A similar approach is surely required with the shared resource that the Mekong is. The nations of Southeast Asia need to develop this resource to achieve the greatest social, economic and environmental outcomes possible.

The Role of Engineers in Ensuring Environmental and Social Justice

The social, environmental and economic impacts of engineering projects such as damming in the Mekong Basin are not only local but also regional and global. Therefore, it is important that engineers consider the wider consequences of their decisions. Engineers have ethical as well as technical responsibilities when they undertake a project. This should encompass identifying all of the options available to resolve a problem, and clearly articulating the social, environmental and economic impacts. They possess the skills to assess the longer-term, farther-reaching impacts of dams, and adjust designs to minimise detrimental impacts. Currently many of these issues are not considered in the traditional environmental and social impact assessments of engineering dam projects, but they can easily be incorporated. Engineers also need to add effective *praxis* to these technical skills, be actively engaged in working with communities, and as experts advocate with other major non-local stakeholders for socially and environmentally just outcomes.

It is essential that future engineering work draws on the knowledge gained through post-development assessment of dam impacts both nationally and internationally, in order to improve dam design, or recommend that dams not be constructed where the impacts will be harmful to society and the environment. Engineers have a role to explain to the decision makers the need to cover this broader scope. If, then, a decision is made that is not an appropriate one, they have an ethical responsibility to withhold participation in the project (Cambodia Engineers Without Borders Returned Volunteer, interviewed 10 Nov 2010; Cambodia Engineers Without Borders Community Partner, interviewed 2 Nov 2010).

Engineers' Role to Inform Decision Making

Large dam projects are generally completed to increase water security for a nation or for the production of hydroelectric power or both. Both of these goals have immediate benefits to the local community and nation, but generally result in other less positive consequences for affected communities. The human impacts and problems associated with large-scale dam projects around the world have already been well documented (Egre & Senecal, 2003). There is a greater role that can be played by engineers to challenge and present solutions to problems determined to arise from specific projects. For example, some alternative options to large dams include small scale *in situ* hydropower systems, utilisation of other power production technologies and improving water consumption and treatment practices. These alternatives may well present a better outcome for local and downstream communities as well as better overall economic results for the country. When impacts are not properly addressed, the project is not accounting for the true cost and risks of substantial mitigation work, the lost revenues for impacted communities or the potential loss of reputation which impacts the license to operate large corporations. In the context of the Mekong, decision makers need to be aware of the options available so that they can make informed decisions for the future of the Mekong River region and, most importantly, impacted communities need to be involved in the decision-making processes in meaningful and not token ways (Cambodia Engineers Without Borders Volunteer, interviewed 5 Nov 2010; Vietnam Engineers Without Borders Volunteer, interviewed 4 Nov 2010; Cambodia Engineers Without Borders Returned Volunteer, interviewed 10 Nov 2010; Cambodia Engineers Without Borders Community Partner, interviewed 2 Nov 2010).

Engineering's Role in Development

Engineering is often touted as being an essential tool for development. Traditionally, development has been defined as increasing the economic wealth and technological means of a society. However, a more current definition is that development aims to assist people in addressing their basic human needs and improving their quality of life (United Nations Development Programme, 2010). Engineers possess skills which may positively impact society, increase sustainable development and reduce poverty. Engineers also possess skills which, in the name of traditional development, have led to the destruction of ecosystems and negative social impacts on communities. This is evident from the outcomes of many engineering projects, including current dam construction in the Mekong Basin.

Monetary concerns are often considered the most pressing consideration in terms of engineering projects, perhaps due to the hegemonic perception of 'The Economy' as primary in the national interest and wellbeing. In times of economic crises, environmental and social considerations are often overlooked, especially when these might be thought of as longer-term problems, not something of immediate concern. Traditional engineering projects have often failed to recognise their broader implications on human life and the environment as a whole. As Riley points out, engineers tend to see science as "objective" and technology as "neutral", and ignore the "social forces that demand certain forms of technology" (2008, p. 42). Instead of being neutral, every engineering project carries with it "a set of values and assumptions" which are often those of the most powerful stakeholders.

Environmental impact assessments focus heavily on the immediate, and often obvious, outcomes of engineering projects. These assessments may not consider the longer-term effects on the physical and human ecology of an area. This is a particularly difficult task in large projects, such as the damming of the Mekong River, where ecological and human impacts can be felt many thousands of kilometres downstream. Hence, the ecological predictions of scientific models and studies of hydropower dams must be considered by engineers early in the design stage as part of good *praxis*. This approach would allow scientific and technical predictions to be combined with political and social assessments to influence decisions over whether dams can be built with minimal environmental impact and in a way that protects the social and environmental rights of affected communities. To date, such concerns have had little consideration in the design and construction of dams along the Mekong (Keskinen & Kummu, 2010).

Social impact assessments, where they are performed, generally consider only the immediate temporal and spatial impacts of projects. Governments compensate (albeit often inadequately) communities around dams (Tilt et al., 2009), where impacts such as displacement and loss of traditional livelihoods are clear and immediate. However, it is contentious as to whether monetary compensation replaces the loss of culture, income-generating activities and ecosystems associated with dam construction. Such compensation schemes do not tend to consider communities downstream of dams or future generations of families relocated by dam construction. It is essential that the impacts of dam construction on all communities influenced by dams are considered early in the decision-making process and that, wherever possible, engineers account for these shortcomings by altering dam designs and/or, acting in an ethically responsible manner, withdraw their services from such projects. Given how problematic these issues are within the context of a single state, the situation along the Mekong River is exponentially more problematic involving six sovereign states. Critically, engineers must also contribute to the debate surrounding whether hydropower dam projects are appropriate forms of development within particular contexts and regions. It is the engineers who have the technical ability to improve practices for better consideration of the environment and communities as well as to help determine where large-scale dam projects might not be the best solution.

Since hydropower dams have often been built in the past without sufficient consideration of environmental and social impacts, engineers from various non-governmental organisations (NGOs) often work with affected communities to restore the ecological and societal damage caused by large dam construction. Grassroots NGOs have a key role to play in the development of the Southeast Asia region, and the technical and managerial skills that engineers possess are a key need for these organisations. Currently, engineers often do not realise that they have the skills to assist these communities to improve their quality of life, due to a lack of exposure in their university education and through the workplace. One NGO, Engineers Without Borders Australia, works in partnership with developing communities both within Australia and over-seas, assisting them to gain access to the knowledge, resources and appropriate technologies they need to improve their livelihoods. This organisation connects students and professionals to developing communities, enabling these engineers or aspiring engineers to provide technical, management and educational support either remotely from Australia or via a direct volunteer placement. Many projects, particularly in Cambodia, are based around water projects along the Mekong River and Tonle Sap, and are an excellent example of engineers utilising their technical skills for environmental and societal benefit. Although this work of engineers in assist-ing affected communities is crucial, it is questionable whether engineering decisions within the dam design and building process could have prevented these consequences from the outset.

There is significant development occurring along the Mekong River which is apparently providing a localised benefit to the communities involved, through job creation or more immediate access to resources. However, the longer-term consequences of these activities in many cases are unclear due to a lack of proper investigation and assessment of downstream impacts. The current development model in the Mekong Region is very focused on national economic aspects, as this is believed to flow through to the community through improved services and employment. The assumption that continuous (and often unregulated) growth is beneficial to communities needs to be challenged (Simms, Johnson, & Chowla, 2010). Feedback received from those working with communities in Cambodia indicates that growth is causing the nation to move away from sustainable development, with sustainability indicators declining in all areas (Cambodia Engineers Without Borders Community Partner, interviewed 2 Nov 2010). If this is allowed to continue it will not only harm the environment, but also decrease the economic benefits from this process. One clear example is the decreasing size of fish and fish stocks in the Tonle Sap region. Osborne (2009, p. 11) notes that "in Cambodia, the country for which the most detailed information is available, fish catches per person have declined from a figure of 350 kg in 1940 to less than 200 kg in 2003". The decreasing fish stocks along the basin are attributed to overfishing and dams upstream. Whilst fishermen may still be able to harvest the same total volume of fish from the lake (with more fishermen operating), the smaller fish they catch are less valuable and a clear indication of long-term ecological change. This is directly impacting their livelihoods and causing an already marginalised group in society to be even more economically disenfranchised (Cambodia Engineers Without Borders Community Partner, interviewed 2 Nov 2010). The engineers who design dams must consider their impact on issues such as fish migration and biodiversity, and whether such consequences are truly justifiable for the benefit of economic growth. Also, emerging engineering techniques may be able to be incorporated into dams to address such issues of environmental importance, and these must be considered by design engineers. Such techniques have not been seen on any existing dams of the Mekong.

The Future

Clearly the issue of rights and of social justice in dealing with such projects raises questions for those who are involved in the planning and construction of large hydraulic schemes such as dams. Osborne notes that one of the reasons for the surge in dam proposals along the Mekong since 2004 is the fact that capital for such projects is now available from "commercial sources rather than from international organisations such as the World Bank and the Asian Development Bank" (Osborne, 2009, p. 22). In the 1980s, organisations such as the World Bank and the Asian Development Bank began to subject loans for development projects to stricter compensation guidelines because of grave concerns about issues of rights and justice with regards to displaced communities. The shift in focus was towards taking greater consideration of social and environmental outcomes. This included "resettlement minimisation" and the focusing in assessment of projects on the link "between the civil engineering solutions adopted … and the social engineering required for their adequate design and implementation" (Cernea, 1988, p. 5). The recent use of more commercial sources of funding begs the question of whether or not, and to what extent, commercial investments and firms/businesses (in the case of dam construction there are any number of international players) are bound by internationally agreed upon ideas about development linked to the rights of stakeholders. How far should interest groups go to ensure that more than just lip service is paid to rights and social justice for those affected by the projects they will initiate? This paper argues that the same question is an important one for individuals such as engineers who might be assigned to work on such ventures by their managers. This is particularly relevant in situations such as one finds along the Mekong, where issues of state corruption and authoritarianism make the entire issue of human rights (never mind environmental concerns) highly problematic. Further, even if a project has clear benefits for the host country, but possible negative impacts for several other riparian states and peoples, what responsibility does the corporation and individual have? Again this is particularly important given that the only bodies with any sort of oversight of development along the Mekong have insufficient power to enforce binding commitments related to hydropower and other development projects.

Engineers are taught technical skills within their degrees, often with little consideration of the global political and economic context within which their work exists. The potential for engineering projects to impact upon communities and the environment suggests that engineers must be educated early on about the impacts of their decisions, and the importance of *praxis*. As previously suggested, engineers have the technical skills to help ensure environmentally and socially just outcomes are achieved via the type and construction features of projects. However, they also need to be able to recognise the importance of the social, cultural and historical environments in which they work and which have shaped their own values and those of other project stakeholders.

Engineers clearly have a role to play in assisting to communicate the impacts that individual nations will have on other nations as a result of development activities. By taking a holistic view of the Mekong Basin and using techniques such as game theory coupled with more traditional approaches such as impact studies and social impact assessments it may be possible to reduce the negative outcomes on downstream nations and generate positive benefits for all involved. To achieve this, an accepted mechanism is required to enable compensation of other countries when activities such as dams and industrial work are undertaken. This compensation would be based on the impacts of the development on other countries and would take the form of either direct compensation or, ideally, the development of infrastructure to prevent or mitigate impacts. Once nations are committed to compensate each other they will be forced to take a more holistic view. Such an approach must ultimately also include decision-making involvement by communities most affected by hydraulic projects.

The challenges that have been observed in past development along the Mekong River demonstrate an opportunity for engineers to play a role in improving regional development outcomes. It has been identified that the utilisation of small-scale, holistic approaches to working with developing communities has enabled them to access their self-identified needs and improve their quality of life (Cambodia Engineers Without Borders Returned Volunteer, interviewed 10Nov2010). These grassroots efforts are proving helpful in offsetting the consequences of both human errors with respect to development projects in the Mekong Basin as well as changes being brought about by climate change. They are also clear evidence of the need for good *praxis* by engineers. These efforts, this paper suggests, need to be taken further, and the technical skills and knowhow of engineers needs to be employed from the outset of projects to ensure the best possible technical solutions to projects are fully understood and acted upon within a framework of meaningful engagement with local communities. It is particularly important in the interests of social justice to ensure that the least politically empowered members of communities have access to such knowledge to inform their own decision making (again the importance of good *praxis* is evident) during the early stages of project planning. There are ample examples of external organisations implementing projects that do not benefit the broader community, but which proceed to advance private interests (Cambodia Engineers Without Borders Community Partner, interviewed 2Nov2010). This demonstrates a need for engineers to broaden their understanding of their roles in projects like dams to incorporate social, environmental and economic factors, and clearly articulate these aspects for each engineering option available (Cambodia Engineers Without Borders Community Partner, interviewed 2Nov2010). As noted already, engineers are not neutral bystanders in these processes, though this is often how they see themselves. Rather, they are political actors whose decisions and actions can well determine the extent to which outcomes are likely to be socially and environmentally just. This paper argues that they have an ethical obligation to be active in *praxis* and to opt out of projects they deem sufficiently problematic in terms of achieving just outcomes.

Acknowledgements

This article was made possible by support from the Australian Learning and Teaching Council Grant, "Engineering Education for Social and Environmental Justice" (CG10-1519). We are grateful to the interviewees for sharing their experiences with us. We would also like to acknowledge the work of IJESJP reviewers and editors in assisting us to improve the manuscript.

Interviewees

Cambodia Engineers Without Borders volunteer. Interviewed by Daniel I. Loden. 5 November 2010.

Vietnam Engineers Without Borders volunteer. Interviewed by Daniel I. Loden. 4 November 2010.

Cambodia Engineers Without Borders returned volunteer. Interviewed by Daniel I. Loden. 10 November 2010.

Cambodia Engineers Without Borders Community Partner. Interviewed by Daniel I. Loden. 2 November 2010.

References

Adeola, F. O. (2000). Cross-national environmental injustice and human rights issues: A review of evidence in the developing world. *The American Behavioral Scientist*, 43(4), 686–706.

Asian Development Bank. (2011). Greater Mekong Sub-Region. Retrieved 13th September, 2011, from http://www.adb.org/gms

Australian Government. (2011*). National Greenhouse Gas Inventory, Accounting for the Kyoto Target, December Quarter 2010*. Barton, ACT: Australian Government.

Baird, I. G., & Beasley, I. L. (2005). Irrawaddy dolphin Orcaella brevirostris in the Cambodian Mekong River: an initial survey. *Oryx*, 39(3), 301-310. doi: 10.1017/s003060530500089x

Bakker, K. (1999). The politics of hydropower: developing the Mekong. *Political Geography*, 18(2), 209-232.

Bangkok Post. (2011a, 13/03/11). Xayaburi dam proposal was "poorly researched", *Bangkok Post*. Retrieved from http://www.bangkokpost.com/news/local/231358/xayaburi-dam-proposal-was-poorly-researched

Bangkok Post. (2011b, 13/03/11). Xayaburi dam work begins on sly, *Bangkok Post*. Retrieved from http://www.bangkokpost.com/news/local/232239/xayaburi-dam-work-begins-on-sly

Benger, S. N. (2007). Remote sensing of ecological responses to changes in the hydrological cycles of the Tonle Sap, Cambodia *Igarss: 2007 IEEE International Geoscience and Remote Sensing Symposium, Vols 1-12—Sensing and Understanding Our Planet* (pp. 5028–5031). New York: IEEE.

Cernea, M. M. (1988). *Involuntary resettlement in development projects: policy guidelines in World Bank-financed projects* (World Bank Technical Paper). Washington D.C.: World Bank.

Chinese National Committee on Large Dams. (2011). Chinese National Committee on Large Dams. Retrieved 13th September, 2011, from http://www.chincold.org.cn/english.asp

Coutant, C. C., & Whitney, R. R. (2000). Fish behavior in relation to passage through hydropower turbines: A review. *Transactions of the American Fisheries Society*, 129(2), 351–380.

Donnelly, J. (2006). *International Human Rights*. Westview Press.

Dugan, P. J., Barlow, C., Agostinho, A. A., Baran, E., Cada, G. F., Chen, D. Q., … Winemiller, K. O. (2010). Fish migration, dams, and loss of ecosystem services in the Mekong Basin. *Ambio*, 39(4), 344-348.

Economy, E. C. (2005). *The River Runs Black: The Environmental Challenge to China's Future*. Ithaca and London: Cornell University Press.

Egre, D., & Senecal, P. (2003). Social impact assessment of large dams throughout the world: lessons learned over two decades. *Impact Assessment and Project Appraisal*, 21(3), 215–224.

Fu, K. D., & He, D. M. (2007). Analysis and prediction of sediment trapping efficiencies of the reservoirs in the mainstream of the Lancang River. *Chinese Science Bulletin*, 52, 134–140. doi: 10.1007/s11434-007-7026-0

Fu, K. D., He, D. M., & Lu, X. X. (2008). Sedimentation in the Manwan reservoir in the Upper Mekong and its downstream impacts. *Quaternary International*, 186, 91-99. doi: 10.1016/j.quaint.2007.09.041

Hall, K. R. (1992). Economic History of Early Southeast Asia. In N. Tarling (Ed.), *The Cambridge History of Southeast Asia* (Vol. 1, pp. 195–196). Singapore: Cambridge University Press.

Hirsch, P. (1998). Dams, resources and the politics of environment in mainland Southeast Asia. In P. Hirsch & C. Warren (Eds.), *The politics of environment in Southeast Asia: resources and resistance*. London: Routledge.

Jacobs, J. W. (1995). Mekong Committee history and lessons for river basin development. The Geographical Journal, 161(2), 146–147.

Jacobs, J. W. (2002). The Mekong River Commission: transboundary water resources planning and regional security. *Geographical Journal*, 168, 354–364.

Kang, B., He, D. M., Perrett, L., Wang, H. Y., Hu, W. X., Deng, W. D., & Wu, Y. F. (2009). Fish and fisheries in the Upper Mekong: current assessment of the fish community, threats and conservation. *Reviews in Fish Biology and Fisheries*, 19(4), 465–480. doi: 10.1007/s11160-009-9114–5

Keay, J. (2005). *Mad about the Mekong: exploration and empire in South East Asia*. London: Harper Collins Publishers.

Keskinen, M., & Kummu, M. (2010). *Impact Assessment in the Mekong: Review of Strategic Environmental Assessment (SEA) & Cumulative Impact Assessment*. Helsinki, Finald: Water & Development Publications.

Kummu, M., & Varis, O. (2007). Sediment-related impacts due to upstream reservoir trapping, the Lower Mekong River. *Geomorphology*, 85(3–4), 275–293. doi: 10.1016/j.geomorph.2006.03.024

Lamberts, D. (2006). The Tonle Sap Lake as a productive ecosystem. *International Journal of Water Resources Development*, 22(3), 481–495. doi: 10.1080/07900620500482592

Live & Learn Environmental Education. (2007). *Tonle Sap Information Guide*. Phnom Penh, Cambodia: Live & Learn Environmental Education.

Lu, X. X., & Siew, R. Y. (2006). Water discharge and sediment flux changes over the past decades in the Lower Mekong River: possible impacts of the Chinese dams. *Hydrology and Earth System Sciences*, 10, 181–195.

McLaren, A. (2011). Environment and cultural heritage in China: Introduction. *Asian Studies Review*, 35(4), 429–437.

Mekong River Commission. (2010). About the MRC. Retrieved 23th May, 2012, from http://www.mrcmekong.org/

Mitchell, M. (1998). The political economy of Mekong Basin development. In P. Hirsch & C. Warren (Eds.), *The politics of environment in Southeast Asia: resources and resistance.* London: Routledge.

Molle, F., Foran, T., & Kakonen, M. (Eds.). (2010). *Contested Waterscapes in the Mekong Region Hydropower, Livelihoods and Governance.* Singapore: Institute of Southeast Asian Studies.

Ngamsiri, T., Nakajima, M., Sukmanomon, S., Sukumasavin, N., Kamonrat, W., Na-Nakorn, U., & Taniguchi, N. (2007). Genetic diversity of wild Mekong giant catfish Pangasianodon gigas collected from Thailand and Cambodia. *Fisheries Science*, 73(4), 792–799. doi: 10.1111/j.1444-2906.2007.01398.x

Nussbaum, M. (2003). Capabilities as fundamental entitlements: Sen and social justice. *Feminist Economics*, 9(2/3), 33–59.

Osborne, M. E. (2000a). *The Mekong: turbulent past, uncertain future.* St Leonards, N.S.W.: Allen and Unwin.

Osborne, M. E. (2000b). The strategic significance of the Mekong. *Contemporary Southeast Asia*, 22(3), 429–444.

Osborne, M. E. (2009). *The Mekong River under threat.* Lowy Institute for International Policy, Sydney: Longueville Press.

Osborne, M. E. (2011, 29/06/11). Mekong dam plans threatening the natural order, The Australian. Retrieved 24th February 2012 from http://www.theaustralian.com.au/news/world/mekong-dam-plans-threatening-the-natural-order/story-e6frg6ux-1226083709322

Rawls, J., & and Kelly, E. (2001). *Justice as fairness: a restatement.* Cambridge, U.S.: Harvard University Press.

Riley, D. (2008). *Engineering and Social Justice.* San Rafael, U.S.: Morgan & Claypool.

Schilt, C. R. (2007). Developing fish passage and protection at hydropower dams. *Applied Animal Behaviour Science*, 104(3–4), 295–325. doi:10.1016/j.applanim.2006.09.004

Scudder, T. (2005). *The Future of Large Dams: Dealing with Social, Environmental, Institutional and Political Costs.* London: Earthscan.

Shaffer, L. N. (1996). *Maritime Southeast Asia to 1500.* Armonk, NY: M. E. Sharpe.

Shiva, V. (2002). *Water Wars: Privatization, Pollution and Profit.* Cambridge, MA: South End Press.

Simms, A., Johnson, V., & Chowla, P. (2010). *Growth isn't possible: Why we need a new economic direction.* London: New Economics Foundation.

Smil, V. (2004). *China's past, China's future: energy, food, environment.* New York: Routledge.

Snowy Hydro Limited. (2011). Snowy Mountains Scheme. Retrieved 13th September, 2011, from http://www.snowyhydro.com.au/LevelThree.asp?pageID=244&parentID=66&grandParentID=4

Tilt, B., Braun, Y., & He, D. M. (2009). Social impacts of large dam projects: A comparison of international case studies and implications for best practice. *Journal of Environmental Management*, 90, S249–S257. doi: 10.1016/j.jenvman.2008.07.030

United Nations. (1948). *Universal Declaration of Human Rights.* Geneva: United Nations.

United Nations Department of Peacekeeping Operations Cartographic Section (Cartographer). (2004). Greater Mekong Subregion. Retrieved from http://www.un.org/depts/Cartographic/map/profile/mekong.pdf

United Nations Development Programme. (2010). *Human Development Report 2010*. New York: Palgrave Macmillan.

Vickery, M. (1998). *Society, economics, and politics in pre-Angkor Cambodia: the 7th-8th centuries*. Tokyo: Centre for East Asian Cultural studies for UNESCO.

Vietnam Business and Economy News. (2011, 23/02/11). Experts worry about Mekong River power plant, *Vietnam Business and Economy News*. Retrieved from http://www.vneconomynews.com/2011/02/experts-worry-about-mekong-river-power.html

Wolf, A. T. (2003). "Water Wars" and other tales of hydromythology. In B. McDonald & J. Douglas (Eds.), *Whose Water is it?: The Unquenchable Thirst of a Water-Hungry World* (pp. 109–124). Washington, D.C.: National Geographic Society.

World Commission on Dams. (2000). *Dams and Development: a New Framework for Decision-making*. London: Earthscan.

Zhai, H. J., Cui, B. S., Hu, B., & Zhang, K. J. Prediction of river ecological integrity after cascade hydropower dam construction on the mainstream of rivers in Longitudinal Range-Gorge Region (LRGR), China. *Ecological Engineering*, 36(4), 361–372. doi: 10.1016/j.ecoleng.2009.10.002

SECTION IV CONCLUSION

What seems certain is that no single energy source or technology is sufficient to meet demand for energy at the global scale. The concern for energy security continues to drive investment in a variety of energy sources and an "all of the above" approach to energy supply in many countries, including the United States and China. There are inherent environmental, social, and economic tradeoffs with every energy source. The decisions of policymakers and energy firms will undoubtedly impact ecosystems and humans, and the question is who and what will be affected and to what degree. The environmental justice approach and Mekong River case study outlined in this chapter illustrate the importance of considering the human cost of energy production. While environmental justice and politics are not the only considerations in energy project planning, they should be directly addressed in impact studies along with assessments of broader, longer-term environmental impacts and economic costs. Environmental movements engaged in energy issues argue for more than local "consultation" in meetings with planning experts and political leaders. Instead, many movements insist on the right to refuse specific energy extraction, production, or other related interventions altogether, as well as the right to shift national and international energy strategies on a more fundamental and genuinely participatory basis.

Section IV Discussion Questions: Energy and Environmental Justice Review

1. Identify 3 environmental justice networks discussed by Claudio. What is the topic of focus for each network, and where else are these topics discussed in the textbook? How do these topics relate across different disciplines?
2. How is ownership and control over river segments determined? How is it enforced?
3. What responsibility do nation states have to minimize environmental impacts on communities/nations downstream?
4. The Barrington et al. case study focuses on the responsibility of engineers to account for the long-term effects of dam construction. What responsibility do other stakeholders, including investors/funders, corporations, and individuals, have to ensure that dam projects protect the environment and human rights?
5. What are the potential benefits of large dam construction? What social and environmental impacts are associated with dam construction?
6. How can the impacts of dam construction be minimized? Who is responsible for this?
7. Should large-scale hydroelectric power be promoted as an energy source? Consider how you would answer based on the following perspectives and scales:
   a. Climate change mitigation
   b. Social justice of local communities
   c. National/regional energy security
   d. Local environmental conservation

References

Barrington, D.J., Dobbs, S., and Loden, D.I. (2012). "Social and Environmental Justice for Communities of the Mekong River." *International Journal of Engineering, Social Justice, and Peace* 1(1): 31–49.

Claudio, L. (2007) "Standing on Principle: The Global Push for Environmental Justice." *Environmental Health Perspectives* 115 (10): 500–503.

Cleveland, C.J. and Morris, C. (eds) (2013) *Handbook of Energy. Volume 1: Diagrams, Charts, and Tables.* Boston: Elsevier.

Cleveland, C. (2013) "Three Gorges Dam, China." *Encyclopedia of Earth.* Updated March 21, 2013.

EIA (U.S. Energy Information Administration)(2012) "International Energy Statistics." (http://www.eia.gov/cfapps/ipdbproject/IEDIndex3.cfm?tid=44&pid=44&aid=2).

EIA (U.S. Energy Information Administration)(2013) "International Energy Outlook 2013." (http://www.eia.gov/forecasts/aeo/index.cfm).

Fargione, J., Hill, J., Tilman, D., Polasky, S., and Hawthorne, P. (2008) "Land Clearing and the Biofuel Carbon Debt." *Science* 319(5867): 1235–1238.

Gallagher, K.S. (2013) "Why and How Governments Support Renewable Energy." *Daedalus* 142(1): 59–77.

IEA (International Energy Agency) (2012) Energy Poverty. "2012 Electricity Access Database." (http://www.iea.org/topics/energypoverty/).

Klare, M. (2012) *The Race for What's Left: The Global Scramble for the World's Last Resources.* New York: Picador (100–127).

McDonald, A. (2008) "Nuclear Power Global Status." IAEA Bulletin 49(2).

Pasqualetti, M.J. (2011) "Opposing Wind Energy Landscapes: A Search for Common Cause." *Annals of the Association of American Geographers* 101(4): 907–917.

Qiu, J. (2011) "China Unveils Green Targets." *Nature* 471 (149).

Scudder, T. (2005) *The Future of Large Dams: Dealing with Social, Environmental, Institutional, and Political Costs.* London; Sterling, VA: Earthscan.

Shapouri, H., Duffield, J.A., and Wang, M. (2002) "The Energy Balance of Corn Ethanol: An Update." U.S. Department of Agriculture. Agricultural Economic Report No. 814, July 2002.

Wong, E. (2013) "China's Plan to Curb Air Pollution Sets Limits on Coal Use and Vehicles." *New York Times* September 12, 2013.

Yee, A. (2013) "India Increases Effort to Harness Biomass Energy." The *New York Times* October 9, 2013.

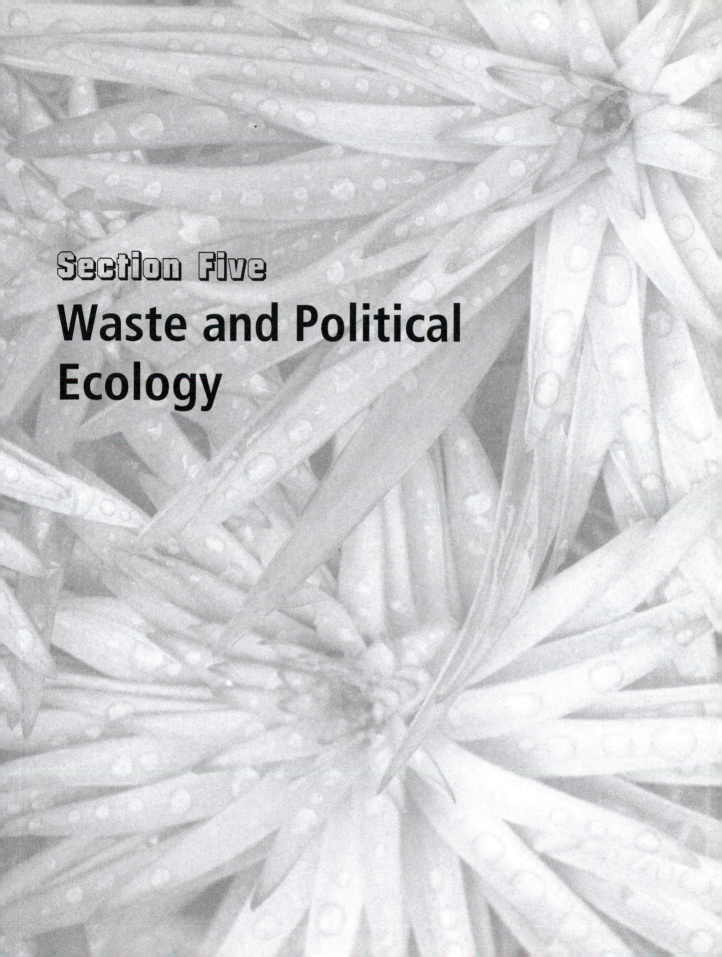

Section Five
Waste and Political Ecology

INTRODUCTION TO GLOBAL WASTE ISSUES

apolitical ecologies biomagnification e-waste	persistent organic pollutants (POPs) scale hazardous waste

KEY TERMS

A cademics, policymakers, development experts, and environmental activists have increasingly focused their attention on the environmental politics of global and local flows of waste. According to Sarah Moore (2011, 133), "as much as countries, people, and companies across the globe are connected (albeit unevenly) by the circulation of goods and services, they are also connected by flows of waste. These flows of waste, moreover, are intimately connected to global flows of capital, processes of uneven development and marginalization." Particular topics of interest related to waste include recycling, reducing industrial waste (pollution), the lucrative global trade in **hazardous waste** and **e-waste**, municipal waste management, sanitation, and garbage scavenging. This section explores waste through a critical examination of the politics of what constitutes waste, who defines waste, and how various forms of waste shape and disrupt broader societal norms and politics.

Hazardous waste presents a hazard to the health of humans or other organisms, due to its toxic, radioactive, or flammable properties.

E-waste includes waste from electronic products such as computers, phones, DVD players, televisions, etc. Many of the components of these items are hazardous to human health and to wildlife (Grossman 2006).

Defining Waste

"Waste" as a term and concept requires significant unpacking. The excretion of waste materials is a major biochemical feature of living organisms in their metabolic processes. Despite this fundamental feature of living organisms, dealing with basic human waste or excrement in the field of sanitation in a social context involves a variety of politics and taboos (e.g., cultural rules) about who can and cannot touch or dispose of waste along socio-economic status because of its association with disgust, revulsion, etc., and specific ideas about where waste should go (Jewitt 2011). Before launching further into studying one particular form of waste (e.g. "shit," Jewitt 2011) among so many other forms of waste, it is important to pause and consider the astounding breadth and complexity of the concept of waste through the following questions:

- What is waste? Is waste a polluting substance? Is waste necessarily toxic or hazardous?
- Is one person's waste or garbage potentially someone else's treasure?
- Who has the authority to define and regulate waste?
- To whom does waste matter, in what ways, why, and where?[1]

Waste can be broadly understood as simultaneously "social" and "natural" and in societal contexts as "that which disturbs or disrupts" day-to-day processes (Moore 2012, 781). More specifically, waste can include food waste, electronic waste (**e-waste**), nuclear waste, wasted energy, a broader category such as "trash" or "garbage," "matter out of place," or useless objects (Ibid.). While waste might be inconvenient or disruptive to a particular person or group in a specific location, that same object can be useful and even represent a lucrative business opportunity to others. For example, many countries export waste (including e-waste and hazardous waste from industrial processes) to be disposed or repurposed in other countries. A common international waste flow is from industrialized countries with tighter environmental regulations to developing countries, although the actual patterns of flow occur within specific regional patterns (Lepawsky and McNabb 2010). In some cases, waste is a welcome source of income for developing countries; however, exposure to waste often leads to health hazards and environmental contamination, representing an environmental justice issue.

The geographies of waste have different political, ethical, and technical implications across different contexts. As substances break down during transportation, reuse, recycling, dispersal/disposal, and other processes, the toxicity of the material can change as it comes into contact with different bodies and environments. For example, when the flame-retardant chemicals in a couch cushion gradually break down and disperse into dust particles inside the home, they can enter and accumulate in the fatty tissue of human babies and household cats through a range of exposure pathways (Slater 2012; Stapleton et al. 2012). Once in a landfill, discarded couch cushions continue to break down and disperse into broader global hydrological, atmospheric, and related biophysical flows in which a disproportionate amount of chemicals converge in the polar regions of the globe and **biomagnify** (or bioaccumulate) in the fatty tissue of fish, other wildlife, and humans (Slater 2012; Muir and de Wit 2010).

---

1   Gregson and Crang 2010

Biomagnification is a process through which species at higher trophic levels eat species at lower tropic levels and accumulate toxins found in the cells of the consumed lower tropic species. These toxins accumulate in the cells of biota (bioaccumulation) as cells absorb nutrients along with associated toxins.

The existence of so many different forms and notions of waste in the world, in addition to broader political-economic interests and histories, means that it is very challenging to regulate transnational flows of waste. Several international conventions and agreements attempt to control the flow of different kinds of waste, including:

- **The Basel Convention** on the Control of Transboundary Movements of Hazardous Wastes and Their Disposal (adopted on March 22, 1989, entered into force beginning in 1992 and amended in 1995 and 1998),
- **The Rotterdam Convention** on the Prior Informed Consent Procedure for Certain Hazardous Chemicals and Pesticides in International Trade (adopted September 10, 1998 and amended in 2004, 2008, and 2011),
- **The Stockholm Convention** on Persistent Organic Pollutants (adopted May 22, 2001, entered into force beginning in 2004 and amended in 2009 and 2011).

These international agreements attempt to set out common definitions for categories of waste such as hazardous waste and **Persistent Organic Pollutants (POPs)**. They also attempt to regulate the transport, disposal, and trade of such materials found in everyday objects from cell phones to detergents and medicine. However, not every country has signed on to these agreements and not every institution gathers the same translatable data about the same substances. The scale of waste production and its distribution also matters in terms of how we analyze the impacts of waste on particular landscapes and livelihoods. When viewing waste production as a personal "consumer" choice, such as deciding whether or not to upgrade to the latest cell phone model and discard an older phone, we produce different solutions to the resulting e-waste problem (e.g., buy fewer or different phones) than if we focus on the waste production of large-scale industrial facilities next to or in vulnerable ecosystems and

Persistent Organic Pollutants (POPs) are mostly synthetic chemical compounds such as PCBs for industrial applications, DDT for pest control, Bisphenol A (BPA) used in plastics, and polybrominated diphenyl ethers (PBDE) used as flame retardants in furniture and electronics. These chemicals persist in the environment in the bodies of wildlife and accumulate in the larger food web, affecting human reproductive, behavioral, endocrine, and neurologic health.

Scale in this chapter refers to the spatial extent of anything from a process to a resource. It is important to examine environmental and social issues at varying scales—local, national, regional, and global—in order to fully understand them.

communities around the globe (e.g., collective *political* as opposed to individual consumer action). Individual consumption often links to larger-scale dynamics but in complex ways. How can scholars, activists, and environmentalists begin to analyze these complex geographies and flows of waste? One approach that combines the biophysical, historical, and political aspects of environmental issues such as waste is political ecology.

Political Ecology: A Transdisciplinary Approach to Human-Environment Analysis of Waste

Political ecology is a critical lens for examining environmental change. Political ecology is a broad community of thinking and practice rather than a particular theory or academic discipline (Robbins 2012). The field of political ecology spans across disciplines of biology, geography, anthropology, history, and political science, among others. Having its roots in both the natural sciences and in social theory inspired by physical scientists, anthropologists, and political theorists, political ecology focuses on the politics and power relations of environmental and landscape change (Biersack 2006). Political ecologists in the 1980s and 1990s focused largely on understanding processes such as soil erosion, deforestation and hunger in developing areas of Africa, Latin America, and Asia. Political ecologists combine localized observations with broad ecological and political-economic and historical analysis to understand why and how a process such as deforestation is happening, and by whom. While some might be satisfied with observing the "proximate" factors that influence ecological change, political ecologists investigate what other political-economic forces in distant places contribute to changes observed locally. This approach challenges "received wisdom" and grand stories about the scarcity of resources (ecoscarcity) or "overpopulation," and it questions the uncritical application of such generalizations across diverse ecological and political-economic contexts.

As Paul Robbins (2012) notes in the following section, political ecology attempts to debunk so-called **apolitical ecologies** that make overly simplistic assumptions about issues such as population growth without engaging per capita consumption, carrying capacities of specific ecosystems, flows of products, and unequal power relations. An apolitical analysis of waste would assume that more people always produce more waste, or that more waste ultimately requires more landfills and dumping sites. Political ecologists would argue that questions about where waste goes, who benefits from the trade in waste, and who suffers from exposure to waste are both biophysical and *political* issues requiring thorough analysis. The Robbins piece serves as a basic introduction to this particular "way of seeing" or analyzing environmental issues.

Apolitical Ecologies generalize about environmental change in ways that obscure complex ethical implications, politics, and power dynamics. Common apolitical ecologies uncritically emphasize the "ultimate scarcity of non-human nature and the rapacity of humankind's growing numbers" (Robbins 2012, 14) while celebrating technocratic, overly optimistic "win-win" solutions based on assumptions about the superiority of "modern" societies, Western societal values, and market-based economic valuation (Robbins 2012, 18).

The second excerpt, by Sarah Moore (2011), applies political ecological questions and analysis to a waste-related sub-topic: the global trade in hazardous waste and garbage. She studies the "global flows of garbage" (137), its management, related policies, and who wins and loses in the local and global trade of various forms of waste. Moore encourages readers to think of waste as more than an object that is inconvenient to deal with, dispose of, and keep away from contaminating food, water, and animal and human bodies. Moore highlights the difficulty of controlling certain forms of hazardous waste, which provoke us to act or respond in ways (fearful responses, entrepreneurial responses, etc.) that are fundamentally unequal.

HIGHLIGHTED APPROACH: POLITICAL ECOLOGY

Political versus Apolitical Ecologies

By Paul Robbins

For many of us who are unable to travel to the plains of East Africa, our images of the region are given life on late-night cable wildlife television, in bold IMAX presentations at natural history museums, or perhaps in the vivid spectacle of Disney's *The Lion King*. The imagined patterns of the "circle of life" in these media—complete with lions, hyenas, and baboons—play out on a yellow-filtered savanna where migrations of wildebeest cross the Serengeti chasing seasonal rainfall, hunted in turn by stoic predators. The scenes are compelling and they inspire in us a justifiable affection for the beauty and complexity of the non-human world around us. These images are also ecologically important, since they give us a picture of connectedness, which is essential to understanding life on the savanna. Across the borderlands of Kenya and Tanzania forage grasses follow rainfall, wildebeest pursue forage, predators pursue wildebeest, scavengers pursue predators, and so on.

The absence of people from these imaginary landscapes seems in no way strange for most of us; these are *natural* landscapes, apparently far from farms, factories, and the depredations of humankind. It is perhaps inevitable, therefore, that an intuitive reaction to the news that wildlife populations are in crisis—including declines in giraffe, topi, buffalo, warthog, gazelle, and cland—is to imagine that the intrusion of humankind into the system is the cause of the problem. Growing populations of impoverished African people, we might imagine, have contaminated the natural rhythm of the wilderness. Indeed, the sense of loss in contemplating the declining biodiversity and destroyed landscapes may inspire frustration, coupled with

Figure 1. Wildebeest crossing the Mara River in Kenya. The migration of wild animals across the region occurs amidst a fully humanized and highly political environment. Copyright © 2008 by iStockphoto.com / Paul Banton

a feeling of helplessness; the situation in the Serengeti and the steady march of growing populations seem far beyond the control and influence of life where we live.

Stepping back from the savanna, however, and gazing across the Serengeti—Mara ecosystem both in time and in space, habitat loss and wildlife decline appear more complex and more connected to the daily lives and routines of urban people in the developed world. Cross-border analysis shows that the decline in habitat and wildlife in Kenya is far higher than in Tanzania. Why? Rainfall, human population, and livestock numbers do not differ significantly. Rather, private holdings and investment in export cereal grains on the Kenyan side of the border have led to intensive cropping and the decline of habitat. These cereals are consumed around the world, as part of an increasingly globalized food economy. As Kenya is increasingly linked to these global markets and as pressure on local producers increases, habitat loss is accelerated. Less developed agricultural markets and less fully privatized land tenure systems in Tanzania mean less pressure on wildlife. The wildlife crisis in East Africa is more political and economic than demographic (Homewood et al. 2001).

These facts undermine widely held apolitical views about ecological relations in one of the most high-profile wildlife habitats in the world. They also point to faulty assumptions about the nature of "wild" Africa. Firstly, the image of a Serengeti without people is a fallacious one. The Masai people and their ancestors inhabited the Central Rift Valley for thousands of years before European contact, living in and around wildlife for generations. Indeed, their removal from wildlife park areas has led to violent conflicts (Collett 1987). More generally, the isolation of these places is also a mistaken perception. Export crops from Kenya, including tea and coffee in other parts of Kenya beyond the Central Rift Valley, continue to find their way to consumers in the first world, even as their global prices fall, constraining producers who must increase production, planting more often and over greater areas, further changing local ecological conditions. With three-quarters of the population in agriculture, economic margins for most Kenyans become tighter every year, and implications for habitat and wildlife more urgent.

The migration of the wildebeest, and its concomitant implications for grasslands and lions, therefore, does not occur outside the influences of a broader political economy. Land tenure laws, which set the terms for land conversion and cash cropping, are made by the Kenyan and Tanzanian states. Commodity markets, which determine prices for Kenyan products and the ever decreasing margins that drive decisions to cut trees or plant crops, are set on global markets. Money and pressure for wildlife enclosure, which fund the removal of native populations from the land, continue to come largely from multilateral institutions and first-world environmentalists. All of these spheres of activity are further arranged along linked axes of money, influence, and control. They are part of systems of power and influence that, unlike the imagined steady march of the population "explosion," are *tractable to challenge and reform.* They can be fixed.

The difference between this contextual approach and the more traditional way of viewing problems like this is the difference between a *political* and an *apolitical* ecology. This is the difference between identifying broader systems rather than blaming proximate and local forces; between viewing ecological systems as power-laden rather than politically inert; and between taking an explicitly normative approach rather than one that claims the objectivity of disinterest.

When the bottom drops out of the coffee market, as it did in the late summer of 2001, what happens to the peasants who depend upon it and the forests in which it is harvested? When the World Bank helps to fund massive afforestation programs around the world, aimed at preserving tree cover and animal biodiversity, what actually happens to the hill forests designated for enclosure and the tribal people who live there?

These are the questions of political ecology, a field of critical research predicated on the assumption that any tug on the strands of the global web of human–environment linkages reverberates throughout the system as a whole. This burgeoning field has attracted several generations of scholars from the fields of anthropology, forestry, development studies, environmental sociology, environmental history, and geography. Its countless practitioners all query the relationship between economics, politics, and nature but come from varying backgrounds and training. Some are physical scientists (e.g., biologists, geomorphologists, and hydrologists), others are methodological technicians (e.g., geographic information or remote sensing specialists), while most are social and behavioral scientists. All share an interest in the condition of the environment and the people who live and work within it. These researchers, moreover, advocate fundamental changes in the management of nature and the rights of people, directly or indirectly working with state and non-governmental organizations (NGOs) to challenge current conditions. Robbins (2012) reviews the work that these people do, pointing towards the common factors evident in a research area often noted for its diversity, and revealing the strengths and weaknesses in a field that has grown far too quickly to prepare a comprehensive survey or census of its accomplishments and failures.

What is Political Ecology?

The term political ecology is a generous one that embraces a range of definitions. A review of the term from its early use (first used to describe this kind of work by Wolf in 1972) to its most recent manifestations shows important differences in emphasis. Some definitions stress political economy, while others point to more formal political institutions; some stress environmental change, while others emphasize narratives or stories about that change (see Table 1). Even so, there seems to be a set of common elements. The many definitions together suggest that political ecology represents an explicit alternative to "apolitical" ecology,

Table 1. Defining political ecology.

Author/Source	Definition of "political ecology"	Goal
Cockburn and Ridgeway (1979)	"a useful way of describing the intentions of radical movements in the United States, in Western Europe and in other advanced industrial countries … very distant from the original rather sedate operations of the eco-lobby" (p. 3)	Explicate and describe first-world urban and rural environmental degradation from corporate and state mismanagement; document social activism in response.
Blaikie and Brookfield (1987)	"combines the concerns of ecology and a broadly defined political economy. Together this encompasses the constantly shifting dialectic between society and land-based resources, and also within classes and groups within society itself "(p. 17)	Explain environmental change in terms of constrained local and regional production choices within global political economic forces, largely within a third-world and rural context.
Greenberg and Park (1994)	A synthesis of "political economy, with its insistence on the need to link the distribution of power with productive activity and ecological analysis, with its broader vision of bio-environmental relationships" (p. 1)	"Synthesize the central questions asked by the social sciences about the relations between human society, viewed in its bio-cultural-political complexity, and a significantly humanized nature" (p. 1),
Peet and Watts (1996b)	"a confluence between ecologically rooted social science and the principles of political economy" (p. 6)	Locates "movements emerging from the tensions and contradictions of under production crises, understands the imaginary basis of their oppositions and visions for a better life and the discursive character of their politics, and sees the possibilities for broadening environmental issues into a movement for livelihood entitlements, and social justice" (pp. 38–39).
Hempel (1996)	"the study of interdependence among political units and of interrelationships between political units and their environment … concerned with the political consequences of environmental change" (p. 150)	Explore and explain community-level and regional political action in the global sphere, in response to local and regional degradation and scarcity.
Watts (2000)	"to understand the complex relations between nature and society through a careful analysis of what one might call the forms of access and control over resources and their implications for environmental health and sustainable livelihoods" (p. 257)	Explain environmental conflict especially in terms of struggles over "knowledge, power and practice" and "politics, justice arid governance"
Stott and Sullivan (2000)	"identified the political circumstances that forced people into activities which caused environmental degradation in the absence of alternative possibilities … involved the query and reframing of accepted environmental narratives, particularly those directed via international environment and development discourse" (p. 4)	"Illustrating the political dimensions of environmental narratives and in deconstructing particular narratives to suggest that accepted ideas of degradation and deterioration may not be simple linear trends that tend to predominate" (p. 5)

that it works from a common set of assumptions, and that it employs a reasonably consistent mode of explanation.

Challenging Apolitical Ecologies

If there is a political ecology, by implication there must be an apolitical one. As such, research in the field commonly presents its accounts, whether explaining land degradation, local resource conflict, or state conservation failures, as an alternative to other perspectives. The most prominent of these apolitical approaches, which tend to dominate in global conversations surrounding the environment, are "ecoscarcity" and "modernization" accounts.

*   *   *   *

Ecoscarcity and the Limits to Growth

The dominant contemporary narrative of environmental change and human–environment interaction is a well-established one with a long history. In Western Europe since the late 1700s, when human influence and response to the environment was first submitted to scientific scrutiny, the central driving explanation for social/ecological crisis has been increasing human population, measured in absolute numbers. Following from Thomas Malthus's *Essay on the Principle of Population,* the argument is straightforward: as human populations grow out of proportion to the capacity of the environmental system to support them, there is a crisis both for humans, whose numbers fall through starvation and disease-based mortality, and for nature, whose overused assets are driven past the point of self-renewal. This argument took many forms during the twentieth century, from the "population bomb" of Paul Ehrlich (1968) to the Club of Rome's "Limits to Growth" (Meadows et al. 1972), but its elements are consistent. All hold to the ultimate scarcity of non-human nature and the rapacity of humankind's growing numbers.

For ecoscarcity proponents, this is nowhere a more serious problem than in the underdeveloped world, where growth rates and absolute numbers of people remain the highest in the world. That the poorest regions of the world are the repositories for what are viewed as important and scarce environmental goods makes the problem doubly serious. In this way of thinking, the perilous decline of Kenya's wildlife, as described above, can be predicted to follow inevitably from the growth of Kenya's population.

The problems with this line of argument are many. In general terms, the demographic explanation is a consistently weak predictor of environmental crisis and change. Firstly, this is because the mitigating factors of affluence and technology (following Commoner 1988) tend to overwhelm the force of crude numbers. A very few members of the global village consume the majority of its resources. When these factors are considered, overpopulation, to the extent that such a thing exists on a global or regional scale, appears to be a problem strictly of smaller, wealthier populations, especially the United States, rather than the apparently larger populations of the global south (Table 2).

The more fundamental problem with this formulation, however, is that it posits the environment as a finite source of basic unchanging and essential elements, which set absolute

Table 2. Who is overpopulated? Comparative per capita consumption of resources and production of waste (World Resources Institute 2010). India is three times larger than the United States, in terms of population, but consumes a comparatively tiny quantity of key resources and produces a fractional amount of waste.

Resource	India	United States
Meat (kg, 2002)	5	125
Paper (kg, 2005)	5	297
Water (m^3)	633	1,687
Energy (kg oil equivalent, 2005)	514	7,921
Carbon emissions (tonnes, 2005)	1	20

limits for human action. However intuitive (divide a limited stock of earth materials by a potentially infinite hungry human population and the result always approaches zero), this assumption has proved historically false and conceptually flawed.

Market "optimists," expressing the problem in economic terms, suggest that any form of resource scarcity creates a response that averts serious crisis. As a good becomes scarcer, they suggest, its price tends to rise, which results either in the clever use of substitutes and new technologies to increase efficiency, or in a simple decreased demand far that good. The result is that apparently finite resources are stretched to become infinitely available as consumers use less and producers supply more efficient alternatives and substitutes (Rees 1990). Even if populations rise on a limited land area, for example, the demand for land and rising land rents will increase its efficiency of use, with more and better production on each unit of land. Even if petroleum becomes scarce, the rising price per barrel will encourage the use of otherwise expensive alternatives like wind and solar power, or simply cause consumers to drive less, endlessly stretching the world's energy supply. While such optimistic prognoses are themselves fraught with problems, they do point to an important and increasingly well-accepted truism: resources are constructed rather than given.

This is not to argue that the number of organisms versus the extent and character of local resources is not an important issue; ask anyone who is in charge of extending water services to suburbs outside of Denver or Phoenix. To be sure, the number of people who use trees, food, water, metals, and other materials in part determines proximate demands on the environment. So too, the adaptation of natural systems to meet changing needs, whether driven by absolute numbers or changing consumption patterns, is an important element of human–environment interactions. Even so, the Malthusian population pressure model poorly reflects the complexity of global ecology. The argument does, however, hold serious implications for the use and management of resources.

When it was first offered up in Malthus's 1793 formulation, the ecoscarcity argument was presented as an explicit justification for social policy. In particular, Malthus insisted that since famine and starvation were essential to controlling runaway human populations, such events are "natural" and inevitable. England's Poor Laws, the modest redistributive welfare subsidies to feed the most marginal groups, were pointless and counter-environmental. By increasing rather than decreasing their numbers, such subsidies were the source not the solution of misery. So too, in such a conceptualization, the crisis for the poor lay not in the larger economy or ecology of their subsistence, but instead in and amongst the poor themselves: "In searching for objects of accusation, [the poor man] never adverts to the quarter from which all his misfortunes originate. The last person he would think of accusing is himself, on whom, in fact, the whole blame lies" (Malthus 1992, book 4, ch. 3. p. 227).

The implications for contemporary global environmentalism are equally programmatic. Environmental crises as demographic problems exist at the site of resource use, in and amongst the world's poor, who are simply too numerous. Subsidies of the poor do little to alleviate the crisis, since they only serve to reinforce the demographic trend. Population control, rather than reconfiguration of global distributions of power and goods, is the solution to ecological crisis. The continued advocacy of an apolitical natural-limits argument, therefore, is implicitly *political,* since it holds implications for the distribution and control of resources.

Demographic explanations of environmental change have become considerably more sophisticated than those outlined by Malthus and the Club of Rome. Attention to high-density urban development and the associated energy costs and infrastructure demands of megacities has created justifiably renewed attention to population as an important driver for environmental change. More recent research has come to demonstrate that the position of women in the workforce and their increased access to decision-making, calories, and education are closely linked not only to changing environmental conditions but also to decreased fertility and population growth. New approaches have come to redefine our ways of thinking about population, power, and environment. Even so, crude Malthusianism regrettably remains a typical way of thinking about environmental change, and so provides a unifying target for many political ecologists.

Other Apolitical Ecologies: Diffusion, Valuation, and Modernization

Other prominent accounts of environmental change also dominate current thinking, asserting apolitical answers to extremely political questions. It is commonly argued, for example, that ecological problems and crises throughout the world are the result of inadequate adoption and implementation of "modern" economic techniques of management, exploitation, and conservation. Generally, this way of thinking is underpinned by a commitment to economic efficiency.

These approaches to environmental management and ecological change generally assert that efficient solutions, determined in optimal economic terms, can create "win-win" outcomes where economic growth (sometimes termed "development") can occur alongside environmental conservation, simply by getting the prices and techniques right. Such approaches are persuasive, at least insofar as they reject the cataclysmic prognoses of Malthusian catastrophe described above. The assertion that economic efficiency pays environmental dividends is further supported by many examples over the recent period of industrial technological change. The historically dirty pulp and paper industry, in a prominent example, has simultaneously increased profit margins and decreased emissions through efficient industrial ecological practices (Pento 1999). By freeing individuals and firms to seek their own best and most efficient use of resources, propelled by competition on an open market and sustained by modern technology, waste, environmental destruction, and resource degradation can be tamed. Moreover, the sometimes perverse influence of strong state bureaucracies over the environment is perhaps avoided through market- and technology-based solutions.

For global ecology, such an approach suggests several general principles and policies. (1) Western/northern technology and techniques need to be diffused outwards to the underdeveloped world. (2) Firms and individuals must be connected to larger markets and given more exclusive property controls over environmental resources (e.g., land, air, wildlife). (3) For wilderness and biodiversity conservation, the benefits of these efficiencies must be realized through institutionalizing some form of valuation; environmental goods like wildebeest, air, and stream quality must be properly priced on an open market.

The debates and critiques surrounding such approaches and the logics that underpin them are too numerous to summarize here; even so, there are some serious general conceptual and empirical problems with this perspective. First, the assertion that modern technologies and markets can optimize production in the underdeveloped world, leading to conservation and environmental benefits, has proven historically questionable. The experience of the green revolution, where technologies of production developed in America and Europe were distributed and subsidized for agrarian production around the world, led to what even its advocates admit to be extensive environmental problems: exhausted soils, contaminated water, increased pest invasions (Lal et al. 2002). Beyond these failings, the more general assertion that superior environmental knowledge originates in the global north for transfer to the global south is in itself problematic, reproducing as it does paternalistic colonial knowledge relations and a priori discounting the environmental practices of indigenous and local communities (Uphoff 1988).

Articulation with global markets, as will be shown in the case materials presented here, has also proved to be a mixed environmental blessing at best. Changes in markets, falling commodity prices, and altered land values that have followed from globalized exchange have often led to land degradation and social disorder in the less developed world. A call to intensify these forms of exchange must be viewed skeptically. More generally, even in free and open markets, monopoly control of resources commonly perverts allocation and distribution, leading to far from optimal social and ecological outcomes. Indeed, the tradition of conservation in the United States is largely based on the understanding that collective control of environmental resources is necessary for fair and sustainable distribution.

Asserting and adopting the apparently apolitical approach to the environment suggested in market and modernization approaches, because of the institutional and political changes that such an approach mandates, is also inherently political. To individuate and distribute "collective" goods like forests or water by necessity requires the alienation of previous user groups. To implement new technological approaches in agriculture, resource extraction, or wilderness management requires a transformation of existing institutions. Increasingly open markets demand deregulation of labor and environmental controls. There is nothing apolitical about such a proposal.

The first lesson to draw is that the dominant contemporary accounts of environmental crisis and ecological change (ecoscarcity and modernization) tend to ignore the significant influence of political economic forces. As we shall see, this is to ignore the most fundamental problems in contemporary ecology. The other lesson is that apolitical ecologies, regardless of claims to even-handed objectivity, are implicitly political. It is not so much that political ecology is "more political" than these other approaches to the environment. Rather it is simply more *explicit* in its normative goals and more outspoken about the assumptions from which its research is conducted.

Common Assumptions and Modes of Explanation

Following Bryant and Bailey, political ecological accounts and research efforts also share a common premise, that environmental change and ecological conditions are the product of political process. This includes three fundamental and linked assumptions in approaching any research problem. Political ecologists: "accept the idea that costs and benefits associated with environmental change are for the most part distributed among actors unequally ... [which inevitably] reinforces or reduces existing social and economic inequalities ... [which holds] political implications in terms of the altered power of actors in relation to other actors" (Bryant and Bailey 1997, pp. 28–29).

Research tends to reveal winners and losers, hidden costs, and the differential power that produces social and environmental outcomes. As a result, political ecological research proceeds from central questions, such as: What causes regional forest loss? Who benefits from wildlife conservation efforts and who loses? What political movements have grown from local land use transitions?

In answering, political geologists follow a mode of explanation that evaluates the influence of variables acting at a number of scales, each nested within another, with local decisions influenced by regional polices, which are in turn directed by global politics and economics. Research pursues decisions at many levels, from the very local, where individual land managers make complex decisions about cutting trees, plowing fields, buying pesticides, and hiring labor, to the international, where multilateral lending agencies shift their multi-billion-dollar priorities from building dams to planting trees or farming fish. Such explanation also tends to be highly (sometimes recklessly) integrative. Bryant (1999) described the field as a series of "disciplinary transgressions," where researchers trace their personal and professional trajectories from political studies arid sociology to geography or from geography to development studies. And as we shall see, a group of people and institutions has emerged around such interdisciplinary transgressions, a global assemblage of diverse practitioners who make certain kinds of movies, write certain kinds of books, and advance certain kinds of arguments.

So, rather than adding yet another definition to a crowded field, it is best to suggest at the outset that political ecology is a term that describes a *community of practice* united around a *certain kind of text*. The nature of this community and the quality of these texts, as well as the theory and empirical research that underpins them, are the topic of the remainder of this volume. But broadly they can he understood to address the condition and change of social/environmental systems, with explicit consideration of relations of power. Political ecology, moreover, explores these social and environmental changes with an understanding that there are better, less coercive, less exploitative, and more sustainable ways of doing things. The research is directed at finding causes rather than symptoms of problems, including starvation, soil erosion, landlessness, biodiversity decline, human health crises, and the more general and pernicious conditions where some social actors exploit other people and environments for limited gain at collective cost. Finally, it is a field that stresses not only that ecological systems are political, but also that our very ideas about them arc further delimited and directed through political and economic process. As a result, political ecology presents a Jekyll and Hyde persona, attempting to do two things at once; critically explaining what is wrong with dominant accounts of environmental change, while at the same time exploring alternatives, adaptations, and creative human action in the face of mismanagement and exploitation: offering both a "hatchet" to take apart flawed, dangerous, and politically problematic accounts, and a "seed," to grow into new socio-ecologies.

Five Dominant Narratives in Political Ecology

In this sense, political ecology characterizes a kind of argument, text, or narrative, born of research efforts to expose the forces at work in ecological struggle and document livelihood alternatives in the face of change. This does not mean that political ecology is something that people must write and think about all the time. Much of this work is carried out by people who might never refer to themselves as political ecologists, who count writing, researching, or arguing as only one part of their job, or who might do so in only one sphere of their work. Neither is political ecology restricted to academics from the "first world." Indeed, the critical ideas and arguments of political ecology are often produced through the research and writing, blogging, filming, and advocacy of countless NGOs or activist groups around the world, surveying the changing fortunes of local people and the landscapes in which they live. This may actually comprise the largest share of work in political ecology. Published only in local meeting and development reports, or uploaded as short documentary videos or slide presentations, this work is as much a part of the field as the well-circulated books or refereed journal articles of formal science.

Big Questions and Theses

What unites the diverse work in these many locations is a general interest in five big themes. Over-simply, political ecology research has demonstrated (or attempted to demonstrate) the general theses shown in Table 3.

The Degradation and Marginalization Thesis

Otherwise environmentally innocuous production systems undergo transition to overexploitation of natural resources on which they depend as a response to state development intervention and/or increasing integration in regional and global markets. This may lead to increasing poverty and, cyclically, increasing overexploitation. Similarly, sustainable community management is hypothesized to become unsustainable as a result of efforts by state authorities or outside firms to enclose traditional collective properly or impose new/foreign institutions. Related assertions posit that modernist development efforts to improve production systems of local people have led contradictorily to decreased sustainability of local practice and a linked decrease in the equity of resource distribution.

Table 3. Five theses of political ecology and the thing they attempt to explain.

Thesis	What is explained?	Relevance
Degradation and marginalization	*Environmental conditions* (especially degradation) and the reasons for their change	Environmental degradation, long blamed on marginal people, is shown in its larger political and economic context.
Conservation and control	*Conservation outcomes* (especially failures)	Usually viewed as benign, efforts at environmental conservation are shown to have pernicious effects, and sometimes fail as a result.
Environmental conflict and exclusion	*Access* to the environment and conflicts over exclusion from it (especially natural resources)	Environmental conflicts are shown to be part of larger gendered, classed, and raced struggles and vice versa.
Environmental subjects and identity	*Identities* of people and social groups (especially new or emerging ones)	Political identities and social struggles are shown to be linked to basic issues of livelihood and environmental activity.
Political objects and actors	*Socio-political conditions* (especially deeply structured ones)	Political and economic systems are shown to be underpinned and affected by the nonhuman actors with which they are intertwined.

The Conservation and Control Thesis

Control of resources and landscapes has been wrested from producers or producer groups (associated by class, gender, or ethnicity) through the implementation of efforts to preserve "sustainability," "community," or "nature." In the process, local systems of livelihood, production, and socio-political organization have been disabled by officials and global interests seeking to preserve the "environment." Related work in this area has further demonstrated that where local production practices have historically been productive and relatively benign, they have been characterized as unsustainable by state authorities or other players in the struggle to control resources.

The Environmental Conflict and Exclusion Thesis

Increasing scarcities produced through resource enclosure or appropriation by state authorities, private firms, or social elites accelerate conflict between groups (gender, class, or ethnicity). Similarly, environmental problems become "socialized" when such groups secure control of collective resources at the expense of others by leveraging management interventions by development authorities, state agents, or private firms. So too, existing and long-term conflicts within and between communities are "ecologized" by changes in conservation or resource development policy.

The Environmental Subjects and Identity Thesis

Institutionalized and power-laden environmental management regimes have led to the emergence of new kinds of people, with their own emerging self-definitions, understandings of the world, and ecological ideologies and behaviors. More firmly: people's beliefs and attitudes do not lead to new environmental actions, behaviors, or rules systems; instead, new environmental actions, behaviors, or rules systems lead to new kinds of people. Correlatively, new environmental regimes and conditions have created opportunities or imperatives for local groups to secure and represent themselves politically. Such movements often represent a new form of political action, since their ecological strands can connect disparate groups, across class, ethnicity, and gender.

Political Objects and Actors Thesis

Material characteristics of non-human nature and its components (dung, climate, refrigerators, bacteria, lawn grass, road salt, goats, and tropical soils) impinge upon the world of human struggles and are entwined within them, and so are inevitably political. Yet as these characteristics and agents assume new roles and take on new importance, they are also transformed by these interactions. People, institutions, communities, and nations assemble and participate in the networks that emerge, leveraging power and influence, just as non-human organisms and communities do. In recent history, hegemonic institutions and individuals (environmental ministries, multinational corporations, corrupt foresters) have gained disproportionate influence by controlling and directing new connections and transformations, leading to unintended consequences and often pernicious results. In the process, resistance emerges from traditional, alternative, or progressive human/non-human alliances marginalized by such efforts (especially along lines of class, ethnicity, and gender).

The Target of Explanation

Of course, each of these theses actually seeks to explain something somewhat different. While degradation and marginalization offers an explanation of why *environmental systems* change (because of capital accumulation), environmental subjectivity research seeks to explain why *social identities* change (because of transformed environmental institutions). This diversity of targets for explanation has been the source of some confusion in the field (Vayda and Walters 1999) and reflects its historic development.

Research linking environmental change to political and economic marginalization emerged first in the 1970s and 80s as an attempt to apply dependency theory to the environmental crises of the period (see Chapter 8). The problematic effects of global and regional conservation efforts, including World Heritage Sites, national parks, and biodiversity zones, also became increasingly apparent in the 1990s, and political ecology on the topic benefited from a growing interest in the historical development of conservation (Chapter 9). Interest in environmental conflict soon followed, as many environmental issues became increasingly politicized in both regional contexts, from Love Canal to the Amazonian rainforest, as well as global ones, with the emergence of global agreements and debates on climate and biodiversity. Interest in the new environmental activism and identities grew from all of the issues above, and was placed squarely on the agenda by local people themselves, including Andean peasant movements, the Zapatistas, *chipko,* and a host of other movements. An interest in political objects and agents is the most recent addition to debate in political ecology, rooted in its deep historical materialism, but also in an emerging concern more generally for the way the non-human world impinges on the human one.

The diversity of political ecology research also results from innumerable, smaller, differing arguments addressing, among many issues:

- possibility for community collective action;
- role of human labor in environmental metabolism;
- nature of risk-taking and risk-aversion in human behavior;
- diversity of environmental perceptions;
- causes and effects of political corruption;
- relationship between knowledge and power.

These many topics and concerns overlap, and a coherent set of answers to these questions is beginning to achieve something of a consensus. They also provide bridges to one another, creating a kind of lattice-work of investigation. Understanding how changing forms of knowledge, like computerized mapping, for example, lead to new systems of control over a forest probably leads a researcher to ask: What are the concomitant changes in the behavior of foresters, and does this create new patterns of actual forest ecology?

Moreover, in their linkages to local communities and NGOs, political ecologists, whether they are more interested in the biophysical or social aspects of a problem, have helped to build practical, detailed, integrated, empirical databases on all these diverse issues, recording land covers, farming practices, wildlife management systems, technological innovations and diffusions, local folk tales and oral histories, and informal markets and economies. These basic empirical findings help communities make decisions, aid in advocacy for social and environmental causes, and serve as a record to future scholars about the way things looked at the dawn of the twenty-first century.

The value of this last contribution, providing an historical record, is not a trivial one. Much of what we know about the political economy of the environment is bequeathed to us by political ecologists of previous generations. Indeed, political ecology can arguably said to be very old, since nineteenth" and twentieth-century environmental research in geography, anthropology, and allied natural and social sciences has a long critical tradition. Even before a semi-coherent body of political ecological theory emerged in the late twentieth century, many explicitly political practitioners emerged from the ranks of field ecologists, ethnographers, explorers, and other researchers. These represent the deep roots of the field.

References

Blaikie, P. and H. Brookfield. 1987. *Land Degradation and Society.* London and New York: Methuen.

Bryant, R. and S. Bailey. 1997. *Third World Political Ecology*. New York: Routledge.

Bryant, R. L. 1999. "A Political Ecology for Developing Countries." *Zeitschrift fur Wirtschaftsgeographie* 43: 148–57.

Cockburn, A. and J. Ridgeway, eds. 1979. *Political Ecology*. New York: Times Books.

Collett, D. 1987. "Pastoralists and Wildlife: Image and Reality in Kenya Massailand." *In Conservation in Africa: Peoples, Policies and Practice, edited by D. Anderson and R. H. Grove*, 129-48. Cambridge: Cambridge University Press.

Commoner, B. 1988. "Crossroads, Environmental Priorities for the Future." I*n Crossroads, Environmental Priorities for the Future, edited by Peter Borrelli*, 121-69. Washington DC: Island Press.

Ehrlich, P. R. 1997. *The Population Bomb*. New York: Sierra Club/Ballantine.

Greenberg, J. B. and T.K. Park. "Political Ecology." *Journal of Political Ecology* 1: 1–12.

Hempel, L. C. 1996. *Environmental Governance: The Global Challenge*. Washington, DC: Island Press.

Homewood, K., E.F. Lambin, E. Coast, A. Kariuki, I. Kikula, J. Kivelia, M. Said, S. Serneels, and M. Thompson. "Long-Term Changes in Serengeti-Mara Wildebeest and Land Cover: Pastoralism, Population, or Policies?" *Proceedings of the National Academy of Sciences* 98: 12544–49.

Lal, R., D. O. Hansen, and N. Uphoff. 2002. *Food Security and Environmental Quality in the Developing World*. Boca Raton: CRC Press.

Malthus, T. 1992. *An Essay on the Principle of Population (Selected and Introduced by D. Winch)*. Cambridge: Cambridge University Press.

Meadows, D. H., E. Goldsmith, and P. Meadow. 1972. *The Limits to Growth*. New York: Universe books.

Peet, R., and M. Watts. 1996. "Liberation Ecology: Development, Sustainability, and Environment in the Age of Market Triumphalism." *In Liberation Ecologies: Environment, Development and Social Movements*, 1-45. New York: Routledge.

Pento, T. 1999. "Industrial Ecology of the Paper Industry." *Water Science & Technology* 40: 21–24.

Rees, J.A. 1990. *Natural Resources: Allocation, Economics and Policy*. New York: Routledge.

Robbins, P. 2012. *Political Ecology: A Critical Introduction*. West Sussex and Malden: John Wiley & Sons.

Stott, P. A., and S. Sullivan, eds. 2000. *Political Ecology: Science, Myth and Power.* London: Arnold.

Uphoff, N. 1988. "Assisted Self-Reliance: Working with, Rather Than for the Poor." *In Strengthening the Poor: What Have We Learned?, edited by J.P. Lewis*. Washington DC: Transaction Books.

Vayda, A. P., and B. B. Walters. 2000. "Against Political Ecology." *Human ecology* 27: 167–79.

Watts, M. 2000. "Political Ecology." In *A Companion to Economic Geography, edited by E. Sheppard and T. Barnes*, 257-74. Oxford: Blackwell.

Wolf, E. "Ownership and Political Ecology." *Anthropological Quarterly* 45(3): 201–05.

World Resources Institute. 1991/2010. "Earth Trends." http://earthtrends.wri.org (accessed June 22, 2011).

CASE STUDY

Global Garbage
Waste, Trash Trading, and Local Garbage Politics

By Sarah A. Moore

Introduction

In September of 2009, Trafigura, a Dutch oil trading company with additional offices in Great Britain, settled a lawsuit brought against it by the people of Abidjan, the main city of the Ivory Coast. The suit alleged that hundreds of tons of waste dumped by the company around the city caused nausea, headaches, vomiting, violent rashes, and even death among thousands of people living near the dump sites. The company denied legal liability, and claimed that the waste was not toxic, but it also agreed to pay out 197 million US dollars.

About a year earlier, in October of 2008, Somali pirates demanded 8 million dollars in ransom for a Ukrainian ship that they had captured. They claimed that the money would be used to clean up toxic waste dumps along the coastal region of Somalia. The spokesperson for the pirates argued that the hijacking of the ship was, in part, a reaction to 20 years of illegal waste dumping on the Somali coast by European firms.

These two events, one a courtroom battle, the other a high seas drama, both point to one undeniable fact: as much as countries, people, and companies across the globe are connected (albeit unevenly) by the circulation of goods and services, they are also connected by the flows of waste. These flows of waste, moreover, are intimately connected to global flows of capital, processes of uneven development and marginalization. Because waste and its disposal are so closely tied to these other global processes, it is imperative to understand that where waste is produced and disposed of are not purely technical matters. Rather, they are inevitably political issues, deeply infused with power relationships, questions of justice and governance, and shaped by representational practices. In this chapter, I discuss several related political and economic aspects of garbage in order to highlight the importance of avoiding technocentric understandings of and solutions to environmental and public health problems. In doing so, I emphasize the roots of our garbage production and disposal practices and patterns in the global capitalist system.

This chapter is divided into the following sections. First, I discuss some basic issues in understanding the global garbage situation including definitions of garbage and waste, estimates of the quantities of waste produce across the globe, and how these definitions and quantities of waste vary spatially. Next, I turn to a larger discussion of the uneven production of waste and the evolution of the international trade in hazardous and municipal solid waste. In the following section, I discuss what happens at the end sites of these global flows of waste (i.e. dump and disposal sites) and issues of environmental justice as well as how garbage can be used as a local political tool by some groups. I conclude by highlighting how a political ecology approach, centered on the relations of capitalism, representation, and citizen/expert knowledge adds to the study of global garbage.

Global Geographies of Garbage

Before evaluating the political ecology of global garbage flows, some basic questions must be addressed. First, it is necessary to define the terms of the discussion. What, after all, is garbage? Second, some basic understanding of where and how garbage is produced and disposed of is essential to understanding the conditions under which garbage has become an important global commodity. These may at first appear to be straightforward questions, but they are not as easy to answer as one might think. In the first case, definitions of garbage differ. Is it simply something that has been thrown in the trashcan? What about items destined for recycling? Should they be considered part of the waste stream? Are garbage, waste, and trash all the same? In the second case, even if we agree on definitions of garbage, how do we collect information about how much of it there is and where it can be found?

There are no simple answers to these questions. For the purposes of this chapter, garbage, waste, and trash will be used interchangeably, but distinguished from hazardous waste. This might be a dubious distinction, given that most waste has some potential to be an environmental or public health risk, depending on how and where it is disposed of. On the other hand, though, most regulations deal differently with wastes identified as hazardous than with another large category of waste, municipal solid waste (MSW). The United Nations defines MSW as "waste originating from: households, commerce and trade, small businesses, office buildings and institutions (schools, hospitals, government buildings)." This, "includes bulky waste (e.g. white goods, old furniture, mattresses) and waste from selected municipal services, e.g. waste from park and garden maintenance, waste from street cleaning services (street sweepings, the content of litter containers, market cleansing waste), if *managed as waste*" (United Nations 2009a). This definition is broad and highlights the importance of the social context in deciding what is and what is not garbage: waste is what is "managed as waste." The management and treatment of MSW represents more than *one third* of the public sector's expenditures on pollution abatement and control (OECD 2008). This means that a large proportion of government money earmarked for all environmental needs goes to the management of MSW.

Hazardous waste, in contrast, can be broadly defined as "waste that, owing to its toxic, infectious, radioactive or flammable properties poses an actual or potential hazard to the health of humans, other living organisms, or the environment" (United Nations 2009b) (see section V, Part A for hazardous waste definition text box). This is also a broad definition, and one that leaves much room for debate over what should and should not be regulated as hazardous waste. For that reason, most waste must be listed in specific annexes according to national or international laws and agreements to be regulated as hazardous waste.

As is hinted at in the definitions of MSW and hazardous waste above, whether or not something is considered trash depends on time and place more than any inherent characteristics of the object itself. Most things bought (commodities) by consumers in wealthy countries end up at a dump, legal or illegal, far or near. But, this is not necessarily the whole story. Old clothes can be given away, handed-down, sold to a consignment store, or torn into rags and used for cleaning. A discarded computer could be smashed along with other items in the dumpster, or it could be carefully taken apart in a recycling center so that its various components can be shipped to Asia and reused. A banana skin could be thrown in a public garbage can, or tossed on the compost pile along with the grounds from your morning coffee. Then again, what if you throw your banana peel or your empty soda bottle in the trash and someone else picks it out of the trash to use in gardening or to return for a deposit. The point is that things can alternate, in the course of their social lives, from trash to treasure, useless to useful, valueless to invaluable, just as easily as they can go in the opposite direction (from treasure to trash, for example).

How garbage is defined and managed, then, are largely influenced by negotiated definitions of waste, like those of MSW and hazardous waste above. This has implications for how statistics on waste are compiled. At what point does something count as waste? Do we count everything disposed of by each household, or only the waste that goes to incinerators or dumps for final disposal? What about items that are disposed of locally, but then make their way overseas where they are recycled into other products? Such issues make it difficult to determine the amount of waste that is generated and disposed of in each household, city, or country. At the international level, efforts have been made over the last decade to keep better data on waste. The United Nations (UN) and the Organization for Economic Cooperation and Development (OECD) keep some of the most comprehensive statistics on garbage generation, disposal and trade.

There are many gaps in the data, and there are significant reporting differences between countries. Further, OECD data reflects only the situation of its 30 member countries. Nonetheless, there are some general trends that the data suggest. In general terms, municipal solid waste in OECD countries increased almost 23 percent between 1990 and 2006 from 530 to 650 million tons (OECD 2008). This is a per capita jump from 509–660 kg/year. This aggregate number, though, masks significant differences between OECD member countries. Some of the geography of global garbage production can be better understood by examining a few ways in which member countries differ, including total garbage production, per capita garbage production, and increases in per capita garbage production.

The overall largest producer of MSW in the world is the United States, with 222,863,000 tons/year. This by far exceeds the next largest producer, Japan, at 51,607,000 tons/year. Germany (49,563,000), Mexico (36,088,000) and the UK (35,077,000) round out the top five. These rankings change, however, if we consider the per capita, rather than total production of MSW in each country. The largest producers of MSW per capita are Ireland, Norway, and the United States. In each of these countries, per capita production of waste is near 800 kg/year. Denmark and Luxembourg also each produce more than 700 kg MSW per capita each year. Japan (400kg), Germany (600 kg), and the UK (580kg), some of the largest aggregate producers of waste, produce less waste per capita. The United States is the only country in the top five, both in total and per capita production of municipal solid waste. On the other end of the spectrum, four member countries have per capita numbers under 400 kgs/capita. These are Poland, Slovak Republic, the Czech Republic, and Mexico (one of the largest total producers).

The country with the largest increase in per capita production of waste since 1990 is Spain (over 70 percent). Other countries with a more than 50 percent increase in per capita waste production between 1990 and 2006 are Italy, Portugal and Greece. Of the countries reporting on this statistic, only Hungary and Poland saw a reduction in per capita waste production (about 10 percent in each case). The largest producers of waste vary in this category. While Ireland did not report on the percent change in per capita waste production, the US had little change (less than 5 percent), but Norway saw a near 50 percent increase in per capita solid waste production during the period. The OECD mean was just under 20 percent.

The country-level data cited above may help in part to indicate some of the factors creating the geography of waste production. While new data indicate that generation intensity per capita grew at a slower rate than the gross domestic product (GDP) and private final consumption expenditure (PFC) (OECD 2008), it is still generally agreed upon that economic growth, urbanization and the structure of consumption are all positively associated with increased garbage production (OECD 2008). These are all factors that many consider to be associated with *development* as popularly defined. That is, the high mass consumption culture often associated with places like the United States, much of Western Europe and Japan. In short, development as the extension of capitalist relations (Wainwright 2008), produces garbage.

The success of global capitalism relies on growth. If, as happened in 2008 and 2009, growth is stopped, things can fall apart very quickly. An average 20 percent increase in per capita garbage production over the last 15 years reminds us that economic growth, while seemingly increasingly created through financial markets that appear detached from patterns of production and consumption, is still dependent on the creation and movement of goods and services across the globe. The creation and movement of goods is inevitably tied to the production of waste. Anything that is traded and consumed makes garbage both as a by-product of production and as a remainder after the good has lost its utility for the consumer.

For people able to afford the high-consumption lifestyle of the "developed world" the most familiar form of waste is packaging. Food and beverages are a good example of the impact of packaging. While most of what is inside the package, (meat, cheese, vegetables, fruits, soda, water) is consumed, the package (deli wrap, plastic bags, Styrofoam containers, aluminum cans, plastic or glass bottles) remains. These are necessary parts of the now global food system, but they present difficulties for waste managers, particularly in places where the consumption of packaged goods has increased quickly.

On the other hand, it is not just food that requires packaging. Most goods that are part of a globalized process of production come in some kind of container. All goods that are shipped across long distances require packaging. Many times, the bulk of the packaging is greater than that of the good itself. Think, for example, of a tiny halogen bulb in a big (nearly unopenable) plastic container. Packaging accounted for nearly one third of the MSW in the United States in 2005 (69,555,000 tons) (OECD 2008).

Clearly, though, if packaging is the first thing thrown out, it is not the last. The bulb, or the TV, or the Ipod or the sweater will eventually need to be disposed of. This too, presents a problem for waste management. The more goods that are produced and consumed, the higher the eventual waste stream. A good example of this is the growing amount of post-consumer electronic or e-waste (see Section V, Part A for e-waste definition text box). According to the United States Environmental Protection Agency, 41,100,000 computers (laptops and desktops) were disposed of in the US in 2007. Although 18 percent of e-waste in the United States was recycled that year, hundreds of millions of computers, televisions and cell phones were trashed, placing pressure on solid and hazardous waste disposal systems across the country (United States Environmental Protection Agency 2008).

Lack of sufficient disposal, though, has not kept companies from continuing to produce and market more and more goods, many of which face planned obsolescence. Even relatively "durable" goods like cars, refrigerators, computers and televisions, can also be replaced with items with more bells and whistles. Not to mention the stock of VCRs, tape players, and certain DVD players for which products are no longer made, due to investment by companies in other forms of technology. All of these end up somewhere, and chances increasingly are that they do not end up in your local dump. For many reasons, these and other items are often shipped to other countries for recycling and disposal. This has resulted in a multi-billion dollar waste trade industry.

In the next sections of this chapter, we will explore the imbrications of the global economy with waste through, first, the international flows of garbage and, second, the conditions associated with garbage's final resting spots, i.e. landfills.

Global Flows of Garbage

Capitalism makes garbage, and when local disposal systems reach capacity, the system is presented with a potential crisis situation. This crisis can be deferred through what many geographers, following David Harvey, refer to as a spatial fix (Harvey 2007). That is, garbage can be shipped to other places, often far removed from producers and consumers. In this way, waste itself has become a commodity. It is now bought and sold on a global market. Both municipal solid waste and hazardous waste are traded internationally. In this section, I focus on the international trade in hazardous waste, though, as discussed above, this can be a dubious distinction, given that all waste has the potential to cause environmental and public health problems.

Between 1976 and 1991, the cost of disposing of hazardous waste in industrial countries increased by a factor of 25 (Asante-Duah and Nagy 1998). This increased disposal cost, contributed to high levels of both legal and illegal transboundary shipments of waste. As transboundary shipments of hazardous waste increased in the 1980s and 1990s, it became increasingly clear that much of the waste was going from more developed countries with stricter environmental regulations to less developed countries with either less strict environmental regulations or without the capacity to enforce the laws in place (Asante-Duah and Nagy l998; O'Neill 2000).

As one example, consider hazardous wastes shipped from the United States. The growth trends in notices to export hazardous wastes (required by the US EPA) between 1980 and 1990 are notable. In 1980, there were only 12 such notices filed. In 1986 there were 286. By 1988 that number had increased to 570. By the end of the decade, over 620 notices were filed each year. In global terms, by the early 2000s, the international trade in hazardous waste was a multi-billion dollar industry (OECD 2008).

International environmental economics suggests that in a "first-best" world of equal trade relationships, international trade in hazardous waste could be beneficial to all countries involved (Rauscher 2001). Indeed, such logic was echoed in the late 1990s by the US EPA, who argued that one reason to export hazardous waste was that in some cases, "hazardous wastes constitute 'raw' material inputs into industrial and manufacturing processes." The report continued: "This is the case in many developing countries where natural resources are scarce or non-existent" (US EPA 1998).

While it is true that hazardous wastes may sometimes be recycled, many are less sanguine about a cost-benefit approach to the waste trade (Asante-Duah and Nagy 1998; O'Neill 2000; Girdner and Smith 2002). In the "second best" world of environmental economics, it is argued that insufficient environmental policies in some countries could distort the market and make the international hazardous waste trade more harmful to the environment and to public health (Rauscher 2001). This is commonly known as the pollution haven hypothesis. The "pollution haven hypothesis" holds that some countries might voluntarily reduce environmental regulations in order to attract foreign direct investment. Some also argue that, even if producers are not inclined to relocate production, they might still decide to export the negative externalities of their production (like hazardous waste) to countries with less regulation and lower disposal costs (O'Neill 2000).

One way to prevent uneven, unjust, and potentially dangerous transboundary waste shipments is to force trading partners into international agreements such as the Basel Convention, which came into effect in 1992. The Basel Convention prevents richer countries from exporting their hazardous wastes to poorer countries. It has been ratified by 172 countries. The United States signed the agreement in the early 1990s but has yet to ratify it. Clearly, however, these regulations only apply to legal trade of hazardous waste. There is a significant illegal trade in hazardous waste, which for obvious reasons has been difficult to document. Lawsuits like the one filed against Trafigura by residents of Abidjan are one source of data on potentially illegal dumping.

In addition to directly banning certain waste transfers, parties to free trade agreements, which are proliferating in this period of global or regional economic integration, might also experience "harmonization" of regulation. This is generally seen as a way to bring regulatory standards of developing countries up to those of developed ones. If regulations are consistent across trading partners, this theoretically eliminates any incentive to ship hazardous waste across borders for treatment (O'Neill 2000).

There is little evidence, though, that harmonization necessarily promotes positive environmental outcomes (O'Neill 2000), despite the fact that it is much lauded as a way of greening environmental agreements. The North American Free Trade Agreement (NAFTA), for example, was originally considered a green free trade agreement because of its side agreements on the environment and steps toward harmonization of regulation across the United States, Mexico and Canada. But the environmental initiatives in the agreement are relatively weak. In fact, the environmental side agreement does not include specific provisions for the management of hazardous waste, but rather cedes these to pre-existing bilateral agreements between the US and Mexico (the La Paz agreement of 1986) and the US and Canada (the agreement was made in 1986 and amended in 1992).

It is not clear what impact these issues actually have on the environmental or public health. There are data to suggest that increased production associated with integration has led to higher levels of pollution along the Mexican border (Di Chiro 2004; Mumme 2007; Simpson 2008) and to an increase in illegal hazardous waste dumping and legal imports of hazardous waste (Slocum 2009).

There is evidence, though, that environmental initiatives created by NAFTA are less important to environmental quality than are some of its free trade articles (Sanchez 2002). One goal of economic integration is to reduce all barriers to trade, not just formal tariffs and quotas. Increasingly, free trade agreements focus on eliminating non-tariff barriers to trade (NTBs). Because environmental regulations have the potential to limit activities and profits of companies investing in foreign countries, such measures are considered NTBs. One important indication of this is the successful use of NAFTA Chapter 11 by corporations who would like to avoid more stringent environmental regulations.

Chapter 11 was written into NAFTA as insurance against expropriation of firm resources by states to protect foreign direct investment (FDI). In the case of NAFTA, it has been used by firms to argue against environmental regulations on the grounds that they represent expropriation because they diminish profits, particularly if they become more stringent over time. A number of prominent lawsuits, based on this interpretation, have been brought against the US, Mexico, and Canada by corporations under Article 1110. Many of these involve the treatment and disposal of hazardous waste. One early example of this is *Metalclad v. Mexico.* The US corporation Metalclad acquired a Mexican hazardous waste company and planned to construct a new waste facility in the city of Guadeleazar, San Luis Potosi in 1993. Metalclad believed that it had permission for the construction, but the municipal authorities shut down the construction after five months. Metalclad brought suit demanding compensation from the Mexican government under Article 1110 of NAFTA. The tribunal found in favor of the corporation, arguing that, since Metalclad was operating under the assumption that they had permission to build on the site, the denial of a permit by the Guadeleazar city council was "tantamount to expropriation." The tribunal also found that Guadeleazar did not have jurisdiction to deny a permit on the grounds of environmental hazards (Chiu 2003).

In these and other cases, it became clear that the interests of international corporations have been privileged over the rights of local people to decide whether or not to allow disposal of toxic substances in their communities. Such precedents ensure the continued growth of the transboundary trade in waste.

Living with Trash: Where the Flows Stop

The global nature of the garbage trade, though, must not be overstated. While the flows of garbage around the world may connect disparate places, the impacts of this trade are felt most deeply by specific people in the places where those flows stop. The garbage trade is truly international, but the effects are largely local. Contaminants leach into a specific community's aquifers, runoff soaks into soil in particular neighborhoods, roaches and rats congregate in locales with dumps. It is true that many of these problems have broader environmental impacts too. Waste incineration contributes to local air quality problems, but also global warming. But, much of the time the brunt of the consequences of the global garbage trade are borne by local communities. In this section, I discuss the politics of deciding who will live with and near waste.

The siting of waste disposal facilities is not primarily a technical issue at any level. Rather, it is always and everywhere a political one. This is well documented by scholars and activists in the area of environmental justice (Gottlieb 1993; Szasz 1994; Liu 2000; Westra and Lawson 2001; Kurtz 2005). Much of the original focus of environmental justice was on waste disposal facilities in the United States. Beginning with Bullard's path-breaking work on dumpsite locations in the Southern US, many scholars and activists brought attention to the fact that disposal sites were disproportionately located in minority and/or poor communities (Bullard 1994). Several potential explanations were put forth. Some argued that the siting was simply the result of land rents being lower in poor and minority neighborhoods. Others argued that such communities had a harder time being successful at NIMBY (not in my back yard) politics. Their marginal status meant that they had less political clout to prevent waste facilities from being located in their neighborhoods. Still others argued that this was a case of simple and blatant racism. In truth, all of these issues might be factors in some specific cases. What was missing in some of the early analyses of the problem, however, were ties to the related processes that created uneven development, marginalization of poor and minority communities, and the very problem of waste itself (Pulido 2000).

These related processes are tied to the way that capitalism works as a mode of production. Accumulation is necessary for the continued growth of the economy. But, it is also an uneven process, one that puts assets and wealth in the hands of the relative few, and forces countless others to meet their needs through wage labor. At the same time, those people fortunate enough to own the means of production are constantly at risk for declining profits, due to the crisis-prone nature of capitalism. In order to stave off under-consumption, firms must constantly create demand for new goods, thus the planned obsolescence of many commodities discussed above. As much as the processes of uneven development and increased production have differential impacts within a country like the United States, they have an analogous effect on an international scale. This is the problem that treaties like The Basel Convention are designed to solve. As noted above, however, such efforts have not been successful at ameliorating the local effects of the transboundary trade in hazardous waste. Moreover, they say nothing about waste that, while not classified as hazardous (a constantly shifting category), could still have negative consequences for public and environmental health.

While there are obvious ethical problems with the fact that a small proportion of people (many of whom produce minimal quantities of waste themselves) are forced to live with wastes resulting from high-consumption lifestyles among a privileged few global citizens, there are other issues at stake when considering solutions to such problems. First, there are millions of people in places like Guatemala, Indonesia, India and Mexico who live on dumps. The plight of such people is well documented (Crocker 1988; Beall 1997). What is also evident, though, is that these dump communities have their own social structures and informal institutions that do provide livelihoods, however marginal, for many families. In many cases, dumps provide resource bases from which people glean materials to build housing, feed themselves and provide income through recycling (Castillo Berthier 1990; Castillo Berthier 2003).

It would be a mistake of course, to glamorize or romanticize life on a dump, but it would also be an error to assume that development institutions, philanthropic organizations and other well-meaning groups have an unquestionable right to interfere in such places, without seeking input from community members. Often, such groups are operating from within a set of discourses that identify waste with chaos, backwardness, and lack of purity. Because of this, they fail to recognize that, in some ways, these are well-ordered spaces complete with their own forms of governance and social practices that must be taken into account in finding just, solutions to the ethical dilemma surrounding the unequal distribution of waste and disposal, locally, nationally, and internationally.

Protesting with Trash

The production of waste is a necessary part of our global economy. But, even though millions of tons of waste flow across the globe into various facilities each year, it is a largely invisible one. In this section I discuss what happens when these flows are stopped short and garbage is left where it does not "belong." In these instances, garbage becomes a political tool.

As environmental justice teaches us, some people in particular places across the globe are forced to live their daily lives near dumps and other places with large quantities of trash. On the other hand, in many modern cities with well developed sanitation systems, the majority of residents are accustomed to relatively clean spaces where litter and debris, though still present, are minimal. In such places, garbage is mostly invisible and well-contained (in its place). This makes the unexpected sight of garbage in such places disturbing and gives a certain amount of power to people who can stop the flow of waste. There are a number of groups capable of employing this politics of manifestation—of making waste visible (Moore 2008). Two of the main groups are municipal sanitation workers and people who live near disposal sites. In the last decade, for example, numerous garbage collection strikes in Europe and North America have been effective in securing job benefits and better pay for workers.

This was the case in Philadelphia 1986, New York City 2006, Toronto, Ontario, 2002, Chicago 2003, Vancouver, British Columbia 2007, Athens, Greece 2006, Alumñécar, Spain 2007. The precise motivations behind these strikes differed, and they ranged in time from a few days to several months. They all, though, have in common the use of garbage as a political tool (Moore 2009). In each case municipal authorities, or private garbage haulers (as in the case of NYC), or legislators (as in Toronto) were forced to negotiate deals with employees and their union representatives to get trash off the streets and out of the sight of angry residents.

A similar way of using garbage as political leverage can be found in cases in which one group simply blocks access to disposal sites, thereby causing uncollected garbage to pile up across and urban area. One example of this comes from Oaxaca, Mexico. Throughout the early 2000s residents of an informal settlement near the municipal dump regularly blocked the city trucks from dumping trash in the large open air dump used by the entire urban area. The blockades played out in a similar way each time. As the municipal authorities halted garbage collection, residents were told to keep their trash in their homes, rather than to pile it in the street. This advice, however, was not heeded by citizens who felt that the municipality was not complying with its obligation to keep the city clean. Hundreds of tons of waste piled up in parks, on street corners, and near market areas.

In addition to annoying residents with its visible presence and increasing smell, the garbage attracted rodents, insects and feral dogs. This, combined with the negative impression on tourists (a key source of the city's income) was enough to lead the municipal authorities to negotiate with the protestors to gain access to the dump. While some of the neighborhood's demands centered on garbage management issues: the inability of authorities to prevent fires on the dump, poor engineering of the landfill, and the fact that the dump was over capacity; the community also received electricity, a medical center and a meeting center as a result of the protests (Moore 2008). In this way, these marginalized citizens were able to use garbage to assert their rights to the city.

Whether wielded by municipal workers or neighborhood residents, the power of garbage as a political tool comes in part from the fact that it stinks and attracts pests. It comes equally, though, from the expectation of many modern urban citizens, particularly in developed countries, that garbage should be out of sight and thus off their minds. In this way, the unexpected presence of garbage reminds people in a visceral way of the consequences of a high-consumption, disposable lifestyle.

Conclusion

This chapter has discussed numerous ways in which garbage is more than simply a technical issue. What garbage is, where garbage is, and how it gets disposed of are political issues. The very definitions of solid waste and hazardous waste are negotiated and differ according to context. Even when there is agreement on what constitutes garbage, questions remain about how to determine who has to live with it. In this way, state power and economic relationships are also important aspects of an international political ecology of garbage. This is as true of the two incidents that began this piece (dumping in the Ivory Coast and hijacking by Somali pirates) as it is of the hazardous waste flows influenced by NAFTA and other free trade agreements. On the other hand, municipal garbage workers and neighborhood protestors have demonstrated the ways that garbage can be used to challenge current power relationships and to improve the economic situation of workers and residents who live with it on a day to day basis.

These contradictory moments (garbage as threat vs. garbage as political tool) in the political aspects of garbage have commonalities that are revealed only by thinking beyond the familiar technological approaches that focus on responsible environmental *management* of garbage. A global political ecology of garbage instead points to how waste production, trade and disposal, just like global flows of (other) commodities, capital and services unfold across an always uneven terrain of development and power. While the former instances demonstrate the lack of local control over garbage flows and disposal and the disconnection between spaces of consumption and spaces of waste, the people who choose to protest with trash highlight the fact that global flows always have local nodes. Moreover, by stopping these flows and making waste visible in central areas, such protestors reconnect spaces of consumption and spaces of waste. This has radical implications for the continuation and extension of the high-consumption style of development associated with global capitalism, because it gives us insight into what might happen when there are no more spatial fixes available to resolve our garbage crisis. If continued production and consumption are enabled by the disposal of goods, what happens when trash remains in place?

References

Asante-Duah, D. K. and I. V. Nagy (1998). *International Trade in Hazardous Waste.* London, E. & F.N. Spon.

Beall, J. (1997). "Thoughts on Poverty from a South Asian Rubbish Dump." *IDS Bulletin* 28(3): 73–90.

Bullard, R. D. (1994). *Dumping in Dixie: Race, Class and Environmental Quality.* Boulder, CO, Westview Press.

Castillo Berthier, H. (1990). *La Sociedad de la Basura: Caciquismo en la Ciudad de México.* México, D.F., Universidad Nacional Autónoma de México.

_____ (2003). "Garbage, Work and Society." *Resources, Conservation and Recycling* 39(3): 193–210.

Chiu, C. (2003). "NAFTA Chapter 11 and the Environment." *Environmental Policy and Law* 33(2): 71–76.

Crocker, G. (1988). "Squatting on Garbage Dumps: Behind the Self-help Housing Debate: A Case Study of a Guatemala City Garbage Dump." *School of Planning,* Universidad Mariano Gálvez de Guatemala: 102.

Di Chiro, G. (2004). "'Living is for Everyone': Border Crossings for Community, Environment, and Health." *Osiris* 19: 112–129.

Girdner, E. J. and J. Smith (2002). *Killing Me Softly: Toxic Waste, Corporate Profit and the Struggle for Environmental Justice.* New York Monthly Review Press.

Gottlieb, R. (1993). *Forcing the Spring.* Washington, D.C., Island Press.

Harvey, D. (2007). *The Limits to Capital.* London, Verso.

Kurtz, H. E. (2005). "Reflections on the Iconography of Environmental Justice Activism." *Area* 37(1): 79–88.

Liu, F. (2000). *Environmental Justice Analysis: Theories, Methods, and Practice.* Boca Raton, LA, Lewis Publishers.

Moore, S. A. (2008). "The Politics of Garbage in Oaxaca, Mexico." *Society & Natural Resources: An International Journal* 21(7): 597–610.

_____ (2009). 'The Excess of Modernity: Garbage Politics in Oaxaca, Mexico." *The Professional Geographer* 61(4): 426–437.

Mumme, S. P. (2007). "Trade Integration, Neoliberal Reform, and Environmental Protection in Mexico – Lessons for the Americas." *Latin American Perspectives* 34(3): 91–107.

O'Neill, K. (2000). *Waste Trading among Rich Nations: Building a New Theory of Environmental Regulation.* Cambridge, MA, MIT Press.

OECD (2008). "OECD Environmental Date Compendium: 2006–8: Waste." Retrieved Nov 1, 2009.

Pulido, L. (2000). "Rethinking Environmental Racism: White Privilege and Urban Development in Southern California." *Annals of the Association of American Geographers* 90(1): 12–40.

Rauscher, M. (2001). "International Trade in Hazardous Waste." In G. Schulze and H. Ursprung (eds), *International Environmental Economics: A Survey of the Issues.* Oxford: Oxford University Press. pp. 148–65.

Sanchez, R. A. (2002). "Governance, Trade and the Environment in the Context of NAFTA." *American Behavioral Scientist* 45(9): 1369–1393.

Simpson, A. (2008). "NAFTA's Failure to Protect Public Health and the Environment: The Case of Metales v Derivados, Tijuana, Mexico." *Epidemiology* 19(6): S16–S16.

Slocum, R. (2009) "Rethinking Hazardous Waste under NAFTA." Americas Program Policy Report.

Szasz, A. (1994). *EcoPopulism: Toxic Waste and the Movement for Environmental Justice.* Minneapolis, University of Minnesota Press.

United Nations (2009a, August 2009). "Environmental Indicators: Waste." Available online at http://unstats.un.org/unsd/environment/wastetreatment.htm (accessed 15 November 2009).

_____ (2009b, August 2009). "Hazardous Waste Generation." Available online at http://unstats.un.org/unsd/environment/wastetreatment.htm (accessed 15 November 2009).

United States Environmental Protection Agency (2008). "Electronics Waste Management in the United States: Approach 1.", Available online at http://www.epa.gov/osw/conserve/materials/ecycling/docs/app-1.pdf (accessed 15 November 2009).

Wainwright, J. (2008). *Decolonizaing development.* Maiden, MA: Blackwell.

Westra, L. and B. E. Lawson (2001). "Introduction." In *Faces of Environmental Racism: Confronting Issues of Global Justice.* Lanham, MD, Rowman and Littlefield Publishers, Inc.: xvii-xxvi.

SECTION V CONCLUSION

This section has elaborated a political ecology approach in the context of the critical environmental issue of waste. Political ecology overlaps with other analytical and applied approaches, particularly environmental justice (discussed in Section IV) and environmental history approaches (Robbins 2012). Deeply rooted in historical, ecological, and political-economic analysis, political ecology urges scholars, practitioners, environmentalists, and others to look beyond overly simplistic explanations for environmental problems. Framing a problem in one particular way can hide the power relations and inequities lying underneath the surface. Thus it is often incorrect to observe a massive electronic waste dump in Ivory Coast and assume that the waste was created by industry or local residents in Ivory Coast. There are global flows of waste that tie diffuse sites of extraction to manufacturing, transport, retail, consumption, waste transport, and further breakdown of materials.

One of the shortcomings of some political ecology studies is that political ecology readily shuts down and critiques optimistic win-win analyses that political ecologists believe obscure power inequities or the fundamentals of ecological processes. To some, this criticism and what Robbins refers to as taking a 'hatchet' to apolitical explanations, is quite strong and can leave readers feeling as though there is no point in trying to intervene in such overwhelming global processes. Robbins has countered this critique in the past by pointing to the so-called seeds of growth of alternative practices and frameworks or suggested points of action of political ecological analysis. Often political ecologists aim to draw our attention to different sets of problems and questions than typical apolitical approaches ask. Such questions move us away from simplistic assumptions and towards an explicitly political engagement with an issue. Rather than blame proximate causes or simplistic overpopulation crisis stories, political ecologists urge major stakeholders to the negotiating table to conduct critical analysis that directly speaks to power. Political ecologists highlight whose voices dominate and who is silenced. Thus, when engaging an exciting win-win solution pitched by a company or development agency, political ecologists would urge the authors of the win-win strategy to be more realistic and consider who will lose under such a strategy and how to address some of the related problems that the project will encounter.

Changing geophysical and biological cycles affect waste flows, just as shifting policies and practices related to waste trade affect how waste flows from one site to another. As community-based and more "official" scientists consider the flows of waste across international borders and through the hydrologic cycle, through soils and biomagnification in the bodies of living organisms, several additional factors must be considered. Changes in climate, glacial cover, and the migration and colonization of species in new distributions will affect where and how waste flows. In light of climate change, researchers are attempting to identify and target their analysis towards the rapidly changing ecological and social shifts that shape how we currently understand everything from hydrologic cycles to future technological innovations (see Sutherland et al. 2013). For example, as the globe experiences climate change–induced shifts in hydrologic systems such as changed precipitation patterns (Trenberth 2011), an accelerated water cycle (Durack et al. 2012) and glacial retreat (Perovich and Richter-Menge 2009), this affects scientists' ability to model and predict where waste will go and how hazardous materials will break down in particular spaces. These ongoing changes in physical process warrant serious attention.

As a final point of consideration, another intriguing technological shift may radically affect waste streams in the future: the three-dimensional (3D) printing revolution (see Sutherland et al. 2013). Researchers and developers now have the technological capacity to print 3D objects—ranging from body parts to working firearm parts to space shuttle parts to toys—including the marketing of personal 3D printers (Lipson and Kurman 2013). Personal 3D printers typically utilize a synthetic (usually a plastic substance) filament that feeds into the printer as the printer receives digital instructions for how to transform the filament bit by bit into a solid object. Will the ability to print 3D objects help reduce waste production by allowing individuals to print missing parts required for repairing otherwise functioning goods, thus reducing demand for purchasing full replacements of household items? (Sutherland et al. 2013) Or, as with paper, ink cartridge and other e-waste production from 2D printing, will users of the new 3D print technology print excessive amounts of mistakes, thus adding more synthetic "junk" to the waste stream? (Ibid.) While there have been some attempts to utilize recycled materials as part of the filament input, this is a pressing area of concern for environmentalists. How will technological innovations shape the global waste trade, and *who* and *where* will the winners and losers of these changes be?

Political ecology and the topic of waste in environmental studies are major areas of future research, action, and organizing. Those interested in pursuing these issues might consider developing their knowledge of chemistry and biology, earth systems and processes. Those interested in the roots of political ecology and how this field has shifted through time can delve more deeply into philosophy and social sciences to understand how capitalism shapes ecological processes, and how particular histories and physical features of materials shape the kinds of solutions and stories defining what waste is and where it should go.

Section V Discussion Questions:
Political Ecology and Waste

1. What images do you associate with the term 'waste'? How is waste defined in this chapter?
2. Name three different categories of waste, and identify a personal experience you have had in producing each category of waste. Where do you think the waste is now?
3. What is the relationship between the size of a population and human impacts on natural resources? What is wrong with the assumption that areas with large populations necessarily cause more environmental degradation? What perspective does political ecology lend to this argument?
4. What factors influence the amount of garbage produced by a country or population?
5. Name at least two examples of the 'one person's trash is another person's treasure' concept from Moore's chapter on global garbage.
6. Explain the 'pollution haven hypothesis' discussed in Moore's chapter.
7. What does Moore's discussion of NAFTA's Chapter 11 illustrate about the role of corporations in transboundary waste disposal?
8. How is the siting of waste facilities NOT a technical issue? What is it? What other environmental issues discussed in this book are similarly complex?

References

Biersack, A. 2006. "Reimagining Political Ecology: Culture/Power/History/Nature." In *Reimagining Political Ecology*, edited by A. Biersack and J.B. Greenberg. Durham: Duke University Press, 3–40.

Durack, P.J., S.E. Wijffels, and R.J. Matear (2012) "Ocean Salinities Reveal Strong Global Water Cycle Intensification During 1950 to 2000." *Science* 336(6080): 455–8.

Gregson, N. and M. Crang (2010) "Materiality and Waste: Inorganic Vitality in a Networked World." *Environment and Planning A* 42: 1026–1032.

Grossman, E. (2006) *High Tech Trash: Hidden Toxics, and Human Health*. Washington, DC: Island Press.

Jewitt, S. (2011) "Geographies of Shit: Spatial and Temporal Variations in Attitudes Towards Human Waste." *Progress in Human Geography* 35(5): 608–626.

Lepawsky, J. and C. McNabb. (2010) "Mapping International Flows of Electronic Waste." *The Canadian Geographer* 54(2): 177–95.

Lipson, H. and M. Kurman (2013) *Fabricated: The New World of 3D Printing*. Indianapolis: John Wiley & Sons, Inc.

Moore, S.A. (2012) "Garbage Matters: Concepts in New Geographies of Waste." *Progress in Human Geography* 36(6): 780–99.

Muir D.C. and de Wit C.A. (2010). "Trends of Legacy and New Persistent Organic Pollutants in the Circumpolar Arctic: Overview, Conclusions, and Recommendations." *The Science of the Total Environment* 408(15): 3044–51.

Perovich, D.K. and J.A. Richter-Menge (2009) "Loss of Sea Ice in the Arctic." *Annual Review of Marine Science* 1(1): 417–41.

Robbins, P. (2012) *Political Ecology: A Critical Introduction*. Malden, MA: Wiley-Blackwell.

Slater, D. (2012) "How Dangerous Is Your Couch?" *The New York Times*, 6 September 2012. Accessed on 10 July 2013 from: http://www.nytimes.com/2012/09/09/magazine/arlene-blums-crusade-against-household-toxins.html?_r=0.

Stapleton, H.M., S. Sharma, G. Getzinger, Ferguson P.L., M. Gabriel, T.F. Webster, and A. Blum (2012) "Novel and High Volume Use Flame Retardants in Us Couches Reflective of the 2005 PentaBDE Phase Out." *Environmental Science & Technology* 46(24): 13432–39.

Sutherland, W.J., Bardsley, S., Clout, M., Depledge, M.H., Dicks, L.V., Fellman, L., Fleishman, E., Gibbons, D.W., Keim, B., Lickorish, F., Margerison, C., Monk, K.A., Norris, K., Peck, L.S., Prior, S.V., Scharlemann, J.P., Spalding, M.D. and Watkinson, A.R. (2013) "A Horizon Scan of Global Conservation Issues for 2013." *Trends in Ecology & Evolution* 28(1): 16–22.

Trenberth, K.E. (2011) "Changes in Precipitation with Climate Change." *Climate Research* 47(1–2): 123–138.

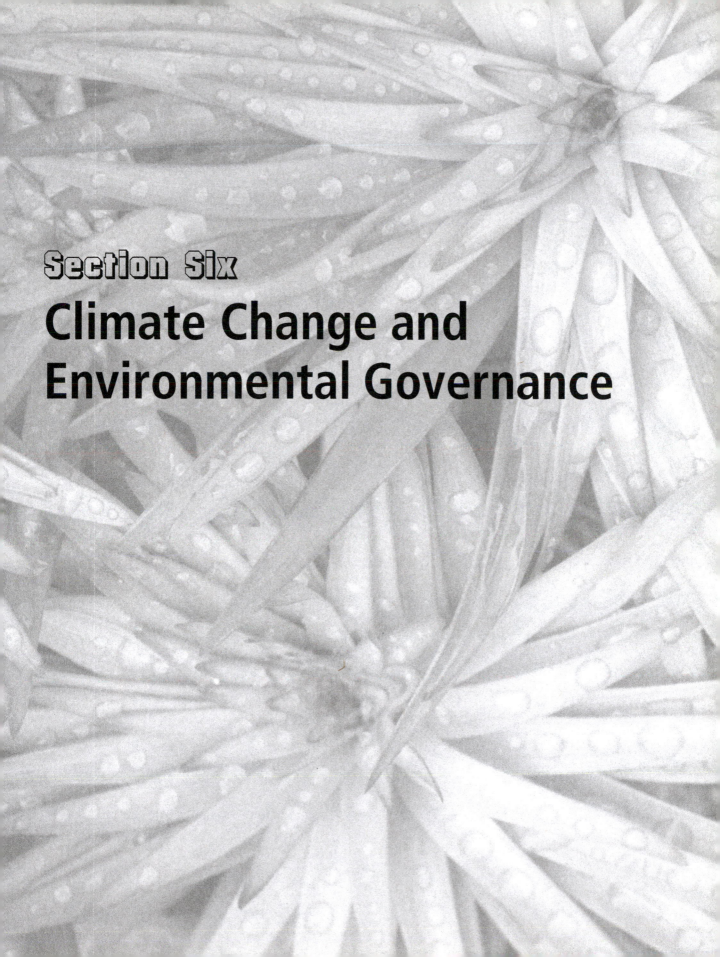

Section Six
Climate Change and Environmental Governance

INTRODUCTION TO GLOBAL CLIMATE CHANGE CONFLICTS

greenhouse gases (GHGs)
united nations framework convention on
   climate change (UNFCCC)

intergovernmental panel on
   climate change (IPCC)
climate change mitigation
climate change adaptation

KEY TERMS

"What we need is an agreement that's ambitious—because that's what the scale of the challenge demands. We need an inclusive agreement—because every country has to play its part. And we need an agreement that's flexible—because different nations have different needs. And if we can come together and get this right, we can define a sustainable future for your generation."

U.S. President Barack Obama, Climate Change Speech at Georgetown University, January 26, 2013

C limate change is arguably the greatest global environmental threat of our time, with implications for every other major environmental issue discussed in this book. Climate change has also proven to be one of the most challenging environmental issues for policymakers to tackle, for a variety of reasons discussed in this section. Scientists have unequivocal evidence for increases in **greenhouse gases (GHGs)**, which trap and radiate heat, and the physical impact of these processes has been well known for decades. However, the interaction of these processes with other natural cycles and the best course of action to deal with such a complex global issue remain contested. Various interest groups that continue to

Greenhouse Gases (GHGs) refers to the release of gases that trap and re-radiate heat in the atmosphere, including carbon dioxide, methane, nitrous oxide, and fluorinated gases (e.g., hydrofluorocarbons). Today's levels of GHG emissions are unprecedented, resulting from anthropogenic (human-caused) activities, including industrial processes, energy generation, vehicle transportation, and agriculture.

challenge each other's credibility have engaged in an increasingly polarized debate on the magnitude and causality of climate change. Even the popular media has picked up on the polarization of the debate exemplified by movies such as *The Day After Tomorrow (2004)* and the documentary produced by former U.S. Vice President Al Gore titled *An Inconvenient Truth (2006)*. Skeptics of climate change have been equally strident in their publications ranging from titles such as *State of Fear* by late bestselling author Michael Crichton (2004) to the book published by the Cato Institute titled *Meltdown: The Predictable Distortion of Global Warming (2006)*. This introductory segment to Section VI attempts to provide clarity to the issues and assumptions affecting policymakers' decisions about climate legislation. In addition, this section highlights environmental governance as an approach to environmental issues and outlines the unique challenges in addressing climate change with international governance.

Institutional Actors

In this section we discuss key climate change actors and policies that currently dominate much of the international debate around how to address the issue today and into the future. The gravity of climate change impacts, both actual and anticipated, has resulted in the formation of several international institutions within the United Nations (UN) seeking to address the issue. One such institution, **United Nations Framework Convention on Climate Change (UNFCCC)**, has a clear cooperative policy mandate[1]. It was formed in 1992 as an international cooperative treaty, and its function is to engage international cooperation to avert the impacts of climate change and cope with any irreversible consequences that have already occurred. Since 1997, the UNFCCC has organized 20 international summits, called "Conference of the Parties" (COP), for signatory nations. One of the most famous meetings was held in Kyoto, Japan, in 1997, where an ambitious series of measures known as the Kyoto Protocol was proposed to reduce GHG emissions from developed countries.

One of the points of contention in international climate negotiations has been determining who should bear the cost of **climate change mitigation** (including which countries are accountable for most GHG emissions), and how and whether industrialized countries

United Nations Framework Convention on Climate Change (UNFCCC) is the international treaty that coordinates cooperation between nations related to climate change policy and organizes Conferences of the Parties (COP).

Climate Change Mitigation is concerned with how to assess and alleviate the effects of human activities (ranging from food production to transportation) through either the reduction of greenhouse gas emissions (for example by using less fossil fuels) or the sequestration of carbon dioxide (CO_2) equivalents (for example, by planting trees or avoiding deforestation) (Metz et al. 2007).

---

1   See: (http://unfccc.int/2860. php)

Table 1. Select policy measures under international climate governance mechanisms

Policy Measure	Focal Areas and Purpose	Key Advantage and Disadvantage
Carbon Taxation	Making polluting industries less cost attractive, leading to alternative sectors for gaining competitive advantage and government support	Adv: Immediate government revenue generation through existing accounting mechanisms Disadv: Creates adversarial relationship with industry with potential for tax-exemption lobbies
Emissions Cap-and-Trade Schemes	Scientifically determined upper limit on emissions (cap) coupled with market mechanism (trade) that creates incentives for cleaner performance as a means of cost savings and business engagement	Adv: Upper limit on emissions easier to manage in terms of mitigation targets Disadv: Complicated enforcement system needed to ensure monitoring of emissions for trading
Clean Development Mechanism (CDM)	Creating a fund for developing countries to adopt clean technologies, acknowledging responsibility of developed world's greater share in GHG emissions	Adv: Fosters cooperation and links climate change to development goals Disadv: Can lead to complacence on emissions reduction, particularly for rapidly developing countries
REDD and REDD+	Reducing Emissions from Deforestation and forest Degradation through carbon credits (REDD). REDD+ includes role of conservation, sustainable forest management, and enhancement of forest carbon stocks.	Adv: Moves conversation from punitive pollution control to alternative 'productive' conservation mechanisms Disadv: Challenges forestry-dependent economies, fundamentally incompatible with diverse land and resource tenure systems and reduces carbon price through flooding market with credits

are responsible for supporting developing countries with **climate change adaptation** (See Section VI, Part B for a thorough discussion of mitigation and adaptation). We summarize some of the recent changes to the climate change convention and mechanisms that have been proposed to address issues of fairness in bearing the cost of climate change mitigation and adaptation across developed and developing countries in Table 1.

The second institution of relevance is the **Intergovernmental Panel on Climate Change (IPCC)**, which was formed by the United Nations Environment Programme (UNEP) and the

Climate Change Adaptation broadly refers to adjustment in natural or human systems in response to actual or expected climatic effects, which may moderate harmful consequences (e.g., risk of flood) or take advantage of beneficial opportunities (e.g., avoid deforestation) (Adapted from Parry et al. 2007).

Intergovernmental Panel on Climate Change (IPCC) is the international panel of thousands of scientists who publish scientific assessment reports evaluating all aspects of climate change.

World Meteorological Organization (WMO)[2]. The IPCC is a panel composed of thousands of scientists from around the world who engage in a rigorous process of scientific assessments evaluating all aspects of climate change. A key function of the IPCC is to publish assessment reports and other technical documents that can be used by policymakers to address climate change[3]. While early assessment reports focused largely on establishing the scientific basis of climate change and predicting ecological outcomes for different emissions scenarios, recent reports also focus on the importance of adaptation given the of climate change.

Climate Change Conflicts and Debates

The last several decades of international climate negotiations and policy have been character-ized by debate over the causes and effects of climate change. In addition, conflict has arisen as to what course of action should be taken to prevent further climate change. Dessler and Parson (2006) provide the first systematic examination of the climate change debate and suggest that four key questions first need to be recognized: 1) *Is the climate changing?* 2) *Are human activities responsible for the observed changes?* 3) *What are the likely climate changes in the future?* and 4) *What will be the impacts of the future changes?*

We could add to this series a fifth question: Can human intervention to reduce these changes have any impact, and if so, on whom and in what ways? This fifth question is par-ticularly important to consider in order to formulate effective policy recommendations at an international level because of the extreme income inequality that the world faces. Limited resources being expended on mitigation (prevention) rather than adaptation by develop-ment donors thus become highly consequential. (See also Ali, 2008 for further analysis)

Scientists' call for immediate, drastic action to stabilize global greenhouse gas emissions has met with substantial resistance. This is in part because the infrastructure of our globalized economy is built on the very activities responsible for emissions (e.g. transportation, industrial agriculture, manufacturing). Another challenge stalling action is the difficulty of assigning responsibility for existing climate change, and the geographic and temporal disconnect between greenhouse gas emissions and the results of climate change.

International negotiations over the past several decades have been slow to produce results. Answering questions such as who is responsible for GHG emissions, how to reduce emissions at the least economic, social, and environmental cost, and what populations will be most affected by climate change has challenged policymakers and delayed action.

---

2   See: (http://www.ipcc.ch/)
3   See: (http://www.ipcc.ch/publications_and_data/publications_and_data_reports.shtml#1)

Environmental Governance Approach

Environmental governance provides a promising approach to analyze and seek resolution to many environmental issues, including climate change. Lemos and Agrawal (2006: 298) define environmental governance as the "set of regulatory processes, mechanisms and organizations through which political actors influence environmental actions and outcomes." Some of the advantages of environmental governance, in terms of its application to climate change, are 1) it addresses issues from a standpoint of dynamic globalization that addresses international rather than national phenomena; 2) it seeks an analysis across scales (i.e., from local to global); 3) it is inclusive of a diversity of relevant actors, including non-governmental organizations, the state, and civil society (individuals or groups); and 4) it explicitly includes market- and agent-focused instruments in its examination. In the article that follows, Lemos and Agrawal outline the potential for environmental governance as a tool to address climate change, as well as the challenges and limitations of a governance approach. The high complexity of social and institutional actors—as well as the ecological processes associated with climate change—requires sophisticated analytical framework. Hybrid forms of governance, including the involvement of social movements, non-governmental organizations, corporations, and states, represent a promising way forward.

Environmental Governance is the set of regulatory processes, mechanisms and organizations through which political actors influence environmental actions and outcomes (Lemos and Agrawal, 2006). A diversity of actors can be involved in environmental governance, including civil society (individuals or groups), non governmental organizations, politicians, businesses, and the media, among others.

European Union Policy on Climate Change Mitigation

The case study by Egenhofer and Alessi (2013) then presents an overview of the ambitious climate change policy adopted by European Union (EU). Until the 2009 UNFCCC Conference of the Parties in Copenhagen, the main focus of EU climate change policy was the Emissions Trading System (ETS). This cap and trade program was designed to incentivize GHG emissions reductions in Europe through the development of a carbon market (see Table 1). However, the 2009 international meeting in Copenhagen failed to instill trust in top-down institutional agreements such as the ETS, and resulted in a shift towards alternative climate change policies in the European Union. New directions of focus include working with transportation and shipping actors to reduce emissions, investing in "green growth," continued support of Reducing Emissions from Deforestation and forest Degradation (REDD) programs, and increased international collaboration on research and technology. A close examination of these alternatives will be needed to assess their effectiveness as cost-effective, culturally appropriate, and politically acceptable means of reducing GHG emissions and supporting climate change adaptation, as these have already met with substantial political resistance.

HIGHLIGHTED APPROACH: ENVIRONMENTAL GOVERNANCE

Environmental Governance

By Maria Carmen Lemos and Arun Agrawal

Introduction

The Millennium Ecosystem Assessment, perhaps the most ambitious and extensive examination of the state of Earth's ecosystems, outlines what might reasonably be expected to happen to them under different future scenarios (1). Its conclusions are pessimistic; the changes required to address the declining resilience of ecosystems are large and currently not under way. It ends with a discussion of the types of responses that can lead to sustainable management of ecosystems. Ostensibly, only the first of these responses focuses directly on institutions and governance—the subject of this review. Others concern economics and incentives, social and behavioral factors, technology, knowledge and cognition, and decision-making processes. Although some of these other responses may seem unrelated to environmental governance, in reality, the effectiveness of every single one of them depends on significant changes in existing strategies of environmental governance.

Our chapter reviews the literature on environmental governance to examine how different approaches have attempted to address some of the most pressing environmental challenges of our time: global climate change, ecosystem degradation, and the like. We find that a significant proportion of this literature has tended to emphasize a particular agent of environmental governance as being the most effective—typically market actors, state actors and,

Maria Carmen Lemos and Arun Agrawal, "Environmental Governance," *Annual Review of Environment and Resources*, vol. 1, no. 1, pp. 297–325. Copyright © 2006 by Annual Reviews. Reprinted with permission.

more recently, civil society-based actors such as nongovernmental organizations (NGOs) and local communities.

Today, a broad array of hybrid environmental governance strategies are being practiced, and it has become clear that seemingly purely market-, state-, or civil society-based governance strategies depend for their efficacy on support from other domains of social interactions. Our discussion examines the importance of spatial and institutional scales to environmental governance, focusing especially on emerging hybrid forms. Of significant interest to our review are (a) soft governance strategies that try to align market and individual incentives with self-regulatory processes and (b) cogovernance, which is predicated on partnerships and notions of embedded autonomy across state-market-society divisions (2, 3). These innovations in environmental governance can potentially be extended to engage multiple types of environmental problems and conflicts.

Defining Environmental Governance

For the purposes of this review, environmental governance is synonymous with interventions aiming at changes in environment-related incentives, knowledge, institutions, decision making, and behaviors. More specifically, we use "environmental governance" to refer to the set of regulatory processes, mechanisms and organizations through which political actors influence environmental actions and outcomes. (Also see Section VI, Part A for 'Environmental Governance' text box) Governance is not the same as government. It includes the actions of the state and, in addition, encompasses actors such as communities, businesses, and NGOs. Key to different forms of environmental governance are the political-economic relationships that institutions embody and how these relationships shape identities, actions, and outcomes (4–6). International accords, national policies and legislation, local decision-making structures, transnational institutions, and environmental NGOs are all examples of the forms through which environmental governance takes place. Because governance can be shaped through nonorganizational institutional mechanisms as well (for example, when it is based on market incentives and self-regulatory processes), there is no escaping it for anyone concerned about environmental outcomes. Environmental governance is varied in form, critical in importance, and near ubiquitous in spread.

To investigate emerging trends in environmental governance in a way that is both sufficiently general for a review and reflects ongoing changes in the world of governance, we focus on four themes around which some of the most interesting writings on environmental governance cluster. The ensuing discussion first reviews the scholarship on globalization, decentralized environmental governance, market-and individual-focused instruments (MAFIs), and governance across scales to uncover how the conventional roles and capacities of important actors and institutions are getting reconfigured. This discussion leads us to a framework through which approaches to environmental governance and the terrain of environmental governance can usefully be explored. We apply insights from this framework to two sets of consequential environmental problems: global climate change and ecosystem degradation. We identify important limitations of hybrid forms of environmental governance and conclude with a discussion of some of the implications of ongoing developments related to environmental governance.

Themes In Environmental Governance

The four themes upon which we focus below—globalization, decentralized environmental governance, market-and individual-focused instruments, and governance across scales—are among the most important emerging trends that are shaping environmental governance. They are generating pressures for innovative ways to address environmental and natural resource crises and challenging existing forms of governance. They are emblematic of the possibilities present in efforts to engage seriously with environmental problems, and their shortcomings are a reason to be concerned about the extent to which environmental actors have the capacity to deal with worsening environmental dilemmas. Although we treat each of these themes distinctly below, it goes without saying that there are close, perhaps even causal, connections among them, even if a review permits only speculation about how they may be related.

Globalization and Environmental Governance

Globalization describes an interconnected world across environments, societies, and economies. Multiplicity, diversity, interdependence, and flows of influence and materials are common themes associated with globalization even if there is significant disagreement about its definition, implications, impacts, and usefulness as a concept (7–10). (See References 11–13 for definitions and implications of globalization.)

From an environmental perspective, globalization produces both negative and positive pressures on governance. Economic globalization produces tremendous impacts on environmental processes at the local, regional, national, and global levels. By integrating far-flung markets and increasing demand, globalization may intensify the use and depletion of natural resources, increase waste production, and lead to a "race to the bottom" as capital moves globally to countries and locations that have less stringent environmental standards (14–17). Most free trade regimes—facilitated by and assisting globalization—provide limited or inadequate environmental provisions and insufficient safeguards for their enforcement (18– 20). Analogously, despite evidence of the negative effect of international trade on carbon-dioxide emissions, it remains uncertain how economic provisions of trade agreements such as those of the World Trade Organization (WTO) intersect with the goals of climate regimes such as the Kyoto Protocol (15). Additionally, the global flow of energy, materials, and organisms through the environment, which Clark labels "environmental stuff," "couples the actions of people in one place with the threats and opportunities faced by people long distances away" (21, p. 86).

By broadening the range of problems national governments are called upon to address, globalization strains the resources of nation states at the same time as it may contribute to socioeconomic inequalities. These pressures can ultimately enhance levels of vulnerability to climate change and other environmental threats (22). Finally, neoliberal policy reforms associated with globalization may complicate the efficacy of state action by shifting power to alternative actors and levels of decision making through decentralization and privatization as well as through the use of MAFIs (see below).

Observers of globalization also argue in favor of its potentially positive impacts on economic equity and environmental standards through a virtuous circle and the diffusion of positive environmental policy initiatives. Clearly, the globalization of environmental problems has contributed to the creation and development of new global regimes, institutions, and organizations dedicated to environmental governance. More efficient use and transfer of technology, freer flow of information, and novel institutional arrangements based on public-private partnerships have the potential to contribute positively to environmental governance (23, 24).

Globalization can also enhance the depth of participation and the diversity of actors shaping environmental governance. For instance, the globalization of social action through international environmental groups expands the role of social movements, so that they can produce deep social changes across national boundaries instead of being limited to negotiations with governments within a nation state (25). By introducing new ways of organizing, interacting, and influencing governmental processes, globalization can help increase the social and political relevance of non-state actors such as NGOs, transnational environmental networks, and epistemic communities—defined as networks of knowledge-based expertise (26). Finally, more accessible and cheaper forms of communication improve access to knowledge and technology and enhance the rate of information exchange, speeding up the dissemination of both technological and policy innovations (21–24).

The analytical argument for global environmental governance lies in the "public bads" implications of processes and outcomes related to environmental problems. Ozone depletion, carbon emissions, and climate change cannot be addressed by any single nation. Global cooperation and institutional arrangements are therefore necessary to address them. Historically, this conceptualization of environmental problems and their solutions meant that nation states were viewed as the appropriate agents of environmental action (27, 28), and international regimes as the appropriate governance mechanism.

Writings about international regimes have tended to cluster around two significant foci: understanding, measuring, and comparing the effectiveness of regime performance (29, 30) and exposing their inherent democratic deficit (31). There are three main aspects to the democratic deficit of international environmental regimes. First, countries participating in the negotiating process may not be democracies. Second, limited participation from nonstate actors (with the exception of large NGOs and at times epistemic communities); the unequal distribution of power, knowledge, and resources among the participant countries; and the ability of some powerful countries to impose their preferences may undermine the capacity of certain participants to make much of an impact on final outcomes. Additionally, the opaque character of the negotiation process itself strengthens the perception that international regimes and negotiations within the scope of multilateral organizations are driven by the more powerful actors (9, 30, 32). Finally, most international environmental agreements lack effective enforcement, especially when the more binding provisions in an agreement are at stake (33, 34).

The failure of state-centered international regimes to address many of the most pressing global problems successfully prompted a search for new institutions, partnerships, and governance mechanisms. A more inclusive global environmental governance paradigm holds the promise not only of innovative governance strategies, but also of expanded cooperation among social actors that may have been previously outside the policy process: corporate interests, social movements, and nongovernmental organizations (21, 35). The fragmentary nature of the sources of complex environmental problems, such as global climate change, and the reluctance or inability of nation states to regulate the sources of these problems, means that nonstate actors and organizations may be able to play an essential role in mobilizing public opinion and generating innovative solutions (36). It is for this reason that scholars of environmental governance such as Haas have proposed multilevel, nonhierarchical, information-rich, loose networks of institutions and actors as an alternative to ineffective state-centric international regimes (37–39).

These new international environmental governance mechanisms are viewed as being superior along a number of dimensions: (*a*) integrating scientific, technological, and lay knowledge and at quickly relaying information; (*b*) providing sufficient redundancy and flexibility in functional performance; (*c*) gaining the involvement of multiple actors; (*d*) recognizing that the relationship between international regimes and nonstate actors is fundamental to address economic and environmental changes; (*e*) identifying modalities of cooperation that go beyond legal arrangements; (*f*) working across scales to develop cooperation and synergy to solve common problems; and (*g*) promoting social learning and compromise seeking. However, these mechanisms may also fail to limit the negative externalities emerging from lack of implementation capacity. Their characteristic reliance on decentralized action and interdependent coordination and their lack of instruments to deal with system disruption and unanticipated systemic effects mean that major environmental problems may be difficult to address directly and efficaciously through them (40, 41).

Decentralized Environmental Governance

Climate change, globalization, recent sociopolitical transformations, and the challenges they pose for environmental processes have been the major concerns occupying many of the scholars who have written and talked about environmental governance. Indeed, for many interested in environmental governance, it is synonymous with what happens on the international or the global stage (42). However, it is at least equally correct that some of the most important contemporary changes in environmental governance are occurring at the subnational level and relate to efforts to incorporate lower-level administrative units and social groups better into formal processes of environmental governance. It is perhaps only a matter of historical record today, but the landscape of natural resource management has undergone a breathtaking shift since the colonial period and its immediate aftermath. Until as recently as the late 1970s and early 1980s, those concerned about loss of biodiversity, soil erosion, desertification, deforestation, decline of fisheries, and other such environmental phenomena used to call for more elaborate and thoroughgoing centralized control. Indeed, the elaborate forms of coercive control that marked governance arrangements for most natural resources continued with little change between the colonial and the postcolonial period. State bureaucratic authority appeared to many policy makers and academic observers as the appropriate means to address the externalities associated with the use of environmental resources. Centralized interventions were therefore essential to redress resulting market failures (43, 44) (for a review of relevant claims, see References 45 and 46).

A loss of faith in the state as a reliable custodian of nature has accompanied the analogous loss of faith in states as effective managers of the economy (47, 48). The reasons for the shift away from centralized forms of governance also have to do, however, with very real forces of change, among them the fall of economies relying on centralized control. Economic pressures on states, resulting both from greater integration of economic activities across national boundaries and a decline in aid flows, have been supplemented by fiscal crises in many developing countries (49). Many nation states no longer have the resources to manage their environments. At the same time, as emerging economic forces have challenged the political and economic capacities of nation states, a shift toward more democratic political processes throughout much of the developing world has facilitated the move toward alternative forms of governance whose effectiveness depends on higher levels of participation and greater involvement of citizens in processes of governance.

In addition, extensive research by scholars of common property and political ecology, emphasizing the capacity of communities and other small-scale social formations to manage resources, has provided the intellectual grounds for a shift toward comanagement, community-based natural resource management, and environmental policy decentralizations (50–54). It has done so by demonstrating that forms of effective environmental governance are not exhausted by terms such as "state" and "free market institutions" and that users of resources are often able to self-organize and govern them. By identifying literally thousands of independent instances of enduring governance of resources and at the same time highlighting arenas in which external support can improve local governance processes, scholars of common property and political ecology have helped prepare the ground for decentralized environmental governance.

Since the mid-1980s, decentralization of authority to govern renewable resources such as forests, irrigation systems, and inland fisheries has gathered steam. Indeed, it has become a characteristic feature of late twentieth and early twenty-first century governance of renewable resources, even if nonrenewable resources continue to be held by state authorities in a tightfisted grip (55–58). As Hutchcroft (59) suggests, "The decentralization of government functions is 'the latest fashion (60),' or at least 'a fashion of our time (61).' " Three distinct justifications for decentralization of environmental governance are available. It can produce greater efficiencies because of competition among subnational units; it can bring decision making closer to those affected by governance, thereby promoting higher participation and accountability; and finally, it can help decision makers take advantage of more precise time- and place-specific knowledge about natural resources.

National governments across the developing world have advanced strong claims about the imperative to establish and strengthen partnerships in which local administrative and organizational arrangements complement or substitute for more central efforts to govern environmental resources (62–64). In many cases, they have backed these claims with changes in renewable resource policies. Whether these changes have occurred because of the alleged advantages of decentralized governance or because of the significant flows of aid funds tied to decentralized governance is difficult to judge. But the shift in favor of decentralization has brought alternative means and new political claimants to the fore in the process of governance as nation states attempt to reclaim governance through partnerships with local organizations.

Indeed, the vast literature on decentralized environmental governance contains many different conclusions regarding the nature and depth of the changes that have occurred since the 1980s. Positions adopted by the participants range from those for whom nothing much has changed (65, 66) to those who see the world of governance to have undergone a major transformation with decentralization (67–69). Much of the debate's heat is explained by the variations in the regional focus and the organizational affiliations of those involved. Because there is enormous patchiness in the reforms different countries have undertaken, indeed even within countries in the case of federal polities, the geographical focus of analysis often leads to different conclusions about the meaningfulness and effectiveness of institutional reforms (70). Similarly, those belonging to organizations involved actively in reforms tend to assess them more positively in comparison to outside observers and academic analysts.

When successful, decentralized governance of natural resources can be seen as effecting at least three sets of changes in the political relationships through which human beings relate to resources (71). The first set of changes concerns how decision makers in lower-level units in a territorial-administrative hierarchy relate to those at higher levels (72). Indeed, much of the existing literature on decentralized governance focuses precisely on this aspect of ongoing changes. A second set of issues is linked with the ways local decision makers relate to their constituents. This aspect of the decentralization of environmental governance has been researched extensively in writings on local resource management, especially by scholars of the commons. However, a third aspect of decentralized governance—alterations of the subjective relationships of people with each other and with the environment as part of changing relationships of power and governance—is also crucial to understand outcomes, an issue that has received far less attention than the preceding two aspects of environmental governance (6).

Contemporary efforts at decentralized environmental governance, like those in earlier periods, aim to make the exercise of control both more thorough and more economical. Decentralization disperses multiple points of political leverage throughout an administrative structure and makes them available to central decision makers (73, 74). It does so by encouraging the systematic creation of legal codes and performance standards that are specified through the exercise of legislative or executive authority. Adherence to these codes and standards is the price of inclusion in decision-making processes. Paradoxically perhaps, decentralization appears to be perfectly compatible with the existence of centralized authority when formal inclusion in decision-making processes occurs together with a clear delineation of spheres of authority within which local actors are supposed to operate. In addition to helping effect fiscal economies, decentralization also serves political and strategic considerations to the extent that dissatisfaction with governance can find local points of authority against which to protest instead of engaging centralized authority.

Contemporary decentralized environmental governance is different from earlier attempts at decentralization of authority in two critical ways. For the most part, earlier efforts in the form of indirect rule in colonial south Asia and Africa and community development programs in the postcolonial developing world relied on existing authority structures and incorporated them into the formal process of the exercise of authority. In contrast, decentralized environmental governance, especially at the local level, has been built upon new organizational entities such as community-based user groups and has established new lines of institutionalized authority. An even more striking difference that characterizes contemporary environmental governance is the way it conceptualizes individual citizens and their responsibilities. By focusing on the incentives that prompt individuals to participate in new institutional arrangements to govern the environment, present day decentralization processes help produce the very individual subjects they require for their effective functioning. The rhetoric of capacity building, local knowledge, and individual rationality is a lynchpin of decentralized environmental governance (6). Ongoing changes in subnational environmental governance hold intriguing possibilities for reshaping the future landscape of political decision making related to the environment. Therefore, further research on environmental policy decentralization holds great promise both for furthering the insights that work on common property institutions has produced and for enhancing the involvement of local decision makers in new forms of environmental governance.

At the same time, it is worth highlighting that ongoing changes are not just an occasion for optimism that less powerful human agents may come to exercise greater voice in how they and their resources are governed. There is also room for cynicism that decentralization policies have typically been motivated by powerful state actors to enhance their own political positions. Without effective safeguards against arbitrary exercise of localized power and clear relations of accountability, decentralization may lead to forms of regulation even more suffocating than those encouraged by more centralized control. The contingent outcomes of contemporary shifts in governance, therefore, depend crucially on the ways local actors mobilize and establish alliances across sociopolitical and administrative scales of governance (64, 75).

Market-and Agent-Focused Instruments

The decline of the state since the 1970s as the prime agent of environmental governance has also propelled market and voluntary incentives-based mechanisms to the fore. Instead of relying on hierarchically organized, regulatory control or even purely participatory structures, MAFIs aim to mobilize individual incentives in favor of environmentally positive outcomes through a careful calculation and modulation of costs and benefits associated with particular environmental strategies. They differ from more conventional regulatory mechanisms along a number of dimensions, including the source of their legitimacy and authority. Cashore (76) suggests that the strength of these instruments lies in their utilization of market exchanges and incentives to encourage environmental compliance.

MAFIs encompass a broad range: ecotaxes and subsidies based on a mix of regulation and market incentives, voluntary agreements, certification, ecolabeling, and informational systems are some of the major examples. At the national level, the popularity of these instruments and frameworks has increased quickly, even if their adoption and implementation can be differentiated by sector and geography rather than being uniform (23, 77). Their popularity seems to relate to a general dissatisfaction with old policy instruments; the influence, transfer, and diffusion of emerging governance paradigms based in neoliberal institutionalism and free trade agreements; and the need for market innovations that keep national economies competitive in a globalizing world (23).

Energy taxes, tradable permits, voluntary agreements, ecolabeling, and certification were introduced as early as the 1960s in a number of western countries (23, 78). However, their adoption has gathered steam especially since the 1990s (24). These instruments are founded upon the bedrock of individual preferences and assumptions about self-interested behavior by economic agents. A strong claim advanced in their favor is their superiority in terms of economic efficiency related to implementation. Although an emerging literature focuses on the extent to which process-oriented evaluative criteria such as popularity, responsiveness, legitimacy, transparency, and accountability may also be associated with market incentive-focused instruments, the extent to which they meet these criteria needs much greater exploration (39, 76).

Environmental taxes of different kinds are among the more common market-based instruments aimed to alter environmental actions of agents (by changing the costs and benefits of environmental choices). Over time, a number of countries have adopted a sophisticated mix of different kinds of ecotaxes as well as distinct policy positions about allocation of revenues generated from such taxes (23). Taxes on commodities and services, such as energy, nutrients used in agriculture, or tourism, are enacted in the belief that existing markets do not fully incorporate the externalities associated with the production and use of these commodities and services and that taxes are an effective mechanism to raise revenues to offset damages associated with the overexploitation of underpriced resources. Similarly, tradable permits are based on the idea that some ecosystem services, such as clean water and air, are not priced fully by existing markets. In such situations, incentives for conservation and economic efficiency of allocation can be improved through economic exchange only if appropriate legal and institutional arrangements are in place and polluters pay a tax on their polluting activities. The resulting markets for some kinds of emissions can reach significant proportions: the total value of trading in carbon markets, according to some recent estimates, may reach 10 to 40 billion dollars by 2010 (1).

Voluntary agreements are negotiated to meet environmental targets regarding, for example, lower waste generation and emissions or higher energy efficiency. Industry and corporate actors often pursue such voluntarily imposed targets as a strategy to preempt legal regulation. It can therefore be argued that the shadow of law is crucial to their emergence and effectiveness (79). Indeed, some researchers of voluntary environmental compliance have argued that without leadership by state agencies, voluntary agreements will produce anemic results at best (80). Others such as Ruggie (35) suggest that the irony of the current reliance on corporate actors to implement environmental sustainability lies in the fact that "the corporate sector, which has done more than any other to create the growing gaps between global economy and national communities, is being pulled into playing a key bridging role between them. In the process, a global public domain is emerging, which cannot substitute for effective action by states but may help to produce it" (35, p. 95).

Primary sector commodities such as coffee, timber, and energy provide familiar examples of ecolabeling and certification schemes (81–83). Both ecolabeling and certification schemes are forms of voluntary agreements wherein producers agree to meet environmental standards related to production and marketing activities. Such standards may be the result of work by third party actors, an industry association, or even the government. The operation of these schemes hinges upon the idea that consumers are willing to express their preferences related to cleaner energy or greener products through their choices in markets and through a willingness to pay higher prices. Perceptions about environment-friendly preferences among consumers have led many corporations to adopt certification mechanisms and advertising campaigns that represent both real and cosmetic shifts in how corporate actors govern their environmental actions.

Some of the drivers of market-based policy instruments in the developed world are analogous to those motivating decentralized environmental governance in much of the developing world (84). Dissatisfaction with regulatory control by state agencies and the bureaucratization associated with their growth play an important role in the expansion of market incentives-based instruments and in their adoption across sectors and national boundaries (85). Difficulties in implementation of traditional regulatory instruments provide a partial explanation of the willingness of governments to experiment with market-oriented efforts. High costs of compliance with environmental regulations and increasing awareness of environmental issues among consumers are other parts of the explanation. Although many economists had argued for the economic superiority of market-based instruments as early as the mid-1960s and 1970s (86, 87), it is only recently that their application to environmental governance is becoming more widespread.

The schematic review of a range of different instruments of environmental governance based on market incentives and exchanges suggests that their success depends significantly on the internalization of positive environment preferences among relevant stakeholders, most importantly citizens and consumers (88), and effective leadership by governments. For example, in their comparative study across eight European Union countries, Jordan et al. (23) found that among the constraints to the implementation of MAFIs was the opposition of environmental policy actors (especially environmental movements) and other vested interests (such as energy-intensive industries). Other constraints to successful implementation are lack of expertise across policy systems, fear among corporate sectors about loss of economic competitiveness, and unequal distributional impacts because of ecotaxing schemes (e.g., fuel taxes). Not surprisingly, corporate and industry actors are less likely to adhere voluntarily to new environmental standards to the extent that they prove more costly in comparison to when such standards are absent or weak (89). Indeed, efforts to induce voluntary compliance by economically motivated actors have been found to be vulnerable to free-riding behavior when effective mechanisms to deter free riding are not in place. For example, in a study of the U.S. Environmental Protection Agency's WasteWise program, Delmas & Keller (90) found that organizations joining the program were likely not to report their creation of waste unless there were private benefits to such reporting.

Other research, especially that focusing on corporate social responsibility, examines the extent to which environmentally oriented actions of market actors are tied to their expectations about consumer preferences—both those specific to their products and to "green preferences" more generally (91, 92). Citizen preferences expressed in the form of a greater willingness to purchase green products and policy environments in which superior environmental outcomes are prized are important drivers of the success of new MAFIs of environmental governance. These considerations suggest that the growing popularity of market incentives-based instruments should not lead to the conclusion that governance is replacing governments. A conclusion more broadly supported by existing evidence would be that there is a complex relationship between governments and governance: governments are the source of credible threats of regulatory action that would require costly compliance and such threats encourage the adoption of voluntary agreements on environmental standards.

Government agencies also remain the monitoring authorities to which appeals regarding violations of environmental standards can be made.

Cross-Scale Environmental Governance

The multiscalar character of environmental problems—spatially, sociopolitically, and temporally—adds significant complexity to their governance (93–95). The implications of spatial scales for environmental governance are twofold. First, the decoupling across scales of the causes and consequences of environmental problems introduces major concerns about the unequal distribution of costs and benefits of environmental issues. For example, a problem such as global climate change may have been caused primarily by the major producers of greenhouse gases in the developed world, but many of their more dramatic effects will negatively affect low-emitting countries in the global south. The spatial distribution of environmental problems, such as acid rain, ozone depletion, and transboundary water pollution, transcends national borders and adds to the challenge of designing and implementing solutions (26). As mentioned above, the main strategy to address these issues has been international environmental regimes. Although more than 1700 multilateral and bilateral environmental agreements have hitherto been signed, their effectiveness is at best mixed (30).

Sociopolitically, cross-scale environmental problems affect and are affected by institutionalized decision making at local, subnational, national, and transnational levels. A common prescription to address the multilevel character of environmental problems is to design governance mechanisms across levels of social and institutional aggregation. Multilevel governance is intended to counteract the fragmentation that is characteristic of sectorally based decision making or, indeed, of decision making that is organized by territorial, social, and political divisions. The involvement of public-private networks in multilevel governance can enhance the representation of the diversity of interests that are affected by environmental problems (39, 96). At the same time, the configuration of cross-scale governance strategies is also conducive to compromise seeking and social learning, often enabling less formal modes of decision making, greater transparency, and higher levels of representativeness (39).

Increasingly, cross-scale governance mechanisms are being shaped by nonstate actors including NGOs, transnational environmental organizations, intergovernmental and multilateral organizations, market-oriented actors (e.g., transnational and multinational companies), and epistemic communities (26, 97–101). These new actors both introduce innovative tools and mechanisms and positively shape power relations within the policy arena (31, 102), even if their transformative potential is contested (103).

The cross-temporal implications of environmental problems are especially severe because of two major obstacles to action: contempocentrism and uncertainty regarding cause and effect relationships involving long-term environmental changes. Contempocentrism, in part a consequence of high market discount rates, is the tendency to disregard the welfare of future generations and believe in the power of technology and technological change to take care of environmental degradation and scarcities. It means humans are likely to "spend" the environment now and discount the future heavily (33, 104). Coupled with the seeming high costs of action that will shift existing trajectories of economic development, the uncertainty surrounding the science of causes and effects of environmental degradation often leads to a "do nothing until we know more" attitude–strongly reflected in the contemporary policy positions of some nations that are the largest emitters of greenhouse gases. Many of the impacts of global climate change on humans and ecosystems are still undetermined, and the design and implementation of policies necessary to reduce emissions are both economically and politically quite costly.

The Terrain of Environmental Governance

The elaboration above of environmental governance-related changes and challenges involving four different themes shows that there are intriguing parallels across them despite the many (and expected) differences in how governance is becoming reconfigured as a result of globalization and decentralization. It also shows the increasing importance of cross-scale governance, market instruments, and individual incentives. Perhaps the most obvious of these parallels relates to the emergence of alternative institutional forms of governance. Some of the new forms of governance are innovative hybrids between the conventionally recognized social roles that markets, states, and, more recently, communities play. Others are the result of a clearer appreciation that the effectiveness of what was conventionally understood as a pure form of governance based in the market or the state may be the result of existing relationships among market, state, and civil society actors. Figure 1 presents a schematic structure to

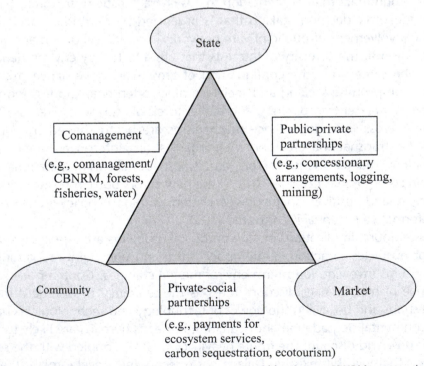

Figure 1. Mechanisms and strategies of environmental governance. Abbreviation: CBNRM, community-based natural resource management.

classify strategies of environmental governance as they are founded upon the actions of three different social mechanisms.

The triangle connecting state, market, and community constitutes the core of the figure. The emphasis in the figure on these social mechanisms is a reflection of early conversations related to the environment that viewed environmental governance strategies as being especially necessary to address the externalities stemming from the public goods nature of environmental resources and processes. To overcome these externalities, some writers saw state action as necessary; others, surmising that externalities could lead to market failure, advocated clearer definition of property rights to allow functioning markets to emerge (43, 105). Arguments advanced by scholars of the commons engaged these policy prescriptions and identified communities as a third potential locus of environmental governance (51). These efforts, championing state-, market-, and community-based governance strategies, were built around perceived strengths of the particular social arena or mechanism being considered: the capacity for action across jurisdictions backed by state authority; the mobilization of basic human incentives through market exchanges; and the deployment of solidaristic relationships and time-and place-specific knowledge embodied in communities (107).

In the past decade and a half, however, an exciting array of research has identified opportunities for more nuanced arguments regarding hybrid forms of collaborations across the dividing lines represented by markets, states, and communities. The three major forms we identify in Figure 1—comanagement (between state agencies and communities), public-private partnerships (between state agencies and market actors), and private-social partnerships (between market actors and communities)—each incorporate joint action across at least two of the social mechanisms/arenas in the core triangle and correspond to scores if not hundreds of specific experiments in which constituent social actors find differing levels of emphasis. They simultaneously illustrate the dynamic and fast-changing nature of contemporary environmental governance. The emergence of these hybrid forms of environmental governance is based upon the recognition that no single agent possesses the capabilities to address the multiple facets, interdependencies, and scales of environmental problems that may appear at first blush to be quite simple.

The hope embodied in hybrid forms of environmental governance is evident in each case. They seek simultaneously to address the weaknesses of a particular social agent and to build upon the strength of the other partner. Thus, the involvement of market actors in environmental collaboration is typically aimed at addressing the inefficiencies of state action, often by injecting competitive pressures in the provision of environmental services. In the same vein, market actors are also viewed as enabling greater profitability in the utilization of environmental resources. The addition of community and local voices to environmental governance is seen as providing the benefit of time-and place-specific information that may help solve complex environmental problems and, at the same time, allow a more equitable allocation of benefits from environmental assets. Higher levels of participation by different stakeholders and the blessings of state authorities can help overcome the democratic deficit and lack of legitimacy often associated with market-focused instruments. Moreover, state actors, ostensibly, create the possibility that fragmented social action by decentralized communities and market actors can be made more coherent and simultaneously more authoritative.

A second obvious parallel across the discussion of the different themes related to environmental governance is that within hybrid strategies one can discern a mobilization of individual incentives that had initially been the core of market-oriented instruments and is now becoming increasingly common. Thus, contemporary cogovernance strategies, in contrast to their historic counterparts, focus on how the individual subject will respond to efforts at governance. Through such a calculation of individual responses, decentralized environmental governance aims to elicit the willing cooperation of those subject to the goals of governance (6, 108). The emphasis on willing cooperation has even prompted some scholars of incentive-based governance strategies to term them "governance without government" (109, p. 652).

In view of the extent to which an appeal to individual self-interest is a part of new environmental governance strategies, it is reasonable to conclude that a pervasive attempt to re-structure agent-level incentives and attitudes toward the environment underpins governance instruments related to civil society-based solidarities, market-based policies, and voluntary compliance mechanisms (110, 111).

The same is true for public-private and social-private partnerships, each of which is enabled by a level of valorization of corporate entities and market actors that would have been quite unimaginable in the 1970s (112–114). Here, the logic of efficiency, which is the hallmark of capitalist organization of production, is also coming to colonize the goal of environmental conservation and sustainable development.

Limitations of Hybrid Governance Strategies

The reconfiguration of environmental governance so that the state is no longer the only actor viewed as capable of addressing environmental externalities has many implications, but not all of them have found an easy acceptance among those concerned about environmental outcomes. The focus on individual incentives, the creation of new property rights and markets in relation to water or carbon, and the encouragement to the corporate sector (insofar as the policy environment enables more extensive public-private and social-private partnerships) have been construed by some scholars as moves toward increasing democratic deficit and higher levels of inequality in the allocation of environmental resources. Those who are able to exercise greater access and expertise in relation to these new mechanisms are more likely to derive greater benefits from them (66). Other scholars have expressed significant concerns about the likely results of market actors being incorporated in a more thoroughgoing manner into environmental governance, which Liverman (115), among others, has called the "com-modification of nature." Greater efficiency in the utilization of natural resources, for many, is equivalent to higher rates of extraction and, thereby, brings up issues of intergenerational equity.

For scholars coming from a radical political economy perspective, there is no new approach to global environmental governance; rather, the supposed new mechanisms of governance are little more than a natural evolution of traditional regime politics because outsiders and disempowered groups continue to have little opportunity to participate in contemporary efforts at governance despite the greater incorporation of civil society actors (31). Here, the key differences between models of new global environmental governance and older conceptions of regime theory concern the role of and the importance accorded to members of global civil society, which is understood as a sphere of voluntary societal associations located above the individual and below the state as well as across state boundaries (31, 98). Ford (31) argues, for example, that the rhetoric of societal participation introduced by the Brundtland Report did little to change regime politics because it failed to democratize the negotiation process itself. New forms of global environmental governance, and their newly incorporated players, can be viewed simply as reflecting existing distributions of power rather than having changed anything fundamental. Indeed, global environmental governance is seen as being embedded in a neoliberal political economy, which is hegemonic in the neo-Gramscian sense that dominant power relations are maintained by consent as well as by coercion (31). In this sense, global environmental governance is part of a broader agenda of corporate interests developed to promote economic globalization and to regulate what both NGOs and nation states do (116). In a world of weak states, deterritorialized action, and concentrated power, corporate interests and multilateral organizations can control and reframe environmental action as a means to legitimize their model of development (117). These dominant interests place greater weight on the problem-solving aspect of new instruments rather than on ameliorating the unequal power relations that the new system also continues to preserve. Indeed, actors who are mostly responsible for nature's degradation are defining the terms of environmental protection. "Governance from below," represented by the role of social movements and protests against organizations such as transnational corporations, the WTO, and the International Monetary Fund, is currently the only recognizable challenge, despite the risk that it too may be coopted (117).

In contrast, the inclusion of a wider array of social actors such as private and corporate interests is justified by the need to guarantee that veto players, whose "voice" or "exit" can jeopardize public action, agree with policy choices. The rationale is that if these elite actors are provided with a privileged space for participation, they will have no incentive to exert their veto power or obstruct the decision-making process. Moreover, the belief in the efficiency of market-led forms of governance to produce positive outcomes justifies compromising for the "greater good." Radical political economists, however, argue that this is hardly a justification for legitimacy (39) and that the mere inclusion of more social actors does not necessarily make governance systems more democratic (118). Although advocates of new forms of governance argue that their democratic deficit is no worse than that of traditional representative democracy (39), critics point out that they fail to meet normative models of deliberative democracy whose fairness is grounded in the equal participation of all stakeholders. The opacity of governance networks may prevent the mass public from identifying and evaluating the role of specific agents, such as experts who play prominent roles in the building of relevant issues and action agendas. For example, in cases of environmental issues with potentially catastrophic impacts (e.g., global climate change), the predominance of "less than democratic" expert politics is justified in the name of the urgency and severity of the problem.

MAFIs and multilevel governance frameworks may also have negative effects on policy capacity, specifically in relation to environmental problems. In multilevel governance systems, the "denationalization" of statehood, reflected empirically in the "hollowing out" of the national state apparatus, reorganizes old and new capacities territorially and functionally—

but not always for the better (119). Indeed, globalization and subnational challenges have led to the emergence of a rescaled state that simultaneously transfers power upward to supranational agencies and downward toward regional and local levels (120), changing the way policy-making capacity is distributed. This transfer of power to different levels of decision making may have already negatively affected policy capacity of the modern state (121). Hybrid modes of environmental governance and emerging partnerships across conventional divisions suggest that the state is not the only, and perhaps not even the most important, actor in governance (119). Yet, advocates of a bigger role for the state contend that, especially in cases where redistributive policy making becomes necessary (e.g., adaptation), it is unlikely that either the market or hybrid forms of governance will be able to accomplish much (122).

Applications: Climate Change and Ecosystem Degradation

The four themes we highlighted above and the framework for viewing emerging hybrid mechanisms of environmental governance are visible in the major problem areas related to the environment. Two significant arenas in which these themes and hybrid governance strategies are especially evident are global climate change and ecosystem degradation. An examination of these areas of environmental concern and crisis provides useful indications about the extent to which contemporary and emerging environmental governance approaches have the capacity to help address major problems.

Climate Change

Among the factors that challenge environmental governance structures, global climate change promises to be one of the most critical. As the need to design policies to respond to the negative impacts of climate change increases, more attention has been paid to emerging modes of environmental governance and to how they can increase the capacity of economic, social, and cultural systems to help humans mitigate and adapt to climatic change. Considering that climate is one of many stressors, the resilience of already overextended economic, political, and administrative institutions may decrease rapidly, especially in the more impoverished regions of the globe (22). Some signs of how environmental stresses may exacerbate governance challenges related to poverty, violence, and authoritarianism are already visible (1). Among the expected casualties of governance breakdown as a result of climate change may be economic growth, democratic institutions, and livelihood possibilities.

Responses to global climate change fall broadly into two main categories: those seeking to curb or stabilize the level of emissions of greenhouse gases into the atmosphere (mitigation) and those seeking to boost natural and human systems' resilience to prevent, respond, and recover from potential impacts of a changing climate (adaptation). Although at this point adaptation may be inevitable, its magnitude and range depends on how much mitigation is successfully implemented to prevent and avoid the most dangerous interference in the climate regime.

Many of the factors that make global climate change unique also make it complex. Global climate change is the quintessential multiscalar environmental problem; because greenhouse gases mix equally in the atmosphere, the costs of the negative effects of climate change are socialized at the global level, but the effects are likely to be felt at the local level. The fragmented and highly politicized nature of the causes of climate change means that it is extremely difficult to assign blame and target offenders. Effective responses to climate change are likely to require a diversity of actors and organizations across the state-society divide. The high level of uncertainty still involving the definition of the magnitude and character of the impacts of climate change in different human and natural systems and the fact they might not be felt for years also make it a politically and financially costly problem (33). Finally, the differences among those causing climate change (large producers of greenhouse gases) and those likely to be more negatively affected by it, including the global poor and natural and biological systems, make it unique in terms of the distribution of costs and benefits and bring up a whole host of equity and environmental justice questions (123). For example, although mitigation actions are likely to fall upon countries and sectors mostly responsible for the production of greenhouse gases, such as polluting corporations and developed countries, adaptation will be realized mostly by affected groups such as the poor, living in less-developed countries, or agencies entrusted with the task of building generic adaptive capacity to climate change such as local governments, NGOs, and aid organizations. In the literature on adaptation, most efforts to compare differential vulnerability identify already stressed countries and regions in Africa and South Asia and small island states as the most vulnerable (124, 125), but the primary burden of mitigation falls on developed countries under international regimes to curb greenhouse gas emissions, such as the Kyoto protocol (127).

Mitigation

The Intergovernmental Panel on Climate Change (IPCC) defines mitigation of global climate change as "an anthropogenic intervention to reduce the sources or enhance the sinks of greenhouse gases" (128)(also see Section VI, Part A for mitigation text box). Mitigation of greenhouse gas emissions has been organized at the international level primarily through the entering into force of the Kyoto Protocol and has been realized at the national level through regulation and implementation of new governance mechanisms across the public-private divide. Mechanisms to mitigate global climate change range from technological fixes to the design of institutions that curb carbon emission practices. Five categories of strategies to mitigate carbon emissions are available: energy conservation, renewable energy, enhanced natural sinks, nuclear energy, and fossil carbon management. Yet the magnitude, complexity, and urgency of the climate change problem suggest that the implementation of any or of a combination of these strategies would require tremendous amounts of financial, human, and political capital (129).

Not surprisingly, the lack of capacity of nation states to implement such strategies (exemplified by the lackluster accomplishments of Kyoto to date) (130), and the general lack of confidence that this capacity will improve dramatically in the near future, suggests that a broader array of hybrid modes of governance is necessary to address global climate change. Comanagement and public-private partnerships in the implementation of Kyoto's Clean Development Mechanism and social-private partnerships to develop community-based carbon sequestration projects are a promising start (131, 132). Carbon taxes and joint development of fuel-efficient technology (e.g., FredomCAR, California Fuel Cell Partnership) are also examples of initiatives involving both public and private actors. Yet, despite the promise of effectiveness, many question the ability of hybrid modes of governance to address mitigation as fast and as broadly as necessary to defuse many of the most negative impacts of global climate change.

Already, in the implementation of mitigation policy, NGOs and businesses have played a particularly important role both in influencing the design and implementation of climate governance mechanisms. Although business interests have focused mostly on flexible mechanisms for carbon trading (see section on market-based mechanisms) and the pursue of fuel efficiency (in addition to playing an oppositional role to the implementation of emission-curbing strategies), NGOs have played a broader role in monitoring implementation and compliance of regulation, lobbying, raising equity issues, and providing scientific and technical knowledge (34, 127, 133, 134). One of the most effective ways NGOs have influenced the global climate change policy process has been through their role as knowledge producers and as members of information networks and epistemic communities seeking to affect the response process.

Adaptation

The IPCC defines adaptation as an "adjustment in natural or human systems in response to actual or expected climatic stimuli or their effects, which moderates harm or exploits beneficial opportunities." (Also see Section VI, Part A for adaptation text box.) Vulnerability in turn is "a function of the character, magnitude, and rate of climate variation to which a system is exposed, its sensitivity, and its adaptive capacity" (128). Adaptive capacity, the third concept important to understand vulnerability to global climate change, is the "potential and capability to change to a more desirable state in the face of the impacts or risks of climate change" (135). It is the ability of a system to moderate and to adjust to global climate change-related damages. Adaptation policy considers the entitlements, assets, and resources that improve the capacity of this system to resist, cope, and recover from a given hazard.

To date, adaptive capacity indicators have been defined mostly at the national scale both because it is an appropriate level to make adaptation decisions and because it allows for comparison of vulnerability across countries (124). Although the reality of building adaptive capacity involves cascading decisions across scales and a diversity of private and public agents and organizations (136), because of the redistributive character of adaptive capacity building, the bulk of action is expected to fall over nation states (22).

At lower scales of government, global climate change critically intersects with decentralization not only in the assessment of different levels of vulnerability within countries but also in the design of policy to enhance adaptive capacity. For example, at the local level, vulnerability assessment (e.g., participatory vulnerability mapping) holds the promise of a more accurate understanding of the "character" of the vulnerability of specific social and human systems (137). At the global level, adaptation policy is influenced by the role that institutions such as the United Nations Framework Climate Change Convention play in coordinating international action, advancing rationales for compensation, and preparing for future impacts (123, 138).

In sum, the panoply of governance strategies related to global climate change are clearly difficult to view as being centered on any single category of social agent as depicted in Figure 1. Although it might have been argued a decade ago that nation states are the only actors who can generate effective measures to address climate change, it is evident that, although their involvement is necessary, they are not adequate to perform the task by themselves. The willing cooperation of civil society and market actors and changes in individual level actions are critically important to the successful implementation of the set of governance strategies that might have some prospect of being effective.

Ecosystem Degradation

Like climate change, ongoing and fundamental alterations of the relationship between humans and ecosystems pose a complex set of multiscalar challenges for environmental governance. Ecosystems and their services are the basis upon which human lives and all human actions are founded; thus it is not surprising that when examining human impacts on the environment, the Millennium Ecosystem Assessment (MEA) focused on ecosystem services. In this section, we draw upon this comprehensive assessment of ecosystems to pursue our arguments about changing forms of environmental governance. The MEA (1) categorized the range of benefits available to humans from ecosystems into "*provisioning services* such as food, water, timber, and fiber; *regulating services* that affect climate, floods, disease, wastes, and water quality; *cultural services* that provide recreational, aesthetic, and spiritual benefits; and *supporting services* such as soil formation, photosynthesis, and nutrient cycling." This assessment concludes that humans have altered ecosystem services more comprehensively in the past half century than in any previous comparable period. Although these alterations in the relationships between humans and ecosystems have led to substantial net gains in economic development and well-being, 60% of ecosystem services are being degraded or used unsustainably. Not only are current use and management patterns unsustainable, they are increasing the likelihood of nonlinear and irreversible changes, such as disease emergence, fisheries collapse, alterations in water quality, and regional climate shifts. Finally, the costs of ongoing changes are being borne disproportionately by the poor, thereby contributing to growing disparities (1).

To address these changes, the MEA evaluates a range of potential responses and focuses especially on those that would (*a*) lead to institutional changes and governance patterns that can manage ecosystems effectively, (*b*) align market incentives better with the real costs of environmental services, (*c*) focus on particular social behavioral obstacles to better utilization of ecosystems, (*d*) promote more efficient technologies, (*e*) provide better knowledge about what is happening to ecosystems, and (*f*) improve the efficacy of environment-related decision making.

Throughout the discussion of these responses, it is evident that the authors of the MEA simultaneously define the terrain of environmental governance quite narrowly and extremely broadly. They identify a specific set of responses, those having to do with institutional and governance-related changes, as properly the domain of environmental governance. Such responses include the integration of ecosystem goals into existing sectoral strategies, for example, in the poverty reduction strategies encouraged by the World Bank, increased emphasis on international environmental agreements and target setting, and greater accountability of environmental decision making.

But they treat environmental governance too narrowly in restricting its scope to specifically institutional responses. In fact, the entire set of responses they identify in relation to markets, social behaviors, technological innovation, and monitoring capacity is contingent on changes in governance. Indeed, without comprehensive changes in contemporary national policies, the basis on which market exchanges are organized, and the incentives on which individuals act, there is little reason to think that the real costs of negative environmental outcomes will be incorporated into economic decision making. Similar arguments are not difficult to advance in relation to desired technological changes, social behaviors, or cultural processes. Although we may, in part as a result of a particular division of social-scientific labors, view the world as being divided into economic, social, political, and cultural domains, shifts in human actions in all of these domains require a reconfiguration of the costs and benefits of given actions. In the absence of changes introduced through shifts in governance patterns, there is little likelihood that humans will change their economic, political, social, or cultural behaviors.

Precisely because of the social interconnections across what we view as local, regional, national, and global levels and what we categorize as the economic, political, social, and cultural domains, successful environmental governance strategies will require heightened cooperation of many different actors across these levels and domains. Thus, not only is it the case that human beings will be able to introduce manageable changes in ecosystems only through significant transformations in environmental governance strategies, it is also very likely that successful outcomes will hinge on environmental governance approaches that are founded upon heightened cooperation involving all actors in all three social locations identified in Figure 1: market, state, and community.

Conclusion

Our review of the changing terrain of environmental governance has emphasized four elements. One, we suggest that environmental governance signifies a wide set of regulatory processes, not just international governance mechanisms and their impacts at the international level or just the state and its agencies at the national and subnational levels. Two, we highlight the hybrid, multilevel, and crosssectoral nature of emerging forms of governance. Our review examines in particular how environmental governance has changed since the 1960s. From a focus on specific agents of change such as state and market actors, advocates of effective environmental management came to view communities and local institutions as important actors to involve in governance. Especially in the past decade and a half, new sets of instruments of environmental governance have emerged. We identify three broad terms that denote these partnerships: comanagement as the form of collaboration between state agencies and communities, public-private partnerships between market actors and state agencies, and social-private partnerships between market actors and communities.

Three, we analyze how emerging forms of environmental governance that have become increasingly popular since the mid-1990s rely, on the one hand, on partnerships and, on the other hand, on the mobilization of individual incentives characteristic of market-based instruments of environmental regulation. Because they seek to gain the willing participation of a range of actors who would be subject to their regulatory effects, they are viewed by many observers as being amenable to more efficient implementation.

Greater efficiency in design and implementation of environmental governance instruments is undoubtedly a major concern of state authorities who may be under fiscal pressures and who may therefore find partnerships with market actors highly desirable. A partnership with private actors may also appear attractive to civil society actors and communities historically strapped for funding. However, a number of observers of changing environmental governance have raised concerns about the degree to which increasing recourse to market actors and processes undermines social goals related to higher levels of democratic participation, creates problems of unequal access to resources, and raises the specter of lack of accountability.

Finally, our review explores valid concerns about the unanticipated consequences of emerging forms of environmental governance. An ethical concern for democratic participation and more equitable outcomes in environmental governance is a welcome development when environmental governance mechanisms emphasize collaboration for greater efficiency. An exclusive focus on greater efficiency in emerging efforts at environmental governance, especially where natural resources are concerned, may yield the unanticipated outcome of increasing commodification of nature. The fact that human interventions in ecosystem processes are already leading to unsustainable use of more than 60% of ecosystems suggests that, together with greater efficiency, it is equally necessary to work toward restraint in human use of major ecosystems. The mobilization of individual incentives and their incorporation into innovative strategies of environmental governance is critical for efficient governance. However, effective environmental governance also requires the incorporation of knowledge about limits on aggregate levels of human activities that rely on high intensities of resource exploitation or lead to high levels of pollutant emissions. In designing and assessing strategies of environmental governance, it is critical therefore to focus not just on efficiency and equity, but also on criteria related to long-term sustainability and a concern for nature.

Acknowledgments

In writing this review, we are indebted to many conversations and insights that proved instrumental in the development of our arguments. Jon Anderson, Charles Benjamin, Edwin Connorley, Benjamin Cousins, Aaron de Grassi, David Kaimowitz, James McCarthy, James Murombedzi, Ebrima Sall, Gill Shepherd, and Ann Thomas gave their time and ideas at short notice. Long-standing conversations with Jesse Ribot and Elinor Ostrom have shaped our arguments and views considerably, especially in relation to subnational forms of environmental governance. Comments from two anonymous reviewers and extensive responses from Duncan Macqueen on an earlier draft of the chapter are also gratefully acknowledged. Finally, we would like to thank Nate Engle for his careful reading of earlier versions of the chapter.

The *Annual Review of Environment and Resources* is online at
http://environ.annualreviews.org

Literature Cited

1. Millenn. Ecosyst. Assess. 2005. *Ecosystems and Human Well Being: Synthesis*. Washington, DC: Island

2. Sonnenfeld DA, Mol APJ. 2002. Ecological modernization, governance, and globalization. *Am. Behav. Sci.* 45:1456–61

3. Evans P. 1996. Government action, social capital and development: reviewing the evidence on synergy. *World Dev.* 24:1119–32

4. Ostrom E. 2001. Vulnerability and polycentric governance systems. *Update: Newsl. Int. Hum. Dimens. Program. Glob. Environ. Chang.* 3 http://www.ihdp.uni-bonn.de/html/publications/update/IHDP Update01 03.html

5. Jagers SC, Stripple J. 2003. Climate governance beyond the state. *Glob. Gov.* 9:385–99

6. Agrawal A. 2005. *Environmentality: Technologies of Government and the Making of Subjects*. Durham, NC: Duke Univ. Press

7. Hirst P, Thompson G. 2002. The future of globalization. *Coop. Confl.* 37:247– 65

8. Newell P. 2002. Globalization and the Future State. Brighton, UK: Inst. Dev. Stud.

9. Nye JS. 2001. Globalization's democratic deficit: how to make international institutions more accountable. *Foreign Aff.* 80:2–6

10. Staeger MB. 2002. *Globalism*. Lanham, MD: Rowman & Littlefield

11. Appadurai A. 1996. *Modernity at Large: Cultural Dimensions of Globalization*. Minneapolis: Univ. Minn. Press

12. Berger P, Huntington S. 2003. *Many Globalizations: Cultural Diversity in the Contemporary World*. New York: Oxford Univ. Press

13. Held D, McGrew A. 2002. *Globalization/Anti-Globalization*. London: Polity

14. Barkin JS. 2003. The counterintuitive relationship between globalization and climate change. *Glob. Environ. Polit.* 3:8–13

15. Frankel J. 2005. Climate and trade: links between the Kyoto Protocol and WTO. *Environment* 47:8–19

16. Santilli M, Moutinho P, Schwartzman S, Nepstad D, Curran L, Nobre C. 2005. Tropical deforestation and the Kyoto Protocol. *Clim. Chang.* 71:267–76

17. Roe E, Eeten MJG. 2004. Three—not two—major environmental counternar-ratives to globalization. *Glob. Environ. Polit.* 4:36–53

18. Liverman DM, Varady RG, Chavez O, Sanchez R. 1999. Environmental issues along the United States-Mexico border: drivers of change and responses of citizens and institutions. *Annu. Rev. Energy Environ.* 24:607–43

19. Harbine J. 2002. NAFTA chapter II arbitration: deciding on the price of free trade. *Ecol. Law Q.* 29:371–94

20. Sanchez RA. 2002. Governance, trade, and the environment in the context of NAFTA. *Am. Behav. Sci.* 45:1369–93

21. Clark W. 2000. Environmental Globalization. In *Governance in a Globalizing World*, ed. JS Nye, JD Donahue, pp. 86–108. Washington, DC: Brookings Inst.

22. Eakin H, Lemos MC. 2006. Adaptation and the state: Latin America and the challenge of capacity-building under globalization. *Glob. Environ. Chang.* 16:7–18

23. Jordan A, Wurtzel R, Zito AR. 2003. "New" environmental policy instruments: an evolution or a revolution in environmental policy? *Environ. Polit.* 12:201–24

24. Busch PO, Jorgens H, Tews K. 2005. The global diffusion of regulatory instruments: the making of a new international environmental regime. *Ann. Am. Polit. Soc. Sci.* 598:146–67

25. Heijden HA. 2006. Globalization, environmental movements, and international political opportunity structures. *Organ. Environ.* 19:28–45

26. Haas PM. 1989. Do regimes matter? Epistemic communities and Mediterranean pollution control. *Int. Organ.* 43:377–403

27. Krasner SD, ed. 1983. *International Regimes.* Ithaca, NY: Cornell Univ. Press

28. Young OR. 1989. *International Cooperation: Building Regimes for Natural Resources and the Environment.* Ithaca, NY: Cornell Univ. Press

29. Young OR. 2001. Inferences and in-dices: evaluating the effectiveness of in ternational environmental regimes. *Glob. Environ. Polit.* 1:99–121

30. Mitchell RB. 2003. International environmental agreements: a survey of their features, formation, and effects. *Annu. Rev. Environ. Resour.* 28:429–61

31. Ford LH. 2003. Challenging global environmental governance: social movement agency and global civil society. *Glob. Environ. Polit.* 3:120–34

32. Stiglitz JE. 1999. The World Bank at the millennium. *Econ. J.* 109:F577–97

33. Hempel LC. 1996. *Environmental Governance: The Global Challenge.* Washing-ton: Island

34. Gulbrandsen LH, Andresen S. 2004. NGO infuence in the implementation of the Kyoto Protocol: compliance, flexibility mechanisms, and sinks. *Glob. Environ. Polit.* 4:54–75

35. Ruggie JG. 2003. Taking embedded liberalism global: the corporate connection. In *Taming Globalization*, ed. D Held, M Koenig-Archibugi, pp. 93–129. Cambridge, UK: Polity

36. Brunner R, Klein R. 1999. Harvesting experience: a reappraisal of the U.S. climate change action plan. *Polit. Sci.* 32:133–61

37. Haas P. 2004. Addressing the global governance deficit. *Glob. Environ. Polit.* 4:1–15

38. Sanwal M. 2004. Trends in global environmental governance: the emergence of a mutual supportiveness approach to achieve sustainable development. *Glob. Environ. Polit.* 4:16–22

39. Papadopoulos Y. 2003. Cooperative forms of governance: problems of democratic accountability in complex environments. *Eur. J. Polit. Res.* 42:473–501

40. Schofer E, Hironaka A. 2005. The effects of world society on environmental protection outcomes. *Soc. Forces* 84:25–47

41. Buhrs T. 2003. From diffusion to diffusion: the roots and effects of environmental innovation in New Zealand. *Environ. Polit.* 12:83–101

42. Claussen E. 2001. Global environmental governance: issues for the new US administration. *Environment* 43:29–34

43. Hardin G. 1978. Political requirements for preserving our common heritage. In *Wildlife and America*, ed. HP Brokaw, pp. 310–17. Washington, DC: Counc. Environ. Qual.

44. Ophuls W. 1977. *Ecology and the Politics of Scarcity: Prologue to a Political Theory of the Steady State.* San Francisco: Freeman

45. Anderson D, Grove R, ed. 1984. *Conservation in Africa: People, Policies and Practice.* Cambridge, UK: Cambridge Univ. Press

46. Peluso NL, Vandergeest P. 2001. Genealogies of the political forest and customary rights in Indonesia. *J. Asia. Stud.* 60:761–812

47. Wunsch JS, Olowu D. 1997. Regime transformation from below: decentralization, local governance, and democratic reform in Nigeria. *Stud. Comp. Int. Dev.* 31:66–82

48. Corbridge S. 1991. Third world development. *Prog. Hum. Geogr.* 15:311–21

49. Silver C. 2003. Do the donors have it right? Decentralization and changing local governance in Indonesia. *Ann. Reg. Sci.* 37:421–34

50. Peluso NL. 1992. *Rich Forests, Poor People: Resource Control and Resistance in Java.* Berkeley: Univ. Calif. Press

51. Ostrom E. 1990. *Governing the Commons: The Evolution of Institutions for Collective Action.* New York: Cambridge Univ. Press

52. Wade R. 1994. *Village Republics: Economic Conditions for Collective Action in South India.* Oakland: ICS Press

53. Blaikie P, Brookfield H. 1987. *Land Degradation and Society.* London: Methuen. 296 pp

54. Bryant RL, Bailey S. 1997. *Third World Political Ecology.* London: Routledge

55. Wantchekon L. 2004. Resource wealth and political regimes in Africa. *Comp. Polit. Stud.* 37:816–41

56. Hardin RD. 2002. *Concessionary politics in the Western Congo Basin: History and Culture in Forest Use.* Washington, DC: World Resour. Inst./Gov. Inst.

57. Watts MJ. 2005. Righteous oil: human rights, the oil complex, and corporate social responsibility. *Annu. Rev. Environ. Resour.* 30:373–407

58. Luong PJ, Weinthal E. 2001. Prelude to the resource curse: explaining oil and gas development strategies in the Soviet successor states and beyond. *Comp. Polit. Stud.* 34:367–99

59. Hutchcroft PD. 2001. Centralization and decentralization in administration and politics: assessing territorial dimensions of authority and power. *Governance* 14:23–53

60. Conyers D. 1983. Decentralization: the latest fashion in development administration. *Public Adm. Dev.* 3:97–109

61. Manor J. 1999. *The Political Economy of Democratic Decentralization.* Washing-ton, DC: World Bank

62. Weber EP. 2000. A new vanguard for the environment: grassroots ecosystem management as a new environmental management. *Soc. Nat. Resour.* 13:237–59

63. Johnson C, Forsyth T. 2002. In the eyes of the state: negotiating a "rights-based approach" to forest conservation in Thailand. *World Dev.* 30:1591–605

64. Lemos MC, Oliveira JLF. 2004. Can water reform survive politics? Institutional change and river basin management in Ceará Northeast Brazil. *World Dev.* 32:2121–37

65. Wunsch JS. 2001. Decentralization, local governance and 'recentralization' in Africa. *Public Adm. Dev.* 21:277–88

66. Ribot JC, Peluso NL. 2003. A theory of access. *Rural Sociol.* 68:153–81

67. Noel E. 1999. Power, politics and place: Who holds the reins of environmental regulation? *Ecol. Law Q.* 25:559–63

68. Campbell T. 2003. *The Quiet Revolution: Decentralization and the Rise of Political Participation in Latin American Cities.* Pittsburgh: Univ. Pittsburgh Press

69. Bardhan P. 2002. Decentralization of governance and development. *J. Econ. Per-spect.* 16:185–205

70. Boone C. 2003. Decentralization as political strategy in West Africa. *Comp. Polit. Stud.* 36:355–80

71. Agrawal A. 2001. The regulatory community: decentralization and the environment in the Van Panchayats (forest councils) of Kumaon. *Mt. Res. Dev.* 21:208–11

72. Andersson KP. 2004. Who talks with whom? The role of repeated interactions in decentralized forest governance. *World Dev.* 32:233–49

73. Bagchi A. 2003. Rethinking federalism: changing power relations between the center and the states. *Publius* 33:21–42

74. Ribot J. 1999. Decentralisation, participation, and accountability in Sahelian forestry: legal instruments of political administrative control. *Africa* 69(1):23–65

75. Prud'homme R. 1995. The dangers of decentralization. *World Bank Res. Obs.* 10:201–20

76. Cashore B. 2002. Legitimacy and the privatization of environmental governance: How non-state market driven (NSMD) governance systems gain rule-making authority. *Governance* 15:503–29

77. Tews K, Busch PO, Jorgens H. 2003. The diffusion of new environmental policy instruments. *Eur. J. Polit. Res.* 42:569–600

78. Lafferty W, Meadowcroft J, eds. 2000. *Implementing Sustainable Development.* Oxford: Oxford Univ. Press

79. Segerson K, Miceli TJ. 1998. Voluntary environmental agreements: Good or bad news for environmental protection? *J. Environ. Econ. Manag.* 36:109–30

80. MacKendrick NM. 2005. The role of the state in voluntary environmental reform: a case study of public land. *Policy Sci.* 38:21–44

81. Bray DB, Sanchez JLP, Murphy EC. 2002. Social dimensions of organic coffee production in Mexico: lessons for eco-labeling initiatives. *Soc. Nat. Resour.* 15:426–46

82. Cashore B, Auld G, Newsom D. 2003. Forest certification (eco-labeling) programs and their policy-making authority: explaining divergence among North American and European case studies. *Forest Policy Econ.* 5:225–47

83. Cashore B, Auld G, Newsom D. 2004. *Governing through Markets: Forest Certification and the Emergence of Non-State Authority.* New Haven: Yale Univ. Press

84. Engel S, Lopez R, Palmer C. 2006. Community-industry contracting over natural resource use in a context of weak property rights: the case of Indonesia. *Environ. Resour. Econ.* 33:73–93

85. Durant RF, Chun YP, Kim B, Lee S. 2004. Toward a new governance paradigm for environmental and natural resource management in the 21st century? *Adm. Soc.* 35:643–82

86. Coase R. 1960. The problem of social cost. *J. Law Econ.* 3:1–44

87. Cheung SNS. 1970. The structure of a contract and the theory of a Non-Exclusive Resource. *J. Law Econ.* 13:49–70

88. Brammer S, Millington A. 2003. The effect of stakeholder preferences, organizational structure and industry type on corporate community involvement. *J. Bus. Ethics* 45:213–26

89. Bartley T. 2003. Certifying forests and factories: states, social movements, and the rise of private regulation in the apparel and forest products fields. *Polit. Soc.* 31:433–64

90. Delmas M, Keller A. 2005. Free riding in voluntary environmental programs: the case of the U.S. E.P.A. WasteWise Program. *Policy Sci.* 38:91–106

91. Auperle KE, Carroll AB, Hatfield JD. 1985. An empirical examination of the relationship between corporate social responsibility and profitability. *Acad. Manag. J.* 28:446–63

92. Cochran PL, Wood RA. 1984. Corporate social responsibility and financial performance. *Acad. Manag. J.* 27:42–56

93. Wilbanks TJ. 2002. Geographic scaling issues in integrated assessments of climate change. *Integr. Assess.* 3:100–14

94. Adger N, Brown K, Tompkins EL. 2006. The political economy of cross-scale networks in resource co-management. *Ecol. Soc.* 10:18

95. Lebel L, Garden P, Imamura M. 2005. The politics of scale, position, and place in the governance of water resources in the Mekong Region. *Ecol. Soc.* 10:9

96. Rival L. 2003. The meaning of forest governance in Esmeraldas, Ecuador. *Oxford Dev. Stud.* 31:479–501

97. Keck ME, Sikkink K. 1998. *Activists Beyond Borders: Advocacy Networks in International Politics.* Ithaca, NY: Cornell Univ. Press

98. Lipschutz RD. 1996. *Global Civil Society and Global Environmental Governance: The Politics of Nature from Place to Planet.* Albany: State Univ. NY Press

99. Wapner P. 1995. Politics beyond the state: environmental activism and world civic politics. *World Polit.* 47:311–40

100. Biermann F. 2002. Institutions for scientific advice: global environmental assessments and their influence in developing countries. *Glob. Gov.* 8:195–219

101. Coate R, Alger C, Lipschutz R. 1996. The United Nations and civil society: creative partnerships for sustainable development. *Alternatives* 21(1):93–122

102. Ford LH. 1999. Social movements and the globalisation of environmental governance. *IDS Bull.* 30:68–74

103. Toke D. 1999. Epstemic communities and environmental groups. *Politics* 19:97–102

104. Speth JG. 2004. Red Sky at Morning: *America and the Crisis of the Global Environment.* New Haven: Yale Univ. Press

105. Alchian A, Demsetz H. 1972. Production, information costs, and economic organization. *Am. Econ. Rev.* 62:777–95

106. Ophuls W. 1977. *Ecology and the Politics of Scarcity: Prologue to a Political Theory of the Steady State.* San Francisco: Freeman

107. Ostrom E, Schroeder L, Wynne S. 1993. *Institutional Incentives and Sustainable Development: Infrastructure Policies in Perspective.* Boulder, CO: Westview

108. McCarthy JJ. 2004. Privatizing conditions of production: trade agreements as ne-oliberal environmental governance. *Geo-forum* 35:327–41

109. Rhodes RAW. 1996. The new governance: governing without government. *Polit. Stud.* 44:652–67

110. Bennett PI. 2000. Environmental governance and private actors: enrolling insurers and international maritime regulation. *Polit. Geogr.* 9:875–99

111. Robertson M. 2004. The neoliberalization of ecosystem services: wetland mitigation banking and problems in environmental governance. *Geoforum* 35:361–73

112. Ashford NA. 2002. Government and environmental innovation in Europe and North America. *Am. Behav. Sci.* 45:1417–34

113. Hardin RD. 2006. *Concessionary Politics.* Berkeley: Univ. Calif. Press. In press

114. Sanderson S. 2002. The future of conservation. *Foreign Aff.* 81:162–82

115. Liverman D. 2004. Who governs, at what scale, and at what price? Geography, environmental governance, and the commodi-fication of nature. *Ann. Assoc. Am. Geogr.* 94:734–38

116. Falkner R. 2003. Private environmental governance and international relations: exploring the links. *Glob. Environ. Polit.* 3:72–87

117. Paterson M, Humphreys D, Pettiford L. 2003. Conceptualizing global environmental governance: from interstate regimes to counter-hegemonic struggles. *Glob. Environ. Polit.* 3:1–10

118. Manor J. 2005. User committees: a potentiality damaging second wave of decentralization? In *Democratic Decentralization through a Natural Resources Lens*, ed. JC Ribot, AM Larson, pp. 193–13. New York: Routledge

119. Jessop B. 2002. Globalization and the national state. In *Paradigm Lost: State Theory Reconsidered*, ed. S Aronowitz, P Bratsis, pp. 185–220. Minneapolis: Univ. Minn. Press

120. Pelkonen A. 2005. State restructuring, urban competitiveness policies and technopole building in Finland: a critical view on the glocal state thesis. *Eur. Plan. Stud.* 13:687–705

121. Painter M, Pierre J. 2005. Unpacking policy capacity: issues and themes. In *Challenges to State Policy Capacity*, ed. M Painter, J Pierre, pp. 1–18. New York: Pal-grave MacMillan

122. Lowi T. 2002. Progress and poverty revisited: toward construction of a statist third way. In *Democratic Governance & Social Inequality*, ed. JS Tulchin, A Brown, pp. 41–74. Boulder, CO: Rienner

123. Adger WN. 2001. Scales of governance and environmental justice for adaptation and mitigation of climate change. *J. Int. Dev.* 13:921–31

124. Brooks N, Adger WN, Kelly M. 2005. The determinants of vulnerability and adaptive capacity at the national level and the implications for adaptation. *Glob. Environ. Chang.* 15:151–63

125. O'Brien KL, Leichenko R, Kelkarc U, Venemad H, Aandahl G. et al. 2004. Mapping vulnerability to multiple stressors: climate change and globalization in India. *Glob. Environ. Chang.* 14:303–13

126. Deleted in proof

127. Streck C. 2004. New partnerships in global environmental policy: the clean development mechanism. *J. Environ. Dev.* 13:295–322

128. Intergov. Panel Clim. Chang. (IPCC). 2001. *Climate Change 2001: Impacts, Adaptation and Vulnerability*. IPCC, Geneva.

129. Socolow R, Hotinsky R, Greenblatt J, Pacala S. 2004. Solving the climate change problem. *Environment* 46:8–19

130. Kates RW. 2004. Beyond Kyoto. *Environment* 46:2

131. Nelson K, Jong BJH. 2003. Making global initiatives local realities: carbon mitigation projects in Chiapas, Mexico. *Glob. Environ. Chang.* 13:19–30

132. Klooster D, Masera O. 2000. Community forest management in Mexico: carbon mitigation and biodiversity conservation through rural development. *Glob. Environ. Chang.* 10:259–72

133. Gough C, Shackley S. 2001. The respectable politics of climate change: the epistemic communities and NGOs. *Int. Aff.* 77:329–45

134. Corell E, Betsill MM. 2001. A comparative look at NGO influence in international environmental negotiations: desertification and climate change. *Glob. Environ. Polit.* 1:86–107

135. Brooks N, Adger WN. 2004. Assessing and enhancing adaptive capacity. In *Adaptation Policy Framework*, ed. B Lim, pp. 165–81. New York: UN Dev. Programme

136. Adger WN, Arnell NW, Tompkins EL. 2005. Successful adaptation to climate change across scales. *Glob. Environ. Chang.* 15:77–86

137. Brooks N. 2003. *Vulnerability, Risk and Adaptation: A Conceptual Framework*. Norwich: Tyndall Cent. Clim. Chang. Res./Cent. Soc. Econ. Res. Glob. Environ.

138. Liverman DM. 2005. *Equity, Justice and Climate Change*. London: Cent. Reform

CASE STUDY

EU Policy on Climate Change Mitigation Since Copenhagen and the Economic Crisis

By Christian Egenhofer and Monica Alessi

1. Introduction

As is well known, the EU has identified tackling climate change as one of the world's greatest challenges. It has repeatedly confirmed its position that an increase in the global, annual, mean surface temperature should not exceed 2°C above pre-industrial levels. After the withdrawal of the US from the Kyoto Protocol, the EU found itself being catapulted into global 'leadership' on climate change. While few had bet at the time that the Kyoto Protocol would survive, instead (not at least owing to active EU diplomacy) Japan, Canada and Russia ratified the Protocol to bring it into force in 2005. As a result, the EU has adopted numerous laws both to fulfil its commitments and to prepare the path for a new post-2012 agreement or at least a framework. Among them have been a host of policies to support renewable energy, improve energy efficiency, decarbonise transport and advance a strategy on low-carbon technology deployment. The centrepiece of the EU's climate change policy has been the EU Emissions Trading Scheme (EU ETS), which started in 2005. Yet the outcome of the Copenhagen summit in December 2009 and the continuing economic crisis have triggered a rethinking of the EU's strategy. The new strategy is still emerging, with its implications for relations with third countries being unclear. Nevertheless, a few pointers and issues for further discussion can be highlighted.

2. The EU's Climate Change Policy in the Run-Up to Copenhagen

Identifying the scope for cooperation between the EU and emerging economies like Brazil requires an understanding of the EU's climate change 'narrative' prior to the 2009 climate summit in Copenhagen. It also requires acknowledging how difficult it is to change a once-achieved consensus or modify a negotiation position of the EU, which for strategically important issues, such as the long-term international strategy, requires a broad consensus within the EU. The current situation, in which Poland plus a number of other Central and Eastern European member states are continually opposed to an increase in the level of ambition, i.e. more onerous targets, is a case in point.

2.1 The climate and energy package

The EU's climate change policy has long been based on the EU's long-term target to limit the global temperature increase to a maximum of two degrees Celsius above pre-industrial levels. To achieve this, the EU set a number of targets as well as a host of accompanying policies, generally referred to as the 'climate and energy package' or the '20 20 by 2020 targets':

1. a binding, absolute, emissions reduction commitment of 30% by 2020 compared with 1990 conditional on a global agreement, and a 'firm independent commitment' to achieve at least a 20% reduction;
2. a binding target to reach a 20% share of renewable energy sources in primary energy consumption by 2020;
3. a binding minimum target of increasing the share of renewables in each member state's transport energy consumption to 10% by 2020 (this target initially focused solely on biofuels, but was later widened to include other forms of renewable energy sources);
4. a 20% reduction of primary energy consumption by 2020 compared with projections (non-binding); and
5. a commitment to enable the construction of up to 12 large-scale power plants using carbon capture and storage (CCS) technology.

The climate and energy package was finally adopted in April 2009 and contains six principal elements. These entail a directive for the promotion of renewable energy sources, a revised EU ETS starting in 2013, an 'effort sharing' decision that sets binding emission targets for EU member states in sectors not subject to the ETS, a regulation to reduce by 2015 average CO_2 emissions of new passenger cars to 120g/km, new environmental quality standards for fuels and biofuels (aimed at reducing by 2020 GHG emissions from fuels by 6% over their entire life-cycle) and a regulatory framework for CCS. Prior to that, the EU had already published the Strategic Energy Technology (SET-)Plan to strengthen research, development and demonstration as well as early deployment help for new low-carbon energy technologies.

While climate change was the main driver, the 'package' was equally meant to address energy policy challenges. Domestic energy resources have been dwindling at the same time as government intervention in the energy industry has been on the rise in precisely those countries that could potentially fill the gap. In this context, the EU and its member states have been examining domestic and external policy options to move to a more sustainable and secure energy supply. These include, among others, investing in renewable energy sources, promoting CCS technology and investing in nuclear energy in member states that wish to do so. Renewables policy has been guided by the need for large-scale deployment to bring down the costs of technology.

Additional real or perceived advantages of the EU's climate and energy package have included the following:

- the renewable energy policy can provide for technological leadership in sun-rise technologies;
- renewable electricity can reduce long-term electricity prices and their volatility;
- the substitution of fossil fuels combined with renewables may reduce the pricing power of Russia (notably on gas); and
- the introduction of the EU ETS can lead to the retention by importing countries of some of the economic rent of producer countries.

To offset the higher prices for both industry and domestic consumers, energy efficiency has been perceived as a central piece, certainly for the transition period until new technologies and new fuels become available on a large scale. With increasing prices, reducing consumption gives a reasonable prospect for keeping the energy bill constant.

There has been an additional aspect of the '20 20 by 2020' targets that is often overlooked. The first phase of the EU ETS showed that setting a hard cap on GHG emissions in the EU is next to impossible without some sort of legally binding constraint. In a scenario of a post 2012 agreement *without* absolute caps, it was and still is difficult to see how the EU ETS could continue to exist in a meaningful way. Member states and the European Commission would most likely not be able to impose an ambitious emissions ceiling on industry without a legally binding constraint. The '20 20' targets were meant to address this risk.

At the heart of the agreement are the '20 20 by 2020' targets. In addition to the revised EU ETS—covering power and industry emissions—which has fixed by law a legally binding target for perpetual, annual reductions by 1.74%,[1] implementation of these targets has been operationalised by the introduction of legally binding targets for GHG emission reductions at the member state level ranging from -20% to +20%, depending on the member state.[2] Also the 20% renewable target by 2020—which translates into roughly a 35% share of renewables in the power sector—has been broken down into differentiated national targets (see Table A1 in the appendix) for the share of renewable energy sources in final energy consumption and introduced. The EU's cornerstone: The Emissions Trading System

The EU ETS has been designed as a domestic policy, largely 'protected' from carbon markets that at the time were seen as emanating from the Kyoto Protocol. The principal reason has been concerns over compliance under the Kyoto Protocol and the Marrakech Accords. For an efficient trading system to work, there has to be a guarantee that compliance is ensured with a possibility of recourse to a court in case of litigation.

---

1   This figure allows for a 21% GHG emissions reduction in 2020 compared with 2005.
2   These are referred to as 'effort sharing' targets, covering transport, building or waste and amounting EU-wide to a 10% reduction below 2005 levels by 2020.

By covering currently some 2 billion of GHG emissions in the EU and the European Economic Area (EEA),[3] the EU ETS by most estimates makes up some 80% of the global carbon market. Strictly speaking a regional carbon market, its size nonetheless means that prices for EU allowances (EUAs) under the ETS set the prices for the global carbon market. With demand from those countries that have ratified the Kyoto Protocol fast decreasing, the EU ETS will become—at least temporarily—an even more important component of the global carbon market.

2.2 ETS Beginnings

The well-publicised initial problems of the ETS were partly the result of the rapid speed with which the ETS was adopted, motivated by the EU's desire to show its strong determination to tackle climate change. This should, however, not hide the fact that the ETS suffered from some serious design flaws (e.g. Egenhofer, 2007; Swedish Energy Agency, 2007, Ellerman, Convery and de Perthuis, 2010). The initial allocation of allowances by member states on the basis of National Allocation Plans led to a 'race to the bottom', i.e. member states were under pressure by industries not to hand out fewer allowances than their EU competitors received. This led to over-allocation and ultimately to a price collapse. During the period when the EU allowance price was high, free allocation also generated 'windfall profits', mainly but not only in the power sector. Some of these issues were addressed in phase 2 (2008–12) as a result of member state cooperation and the European Commission being able to reduce member states' allocation proposals. Still, throughout both phases, by and large the ETS has managed to deliver a carbon price. One result has been that the carbon price has now clearly entered boardroom discussions (Ellerman and Joskow, 2008).

In the absence of a global agreement and 'uneven' carbon constraints, the answer to concerns over competitiveness and carbon leakage has been free allocation. Free allocation constitutes compensation, potentially creating an incentive to continue producing carbon in Europe (Ellerman, Convery and de Perthuis, 2010).

2.3 Overhaul in Two Steps

Experiences from phase 1 and 2 have greatly helped the European Commission to propose and adopt radical changes to the EU ETS, which were not even thinkable before its initial adoption in 2003.[4] The principal element of the new ETS is a single EU-wide cap, which will decrease annually in a linear way by 1.74% starting in 2013. This linear reduction continues beyond 2020, as there is no sunset clause.

The revised ETS Directive also foresees EU-wide harmonised allocation rules. Starting from 2013, power companies will have to buy all their emission allowances at an auction with some temporary exceptions for 'coal-based' poorer member states. At the same time, the industrial sectors under the ETS that are exposed to significant non-EU competition and

---

3   The EEA countries Norway, Iceland and Liechtenstein are fully integrated into this market.
4   See e.g. Ellerman, Convery and de Perthuis (2010), Skjærseth and Wettestad (2010) and Egenhofer et al. (2011) for a full overview.

thereby potentially subject to carbon leakage will receive 100% of allowances free of charge up to 2020.

Other changes include restrictions to the total volume of Clean Development Mechanism (CDM)/Joint Implementation (JI) credits, the use of 300 million EU allowances to finance the demonstration of CCS and innovative renewable technologies. Furthermore, there is a general—non-legally binding—commitment by EU member states to spend at least half of the revenues from auctioning on tackling climate change in both the EU and developing countries, including on measures to avoid deforestation and increase afforestation and reforestation in developing countries. In addition,

- the system will be extended to aviation, the chemicals and aluminium sectors and to other GHGs, e.g. nitrous oxide from fertilisers and perfluorocarbons from aluminium; and
- member states can financially compensate electro-intensive industries for higher power prices. The European Commission has drawn up EU guidelines to this end.

As in the previous periods, access to project credits under the Kyoto Protocol from outside the EU will be limited. The revised ETS will restrict access to no more than 50% of the reductions required in the EU ETS to ensure that emission reductions will happen in the EU. Leftover CDM/JI credits from 2008–12 can be used until 2020.

2.4 The Economic Crisis

At the time of the hard-won compromise of the ETS review for post-2012, there was a general conviction that the new ETS would be 'future-proof', i.e. be able to cope with the *temporary* lack of a global climate change agreement and address competitiveness, yet able to drive decarbonisation of the EU economy. The 2008–09 economic crisis, however, has destroyed that confidence by a seemingly permanent dramatic lowering of EUA prices due to a rapid and dramatic decline in economic output. Ever since, EUA prices have been lingering below €5 per tonne of CO_2, going as low as around €2. Without political intervention, EUA prices are not expected to climb much higher throughout the period of up to 2020, largely because of the possibility to bank unused allowances between the second and third phase (European Commission, 2012).

When measured against 2007 levels, the EU's current pledge of 20% compares poorly with the pledges of other industrialised countries. The current −20% pledge is inferior in terms of the effort required to those of the US or Canada, while a 30% reduction pledge would still be weaker than the upper-end pledges of Australia and Japan (e.g. Spencer et al., 2010; Den Elzen et al., 2009).

The implication of the lack of ambition goes beyond the EU's domestic decarbonisation strategy. The EU's minimum target is likely to lie above the trajectory implied by a linear reduction from current levels towards a 2050 target to reach the long-term target of reducing "emissions by 80–95% by 2050 compared to 1990 levels", the EU's politically accepted objective. This would mean that an EU reduction target of 20% would not seem to enable the world to reach its envisaged objective under reasonable assumptions (e.g. Ward and Grubb,

2009). This has been indirectly acknowledged by the European Commission in the Staff Working Paper accompanying the 26 May 2010 Communication, which states that "internal reductions by 2020 at a higher level than the reference case (which achieves the −20% target internally) is more in line with a 2°C compatible scenario" (European Commission, 2010b).

A low level of ambition in the EU is equally unlikely to facilitate an ambitious international agreement consistent with long-term objectives and economic efficiency. The European Commission's own analysis already in 2009 (European Commission, 2009) noted that a 30% reduction target combined with a carbon market for the group of developed countries would cut global mitigation costs by about a quarter. Sticking to a 20% target would forego these potential benefits.

Finally, a lack of ambition is in gross contradiction of the EU's rhetoric on how to generate financing for mitigation and adaptation to climate change in developing countries. The EU envisages the majority of these financial flows coming through the carbon market. Under a 20% reduction pathway and the possibility to import credits through the Kyoto Protocol's flexible mechanisms, the resulting EU carbon price is likely to be too low to generate a significant portion of the $100 billion p.a. post-2012 that has been agreed.

3. Implications

The EU's low level of ambition affects its influence in international fora when discussing climate change policy. The emergence of new, important global players (in particular BRIC[5] countries) with a large potential to reduce emissions – but also to increase them if no action is taken—requires a delicate diplomatic effort, as well as willingness to support effectively a change of track. The share of EU emissions in global emissions is decreasing (due in large part to the increases in emerging economies), which in turn brings adverse domestic incentives and puts into question the EU's climate policy. There is thus a need to reconcile the EU's rhetoric with its own ambitions, first by getting its house in order and second by engaging more meaningfully with emerging countries willing to participate constructively in reducing emissions.

3.1 Getting its House in Order will Take Time

The first implication is that the EU will need to get its house in order. An initial step has been taken with a European Commission proposal[6] to stagger the release of EUAs to be auctioned, a practice that is generally referred to as 'back-loading'. Once adopted, this would mean that fewer EUAs are released for auction initially and more later, towards the end of the trading

---

5   BRIC refers to Brazil, Russia, India and China.
6   The proposal consists of the following elements: i) a proposal to amend the EU ETS Directive and clarify the prerogative of the EC to make changes to the auctioning profile within a trading period through the Climate Change Committee; ii) an amendment to the Auctioning Regulation that does not include the number; and iii) a Staff Working Document (SWD) that outlines, in some detail, the rationale behind back-loading as well as at least three different options on how to implement such action. The SWD showed, by calculations using three different models, the potential impact of back-loading.

period in 2020, which in the Commission's view would be able to address this 'temporary' market imbalance. At the same time, the European Commission has initiated a discussion on the need for 'structural' measures, in particular to address the root cause of the current imbalance (European Commission, 2012). Numerous options exist, including such one-off measures as cancelling a certain amount of allowances, introducing systemic adjustment measures or even creating new bodies (see e.g. Egenhofer et al., 2012). Whatever the final political solution, decision-making will take years to complete. The development of the EU's international strategy cannot be seen in isolation from the intricacies of the international discussion, notably since there is no consensus on either the domestic or the international aspects.

Differences of interest among member states within the Council are multi-faceted, and there is a cleavage between the 'new' and 'old' member states, i.e. those member states that were already members in 2004 when the new and newly 'independent' member states of the former Soviet area of influence joined the EU. These internal differences bear some resemblance to tensions at the international level, and this is often not understood by negotiating partners. Generally, the new member states have a far lower GDP per capita than the older member states. The poorest EU member states recorded a GDP per capita of €12,600 (Romania) and €13,800 (Bulgaria). These are levels comparable to Brazil at €11,900 and South Africa at €11,100. In many cases, this is coupled with a power sector that is predominantly coal-based. Poland is the most extreme example, with coal-based power production being responsible for a bit more than 90% of total power, which translates into 56% of total primary energy consumption. The Europe OECD average figures for comparison are 24% and 17% (Spencer, 2012). Finally, energy efficiency in industry is considerably below that in old member states. Polish energy intensity is about 2.2 times higher than the EU-27 average and 2.5 times higher than that in the old member states.[7] This situation represents a kind of contradiction between intra-EU developed versus developing countries.

3.2 The EU's Share of Global Emissions is Falling Fast

It is also increasingly becoming clear that the EU's share of global GHG emissions—currently at around 13% of the global share—is decreasing fast and will fall to around 10% in 2020. This compares with shares for China and the US each of around 20%. According to the International Energy Agency (IEA) in Paris, the EU's cumulative savings over the period 2008 to 2020—the period for which the EU has capped its emissions – would represent around 40% of China's expected, annual CO_2 emissions (IEA, 2008).

Figure 1 shows that even if the EU, the US and other developed countries follow an aggressive reduction pathway, such as reducing total emissions by 90% in 2050 compared with 1990, emerging economies (possibly excluding India due to its low per-capita GHG emissions) will need to reduce their emissions equally by a similar degree, although with a delay of one decade. To be able to reach a situation in which the global average mean temperature increases do not exceed 2°C, the GHG emissions of emerging economies would need to start falling absolutely by 2020.

---

7   This is based on Eurostat figures: Polish energy intensity is 373.859 kgoe/€1,000 GDP; that of the EU27 is 167.99 and the EU-15 is 150.942.

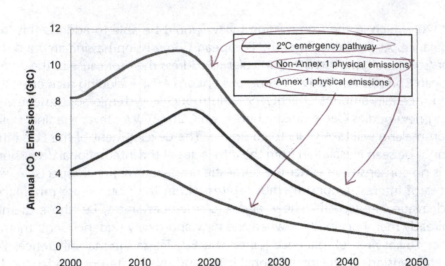

Figure 1. A thought experiment, showing the global emissions budget that entails a 15–30% risk of exceeding 2°C (top line), the Annex 1 trajectory assuming an aggressive reduction of 90% below 1990 levels by 2050 (bottom line), and the remaining carbon budget available to the non-Annex 1 (middle line)

Source: Kartha et al. 2008 (ECP Report No. 5).

While there is no renouncing the notion of "common but differentiated responsibilities and respective capabilities", as enshrined in the UN Framework Convention on Climate Change (UNFCCC) ratified by more than 190 nations worldwide (including the US), it is nonetheless clear that EU reductions on their own may be laudable but are far from sufficient to address the problem. Hence, the EU's insistence on a common framework for all Parties, which was subsequently agreed in Durban when Parties agreed to "launch a process to develop a protocol, another legal instrument or an agreed outcome with legal force under the UNFCCC applicable to all Parties" to be finished by 2015 (for 2020). The increasing awareness of this situation makes the EU's unilateral commitments increasingly a hard sale.

3.3 Industrial Competitiveness Does Matter

Closely related to the differentiation between developed and developing countries has been the lack of progress in 'industrial competitiveness'[8] issues. The risk of carbon leakage, whether real or perceived, will become an increasingly important impediment in the EU to raising its ambition level. Prior to Copenhagen, pressure from EU industry was relatively modest, essentially for two reasons. First, there was a prospect of some sort of global deal able to establish a 'level playing field'. Second, ETS design has been able if not to address for good, at least to park the issue. With the prospect of a global deal pushed farther away, competitive-

---

8   This term has never been defined, although roughly speaking 'competitiveness' in the context of EU climate change policy and the ETS has assumed a micro (i.e. firm or sector-specific) perspective, meaning the ability to sell, keep or increase market share, profits or stock market value or all of these at once.

ness has again become an important matter on the EU's agenda. Competitiveness issues will be further aggravated because more European industry will need to contribute to the 'deep' costs of decarbonisation or energy transition, such as for renewable intake and massive new investment in energy infrastructure. To date, industry in all member states has largely been exempted from contributing. But as costs rise, households will decreasingly be willing or able to cover the full burden.[9]

In the past, 'competitiveness' was addressed by free allocation in the ETS. Free allocation constitutes a form of compensation, potentially creating an incentive to continue producing in Europe. Electro-intensive industries can be compensated by state aid for additional costs stemming from carbon-induced increases in power prices.

Carbon crediting mechanisms are a second tool to address competitiveness. The extent to which crediting mechanisms are able to positively affect the competitiveness of industry in Europe by reducing compliance costs remains complex and depends on numerous conditions.

A third possibility is to include importers in the ETS or to impose an import tax on the content (i.e. including the embedded carbon) of CO_2 of all goods imported into the EU from countries that do not have their own cap-and-trade system or equivalent pricing measures (see the further discussion below, in section 5.2).

A fourth possibility to deal with competiveness is to reinforce innovation and innovation policy to facilitate the transition of an industrial sector towards a low-carbon future. Such a transition will require a focus on the new value chains that a low-carbon sector could unlock. The paper and pulp industry's *2050 Roadmap to a low carbon bio-economy* (CEPI, 2012) takes such an approach. According to the document, the "sector has the ambition to be at the heart of the 2050 bio-economy, an essential platform for a range of bio-based products and the recycling society". Transitions towards unlocking new value chains have happened and continue to happen in other sectors, such as steel and chemicals (see also CCAP, 2013).

4. Building a Global Carbon Market

The above analysis makes it clear that the principal direction for the EU's domestic and international climate change policy will be to establish a global carbon market as soon as possible. Cap-and-trade programmes to reduce GHG emissions, or at least as a substantial element of a climate change policy, are proliferating in many regions of the world. The Kyoto mechanisms of CDM and JI have created a constituency that is likely to promote the use of emissions trading.

For the EU, emissions trading has the following attractions:

- over time it will create a global carbon price or at least a bandwidth of prices;
- such a price has the credible potential to address EU competitiveness concerns;
- carbon crediting mechanisms as an integral part of emissions trading operate in several ways; in the transition towards a global carbon price, they can address competitiveness concerns in the short term, they help capacity building and they link different markets;

---

9 In the case of Germany, all costs related to the 'energy transition' of the power sector are borne by household customers. In 2012, these costs amounted to almost a quarter of the retail electricity price.

- a global net of emission trading systems—as long as they are linked—will go a long way towards meeting the EU's aspirations for a global framework;
- if properly regulated, emission markets are efficient tools to achieve climate change objectives; and finally,
- they can be a major source of financial transfers to support least developed countries in their decarbonisation efforts.

For the EU, it can be seen as a success that the international climate change negotiations in Durban in December 2011 opened the way towards the creation of new market mechanisms (Marcu, 2012).

In parallel, this has triggered a review of the existing or planned mechanisms that have been under discussion for some time, for example a bilateral offset credit mechanism, sectoral crediting mechanisms, REDD-plus markets and NAMA (nationally appropriate mitigation action) crediting.

5. Raising the Ambition Level

It has become increasingly clear that raising the ambition level within the UNFCCC framework beyond the pledges in Copenhagen is extremely difficult. Therefore, there are attempts at doing so 'outside' or 'around' the UNFCCC. Several examples can be mentioned.

5.1 Aviation and Maritime

Following the lack of progress in international fora such as the UN, or within the International Civil Aviation Organisation (ICAO) on international aviation, the EU decided that at the start of 2012 emissions from all domestic and international flights arriving at or departing from an EU airport would be covered by the EU Emissions Trading System. The EU decided that the aviation sector would have to surrender allowances, which they receive for free or would be required to purchase.

The EU's right to cover international flights was contested by many other countries, either by political pressure or legal complaints. The most vocal opposition came from China and the US. As a result, in November 2012 the EU suspended the inclusion of international aviation following the ICAO Council meeting of 9 November, in which, according the EU, significant progress was made towards the goal of global regulation of aviation emissions.

In parallel, a similar approach is being pursued for maritime. The EU has confirmed its commitment to include these emissions in the existing EU reduction commitment should the UNFCCC processes fail to tackle them and has announced a proposal in this case. After the experience with aviation, however, it is more likely now that a solution is sought through the International Maritime Organisation.

5.2 Carbon Border Measures

Conceptually speaking, the inclusion of aviation in the ETS is comparable to a 'carbon border tax' to pursue a global 'level' pricing of carbon, i.e. to include importers in the ETS or to impose an import tax on the content (i.e. including the embedded carbon) of CO_2 of all goods imported into the EU from countries that do not have their own cap-and-trade system or equivalent pricing measures. If levied by major economies, such as the US and the EU, this would most likely create a global 'shadow' carbon price even in the rest of the world. This would at least partially, through trade flows, establish carbon transfer pricing even in those parts of the world where governments have so far refrained from imposing domestic measures of any magnitude.[10] Nevertheless, carbon border measures would have potential implications for world trade, international relations in general and climate negotiations, as witnessed in the controversy on including international aviation in the ETS.

5.3 The Climate and Clean Air Coalition

While within the UNFCCC policy discussions on emission reductions concentrate on long-lived greenhouse gases, and in particular on CO_2, the role of short-lived climate pollutants (SLCPs) in reducing global warming levels and impacts in the shorter term has received less attention. Recent studies by the United Nations Environment Programme (UNEP) (2011 and UNEP & WMO, 2011) estimate that a portfolio of low-cost abatement measures of black carbon, tropospheric ozone and methane can reduce temperature increases by 0.4–0.5C between 2010 and 2050. While the abatement of SLCPs can in no circumstances replace CO_2 measures, addressing them in parallel has considerable benefits in the near term. Launched in February 2012, the UNEP-based Climate and Clean Air Coalition (CCAC)[11] was created to develop a number of initiatives addressing i) black carbon emissions from heavy-duty diesel vehicles and engines, ii) black carbon and other pollutants from brick production, iii) SLCPs from municipal solid waste, iv) HFC alternative technology and standards, v) methane and black carbon emissions from oil and natural gas production, and other measures.

5.4 Green Growth

More recently also within the EU, the concept of 'green growth' has gained popularity. This is partly owing to the failures of international climate negotiations, and partly to the economic stagnation following the 2008 financial crisis. The notion of green growth increasingly seems to suggest a way out of both the 'economic' and 'climate' crises. The shift to a low-carbon economy would unleash a wave of investment, innovation and more jobs. Developed countries would re-establish economic competitiveness partly due to high-tech green technologies, while developing countries and emerging economies would move on to more sustainable paths of economic development (Zysman and Huberty, 2012).

---

10 In other words, it creates a mechanism that enforces the pass-through of carbon costs across the globe, therefore making domestic consumers pay the full cost of carbon. In principle, solutions to such issues as WTO compatibility, estimating the embedded carbon or equity concerns can be found, e.g. Gros & Egenhofer (2012).

11 The state members are Australia, Bangladesh, Canada, Colombia, Denmark, Finland, France, Germany, Ghana, Israel, Italy, Japan, Jordan, Mexico, Nigeria, Norway, Sweden, the UK, the US and the European Commission. Other members include international organisations and NGOS.

5.5 Reducing Emissions from Deforestation

Reducing emissions from deforestation or forest degradation (REDD-plus) as part of the international negotiations is a controversial issue. Within the EU, there is a consensus on the importance of attributing a value to environmental services, such as those avoiding deforestation. The importance of avoided deforestation was discussed in detail during the review of the ETS and is recognised in Article 10(3) of the ETS Directive.

To date, the sovereign participation of EU member states in the international REDD-plus market generally appears to be the most likely avenue for the EU and its member states. This approach is also seen as preferable to linking to the ETS and international carbon markets. Full linking to international carbon markets would first require more clarity in the design of REDD-plus markets, notably addressing questions of permanence, monitoring, reporting and verification and more generally compliance, as well as a solution to the tricky question of how to absorb the expected volumes of credits (e.g. O'Sullivan et al., 2010).

To date, the link to the EU ETS is the auctioning of EUAs, which will supply EU governments with funds for sovereign participation. Yet, current and expected EUA price levels are insufficient for EU financing commitments.

5.6 Technology

While there may be different views on whether the stabilisation of GHG emissions in line with the UNFCCC's objectives can be achieved with technically proven technology, the need to bring carbon-efficient technologies to the market at scale more quickly is uncontroversial. Also undisputed is the need to develop, demonstrate and deploy as yet unproven technologies, in order to reach climate change targets beyond 2050. This is evidenced by the EU's SET-Plan, which has put a special emphasis on a long-term agenda of energy research, demonstration and innovation for Europe in order to make low-carbon technologies affordable and competitive and thereby enable market uptake to meet the EU 2020 targets, as well as to realise its 2050 vision of a low-carbon economy.

The IEA's *Energy Technology Perspectives 2012*, however, finds that progress in almost all technologies (i.e. nuclear, clean coal, CCS in power, CCS in industry, buildings and biofuels in industry) is not where it needs to be to meet global ambitions for GHG emission reductions. The notable exceptions are renewables and to a degree industry, vehicle fleet economy and electrical vehicles, where there is progress but additional effort would be required to meet targets.

6. Areas for Cooperation

Both the failure of the Copenhagen climate change negotiations and the economic crisis caught the EU off guard. Since the demise of the Kyoto-style top-down world of legally binding emission 'targets' for developed countries and 'actions' for developing countries, and the subsequent substitution by a bottom-up approach based on voluntary pledges (with or without review), the EU has struggled to find a new climate change consensus. Although support for climate change policy is still very high among politicians and citizens alike, discussions on the distribution of costs and benefits among sectors, regions and member states have become more acrimonious.

The EU has also realised that 'leadership' requires followers. In Copenhagen, there was little if any interest in the EU's offer to increase its ambition level to 30% GHG emission reductions in 2020 compared with 1990. The EU's negotiation partners were rather preoccupied with replacing the top-down architecture of the Kyoto Protocol with a bottom-up model of voluntary pledges.

While there might be a comprehensive and legally binding, global climate change agreement that the EU had so hoped for, it will significantly fall short of the EU's declared ambitions. Hence, the matter of a level playing field for EU industry, especially in times of economic crisis and uncertainty, will become more important and may hold back a new EU consensus.

The best way to address this from the EU perspective is through the (gradual) establishment of a global carbon market. In addition to being able to address competitiveness in both the short and long term, a global carbon market would go a long way towards setting up a framework for global climate change policy as well as offering the possibility to address climate finance. This could also give a boost to low-carbon technology deployment and possibly to technology development.

While all this does not offer any hope of keeping the global average increase in mean temperature to below 4°C or 3°C at best, the EU along with other countries is trying to increase the level of ambition, mainly by working outside but not against the UN framework. Aviation, shipping and short-lived climate pollutants are examples in this regard. Other potential areas might be REDD-plus or certain 'green growth' themes, including finance.

This opens the door to a different approach. Owing to positive domestic changes in Brazilian climate policy, as well as Brazil's willingness to collaborate, the EU may seize the opportunity to counterbalance the present lack of influence originating from its own domestic climate policy by engaging in effective bilateral assistance to Brazil. In doing so, the EU may also be able to engage further with other BRIC countries, by demonstrating the benefits of collaboration. The EU could regain some influence as well as bring some additional momentum to its industrial policy in the area of low carbon technologies.

There is actually strong interest in technology cooperation on the part of Brazil. First, this would point to joint research cooperation with the EU and its member states, and capacity building would be a key building block in this respect (e.g. transferring managerial and organisational capabilities). Fields for 'technology transfer' that regularly appear on the list of areas for cooperation (such as CCS, smart grids, solar and wind energy, and energy efficiency), on the other hand, will require further work to identify the public policy issues. Technology transfer typically is integral to trade and notably investment, where industry deploys and therefore transfers technologies. Public policy issues outside R&D cooperation remain limited in scope.

Possible initial actions might be for the EU to offer better market access to bio-ethanol or reduce trade barriers for second-generation ethanol. Still, it must be said that the high number of cars with diesel engines in the EU somewhat reduces the market potential for bioethanol.

Of course, a move to increase its domestic ambition level from a situation in which it is very close to having achieved its unilateral targets of −20% because of the economic crisis and other events unrelated to climate change policy would support the EU's position towards its partners. How this will play out is impossible to say at this stage.

Bibliography

Center for Clean Air Policy (CCAP) (2013), *The New Deal: An Enlightened Industrial Policy for the EU through Structural ETS Reform*, CCAP, Washington D.C. and Brussels.

Confederation of European Paper Industries (CEPI) (2012), *Unfold the future: The forest fibre industry 2050 Roadmap to a low carbon bio-economy*, CEPI, Brussels.

Den Elzen, M., M.A. Mendoza Beltran, J. van Vliet, S.J.A. Bakker and T. Bole (2009), *Pledges and Actions*, Report No. 500102 032 2009, Netherlands Environmental Assessment Agency, The Hague.

European Environment Agency (EEA) (2009), *Annual European Community greenhouse gas inventory 1990–2007 and inventory report 2009: Submission to the UNFCCC Secretariat*, EEA Technical Report No. 4/2009, EEA, Copenhagen.

Egenhofer, C. (2007), "The Making of the EU Emissions Trading Scheme: Status, Prospects and Implications for Business", *European Management Journal*, Vol. 25, No. 6, December, pp. 453-463.

Egenhofer, C., M. Alessi, A. Georgiev and N. Fujiwara (2011), *The EU Emissions Trading Scheme and Climate Policy towards 2050*, CEPS Special Report, CEPS, Brussels.

Egenhofer, C., A. Marcu and A. Georgiev (2012), *Reviewing the EU ETS Review?* CEPS Task Force Report, CEPS, Brussels, October.

Ellerman, A.D. and P. Joskow (2008), *The European Union's Emissions Trading System in Perspective*, Pew Center on Global Climate Change, Arlington, VA, May.

Ellerman, A.D., F. Convery and C. de Perthuis (2010), *Pricing Carbon: The European Union Emissions Trading Scheme*, Cambridge: Cambridge University Press.

European Commission (2009), *Stepping up international climate finance: A European blueprint for the Copenhagen deal*, Communication from the Commission, COM(2009) 475/3, Brussels.

———— (2010a), *Analysis of options to move beyond 20% greenhouse gas emission reductions and assessing the risk of carbon leakage*, Communication from the Commission COM(2010) 265/3 (unofficial version), Brussels.

———— (2010b), Commission Staff Working Document, accompanying the European Commission Communication, *Analysis of options to move beyond 20% greenhouse gas emission reductions and assessing the risk of carbon leakage*, Communication from the Commission, SEC(2010) 650/2, Background information and analysis, Part II (unofficial version), Brussels, p. 40.

———— (2012), *The state of the European carbon market in 2012*, Report from the Commission to the European Parliament and the Council, COM(2012) 652, 14 November, Brussels.

Gros, D. and C. Egenhofer (2011), "The case for taxing carbon at the border", *Climate Policy*, Vol. 11, No. 5, Special Issue, pp. 1212-1225.

International Monetary Fund (IMF) (2009), *World Economic Outlook Database*, IMF, Washington, D.C., October.

International Energy Agency (IEA) (2008a), *World Energy Outlook 2008*, OECD/IEA, Paris.

————— (2008b), *Climate Policy and Carbon Leakage*, IEA Information Paper, OECD/IEA, Paris, October.

————— (2012), *Energy Technology Perspectives 2012*, International Energy Agency, OECD/IEA, Paris.

Kartha, S., B. Kjellen, P. Baer and T. Athanasiou (2008), *Linking measurable, reportable and verifiable mitigation actions by developing countries to measurable, reportable and verifiable financial and technical support by developed countries*, Background Paper No. 1 of ECP Report No. 5, European Climate Platform, CEPS, Brussels.

Marcu, A. (2012), "The Durban Outcome: A Post-2012 Framework Approach for Greenhouse Gas Markets", in UNEP Risoe Centre (ed.), *Progressing towards post-2012 carbon markets*, UNEP Risoe Center, Roskilde, pp. 127–138.

O'Sullivan, R., C. Streck, T. Pearson, S. Brown and A. Gilbert (2010), *Engaging the private sector in the potential generation of carbon credits from REDD+: An analysis of issues*, Report to the UK Department for International Development, Climate Focus, Amsterdam.

Skjærseth, J.B. and J. Wettestad (2010), "Fixing the EU Emissions Trading System? Understanding the Post-2012 Changes", *Global Environmental Politics*, Vol. 10, No. 4, pp. 101–123.

Spencer, T., K. Tangen and A. Korppoo (2010), *The EU and the Global Climate Regime: Getting back into the game*, Briefing Paper No. 55, Finnish Institute of International Affairs, Helsinki, February.

Spencer, T. (2012), "Time for a grand bargain with Poland on energy and climate", *European Energy Review*, 8 March.

Swedish Energy Agency (2007), *The EU Emissions Trading Scheme after 2012*, Swedish Environmental Protection Agency and Swedish Energy Agency, Eskilstuna.

United Nations Environment Programme (UNEP) (2011), *Near-term Climate Protection and Clean Air Benefits: Actions for Controlling Short-Lived Climate Forcers*, UNEP Synthesis Report, UNEP, Nairobi.

United Nations Environment Programme (UNEP) and World Meteorological Organization (WMO) (2011), *Integrated Assessment of Black Carbon and Tropospheric Ozone—Summary for Decision Makers*, UNEP, Nairobi.

Ward, M. and M. Grubb (2009), *Comparability of Effort by Annex 1 Parties: An Overview of Issues*, Climate Strategies, London.

Zysman, J. and M. Huberty (2012), "Religion and Reality in the Search for Green Growth", *Intereconomics*, Vol. 45, No. 3, pp. 140–146.

Appendix

Table A1. National overall targets for the share of energy from renewable sources in gross final consumption of energy in 2020 and member state GHG emission limits in non-ETS sectors for the period 2013–20 (%)

Member state	Share of energy from renewable sources in gross final consumption of energy, 2005	Target for share of energy from renewable sources in gross final consumption of energy, 2020	Member state GHG emission limits in 2020 compared with 2005, GHG emission levels (from sources not covered by the ETS)
Austria	23.3	34	-16
Belgium	2.2	13	-15
Bulgaria	9.4	16	20
Czech Republic	6.1	13	9
Cyprus	2.9	13	-5
Denmark	17	30	-20
Estonia	18.0	25	11
Finland	28.5	38	-16
France	10.3	23	-14
Germany	5.8	18	-14
Greece	6.9	18	-4
Hungary	4.3	13	10
Ireland	3.1	16	-20
Italy	5.2	17	-13
Latvia	32.6	40	17
Lithuania	15.0	23	15
Luxembourg	0.9	11	-20
Malta	0	10	5
The Netherlands	2.4	14	-16
Poland	7.2	15	14
Portugal	20.5	31	1
Romania	17.8	24	19
Slovak Republic	6.7	14	13
Slovenia	16.0	25	4
Spain	8.7	20	-10
Sweden	39.8	49	-17
UK	1.3	15	-16

Source: European Commission website.

SECTION VI CONCLUSION

G iven the complexity of climate change causality and the difficulty in empirical observation and ascription, it is unlikely that purely scientific terms will resolve the issue. If we continue to articulate our call for action on purely scientific terms about diagnosing the problem, we are likely to remain entrapped in the cycle of further research or incremental policies without achieving results. Even with scientific consensus through bodies such as the IPCC, the dissenting voices will remain in the background and polarization is likely to continue. Conflict over the science and policy of climate change will require us to be innovative in designing solutions that tap into many of these disparate constituencies. We also must be careful not to let expeditious action on climate change lead to spill-over problems from alternatives, such as promoting nuclear power without considering safety risks and long-term storage. By clearly delineating issues and priorities related to climate change, we may finally reach resolution to this confounding challenge of our times. Climate change has defied effective international environmental governance, as discussed in the preceding two articles. However, the shifts presented in the European Union's climate policy case study, examined through an environmental governance perspective, provide some lessons as to how to better understand and potentially direct climate policy in the future.

Section VI Discussion Questions: Climate Change and Governance

1. What is environmental governance? What actors and entities can be involved environmental governance?
2. Why is climate change a particularly difficult international environmental issue to tackle? Cite specific reasons given throughout Section VI. What solutions and strategies discussed in the preceding chapters are most promising for addressing climate change?
3. What is the EU ETS? Has it been an effective mechanism at reducing GHG emissions? Why?
4. Name three specific policies the EU adopted to reduce GHG emissions.
5. What percent of the world's greenhouse gas emissions are generated by the European Union? What percent from China? The United States of America? Why is this significant?
6. How can globalization impact the effectiveness of international environmental governance, both negatively and positively?
7. What is the role of market-based mechanisms in driving environmental change? (eco-labels, etc)
8. What lessons from the EU ETS experience could be applied to other countries/regions in order to reduce greenhouse gas emissions?

References

Ali, S.H. (2008) "Climate Conflicts: Extricating Post-Kyoto Debates in Science and Policy." In Velma Grover ed. *Climate Change: Kyoto—Ten Years and Still Counting.* Science Publishers. New Hampshire.

Dessler, A.E. and E.A. Parson (2006) *The Science and Politics of Global Climate Change: A guide to the Debate.* Cambridge University Press. Cambridge, UK.

Metz, B., O.R. Davidson, P.R. Bosch, R. Dave, and L.A. Meyer (Eds.) (2007) *Mitigation of Climate Change. Contribution of Working Group III to the Fourth Assessment Report of the Intergovernmental Panel on Climate Change, 2007.* Cambridge University Press. Cambridge, UK.

Parry, M.L., O.F. Canziani, J.P. Palutikof, P.J. van der Linden, and C.E. Hanson (Eds.) (2007) *Climate Change 2007: Impacts, Adaptation and Vulnerability. Contribution of Working Group II to the Fourth Assessment Report of the Intergovernmental Panel on Climate Change (IPCC).* Cambridge University Press. Cambridge, UK.

INTERNATIONAL ENVIRONMENTAL STUDIES: CONCLUSION

We environmentalists struggle to stay positive in the face of the multitude of challenges facing our planet: deforestation, food insecurity, soil degradation, rising sea levels, fresh water scarcity, and other issues. We may alternate between feeling hopeful that our efforts will make a difference, and feeling despair that environmental problems are too numerous and too great to solve. There are no easy answers or silver bullets to all of the global environmental problems outlined in this book. However, there is a diversity of approaches and potential solutions available, or "tools in the toolbox." This text has highlighted six major environmental issues of global concern and shown a variety of ways to think about environmental problems and solutions through examples, approaches, and case studies. Each problem has differentiated local manifestations and interpretations across the globe, so it is important not to read each case study as fully representative of how the problem plays out in another region. Rather, each problem connects with local, regional, and global political-economic forces and histories in different ways. We hope that this inspires curiosity and critical engagement to follow these issues through their different contexts and challenges. We believe that this approach is ultimately more realistic and moderate than either despair or uncritical desires to "save the environment."

Beyond the biophysical challenges of issues such as fresh water scarcity and climate change, one of the greatest challenges we face is the difficulty of consensus on what course of action to take in addressing environmental problems. Dialogue between environmental delegates from different nations has often resulted in disagreement and ultimate impasse. Climate change is perhaps the best contemporary illustration of the difficulties of orchestrating an international agreement to address a pressing environmental problem that requires cooperation. Even reaching consensus as to the causes of climate change, the degree of severity of the problem, and the likely outcomes has been a decades-long (and continuing) process. Every country has its own interests and agenda, often in direct competition with the interests of another country. Indeed, some scholars argue that massive "global conference sites" might not be the best strategy for resolving "global" problems in all of their localized and regional diversity.[1] The divide between industrialized and developing countries has also presented challenges, in terms of who has the responsibility to mitigate climate change and the resources to adapt to its effects.

The international scale is not the only level in which consensus has proved challenging. Within countries and even at regional and local levels, communities and policymakers disagree on natural resource issues. The decisions that they ultimately reach have serious consequences for resources and people's lives. There are tradeoffs inherent in nearly every decision of how to meet human needs, from food production to transportation to energy generation. For example, while a coal power plant provides a public good of electricity, it also produces a "public bad" of sulfur dioxide emissions, illustrating that in many cases there are both winners and losers. Who wins and loses is often dictated by who has the political and economic power to influence decisions. Because these tradeoffs and issues of inequity exist within nearly all environmental issues, this text has dedicated several sections to approaches such as environmental justice and political ecology, which explicitly address power dynamics within environmental issues and bring these questions to light.

By illustrating the breadth of approaches to different environmental issues, we have shown that not only is it possible to address environmental problems from a transdisciplinary perspective, but that it is essential. Our first step in working towards environmental solutions is to have conversations among ourselves: concerned citizens, environmentalists, academics, no matter the discipline or particular environmental issue with which we most identify. As editors, it is our hope that the approaches and cases presented in this textbook have encouraged students to ask critical questions moving forward. Whether students use these skills and knowledge as government employees, international development workers, teachers, environmental consultants, or even in day-to-day conversations with peers and family, it will play a part in the collective effort to better understand and resolve the environmental issues of our time.

1 For example, see Corson, C. and MacDonald, K. I. (2012) "Enclosing the Global Commons: The Convention on Biological Diversity and Green Grabbing." *The Journal of Peasant Studies* 39 (2): 263–283.

CPSIA information can be obtained
at www.ICGtesting.com
Printed in the USA
FSOW04n1006151217
42448FS